DISTRICT ADMINISTRATION AND RURAL DEVELOPMENT IN INDIA

Policy Objectives and Administrative Change in Historical Perspective

B. B. MISRA

DELHI
OXFORD UNIVERSITY PRESS
BOMBAY CALCUTTA MADRAS
1983

Oxford University Press, Walton Street, Oxford OX2 6DP

LONDON GLASGOW NEW YORK TORONTO
DELHI BOMBAY CALCUTTA MADRAS KARACHI
KUALA LUMPUR SINGAPORE HONG KONG TOKYO
NAIROBI DAR ES SALAAM CAPE TOWN
MELBOURNE AUCKLAND

and associates in
BEIRUT BERLIN IBADAN MEXICO CITY NICOSIA

Filmset by N. K. Enterprises, 23 Daryaganj, New Delhi 110002
Printed by Rekha Printers Private Ltd., New Delhi 110020
and published by R. Dayal, Oxford University Press
2/11 Ansari Road, Daryaganj, New Delhi 110002

PREFACE

Rural development in modern India was initially the work of European free traders, a body of commercial entrepreneurs or colonizers, more especially from Britain, who were emerging in the second half of the eighteenth century as the antithesis of the monopoly rights of the East India Company. The Regulating Act (1773) and Pitt's India Act (1784) were two important measures enacted by the British Parliament to invest the Company with powers to check their activities and control their Indian interest operating from within its own infrastructure, commercial as well as administrative. But these could not succeed. For even the Company's covenanted servants were no exception. In the absence of adequate provision for security in the rural districts, they not only advanced loans to private entrepreneurs, but themselves got involved in the development of such commercial crops as tea and coffee, jute and cotton, indigo and sugarcane. They functioned more or less as the first rural banks.

By the turn of the nineteenth century *laissez faire* had emerged as a major economic force. It led to a strong political pressure group which resulted in the opening of the Company's trade in 1813 and to the abolition of its very trading rights in 1833. The exigencies of imperial control over the free trade movement, however, were always recognized. The Charter Act of 1833, which abolished the Company's rights, made that control even more rigorous. The Government of India, reconstituted in 1834, was invested with a highly centralized authority. Its civil service was reorganized first on the principle of a four-fold limited competition and, later, on the basis of a full competitive system in 1855. In their reorganized form, the Government of India and its civil service were together to represent a potentially powerful and countervailing imperial force, not necessarily meant to act as the antithesis of *laissez faire*, a purely commercial development, but to serve in principle as an instrument of protection against human suffering caused by natural calamities or by the advocates of free trade who were actuated by motives of sheer profit and commercial gain.

To a casual observer the two forces seemed overlapping because of inter-relatedness. But a distinction was never absent. It surfaced, for example, in the course of recurrent famines, especially during the first few decades after 1858. Several district officers were found to have proceeded on humanitarian grounds to restrict, without any legal sanction, the free movement of trade and to control the market to ensure the distribution of foodgrains by seizing stocks. Considerations of rural welfare in fact called for executive action to bend profiteers to the collective will of the community. The judiciary could not do this. On the contrary, it actually helped moneylenders to grab the lands of the rural poor judicially transferred in satisfaction of debts incurred at exorbitant rates of interest. The report of the Deccan Riots Commission (1873–4) provided full justification for executive interference as an instrument of welfare.

The business communities, both European and Indian, complained. But since no government could, in the interest of its own stability, afford to overlook the sufferings of the mass of people, it had to recognize in principle the necessity of executive control as part of welfare measures. In the post-1880 period, the government in India actually took a number of steps to protect tenancy rights, to acquire knowledge of agricultural statistics, and to promote local self-government to acquaint district officers with the needs of the rural population. A separate committee of the Aitchison Commission (1886-7) even studied the technical aspects of development and suggested measures for the reorganization of technical services.

These and other steps indicating governmental involvement in rural welfare proceeded in fact from the recommendations of the Famine Commission (1880). But as both European and Indian business houses and the educated elites functioned as collaborators, the emphasis on centralized executive control for development remained on the whole weak. It was Lord Curzon who first pushed reliance on imperial agencies and centralization for rural development to an extent where urban business and politics both united to force the appointment of the Royal Commission on Decentralization in 1907. For while the excessive use of executive power ran counter to commercial operations for private gain, an exclusive reliance on Europeans as an agency of modernization, especially in the field of agricultural science and technology prejudiced the growth of indigenous talents. In its report published in 1909, the Commission therefore recommended a middle course for purposes of rural development, a policy in practice, however, weighted more on the side of free enterprise than the unorganized rural masses who later, with the introduction of democracy, came under the influence of power elites of varied complexions. The progress of rural development took place in this context of history. In the post-Independence period, it had not only to reckon with such elites and business interests, but also with bureaucratic hierarchies, more career-minded than service-oriented.

This study is designed to serve in the field of public administration as a complement to the author's two earlier works—*The Central Administration of the East India Company (1773–1834)* and *The Administrative History of India (1834–1947)*—which deal with general administration. It goes further and attempts, in the field of development administration, an analysis of the policy objectives of government and its organizational problem, with special reference to district administration in the post-1947 period where it is again complementary to two other works—*The Bureaucracy in India: An Historical Analysis of Development up to 1947* and *Government and Bureaucracy in India after 1947*.

I must express here my sincerest gratitude to the Indian Institute of Public Administration, New Delhi, which initially encouraged me to undertake this study and made available to me the services of a couple of research assistants. I am especially thankful to its former Director, Shri T.N. Chaturvedi, and its Librarian, Shri Mohinder Singh. My thanks are equally due to the Ministry of Home Affairs, Government of India; to the Ministry of Community Development and Cooperation, and the Directorate of Public Health, who all ungrudgingly permitted the use of their files.

I owe a special dept to the Director, National Archives of India, more especially to Shri R. C. Gupta, Shri S. A. Tirmizi, Shri H. N. Mathur, as well as to such of their staff as Shri S. K. Dogra who took pains to get my research material duly typed and xeroxed. I am similarly indebted to Shri J. C. Srivastava, the Librarian of the National Archives, and his entire staff. It is a pleasure to acknowledge with thanks the assistance extended to me from time to time in the preparation of the manuscript by Shri Sundaram of the National Archives.

I shall be failing in my duty if I omit to mention the help I received from my friend, Shri Tara Sharan Sinha, Director of Archives, Government of Bihar, and his colleagues, who made available to me copies of all the necessary papers connected with the 'Grow More Food Campaign', a campaign started in 1942 and extended later for a period of five years after the Congress had taken over in 1946. I am also thankful to the Directorate of Rural Development, Government of Bihar, especially to Shri Bhoodeva Ojha, a knowledgeable Assistant, who enlightened me on the several structural changes effected from time to time in the Department of Community Development and Co-operation.

B. B. Misra

CONTENTS

I

EVOLUTION OF DISTRICT ADMINISTRATION UP TO 1858

General Features

District administration in modern India has changed from time to time in terms of both its goal and structure, a change resulting from an interaction between the exigencies of regulatory functions and demands for 'development' to satisfy emergent social and political urges.

In spite of periodical changes, the general executive administration of the districts has remained the core, the central agency invested with an overall responsibility under the Collector and District Magistrate functioning as the head of the executive administration. In the discharge of his functions he not only controls the machinery of law and order and the management of most branches of the revenue system, but also handles the manifold relations between government and the people within the limits of his jurisdiction. As District Officer he is required in fact to remain concerned with the general circumstances of his district, touching not only on the problems of peace and fiscal administration, but also on other related matters affecting its economy and general well-being. There are, of course, variations in the pattern of district administration. The District Officer none the less remains its main central pillar.

Two other elements of interaction that later developed to effect changes in policy objectives and administrative structure were technical and political: one lead to the gradual establishment of 'special departments' as part of the machinery of government providing for separate staff and heads appointed for developmental purposes; the other injected a political dimension which, on the one hand, contributed to the emergence of local bodies as an agency of local self-government for rural development and, on the other, created conditions for the growth of representative and parliamentary institutions to guide the course of administration at all levels. The administration of districts in modern times was thus a function of interaction among three main constituents, including the panchayati raj institutions which later came virtually in succession to local bodies.

Prior to 1858, however, there was practically little or no scope for any such interaction. It is true that the government of Lord Bentinck (1828-35) attempted to get the London authorities directly involved in the modernization of the Indian economy, communications, society and agriculture. But, as we shall see, financial considerations blocked progress, and even the basic condition of higher education, so essential for modernization, was found lacking as Bentinck's Council was divided on the question of promoting education through western literature and science. And although with the arrival of Macaulay the weight of official opinion steadily supported Western education from 1835 onwards, it took several years after that before three Indian universities could be established in 1857, and that, too, only at the headquarters of the presidency governments of Madras, Bombay and Bengal. In the field of district administration, however, considerations of economy and justice led Bentinck to create a subordinate Indian agency of deputy collectors and Sadr Amins, and unite in the office of Collector the powers of Judge-Magistrate, functioning under the supervision of Divisional Commissioners appointed in 1829.

The Collector of the East India Company became the supreme arbiter in the administration of the districts. The Board of Revenue or Commissioner exercised only an appellate jurisdiction. The executive head of district administration or district officer was the Collector himself. The police, too, did not have on a firm basis a separate departmental head of its own until 1861. The directorate of education and the public works department had of course been established in 1855. But it was only after 1858 that most of the other special departments came into being. The Department of Forest, for instance, was created in 1861, of Revenue and Agriculture in 1871, of Medical and Sanitation in 1896, of separate Agriculture in 1905, of separate Irrigation in 1906, and so on. The position of Collector dimmed gradually when these special departments began to operate under separate heads at the district level and came to be managed by the officers of the separate All-India Services recruited by the same agency as that of the Indian Civil Service to which the district officer belonged.

Similarly, on the political side, while Lord Ripon's scheme of local self-government was intended to effect a shift of emphasis from executive direction to welfare activity in the administration of the districts, the Indian Councils Act of 1892 was designed to promote the growth of a separate legislative authority, a potential check on the exercise of executive power in district administration. The position of district officers, however, remained virtually unimpaired before the introduction of diarchical democracy, which, even in its limited form, brought them under ministerial control in respect of all 'transferred' subjects, including local self-government itself.

The strength of district officers had in the past flowed from a highly centralized Government of India created by the Company's Charter Act, 1833. The despatch which the Court of Directors addressed to the Government of India on 10 December, 1834, laid down the principles governing relations with provincial governments under the Act. These principles reduced the provincial governments to the status of mere agents of the Central Government, which was to exercise constant check even over matters primarily assigned later to the provinces, such as police, civil and criminal justice, the assessment and collection of the revenues, education, medical and sanitation, irrigation, roads and buildings, forest, agriculture and control over municipal and rural boards.

This supremacy of the Centre was reflected in the dominant position held locally by district officers who were firmly wedded to the Government of India in the protection of imperial interests. The norm so established under the Company's rule continued until educated Indians started demanding their due share in government and administration. They created a situation where their political pressure found lateral expression for the removal of the economic distress arising particularly from recurrent famines which, in course of time, dictated a reorientation of administrative policy in favour of agricultural development and rural welfare. It was these trends and the consequent extension of special departments to the districts that tended to effect a change in the direction and policy objectives of district administration.

For a clear understanding and appreciation of these developments an attempt will be made in the course of this chapter to review the circumstances that led to the evolution of three of the main patterns of district administration that emerged from differences in the nature of land tenure and history. These were crystallized during the formative phase of British rule, the rule of the East India Company.

The Bengal Pattern

The Bengal pattern of district administration was based on the zamindari system of land tenure. It emerged from historical circumstances and political compulsions which induced Lord Cornwallis to enact a measure declaring the Permanent Settlement of land revenue made with the zamindars in 1793.

Pre-British Position

In pre-British days the zamindars were a class of landed aristocracy entrusted with the collection of government revenue and the maintenance of local peace. They belonged either to ancient families of rajas, such as the Rajput chiefs of Monghyr, Ramgarh and other frontier districts, or to other families of local influence, who stipulated to do the collection on payment of only a fixed sum to the royal exchequer. The zamindar had the jungles cleared and colonized by a settlement the land so cleared. He did it so on the payment of a small quit-rent to the sovereign. There was yet a third category of zamindars, a category of 'asignees', not of the land itself, but of the revenue to which the state was entitled. These assignments were often granted by the Mughal government to favourites of the Crown. The revenue was in some cases entirely remitted, while in others a quit-rent was retained.But these were in most cases usually hereditary and were called *nankar*, if granted for the maintenance of the zamindars and their families. The right to collect revenue in any form in fact symbolized social status and, in addition, acted as a source of all sorts of perquisites.

The zamindar functioned more or less as a semi-official agency operating locally in subordination to a district executive officer called the *faujdar*, whom he assisted in the preservation of the peace by placing at his disposal, if necessary, the entire rural police contingents employed in the collection of revenue or night patrolling. Some zamindars maintained even auxiliary armed forces which they supplied to the government in an emergency. They served in fact as a link between the government and society. There were, in addition, 'farmers' of land revenue who undertook on lease to pay a fixed sum annually to the royal exchequer. They were treated as inferior in status to hereditary zamindars who, unlike them, were not required to furnish any security for payment.

However, the zamindar as well as the revenue farmer stood on equal footing in respect of functional subordination to the executive authority of a district. Each was required to assist the *faujdar* in the administration of his district, especially in police administration. While defining the relationship that existed under Mughal rule between the landed aristocracy and the official bureaucracy of the district, Warren Hastings pointed out in 1775 that the zamindar or revenue farmer did the policing in his area.

> as the subordinate Instrument of a larger System. The Land Servants, or the ancient Militia of the Country, were under his immediate charge; and being distributed throughout the Zemindarry, enabled the Zemindar both to watch over its internal Quiet, and to obtain Information of whatever passed in any Part of it; and so far the foujedarry jurisdiction is inherent in the Zemindar. In the Exercise of it, he was subject to a Foujedar, who had the Superintendence of a District comprehending many Zemindarries. . . . It was the zemindar's Duty to give constant Intelligence . . .and to assist the Foujedar in the Apprehension of Robbers, and in executing the Measures which were required of him for preserving the Peace of the Country; but this duty first and immediately belonged to the Foujedar, who was the Representative of the Nazim [provincial governor] and to him the People, looked up for Justice and Protection, even against their Chiefs.[1]

Apart from the rajas and zamindars who owned lands and received perquisites and allowances by virtue of their hereditary rights or grants from the sovereign for a variety of purposes, there were holders of subordinate tenures called taluks. These were grants from a prince or governor of a province, the grantee or talukdar being required to pay his revenue through the zamindar, not directly to the royal exchequer. The zamindars and the various types of assignees constituted the elements of what might be called a feudal structure of society, the actual tillers of the soil of the cultivating community forming the base which supported the superimposed elements of the landed aristocracy. The seignorial rights and privileges of that aristocracy, however, arose from tax farming as well as from military and fiscal obligations to a bureaucratic state, rather than from any legal recognition in respect of village lands under the actual occupation of tillers.

The chief revenue officer of a district (*sarkar*) with direct responsibility for revenue administration on behalf of the government was called the *amalguzar* or *amil*. His function was to bring waste lands into cultivation, to do everything to promote agriculture, and to secure the protection of peasants either against natural calamity or the oppressive conduct of individuals. He exercized a limited executive function and a certain degree of judicial power in the settlement of disputed claims during assessment. But he was neither a magistrate nor a judicial officer. The district revenue officer under the Mughals did not hold a dominant position in the scheme of district administration; for the local communities or individual zamindars of different shades were associated with the performance of two of the main functions of the state, the collection of revenue and the preservation of local peace. They did so as the subordinate instrument of the *faujdar* who had the superintendence of district administration as a whole, an administration which, in spite of its despotic character, was tradition-bound, not change-oriented. Its influence did not go deep in terms of social and economic change.

The administrative arrangements so organized in the districts under the controlling authority of a *Nazim* and his Diwan at the provincial headquarters had both strengths and weakness. Its strength lay in the diffusion of responsibility among zamindars and their local militia of ancient rural police, all tradition-bound and rooted in the community. This diffusion of power, based on the principle of limited bureaucratic functioning, conduced to stability, both political and social. However, its resistance to change caused stagnation. It worked well only so long as the directing force of the Mughal central authority kept both the official and the non-official organs of administration in proper place. But with the disintegration of that central authority they both started working at cross purposes. The district bureaucracy, which mostly depended on the military and financial resources made available to it locally, found itself crippled when zamindars and other landed interests chose to withhold these and declared themselves independent. The erstwhile limited scope of bureaucratic operation and the absence of anything like an organized legal framework of centrally supported local authority created a condition where, in the absence of a regular control by provincial governors, such independence remained largely unchecked. It led to anarchy and disorder, with the result that zamindars and revenue farmers assumed virtual control of rural districts, while the authority of the Nawab of Bengal became restricted to the provincial headquarters and certain other urban centres. Murshid Quli Khan (1712-27) and Alivardi Khan (1740-56) were two Governors of Bengal who tried to check the forces of disintegration. But conditions worsened when Alivardi was succeeded by Siraj-ud-daula in 1757 and created a situation where the involvement of the East India Company added to the confusion.

The East India Company up to 1793

In this state of political uncertainty the East India Company secured from Shah Alam, the Mughal Emperor, the diwani of Bengal, Bihar and Orissa in 1765. It was in the nature of an assignment which invested the Company with the civil administration of the districts. Motivated by considerations of immediate gain the Company did nothing but recognize the *status quo ante*. Four years later, in 1769, it proceeded to appoint to each of the large districts its European convenated servants as *Supervisors* who were nominated as 'Collectors' under Warren Hastings in 1772. It made no appreciable change, however, in the prevailing state of district administration. For, as the *Sixth Report from the Committee of Secrecy of the House of Commons* pointed out in 1773, no regular process had yet been formed for the conduct of business in the districts. Every zamindari and taluk was left to its own peculiar customs and these too were not inviolably adhered to. The effects of the earlier practices were still continuing.

> The Nazims exacted what they could from the Zamindars and great Farmers of the Revenue, whom they left at liberty to plunder all below, reserving to themselves the prerogative of plundering them in their Turn, when they were supposed to have enriched themselves with the Spoils of the Country. The Mutteseddees [revenue agents] who stood between the Nazim and the Zamindars, or between them and the People, had each their respective Shares of the public Wealth. These profits were considered illegal Embezzlements, and therefore were taken with every Caution which could ensure Secrecy..... It therefore became a Duty in every Man to take the most effectual measures to conceal the Value of his Property, and elude every Enquiry into his Conduct; while the Zemindars and other Landholders who had the Advantage of Long Possessions, availed themselves of it by complex Divisions of the Lands, and intricate Modes of Collection, to perplex the Officers of the [Company's] Government, and confine the knowledge of the Rents to themselves. It will be easily imagined that much of the current wealth stopped in the way to the public Treasury.[2]

It is clear from the 1773 Parliamentary Committee Report that zamindars and their allied groups of landholders as a class continued to do everything possible to preserve the commanding influence acquired under the later Mughals. This they tried to achieve by confining, in the words of the Committee, 'the knowledge of the Rents to themselves'. Naturally, the Company's problem was to ascertain the state, produce and capacity of the lands; to know the amount of revenues, cesses or arbitrary taxes which the zamindars and other landholders actually collected from tenants, and to make inquiries into the manner in which these were collected in every district. As the administration of justice also formed part of civil administration a knowledge of it had to included in the inquiry by Collectors.

In the course of a couple of decades from 1769, the year when a plan of supervision was first introduced and European covenanted servants sent into each district to investigate and find answers to the queries entrusted to them, the Company's government enacted a series of measures to know the difference between collections made from the raiyats and the revenues received in 'the public treasury'. These and the various reforms introduced periodically to ascertain the revenue capacity of each district in the interest of both government and the people have already been discussed in some depth in earlier works.[3] In this work the pre-1793 developments are resolved into issues and analysed in terms of district administration by reference to the principle of the Company's policy and the incapacity of its bureaucracy to devise any alternative to the Permanent Settlement. This approach is peculiarly relevant to present-day experience.

There were two main objects in the Company's plan for supervision: to secure for it commercial interest to the extent that the potential resources of the diwani provinces permitted; and, consistent with those resources, to reorganize district administration so as to secure the protection of the peasantry against the rapacity and exactions of intermediaries. How best could these objects be achieved? Should the erstwhile indigenous agency be continued for the purpose, or should the agency of the Company's convenanted servants be employed to achieve necessary goals? The continuance of the indigenous agency involved an attempt to restore it to the vigour of the original constitution of the Mughal government. The exclusive employment of the Company's covenanted agency as an instrument of change meant, on the other hand, a gigantic task of transforming a profit-motivated commercial apparatus into a service-motivated administrative structure. Both the alternatives were equally difficult. Opinion, too, was divided on the question of accepting one to the exclusion of the other. Even so, a beginning had been made in favour of the former. Muhammad Reza Khan was appointed both as *naib diwan* and *naib nazim* to look after the civil and criminal administration in the districts throughout Bengal, Bihar and Orissa.[4] For, as Clive wrote to the Court of Directors, 'In the infancy of the acquisition [of diwani] we were under the necessity of confiding in the old officers of the Government, from whom we were to derive our knowledge, and whom we therefore endeavoured to attract to our Service by the ties of interest, until experience should render their assistance less necessary. Policy required that we should pursue every step to conciliate the natives to our government.'[5]

The policy so pursued accomplished the object intended. It is borne out by the *Sixth Report from the Committee of Secrecy*. Quoting figures of revenue collection it noted 'the dreadful Famine' which visited the diwani provinces in 1770 and which 'raged during the whole course of that year'. Referring further to the sufferings caused the Committee observed:

> But its influence on the Revenues has been yet unnoticed, and even unfelt but by those from whom it is collected; for notwithstanding the Loss of at least One Third of the Inhabitants of the Province, and the consequent Decrease of the Cultivation, the Net Collections of the year 1771 exceeded even those of 1768.[6]

However, this was no indication of the total amount of the revenues, cesses or arbitrary collections of the zamindars and other landholders; nor did it help provide the requisite knowledge of the manner in which these collections were made from raiyats. In the absence of any regular process, they followed their own custom, based on arbitrary will, a will which could not be controlled except by an interposition of the executive authority of the Company's government.[7] The Supervisors were of course commissioned to look into the numerous 'oppressions' which happened to be 'as grievous to the poor as they are injurious to the government'. They were in fact asked to raise 'the heart of the ryot from oppression and despondency to security and joy'. But they had no executive authority. Their attempt to detect abuses was counteracted by the power of zamindars and others of their kind whose interest it was to keep them ignorant. In these circumstances Warren Hastings nominated them as Collectors in 1772 and invested them with executive authority in the administration of districts. This united in their office both revenue and civil judicial functions of a regular *diwani adalat*.

Educated at Westminister and appointed to the covenanted service of the Company at seventeen, Hastings acquired a knowledge of Bengali, Urdu and Persian which enabled him to master the details of the Company's affairs in Bengal. Unlike most of his colleagues, he possessed a clear mind, a fertile intellect, a rare talent for command, a genuine taste for administration and a fervent zeal for the interest of the state. These qualities were united with his love for order and recognized methods, his dauntless courage and belief in the need to promote the public interest. He was thus appointed second of Council at Fort St. George (Madras) in 1769 and raised to the position of Governor at Fort William in Bengal in April, 1772. Both he and the Court of Directors wanted sovereign powers to be exercised in the administration of the *diwani* provinces. But while the Court suggested the expediency of a partial continuance of veil by an attempt to conceal the source of authority, Hastings insisted on an open avowal of British sovereignty as the first step to put an end to the evils of double government through clean administration in the districts under the executive authority of Collectors. His approach in fact was purely political, while that of the Directors largely commercial.

A harder nut to crack, however, was the majority in the Council at Fort William which came to be formed under the Regulating Act (1773) with Warren Hastings as Governor-General and President, and Richard Barwell, General Clavering, Colonel Monson and Philip Francis as Members, all being named in the Act itself. The majority, with the exception of Richard Barwell, lent support to the zamindars who had in several cases been thrown out by revenue farmers and others under the terms of the Quinquennial Settlement[8] introduced in 1772, which let out lands to the highest bidders in order to ascertain the revenue capacity of each of the districts. This mode of settlement, it is true, did provide a new basis of assessment and discovered the revenue resources of the zamindaries to an extent never done before. But letting the lands opened the door to speculators, which, in turn, brought discredit to the government. The Council majority exploited the situation against Warren Hastings who was obliged to go slow.

The active opposition of the majority on the spot and the lukewarmness of the political authority at home tended in fact to put the clock back. The Collectors were thus recalled from the districts which were placed under Indian *naibs* or deputies invested with both revenue and judicial powers to be exercised under the immediate control of six of the provincial councils established on the recall of Collectors in 1773. Policy decisions were clouded by clash between continuity and change. Muhammd Reza Khan was reappointed in 1776 and the Mughal institution of *faujdar* was sought to be revived as an instrument of law and order. Some districts in the course of time were placed later under Collectors, while others remained under *naibs*. Separate civil courts called provincial *diwani adalats* were established in certain districts for the determination of civil suits relating to property as well as those of inheritance and succession to zamindaries and talukdaries, which formerly constituted the jurisdiction of the Governor-General and Council. But no Superintendent of the *adalat* so established was authorized to compel the appearance of any zamindar or revenue farmer to any action except with the written permission of superior revenue authorities. The zamindars and talukdars were not subject to the ordinary process of civil courts.[9] They had regained their freedom as a result of the favour shown to them by the Council majority.

Despite the opposition of his Council majority, Warren Hastings, by a resort to his casting vote, instituted in 1776 a temporary office called the Amini Commission to tour the districts and collect information on the value of the lands. The report presented by the Commission in 1778 contained useful information on the immediate subject of inquiry and, in addition, threw light on the original object of the old institution of *kanungo*, an office of land registry and agricultural statistics which under the Mughals secured the interest of government and the rights of the raiyat. However, the Directors censured Warren Hastings for using his casting vote and warned him against what they regarded as an abuse of authority. Politics was found lagging behind administration.

The interest of the rural cultivating community thus continued to be governed by the arbitrary conduct of landholders. No fixed pattern of district administration could therefore be established until 1781, by when the old Council majority had ceased to exist. Such districts as Burdwan, Murshidabad, Dinajpur, Dacca and Patna had, for instance, continued under the chiefs of the provincial councils of revenue established on the recall of Collectors in 1773. Chittagong, on the other hand, was administered by the Chief of the local Factory, while Rajmahal, Bhagalpur and Palamow remained under military Collectors, exercising both revenue and judicial functions. In the course of 1774-9 several districts were separated from the provincial councils and formed into distinct Collectorships on a different footing. The remaining districts continued to be under their Indian *naibs*. Yet another factor involving legal and constitutional dimensions added to the confusion—the continuance of the Company's muddled thinking on the related subjects of commerce and politics. That perhaps was the reason why the Regulating Act created, without any avowal of the Company's sovereignty, two concurrent and coterminous jurisdictions exercisable by the Governor-General and Council on the one hand and the Supreme Court of judicature, a King's Court, on the other. It led to a series of conflicts[10] beween the Council and the Court, which could not but leave its own stain on district administration.

However, the political principle that Hastings had emphasized on his accession to the Government of Bengal did not long remain unrecognized. While the Amending Act (1781) recognized the legislative authority of the Company's Supreme Government in Bengal and reduced the powers of the Supreme Court, Pitt's India Act (1784) provided for Parliamentary control over the Company's Indian affairs in a manner which continued with certain changes till 1858. Hastings, who shaped the character of the Company's government, firmly believed in the soundness of the Mughal principle of government based on the union of legislative, executive and judicial functions. On this principle his government enacted in 1772 regulations investing the Collector with executive, revenue and judicial powers. There were of course separate officers of justice. But their determinations were to be subject to approval by the Collector who was to preside over the district *adalat* in the same way as Members of Government did over the Sadar court. This was no less than a concept of despotism, although based on the Committee form of government and the rule of law which distinguished Hastings' administration from that of the Mughals, a distinction intended to impart security. Separate Civil Courts were of course established during 1780-1 with a view to separating title suits from revenue cases. But the Sadar Court which consisted of Members of Government remained the final arbiter.

Sir John Shore, an able civil servant and Member of Council, fully shared the views of Warren Hastings on the question of district administration. The heterogeneous form developed during 1774-9 became unacceptable not only to him but to other experienced and honest civil servants also. They pressed for the introduction of a uniform principle of district administration on the pattern of 1772 and recommended that a covenanted servant of the Company should be appointed to every district with powers to administer both revenue and civil justice. In a note of 13 January 1782 Shore justified his proposal on political as well as administrative considerations.[11]

The existing arrangements were, however, allowed to continue thanks to wars and financial stringency. Besides, Hastings himself had to quit in February 1785. Macpherson, who succeeded him, was guided by an exclusive regard for economy and retrenchment. Stuart, who opposed reduction in the number of Collectorships, however, met Macpherson's argument by a suggestion to unite revenue and civil justice in the office of Collector, a suggestion, which, apart from considerations of economy, satisfied the principle of Shore's proposal also. The Governor-General ultimately gave in and accepted his Council's proposal to place all the districts in the neighbourhood of Calcutta under covenanted servants. The Indian diwans, who under the plan of 1772 acted jointly with Collectors, were to be struck off from districts to which covenanted Collectors were appointed. The Court of Directors, too, approved in the meantime the principles underlying the proposals of Shore and Stuart. They realized that the executive authority of government and the Company's own sovereignty could not be strengthened except by the vigour of the European agency of covenanted servants. In their despatch of 12 April 1786, therefore, the Directors asked the Governor-General in Council to place all the districts in the hands of their covenanted servants under the title of Collectors,[12] they were authorized to appoint or dismiss their Indian subordinates, subject only to information being submitted to the Committee of Revenue at Calcutta which was established on the abolition of the provincial councils in 1781.

The Court of Directors even went a step forward and, under the influence of the Board of Control, a Parliamentary body, approved Stuart's plan to re-unite revenue and civil justice in the office of the Collector himself. It was justified on the grounds of simplicity, energy, justice and economy. The Magistracy, created in 1781 in place of the indigenous *faujdar* and transferred to the office of district judge to enable him to function as judge-magistrate, came now to be also united on the same grounds with the office of Collector. In addition to his immediate function of revenue collection and rural relief he became judge and magistrate too. These changes restored him to the status to which Warren Hastings had ceaselessly endeavoured to raise him. Controversies arose from time to time on the question of the union or separation of powers. But the policy that the head of district administration should be an exclusive preserve of the covenanted service remained unchallenged.

In his revenue capacity the Collector was subject to the control of the Board of Revenue created in place of the Commitee of Revenue in

1786, while as magistrate and judge he corresponded directly with Government. His writ ran over the whole of his district, the extent of which could be imagined from the fact that there were at the time only 38 districts in all the diwani provinces of Bengal, Bihar and Orissa, a number reduced to 23 in April 1787.[13] His power and prestige was further enhanced by a regular salary. The economy effected by Macpherson enabled his government to fix the salary of a Collector at 1200 sicca rupees per month. A sum of Rs 500 was allowed to those who presided in civil courts. Every Collector was in addition to be paid a commission on the revenues realized according to certain fixed rates. These were all measures enacted to impart to him and his office a public character, separate and distinct from the commercial tradition of the Company.[14]

Cornwallis, who succeeded Macpherson in 1786, put the seal of approval to these changes in district administration. Differences, however, developed over the policy relating to land settlement, and the Shore-Cornwallis controversy that followed forms part of known history and required no repetition. Lands were settled with zamindars in perpetuity in 1793.

But what needs to be emphasized are a couple of factors that have not received the attention they deserve. The first, of course, is the reinforced recognition of the case of zamindars and other landholders by a statutory order of Parliament to institute inquiries into their claims. Where was the agency then for the conduct of such inquiries? Obviously, the answer was the Company's covenanted service. But was this service a fit instrument for the accomplishment of the task in terms of ability, honesty and experience? This is the second and perhaps more important question. There were doubtless some individual administrators known for their ability and uprightness but the covenanted service as a class was not able or willing to work out an alternative to the zamindari system.

In fact, the Company's servants themselves had developed landed interests comparable to those of the zamindars, to whom they had started giving loans on lease or mortgages once the Company gained possession of the 38 villages[15] around Calcutta on the defeat of Siraj-ud-daula at Plassey in 1757. For instance when the Governor and his committee at Fort William let the lands of the Calcutta pargana for a period of three years by public auction, 'some of the Company's Servants took and leased a Part of the Lands of the said Purgunnahs'.[16] In a letter of 23 March 1759 the Court of Directors in fact issued an advice prohibiting 'their Covenanted Servants from holding any lands, Towns, or Villages, directly or indirectly [through their agents] within or without the Company's jurisdiction'.[17]

This advice of the Court of Directors remained inoperative. It was later 'revoked' in their letter of 13 March 1761 which said that if 'the Governor and Council' at Fort William 'were perfectly satisfied, and no Inconveniencies could arise from the Company's Servants farming any Part of the newly acquired lands, they should not object to it'.[18] The result was that, like employees of the Mughals, the covenanted servants of the Company came to hold farms not only in the Calcutta pargana, but also in the districts of Burdwan, Midnapur and Chittagong ceded in 1760 by Mir Kasim in return for the ouster of Mir Jafar from the governorship of Bengal. And, as Verelst, the Supervisor of Burdwan reported in a letter of 13 September 1765, these covenanted servants had taken for themselves on lease at reduced rates the best lands in the district and it became difficult to find bidders for the rest.

In their letter of 17 May 1766, the Court of Directors mentioned Verelst's earlier report and regretted the permission extended to the Company's servants to farm lands for themselves directly or indirectly.

> We have on a former occasion [the letter said] permitted our Servants to bid at the public Sale of the Calcutta Lands, but we could not conceive such an Indulgence could ever be construed to admit Servants employed in the Collection of the Revenues of a Province, to select out the most profitable Lands for themselves . . . and it is one more striking proof of the general corruption, with which all Ranks were tainted, and of the ill use that has been made of every Indulgence: We direct a strict Scrutiny into this Affair.[19]

The Directors in fact 'positively' ordered that 'no Covenanted Servant, or Englishman, residing under our Protection, shall be suffered to hold any Land for his own Account, directly or indirectly, in his own Name, or that of others, or to be concerned in any Farms or Revenues whatsoever'.[20] The order did not work, however, for the Company's covenanted servants continued to hold lands either in their own names or in those of their *banyans* with whom they shared the profits.

In districts where the Company had been granted the diwani the position was only slightly different. There the covenanted servants lent money to zamindars and held farms through them. They developed an identity of interest with the zamindars and protected them against the *amils* employed by Muhammad Reza Khan, the *naib diwan*, to collect the revenue from them for the Company. On the complaints made by the *naib diwan* the Company's government in Bengal issued 'positive orders' to the chiefs of subordinate factories, commanding officers and other servants 'prohibiting them from lending Money to the Zemindars, or other Servants of the [Nawab's] Government, on the security of Lands by Lease or Mortage, and also from exerting any Degree of Influence in the Appointment to the public offices, or otherwise interfering, directly or indirectly, with the Business of the [Nawab's] Government, on Pain of Suspenson.[21] In a Minute recorded by Clive and his Select Committee on 31 December 1766, however, they noted with concern that these orders had been 'disregarded to the great prejudice of the Revenue, and injury of the Company'.[22] But the Select Committee did nothing beyond suggesting that 'strict inquiry' should be made as to who the 'transgressors' were and that the names of those who had lent money at rates higher than 12 per cent should be transmitted to the headquarters for such action as the authorities deemed fit. Clive introduced a number of changes to improve the situation but failed to create any impression because of his own involvement in the jagir of the 24 Parganas earlier secured for himself.

Regardless of whether it is the zamindars or revenue farmers, the officers of the Nawab's government of even of the Company's European Servants, it is clear that categories acted and behaved according to the norms prevalent in later Mughals times. The Collectors whom the Company's Governor and Council nominated in 1772, were little different in this respect, despite the regulations enacted in that year and the Quinquennial Settlement which involved public auctions.

Certain proceedings against some military and other officers of the Company show that the rate of accumulated interest on money lent to zamindars, revenue farmers or raiyats was 'rarely less than 3, and often as high as 15 per cent per Mensem'. The Committee of Secrecy (1773)[23] found that with monthly accumulation, including fees to agents, *banyans*, peons and sepoys, the rate of interest amounted to '200 per cent per Annum'. Hastings' Government admitted this:

> Every Rupee thus squeezed from the People is in effect taken from the government, which can receive from the People no more than they have to give. We lament that it is not in our Power wholly to repress this Evil: The only way by which such an end could be accomplished, would be the absolute prohibition of all Loans, or, which would, in effect, prove the same, by refusing the Aid of Govemment to the Recovery of them.

Another alternative suggested under the rules was that 'the Collector be forbid, on Plain of Dismission from his office, to be concerned, directly or indirectly, to the purchase of sale of Grain' effected in the process of realizing the dues of government.

While letting the lands by public auction in 1772, the Government of Bengal was fully aware of the continuing evils of money-lending. But it could do no more than enjoining Collectors to stop the evil by avoiding involvement in the purchase or sale of farms. Even so, one particular Collector was warned that he would be removed from office if he lent money himself to zamindars, farmers or talukdars of his district or suffered 'his Banyan or any other of his servants or dependants' to do so.

The government regretted its inability to stamp out bureaucratic corruption, but effective check could not be exercised on Collectors attempting to hold land on lease or bidding at a public auction either himself or through his favourites. Naturally, the Quinquennial Settlement of 1772 brought discredit on Warren Hastings, its author, who was called upon to recall Collectors from the districts and replace them by *naib diwans*. The zamindars whose interest was seriously affected by Hastings' decision to let the lands to the highest bidders, worked against the success of his plan. But the bureaucratic agency that viewed the continuance of the zamindari system as immediately profitable to itself was perhaps the basic cause of its failure. The difficulty of the government continued even after the recall of Collectors, for, as noted earlier, the Council majority ceaselessly worked against any action Hastings took to weaken the intermediaries between government and the communities who bore the tax-burden.

Doubtless, there were some Collectors who were men of 'probity and honour'. They needed no check or restraint. But restraint was necessary for the Company's covenanted servants as a class so that they might develop the qualities of public service. Its object was in fact to 'make the Interest of Individuals coincide with their duty'. It was here that Warren Hastings, despite obstacles, laid foundations for the development of those qualities. 'To presume', as his Committee of Revenue said, 'that all Men are possessed of Integrity, and to trust entirely to this Principle, is to leave a Door open for every Species of Depravity; for many will abuse the Confidence thus tacitly reposed in them; and under the specious Appellation of Perquisites, the most flagrant corruption will be admitted, even by Men whose natural Principles, without such a Bias, would receive the offer of them with Abhorrence.'[24] It is thus not unreasonable to conclude that, barring certain exceptions, the Company's covenanted service as a whole had not yet developed the requisite character, ability and experience to evolve, any positive and precise answer to the problems of land policy raised since the appointment of supervisors in 1769 and their subsequent nomination as Collectors in 1772.

Apart from the profit motivations of the bulk of its own bureaucracy, a most serious handicap of the new government proceeded from the fact that the institution of *kanungo* under the later Mughals had become dysfunctional and developed a degree of landed interest which differed but little from that of the zamindars themselves. The original object of the *kanungo* was to attest and register grants and transfers of landed property; the records showed the names of parties, the nature of their tenures, the quantity of lands under cultivation or waste, the nature of produce and current prices, the rates of assessment, the total demand, receipt and balance of land revenue within the limits of his jurisdiction. He also maintained the genealogies of zamindars, registered judicial degrees of estates and kept copies of every document which he was in law required to authenticate. His office thus secured the interests of the state against the dissipation of revenues by zamindars, and protected at the same time the cultivating community from exactions and illegal impositions. The *kanungo* was, in fact, a key institution which kept in shape the rural economy of the Mughals by functioning as a check on the landed aristocracy.

Like most other institutions, however, the office of the *kanungo* also became hereditary, He developed a vested interest; and, instead of serving as a check on zamindars, he became their ally. It was these *kanungos* who, on the Company's accession to the diwani of Bengal, tried,either from fear or self-interest, to conceal the real value of the lands. Warren Hastings attempted to convert them into paid servants by a suspension of their grants in the districts. But on the recall of the Collectors this decision had to be revoked. The Amini Commission appointed in 1776 studied the original objects of their institution. But for reasons already pointed out its effort remained largely academic.

Indeed, while the old agency of control over zamindars had for all practical purposes come to partake of the character of zamindars themselves, the new agency of the Company's covenanted service had not yet emerged as an effective check in terms of experience, honesty and public spirit. Consideration of political stability and vague notions of respect for what was claimed as the private property of zamindars added weight to Cornwallis's decision to declare Shore's decennial settlement permanent in 1793.

The Permanent Settlement thus recognized the zamindars as the dominant element of society in Bengal and Bihar. The administrative arrangement introduced with it naturally affected the position of the Collector, who ceased to be both Magistrate and Judge. He was completely divested of all judicial powers, including even those connected with revenue cases. The scope of his functions became limited merely to the collection of the revenues. Differing from the Court of Directors, Cornwallis deemed it incompatible with the principles of his system to permit revenue officers to decide even on civil suits originating in their own departments. All judicial powers were transferred to a new court of *diwani adalat* established in every district. The new Judge was a European covenanted servant of a higher official rank than the Collector who uniting in his person the function of Magistrate. In actual practice the existing Collectors were appointed Judges, while their covenanted head assistants were appointed to the several Collectorates.[25] The arrangement so made by Cornwallis met the demands of zamindars but weakened the authority of the Collector in the districts of Bengal and Bihar, which, in consequence, were the first to witness the emergence of revolutionary nationalism a century later.

The appointment of Indian civil judges called munsifs was another measure enacted in 1793 to hear and decide, in the first instance, suits of personal property not exceeding a certain value. They were paid by commission on the amount of causes investigated by them. Appeals lay from their decision to the District Judge.

Appeals from the Court of the District Judge lay before one of the four Provincial Courts of Appeal established under Regulation V of 1793 at Dacca, Patna, Murshidabad and in the vicinity of Calcutta. This arrangement was designed to lessen the burden on the Governor-General in Council who previously received appeals directly from the districts. The Executive Government, however, continued to function as the highest court of appeal called Sadar Diwani Adalat.

As regards criminal administration,[26] Warren Hastings had on the advice of Muhammed Reza Khan reorganized it in every district under a *faujdar* as police officer and a *daroga* of the *nizamat adalat* as a superintendent of criminal justice who tried criminal cases with the assistance of Muhammadan Law Officers, subject to final determination by the Sadar Nizamat Adalat presided over by Muhammad Reza Khan as the Nawab's Deputy at Murshidabad. While the *faujdar* was replaced by the European Magistrate in 1781, the criminal judicial arrangement for the trial and punishment of offences continued till 1790. Certain zamindars were in the meantime invested by Government with such police duties as they once performed under the Mughals. In such cases the European Judge, in his capacity as Magistrate, the *daroga* of the *faujdari adalat*, and the zamindar were all to exercise concurrent jurisdiction in the prevention of crime. The only change that took place in 1786 was the union of the magistracy with the function of the civil judge in the person of the Collector, which until he was divested of both in 1793.

The change that Cornwallis effected in the administration of criminal justice was a radical departure from the old tradition of functional overlapping. Towards the close of 1790 it was declared that in order 'to ensure a prompt and impartial administration of criminal law' and to enable 'all ranks of people' to enjoy 'security of person and property the Governor-General in Council has resolved to accept the superintendence of the administration of criminal justice throughout the Province'. Muhammad Reza Khan was accordingly discharged and the *nizamat adalat* or the chief criminal court was brought to Calcutta where it consisted of the Governor-General and Members of his Council. The native *darogas* of criminal courts were also discharged and four Courts of Circuit were constituted for the trial of cases not punishable by the Magistrates in the districts. Each of these four courts established for each of the four divisions of Calcutta, Murshidabad, Dacca and Patna was presided over by Indian law officers. The courts of circuit were manned by the same officers, European and Indian, for the trial of civil and criminal cases. Their judges moved round their respective circuits twice a year and superintended trial in the districts in their jurisdiction.

In the districts, every Judge-Magistrate in his magisterial capacity functioned as the chief police officer or superintendent of his district. He was assisted by police *darogas* or *thanadars* appointed by the government and put under his immediate control in place of zamindars who were divested of their entire police function in 1792. The powers of the Magistrate had in fact started increasing ever since 1787 when, apart from being the chief police officer of his district, he was, contrary to the constitution of the Mughals, invested with the trial and punishment of offences to the extent of fifteen *ratans*, or imprisonment not exceeding fifteen-day terms and fines within a limit of Rs 200. His power of punishment did not remain limited to imprisonment only for the term laid down in 1787, but kept increasing gradually till it reached the maximum term of two years in 1818. He was in the meantime also authorized to appoint his *darogas* of police, a power earlier subject to approval by the government. While the zamindars under the Cornwallis Code were deprived of their powers to preserve the peace, the entire body of rural police consisting of different varieties of chaukidars was placed at the disposal of the government police, administered locally by the Magistrate and his *darogas*.

Though discussed at length in the *Central Administration of the East India Company, 1773-1834,* this brief recapitulation is necessary for a clear grasp of the Bengal pattern of district administration that developed on the principles laid down by Cornwallis in 1793. The first of these principles was the security of person and right to private property recognized by law and ascertained by the judiciary, not by custom, which differed from place to place and would not easily be reduced to uniformity for legislative and administrative purposes. That gave the zamindar a clear edge over the Collector whose jurisdiction did not extend beyond the collection of revenue, and there, too, his decisions were subject to revision by the civil court. The Collector, whose rank was also reduced, could no longer make justice executively available to those who could not afford any resort to judicial proceedings in a regular court of law. The second important principle was that criminal judicial function was united with the executive and police authority of the Magistrate who was also a civil judge. As the Judge-Magistrate was not in any way associated with the promotion of agriculture or rural development, as the Collector once was, this union of functions in the office of the Magistrate bred bureaucratic despotism for its own sake, or, at best, for the sake of British imperialism. There was a third important dimension to district administration which Cornwallis introduced in 1793. This was an attempt to bring under the aegis of the state all such functions as were earlier performed by local communities, including the zamindars who after all not only formed part of those communities but also led them.

These measures which went into the formation of the Cornwallis Code, doubtless conduced to modernization in terms of reducing by law and legislative authority the operational area of custom and consensus. But since the precondition of social and economic advance was largely missing, this type of modernization was more formal than real. It was based on the concept of legal contract without a corresponding support of modern education and economic development, the *sine qua non* in the growth tort or contract. The creation of the right to property by law and the reorganization of a judicial system to ascertain and enforce that right according to a legally recognized process encouraged, in the absence of that socio-economic precondition, a tendency among the rich to exploit the poor and the ignorant. It led to the growth of a modern legal profession which, together with the propertied classes, developed a vested urban interest of its own that was hardly conducive to rural welfare. The Code tended in fact to destroy the benefits of a status society based on the popularly recognized concept of natural justice, and introduced, instead, an alternative system which, though designed conceptually to promote equality before law, dissipated it and encouraged inequality. Justice could no longer be made executively available to the poor and needy under the Judge Magistrate system.

Like Cornwallis, Warren Hastings, too, had implicit faith in the European bureaucracy as an instrument of administrative reconstruction at the district level. But he was radically different from Cornwallis in two respects. First, though both wanted the Magistracy to be the head of district administration, Hastings' preference was for the Collector who had the promotion of agriculture and the care of public finance as part of his immediate duty, not the Judge-Magistrate who was unconnected with the problems of rural communities. Secondly, as a civil servant Hastings possessed a knowledge of indigenous languages and cultures. He believed in the soundness of the Mughal constitution in its original form, which was more in keeping with the status-bound and authoritarian society of the country than the concept of the rule of law which was destructive of both status and caste order. His policy to combine powers in the office of Collector proceeded from the peculiar construction of the indigenous society, not from any theoretical formulation of legal principles or a desire to introduce innovations as an imported artefact to encourage change without reference to reality. During this formative period of the Company's rule in Bengal both principles emerged and started competing for recognition in the field of district administration. The higher echelons of the bureaucracy who had direct experience of local conditions, cast their weight in favour of the authority of the Collector. But Cornwallis' emphasis on the rule of law was not in vain and continued after him. District administration in modern times grew both structurally and functionally from the interaction between these two principles.

The first of the two principles was conducive to continuity, while the second contained the seeds of change. But in a society where the balance of both social and economic forces was weighted heavily in favour of the propertied classes, any provision for compulsory resort to court as a *sine qua non* for relief signified a virtual denial of justice to those who did not possess means to carry on litigation for years on end. Though devised as an instrument of change, Cornwallis' emphasis on the rule of law was used by landholders not only to maintain the *status quo ante* but also to enable the rich to become richer by making the poor poorer. The dichotomy naturally continued and continues even now without any prospect of a resolution. The 42nd Constitution Amendment Act (1976), which sought to curtail the powers of the judiciary in an 'Emergency' is clear evidence of the continuance of that dichotomy. The success or failure of one principle or the other, however, depended on the administrative skill which individuals brought to bear upon the administration of law to make justice available to the rural poor. It was in the light of experience that changes were effected in the system of district administration established in 1793.

The Cornwallis System in the North-Western Provinces

The Upper or North-Western Provinces consisted of the territory ceded by the Nawab of Oudh in 1801 to the British and conquered by them from the Marathas in 1803. By a proclamation issued on 14 July 1802 the Central Government in Bengal declared its intention to introduce a permanent settlement after ten years, covering a couple of triennial settlements in the first instance and a quadrennial settlement which was to be concluded in 1813 in the case of the ceded districts and in 1815 in respect of the conquered areas. This intention was announced without any reference to the Court of Directors. It was assumed that since the merits of a settlement in perpetuity had already received approval in the case of the *diwani* provinces in 1793, its extension to the ceded and conquered districts would be only a matter of course. The announcement to have the settlement of land revenue made in perpetuity preferably with 'the zamindars or the other actual proprietors of the soil' occurred without ascertaining who the actual proprietors were.

The Court of Directors, however, withheld their approval. The

Governor-General in Council then appointed a Commission in 1807 with Cox and Tucker as two of its members. The object was to secure a local report to confirm the policy already announced. But the Commission's report did not conform to the expectations of the Government. On the contrary, the Commissioners raised serious objections to a permanent settlement even on the score of political expediency. For the resources of the newly-acquired districts had not yet been assessed and no decision had been made on the question of proprietorship which was being contested by all sorts of people.

There were in fact four categories of landed interests in the newly acquired districts of the North-Western Provinces. These consisted of big zamindars, subordinate *talukdars*, joint village proprietors and resident raiyats with no proprietory rights but tilling the lands on payment of rent. The taluks or smaller estates in a large zamindari stood in the same relation to their zamindar as the village proprietors to their immediate overlord, the *talukdar*. As part of its policy to reduce refractory zamindars, however, settlement could be made separately with subordinate *talukdars* with permission to pay their revenue immediately to Government through its *tahasildars*. But where there were no *talukdars*, a settlement could as well be concluded with the chiefs of village zamindars holding lands in co-parcenary tenure on the principle of kinship and common heredity. Confusion arose because of hasty government action which involved the zamindars, *talukdars* and village proprietors in a triangular conflict, where each class started vying for recognition of its own rights to property. In the melee which followed, the more respectable class of village zamindars happened to be the worst sufferers. Their estates were in several cases sold out for default of a few principal shareholders in whose names these estates were exclusively recorded in government registers (and not in those of all the co-parceners). Even officers of civil courts colluded with the principal shareholders and innumerable transfers of landed property were fraudulently effected on payment of nominal sums of money, transfers which were legally confirmed even by the Company's higher courts of appeal. The Collectors could do little to help, for they had no civil judicial powers even in revenue cases.

Such developments dictated the need for a revision of the Cornwallis system, not only in respect of the principle and mode of settlement, but also of the Judge-Magistrate system in the administration of the districts. The person who led the move in favour of this revision was

Holt Mackenzie, by far the ablest of the civil servants who believed in the soundness of the raiyatwari system introduced in Madras by Sir Thomas Munro. As Secretary to the Government in the Territorial Department he personally made local investigations into the nature of land tenures in the ceded and conquered provinces, studied their main features in the context of historical developments, and drew from his researches a principle of settlement to the Government for acceptance on 1 July 1819.[27] His discovery of the existance of villages held in joint property and comprehended in the estates of major landholders led him to recommend that the revision of settlement should in all cases be made village by village and that with joint villages separate engagements should be entered into with one or more principal co-parceners, or with any trustworthy manager to be elected with the consent of inferior shareholders whose names had not yet found place in government registers. He emphasized the necessity of a systematic survey as the only effective means to determine not only the respective rights of parties in a village, but also the precise point of improvement in the state of agriculture.

Mackenzie's recommendations were perfectly in line with the policy of the London authorities. His emphasis on a systematic survey was in principle a recognition of the essential feature of the raiyatwari system. He called for the restoration of the importance of the office of Collector, reduced under the Cornwallis Code. Consistent with his recommendations a Special Commission was appointed in 1821. This was done in the teeth of opposition from the Sadar Diwani Adalat. For the Commission was a purely executive agency and authorized to revoke the decisions of the court in order to make relief available to those co-parceners whose property had been sold in the absence of any record of right being separately maintained in their own names. The Special Commission was in addition guided by its own rules, which were less rigid than those required in regular judicial process.

In the same order of developments the Governor-General in Council enacted Regulation VII of 1822 under which the Collector or his settlement officer was required to conduct inquiries on the spot, village by village, proceeding upwards from those who tilled the ground to the government itself, noting all the classes who shared in the produce or rent of land, the extent of the interest of each, and the nature of the title by which it was held. The new task could not obviously be accomplished except by reinvesting the Collector with a measure of executive and judicial authority. His decisions were of course to be subject to review by a regular civil court. Even so, it was to remain operative unless otherwise determined on appeal to a civil judge.

However, not only the new approach to land policy called for a strengthening of the powers of Collectors, but the exigencies of nascent British capitalism which was emerging as an imperial and liberal force. This also dictated the need for a highly centralized government and a well-knit administration in India, an administration which might function efficiently as an agent of the parliamentary body, the Board of Control. In a Minute of 1 October 1830, Holt Mackenzie gave clear expression to this new trend which shaped district administration under the government of Lord Bentick. He emphasized in this Minute that there should be 'the completest possible unity of purpose throughout all the departments' in the districts. This, he pointed out, could be achieved by making the Collector a 'sufficiently strong connecting link' between the government and the district, an object which could be accomplished only by uniting in that office magisterial, revenue and, in a certain measure, judicial functions. For, as he argued, 'to disjoin the several parts of government in a country, which is not self-governed, is like placing the different members of the body in charge of different physicians, severally acting with their respective limbs according to individual theory, without reference to the treatment of other parts, and each holding in his hand the power of destroying life, but helpless to save, from the blunders of his brethren.'[28]

The principle so recommended for the reorganization of district administration had already been recognized by a Regulation of 19 January 1821 which declared the Governor-General in Council competent to authorize a Collector or other revenue officer to exercise the power of a magistrate or joint magistrate, or to invest magistrates with the powers of a Collector. Sir Thomas Munro, who had gained eminence for his liberal reforms, justified this union of revenue and magisterial functions in the office of Collector as most essential in the context of Indian society. 'We should form a very erroneous judgment of the important influence of the office of Collector,' he pointed out, in a Minute of 22 January 1822, 'if we supposed that it was limited merely to revenue matters instead of extending to everything affecting the welfare of the people. In India whoever regulates the assessment of the land, really holds in his hand the mainspring of the country.'[29] This principle was reinforced by Bentinck's Government in 1831.

While Regulation VIII of that year divested civil judges of their powers to receive any claims of rent or revenue unless the complaint was preferred as a regular civil suit in their court, the Governor-General in Council transferred on a general plan the office of Magistrate to the Collector in most districts. Under Regulation VII of 1831, the Collector became the district officer, invested not only with the executive authority of Magistrate with powers of arrest and punishment of offences, but also with the summary trial and determination of rent or revenue cases arising from disputed claims to landed property.

Bentinck felt that, apart from the importance of forming individual records of rights under the supervision of Collectors to promote mobility in the transfers of land for purposes of agricultural development, the union of powers in the office of Collector would be able to provide administrative unity for a quick and effective change for good in Indian Society. From a perusal of printed correspondence of Bentinck which Sir Cyril Philips has edited, it appears that Bentinck regretted the virtual absence of improvement in such fields of administration as agriculture and irrigation, roads, and communication, canals and drainage, manufactures and the use of machinery, education and social reforms. He realized that since India under the Company's government had moved into a period of peace, 'its principal business is to improve the condition of the tenantry' by reorganizing its economy and its civil government and administration in the districts. This he found to be 'miserably inefficient', because the separation of judicial and revenue powers had over the years become a source of misrule and injustice, The boards of revenue in the Western provinces had, on the other hand, signally failed to control the excesses of field officers. The need to streamline district administration by a concentration of power in the office of Collector was thus considered necessary not only for the sake of efficiency in the conduct of routine business, but more especially for the development of the economy and modern education involved in the process of modernization.

Bentinck's emphasis on administrative modernization through uniting functions in the office of Collector proceeded from his belief that quick and beneficial socio-economic development in India could 'come mainly from direct action through the formal processes of government by law and official regulation', not from the indigenous society, especially the 'Hindus' who could not accomplish the task of modernizing society unless they were emancipated from 'those chains and shackles upon their minds and actions' which in the past had made them 'the slaves of every foreign conqueror'. For, although in Bengal they were acquiring new vested interests in land, banking shipping and trade, they still clung to orthodox beliefs and opposed the efforts of government, for example, to abolish *sati*.

The modernization of district administration as a link between government and people was thus designed not only to secure efficiency in the discharge of regulatory functions, but also to promote as a direct instrument of government the development of such resources as were immediately related to improvement in the condition of the tenantry. And since to Bentinck the elites of Indian society did not seem equipped to assume 'their just places among the great families of mankind', the Governor-General and Members of Council, in spite of differences on other counts, were unanimous in assuming that, 'if India was to be westernized and modernized, the creative forces to produce change and development in the civil service and in India generally had to be European, and that European colonization in India was therefore immediately desirable on some scale'.[30]

But to Bentinck colonization was to be 'by a small sober class of British with capital and skill, mainly artisans, teachers, and craftsmen,' with, as he said, 'a character of solidity'. This concept of colonization was a product of his imagination, perhaps an expression of basically noble intentions, but it was hardly related to reality. Wedded to the rising wave of *laissez faire* after the opening of the Company's trade and the infiltration of other private interests, its directorate was obliged to release the forces of capitalist enterprise in the exploitation of Indian resources. These included free-lancers of dubious character, speculators and money-lenders, planters and publishers, entrepreneurs and manufactures. In England, the dichotomy of *laissez faire* and strong executive control was resolved by Bentham and other Utilitarian leaders who wanted that control to remain subject to a free, representative legislature which the Reform Act of 1833 sought to provide. In India, where there was yet no possibility of a free legislature, the Charter Act of 1833 provided for the establishment of 'good government'. Bentinck's government enacted regulations for the appointment of uncovenanted Indian officers to assist European civil servants in the discharge of their executive and judicial functions. His policy to promote development with direct, government participation did not work, thanks to financial difficulties and the Home Government's support for private enterprise. But the agency of modernization remained European. It created conditions for the emergence of technical services on the one hand, and the growth of politics which sought representative and parliamentary government on the other.

Post-Bentinck Development in Bengal

Bengal itself did not long remain outside the influence of this new trend of thought. At the time of the permanent settlement large tracts of land had been declared revenue free. The Government, however, reserved to itself the authority to scrutinize such revenue-free grants and to annex them in case they were found invalid. These grants were of two types—*badshahi* and *hukumi*, the former being those granted directly by the Mughal Emperor himself and the latter by Mughal officials. These were dealt with under two Regulations of 1793.

Badshahi grants were later recognized as valid (*bahali*) if the holder could prove that his *sanad* or grant was hereditary and that he was in possession. Though in their nature invalid, *hukumi* grants were, on the other hand, accepted as valid if dated prior to 1765, when the Company first became the diwan of the Mughal Emperor, Shah Alam. All grants of a subsequent date were to be treated as invalid and subject to being resumed, although *hukumi* grants made during 1765-90 were accorded a privileged rate of assessment. All *lakhiraj* or rent-free grants made by zamindars after 1790 were, however, invalidated and they were authorized to nullify their own grants.

These Regulations remained inoperative till 1800, when an attempt was made to introduce compulsory registration of *lakhiraj* grants in registry offices. This, too, proved abortive. The Governor-General in Council had then to enact Regulation II of 1819 which transferred the power of resumption from the civil to the revenue courts. This enactment was reinforced by Regulation III of 1828, which appointed an executive agency of a special Commissioner to implement the policy of resumption. It was under his guidance that resumption proceedings were systematically undertaken between 1830 and 1850. Thousands of estates were consequently added to the revenue roll of the Government. In the post-Mutiny period, when land policy assumed once again a pro-zamindar trend, the jurisdiction of resumption cases was transferred to civil courts under Act VIII of 1869. The question was finally set at rest by the limitation law (Act XV of 1877) which expressly provided for a limit of 60 years in the case of suits instituted by the Secretary of State.

The Judge-Magistrate arrangement of Cornwallis was likewise

modified. The two functions remained united in a single person for nearly forty years after 1793, although in 1810 Regulation XVI had been enacted by which the Government was empowered to make a separate and distinct appointment of a Magistrate. A change in the new direction first came about in 1829 when under Regulation I of that year Divisional Commissioners were appointed over four or five Collectors in a division to supervise the conduct of revenue administration. To the Commissioners so appointed were assigned the functions of the provincial courts of appeal and circuit which were abolished for reasons of economy. They were required to go on circuit as Sessions Judges, in addition to acting as appellate revenue courts under the Sadar Board of Revenue at Calcutta. To these functions was added the superintendence of police. They became divisional superintendents of police: under the earlier arrangement a Superintendent of Police was appointed for several divisions of Bengal in 1808 and another for the divisions of Patna, Banaras and Bareilly in 1810.

However, these arrangements did not work with any measure of success. The judicial powers of Commissioners were transferred after a few years to Civil Judges. Regulation VII of 1831, for instance, authorized the Government to invest the Civil Judges with full powers to perform the duties of the Sessions. Act III of 1835, on the other hand, invested the Government with powers to transfer any part or the whole of the duties connected with criminal justice from any Commissioners of Circuit to any Sessions Judges, and to define the powers which shall be exercised by each respectively.' Even so, Commissioners continued to hold judicial powers and were at times so employed. Regulation VII of 1831 and Act III of 1835 were both repealed by Act VIII of 1868. The result was that all Divisional Commissioners ceased to have powers of Sessions Judges. The appointment of officers as Sessions Judges was thereafter governed by the rules laid down by the new Code of Criminal Procedure.

Under Bentinck's arrangement of 1831, judges were required to hold jail delivery every month. They could not however discharge their Magisterial duties adequately for the demands of the Magistracy. Civil Judges were, therefore, divested of their Magisterial responsibilities, which were transferred to the Collector in 1831. The Collector-Magistrate became once again the executive head of each district.

The criminal branch of the judicial departmet was later

strengthened by the extended employment of uncovenanted civilians, which led to the creation of a separate cadre of Deputy Magistrates under an Act of the Legislative Council in 1843. The gradual extension of the uncovenanted agency to criminal administration after Bentinck tended to reduce the Magisterial work of the Collector, who was called upon to devote greater attention to the increasing operatons for the resumption of revenue-free tenures which had come to be treated virtually as a permanent job. In 1837, the Court of Directors and Lord Auckland both agreed on a plan of the gradual separation of the offices of Magistrate and Collector. This went on until 1845 when the magisterial and fiscal offices were separated everywhere, except in three districts of Orissa and in the Joint-Magistracies or sub-divisions of Pabna, Malda, Bogra, Noakhali, Faridpur, Bankura, Barasat and Champaran.[31]

The major consideration for the separation of the magistracy from the Collector in 1845 was, however, fiscal, a consideration which did not take into account the relative importance of the magistracy as an integral part of the office of Collector, who held a commanding position by virtue of his direct contact with the rural population. This was the political dimension of the administrative arrangement of both Hastings and Bentinck, but the separation of 1845 seemed to have disregarded it perhaps out of a conviction that the progressive character of British land policy could act as the best guarantee for security against any rebellion. The Indian Mutiny of 1857, however, belied this fond hope. The peasantry whose landed rights had been secured against their landlords rallied round their erstwhile oppressors in their attempt to overthrow British rule.

In the light of experience gained at great cost, the offices of Magistrate and Collector were united again in 1859. Besides being the executive head of the district, the Collector-Magistrate was reinvested with judicial powers in the administration of revenue and criminal cases, over crimes punishable with up to two years' imprisonment at the discretion of the District Magistrate.

The administration of police in the districts, however, remained in a state of confusion. The police force was administered by the Collector-Magistrate who united in his office both revenue and magisterial functions under Regulation VII of 1831, under the immediate supervision of the Divisional Commissioner who also combined both revenue and Magisterial functions. These were gradually separated in the districts between 1837 and 1845, a period when the revenue establishments of the Company exercised a general and ill-defined control over the police within their charge, and separate police officers were gradually appointed to administer the police forces under the general instructions of the head of the district. The gradual separation of the revenue and the Magistracy between 1837 and 1845 thus meant a corresponding separation of the Magistrate's judicial and police functions in the same period. This proved a failure and had to be abandoned in 1859.[32]

In 1837 yet another spot weakness in the organization of the Magistracy and police in Bengal became evident. Under Act XXIV of that year the Magisterial and police authority of the Commissioner was affected by a provision which again empowered the Government to appoint a Superintendent of Police, so that the Commissioner should cease to exercise any powers in regard to the Magistracy and police. In Bengal, a single Superintendent of Police was accordingly appointed. The separate police officers appointed on the gradual separation of revenue and Magisterial functions in the districts during 1837-45 and after were perhaps to act under the direction of the single Superintendent of Police so appointed. After a short experience, however, it was considered advisable to exempt from his jurisdiction the non-regulation districts of Assam, the South-Western frontier and Orissa, which were placed again under Commissioners. The Chittagong Division too was similarly removed from the jurisdiction of the Superintendent of Police. These experiments continued on the principle of trial and error. On 23 March 1854 the Court of Directors sanctioned the abolition of the Superintendent of Police and transferred his functions to the Commissioners of Revenue.

The foregoing account of district administration in Bengal brings into relief two well-defined trends emerging from the creation of property under the terms of the permanent settlement. The first was the emphasis which Cornwallis laid on the rule of law and legislative authority as an instrument for the protection of property so created. The rights of the landlord as against the state were, for instance, well defined by the Regulations of 1793. But the rights of tenant as against landlord were left to the law courts to decide. Moreover, the zamindars in 1799 were invested with greater powers of distraint to recover rents from the raiyats, and these powers were further increased in 1812. Landholders thus came to exercise over the years an authority far in excess of that given to them by the original settlement of 1793. Consistent with considerations for the protection of property rights, the Government even ceased to function as the final court of appeal in both civil and criminal cases. Under Regulation II of 1801 it was determined that the Government should relinquish the chief civil and criminal jurisdiction and place it in the hands of a court of justice consisting of three judges, the chief judge being a member of the Council, and the other two selected from the covenanted civil service.

The object of the second trend was to strengthen the executive apparatus of the state as a medium of direct contact with all the classes engaged in agriculture and to know the conditions under which subordinate tenures subsisted. Its origin go back to a letter of 28 August 1771 from the Court of Directors to the Government of Bengal, asking the Government to stand forth as diwan and directly take over through its own servants the entire care and management of the revenues. The administrative arrangement that Warren Hastings introduced in 1772 was in fulfilment of that plan. For reasons analysed before, it did not succeed. The permanent settlement intervened. The experience gained from the Mahalwari Settlement in the North-Western Provinces, however, renewed the importance of the original plan of 1772, an importance reinforced ideologically by the nascent capitalist philosophy of the English Utilitarians. Even so, the Judge-Magistrate system as well as the various experiments tried from time to time in the field of district administration left the position of the Collector-Magistrate relatively weak in Bengal and Bihar before it was sought to be finally restored to strength in 1859.

The position of the Collector in the Upper Provinces was, however, stronger. The Cornwallis system was exposed to severe criticism before it could take root. The rejection of the permanent settlement and the Mahalwari system of periodic settlements were both responsible for the strength of that office. The permanent settlement and the invariable rule of sale in case of default were said to have rendered unnecessary any further information than the great book of the Collector which showed the revenue payable for each estate. Most districts were later surveyed, but this was only for the exterior boundaries of these estates. Nothing like an exact census of the population had been attempted. The districts of the North-Western Provinces were, on the contrary, provided with large establishments which over the years were brought by close supervision to a high state of efficiency. These kept the Magistrate and Collector in intimate communication with every part of his district. The tahsildars and their subordinates, the *kanungos* and patwaris, furnished from year to year fiscal and agrarian returns of the most minute description.[33] Such establishments were found wanting in the lower Provinces of Bengal and Bihar where the Collector had neither executive establishments at lower levels nor statistics. Districts were later subdivided into what came to be known as Joint-Magistracies or Sub-divisions. But the Joint-Magistrate was more a judicial officer than a revenue functionary concerned with the rural economy. Even so, the ease-loving Bengal Collector viewed with dismay any attempt to reduce his territorial jurisdiction by the creation of independent Joint-Magistracies.

The importance of both substantive and procedural laws which the Cornwallis Code emphasized stayed nevertheless, and stayed as a permanent feature of public administration in the country as a whole. It was a radical departure from tradition, not only subjecting executive action to judicial review, but bringing under its jurisdiction an ever increasing number of functions previously recognized as the exclusive domain of the tradition-bound local custom and usage, administered locally by consensus-bound rural communities. The complexity of the modern legal system as an alternative to custom encouraged litigation and led to the expansion of the executive and judicial hierarchies causing delay in the making of decisions in the districts. A remedy was, therefore, sought to be found in functional specialization, which, in turn, meant diversification at both administrative and executive levels. These trends which formed part of the philosophy of bureaucratic rationalization, had already started emerging towards the close of the Company's rule. The gradual separation of the police from the Magistracy after 1837 was, for instance, in line with the development of functional specialization in the administration of the police. Imperial interests, however, called for a concentration of authority. That is why the Magistracy was united again with the office of Collector in 1859. But that was now more for purposes of coordination than direct executive action. The creation of a separate and systematic police organization under the Police Act of 1861 was in fact clear evidence of the new trend of specialization which had been proceeding in the wake of western education, commerce and industry.

Indeed, the need for coordination in district administration first arose on the creation of Joint-Magistracies 'as quasi-subdivisions' in the early part of the nineteenth century.[34] At first these were off-shoots from large districts, which were placed under Joint-Magistrates to stern the tide of dacoity and other crimes committed in localities remote from the headquarters of a district. Starting from an exercise of joint jurisdiction with the Magistrate of the district the Joint Magistrate of such sub-divisions gradually came to wield independent criminal powers, uniting in his office both police and criminal judicial authority. In revenue matters, however, he was invested with more powers than those of a Deputy Collector, a subordinate revenue officer organized into a separate cadre in 1833. The land revenue of a Joint-Magistracy was always paid at the headquarters' treasury.

Of the eight independent Joint-Magistracies where magisterial and fiscal functions remained united in spite of the general separation effected in 1845, four were on Rs 18,000 per annum and the remaining four on Rs 12,000. At the time of the reunion of the magistracy with the Collector in 1859, one was reduced to an ordinary sub-division and the remaining seven were raised to the status of full Magistracies and Collectorates.

The regular cadre of Joint Magistrates that developed later in modern times was, in fact, the creation of Lord Bentinck. He established two classes of covenanted officers functioning as subordinates to the district officer. One was the Joint Magistrate and Deputy Collector on a salary of Rs 1,000 a month, the other a Head Assistant on Rs. 700. The latter was abolished by an order of 16 August, 1836 and in its place a second grade of Joint-Magistracy was created on the same salary but with the full powers of a Joint Magistrate and Deputy Collector. The first category of Joint Magistrates became Magistrates when the magisterial and revenue functions were separated. But their salary was then reduced to Rs 900 a month. It was this category that later corresponded to first-grade Joint Magistrates.

The necessity of the co-ordinating or controlling authority of the district officer thus arose, in the first instance from the creation of sub-divisions under separate Joint-Magistracies which subsequently became full Magistracies and then from the gradual appointment of separate police officers acting under general instructions from the executive head of the district. Of these two developments in the administration of districts, the separation of the police from the Magistracy became important after the expense of the Mutiny, and led to the establishment in 1861 of a separate Department of Police under the District Magistrate.

Indeed, the question of separating the police from judicial functions had first engaged the attention of Sir Charles Napier after the conquest of Sind in 1843. Apart from his attempt to organize the police on a self-contained basis, his system involved a regular course of training, which was extended in 1853 by Sir George Clark to the rest of Bombay Presidency. A police force on the Sind Model was in the meantime also organized in the Punjab in 1849, with the difference that it consisted of two branches, one military and the other civil.

No legislative sanction, however, was given to the organization of the police as a separate branch of the administration until 1859, when the Madras Government reorganized its police under Act XXIV. This Act was a result of the findings of a Commission of Inquiry into certain abuses which had crept into the Madras police. The attention thus drawn to the defects of police organization in the country as a whole led the Government of Lord Lawrence to appoint a Commission in 1860. On the basis of its recommendations the Governor-General passed the Police Act V of 1861. It provided for the appointment of District Superintendents and Assistant Superintendents of Police in addition to an Inspector-General and Deputy Inspector-General who were placed at the head of the police to supervise and inspect the new department. The Act made the District Superintendent responsible for the discipline and internal management of the force. He was to remain subordinate to the District Magistrate in all matters connected with the preservation of peace and the detection and suppression of crime. This was in fact no more than statutory confirmation of a *fait accompli*, the separation of police and judicial functions that had started in 1837.

As regards the controlling authority of the Inspector-General of Police, not all Provinces made the appointment immediately after the enactment. Bombay, for instance, was the last Province to appoint a separate Inspector-General in 1885. 'In some other Provinces', as the Decentralization Committee for the Royal Commission on Decentralization pointed out in its Note on Police in 1907.

> although Act V of 1861 gives no specific recognition to Commissioners, the same traditions, coupled with the consideration that a Commissioner, as the Chief administrative officer in his division, should have cognizance of, as he is generally regarded as responsible for, all matters relating to his territorial charge, have resulted in the issue of regulations by the Local Governments, which have given Commissioners authority in the Police administration parallel to that of the Inspector-General.[35]

It was a case of continuity rather than change. The control of the covenanted civil service over the police remained more or less unrelaxed.

This continuity, however, did not signify the strength of the Collector's magisterial authority. For, as already noted, the Bengal pattern of district administration was dominated by the desire to protect zamindars' rights to landed property, without ascertaining the nature of subordinate tenures or even the correctness or otherwise of the grounds on which the claims of zamindars were founded. It reduced the position of the Collector by divesting him of all his judicial powers and increased the powers of the zamindars who, under Regulation VIII of 1799, were authorized to enforce their demand by means of a destraint of the raiyat's property without prior notice to a court of law. The executive authority of the Collector was later restored, but the damage done over the years after 1793 left a scar which could not be removed entirely. The zamindari system contributed to aristocratic affluence in Bengal and led to the emergence of a western-educated class of élites who hastened to compete for power in a manner hardly consistent with ordered progress, or the interests of the lower orders of society.

The Madras Model

Structurally, the system of district administration which Warren Hastings introduced for Bengal in 1772 was adopted in Madras with only such modifications as local requirements demanded. Unlike Fort William which grew as a centre of British power in Bengal with the assent of Mughal governors given from time to time from 1696 onwards, the Government of Madras Presidency was formed on the model of the governing body of the old Factory at Fort St George, which for many years remained the headquarters of the Company's settlement in the East. It consisted of a President and a certain number of Councillors. In his executive capacity the President functioned as Governor. It was to the Council at Fort St George that Warren Hastings was appointed in 1769 before being nominated as Governor at Fort William. What he did in Bengal even as Governor had a sympathetic impact on the administration of districts in Madras.

The Presidency was divided into districts, the traditional units of administration being called zillah. These were placed under *tahsildars*. The chief executive officer of the district was the European Collector of the covenanted service who exercised, as in Bombay, revenue, judicial and magisterial functions, including those of the police. This principle of district administration was finally established by the Madras Regulations of 1816, and its operation extended to the levels of *tahsildars* and village munsifs also.

In the field of revenue administration, the Collector was immediately responsible to the Board of Revenue established in 1786. As the average size of districts in Madras happened to be larger than elsewhere,[36] steps were taken as early as 1792 to assign to the office of the Collector covenanted Assistants who, for reasons of economy, were later allotted fixed territorial jurisdictions as Head Assistants or Sub-Collectors, a development comparable to the Joint-Magistracies or sub-divisions in Bengal.

In *The Administrative History of India* I have discussed the peculiar features of the Madras system which retained the dominance of the Collector envisaged in 1772, and shall thus not cover the same ground again. However, it is important to note that the ease and competence with which the professional use of land survey was made by military officers like Colonel Read or Thomas Munro enabled them to introduce in Madras the raiyatwari system and finally reject the zamindari settlement of revenue or even the 'village system', which was unsuccessfully tried and finally given up. Perhaps a more important factor was the active support lent to the raiyatwari settlement by Munro who rose from the position of a settlement officer to that of Governor of Madras in 1821.

Doubtless, the duties and powers of the Collector were sought to be defined by Madras Regulation I (1803) enacted at the instance of Lord Wellesley who influenced Clive, then Madras Governor. Modelled after the principle of the Cornwallis Code, this Regulation was designed to protect the interest of the *poligars* (zamindars) with whom lands had earlier been settled in perpetuity in the Northern Circars and Bara Mahal. On the lines of Bengal Regulation II (1793), this Madras enactment, too, divested the Collector of his judicial and magisterial functions and united them in the office of the Civil Judge of the district. But the land revenue system in Madras being in the main raiyatwari, the Collector exercised an executive authority and the Board of Revenue a degree of supervision and control hardly known to their counterparts in Bengal. Their judicial powers were only formally abrogated and that, too, in the districts where zillah courts had been established. Besides, the Judge-Magistrate system so introduced did not last long. Thomas Munro, it is true, could not influence Lord Clive. But he did influence the Court of Directors. 'In India whoever regulates the assessment of the land', he argued, 'really holds in his hand the mainspring of the country'.[37] The Directors cast their weight in favour of Munro, and suggested a more extensive use of Indians under the Collector whose powers were to be increased by a revision of the Cornwallis Code. This was done by the Madras Regulations enacted in 1816. The village headmen, called munsifs, were re-invested with civil and criminal jurisdiction and the Collectors with their Magisterial powers and control over the police. The separation of the magistracy and police from the office of Civil Judge and their reunion with the office of the Collector were perhaps the most important reforms effected in Madras under Munro's immediate influence. In 1822, the Collector was authorized by Regulation V to arbitrate summarily to even between a zamindar and his tenant in the permanently settled area of the Northern Circars where the zamindars had powers of distraint and ejectment on the lines of Bengal. The union of the revenue, judicial and police functions from the Collector downwards to village level officers in fact made official influence pervasive throughout Madras, a situation which was different from that in the permanently settled districts of Bengal and Bihar, where the zamindar dominaed the social scene.

The restoration of Magisterial powers to the Collector in Madras was, however, not without reservation. Unlike Bengal, where the Magistrate himself committed prisoners for trial to the Sessions, in Madras there was an intermediate functionary or criminal judge between the Magistrate and the Sessions. He was either a subordinate judge of the covenanted service or a principal *sadar amin*. In the exercise of their original jurisdiction these judges tried, subject to an appeal to the Sessions, such cases as the Magistrate and head of the district police forwarded to them, and committed to the sessions those which they were not entitled to try. Their powers of punishment were, however, generally the same as those of Magistrates in Bengal.

The judicial powers of the Magistrate in Madras were limited only to petty offences. He could take cognizance of petty thefts, but his powers to punish did not extend beyond 90 lashes or imprisonment for a term of one month. In 1843 his powers were increased slightly; the maximum limit of corporal punishment was raised to 150 lashes, and imprisonment to six months.

The criminal judicial powers of the Magistrate in Madras were thus not excessive. These were for the most part vested in the intermediate agency of criminal judges. The Madras system of district administration made the Collector all powerful without the Magistracy being in any way oppressive at the level of the covenanted service. What led to oppression and torture was the union of revenue and police functions at the taluk and village levels, where the tyrannies of Indian officials led to the appointment of the Torture Commission in 1855. It recommended the separtion of revenue functions and the appointment of European officers for the exclusive control of the police force in every district. Legislation was, however, delayed by the outbreak of the Mutiny. The Madras Government none the less accepted the Commission's recommendations and the Bill it drafted passed into law as Act XXIV of 1859. This provided for the establishment of a separate police force to be administered by a Superintendent of Police in every district under the immediate control of the District Magistrate. Departmentally, however, he was responsible to a Commissioner of Police who looked after the entire Presidency. Here, as elsewhere, the creation of a police department, separate and distinct from the Magistracy, tended to compromise the old supremacy of the District Magistrate who naturally viewed with disapproval this new and specialized trend in the field of district administration, a trend which had already been preceded by the emergence of Joint-Magistracies or sub-divisions exercising independent criminal jurisdiction within the limits of a recognized district itself.

In the administration of civil justice, there was little difference between Madras and Bengal except that the judicial apparatus of the Madras Government was extended to the village level. In 1793 Cornwallis had established a three-tier system of civil justice presided over by European judges. It consisted of the Sadar Diwani Adalat, on top, the provincial cours of appeal in the middle and the zillah judges in the districts. The provincial courts of appeal were abolished generally by Regulation II of 1833 and their powers transferred to the zillah or district judges who also functioned as sessions judges on the abolition of the provincial courts of appeal which also acted as circuit courts. The Divisional Commissioners exercised these functions for a few years in Bengal. But as Madras had no Commissioners, the functions were transferred to the zillah civil and sessions judges. These and the courts of Sadar Amins and principal Sadar Amins presided over by Indian judges were similar to those of Bengal except that the Sadar Diwani Adalat was composed of a Chief Judge who, unlike in Bengal, was a member of Council, and three puisne judges selected, as in Bengal, from among the Company's covenanted servants. The characteristic feature of Madras, however, was the constitution of the Courts of Munsifs and panchayats at both village and district levels, established as courts of primary jurisdiction respectively under Madras Regulations VI and VII of 1816. Unlike Bengal, Madras maintained its local indigenous institutions through which the influence of district administration and its Collector filtered down to the grass-root level.

Modifications in Bombay

The old Surat Factory of the East India Company provided the model for the Government of Bombay Presidency. It was a form of administration composed of a President and a certain number of Councillors. The whole body was called the President in Council and the Factory itself a Presidency, a term which later spread over India.

The Presidency of Bombay included at the start of the nineteenth century the town and island of Bomaby, the island of Salsette, Fort Victoria in South Konkan, and the town and district of Surat. The Northern Konkan and other territories ceded in 1817 by the Peshwa and the Gaekwar in Gujarat were all added to these along with the Southern Konkan which was partly ceded and partly conquered during the last Maratha War of 1817-18, which brought under British sovereignty the whole of the Deccan consisting of such districts as Khandesh, Ahmadnagar, Nàsik, Poona, Sholapur, Satara as well as the Bombay Karnatak, including the districts of Belgaum, Dharwar and Bijapur.

Elphinstone as Commissioner (1818-19)

In 1818 Mountstuart Elphinstone, a Sanskritist and Orientalist by training at the Banaras Sanskrit College, was appointed Commissioner for the Deccan on its conquest from Baji Rao, the head of the great Maratha Confederacy. The administrative norms he established in district administration were later codified by him in 1827 when he retired after eight years as Governor of Bombay Presidency.

In pre-British days most districts in the Deccan were inhabited by a class of peasant proprietors called *mirasidars* who possessed heritable and transferable rights to property. There existed side by side another class of tenants-at-will called *upries*, Comparable to the co-parceners of the North-West Provinces and the *bhagdars* or the owners of joint villages in Gujarat, the *mirasidars* undertook joint responsibility for the payment of public dues on the principle of village assessment.[38]

The system of revenue farming under the Peshwas had for all

practical purposes weakened the corporateness of the joint villages in the Presidency. There were, of course, district revenue officers called *mamlatdars*. But even their offices were mostly put to auction and given to the highest bidder from among the attendants of the Peshwa who let out his district at an enhanced rate to under-farmers. The operation of this process was repeated till it reached the village headmen (*patels*) who allotted among cultivators the sum assessed for the whole village. This represented a situation not dissimilar to that found by Warren Hastings seven years after the grant of the diwani in Bengal in 1765. In the early days of Maratha rule the Government operated as a check on the *mamlatdar*, as he did on the *patel*. But the officers whose duty it was to look into popular grievances had become involved in local tyrannies. In the meantime, individual tenants tended to deal directly with the officers of the government or with their revenue farmers. The *mirasi* tenure or the joint village system had in fact yielded place to individual raiyatwari practice in most districts, if not everywhere, in the Pesidency.

The British proceeded cautiously when they took over in this state of transition, and introduced survey settlements on the raiyatwari lines. They did not abolish the system of revenue farming altogether but took care to make sure that it was done by the headmen of villages, not by outsiders as Warren Hastings had earlier attempted to his discredit in Bengal. This was in keeping with a principle which Elphinstone had laid down as Commissioner of the Deccan, where he first attempted to renovate the existing structure of administration by re-officializing the indigenous agency and reducing it to the control of European Collectors, each presiding over a number of erstwhile districts which had earlier been under *mamlatdars*.

Elphinstone acted on the assumption that institutions which had lasted for centuries on the strength of social usage could not be entirely devoid of merit. He therefore assured the people that they should 'expect no change but in the better administration of their former laws'. He justified this assumption to the Governor-General by telling him 'that even just Government will not be a blessing if at variance with the habits and character of the people'.[39]

Elphinstone had respect for hereditary rights. He not only gave back the jagirs to their owners, but ordered the restoration of all rent-free lands, all established pensions, all charitable and religious endowments. 'The preservation of religious establishments', he wrote, 'is always necessary in a conquered country; but more particularly so in one where the Brahmins have so long possessed the temporal power' under the Peshwas.[40] He realized that it was not easy to conciliate the Brahmins who were by tradition revivalist, authoritarian and power-hungry. Some even hatched a conspiracy to kill Europeans in order to restore the Peshwa. But this did not make Elphinstone swerve from his regular policy decisions.

The land revenue system introduced by Elphinstone as Commissioner in the Deccan did not essentially differ from that of Nana Fadnavis under whom the agents of government settled directly with raiyats. He appreciated the advantages of the raiyatwari system which provided direct contact between the rulers and the people. The abolition of the farming system of Baji Rao, by which districts were rented to contractors, removed many grievances. Even so, he tried to maintain moderation and ordered his Collectors to use discretion and revive the public spirit by encouraging the village communities, ancient institutions which even centuries of tyranny and anarchy had failed to extinguish in the Maratha country. Indeed, Elphinstone realized that the assembly of village panchayats was consistent with the state of Indian society and civilization which called for a simple, cheap and expeditious administration of justice. He therefore refrained from introducing new institutions at this level, for innovations could disturb to popular sentiment and the security of British interest. The panchayats system had its defects: it resisted social mobility and was not free from corruption. Elphinstone was aware of this, but nevertheless asked his Collectors to preserve them, for he argued that the object of the conquerors was not to destroy the native system but to remove its abuses and revive its energy.

Like the eminent Bengal civilian, Sir John Shore, Elphinstone believed in the efficacy of personal rule at the district level. Indian officers were retained in both revenue and judicial departments. But appeals in all cases were allowed to the European Collector with whom all powers of Criminal and civil administration remained. He was not a supporter of the secretariat system at the district level, where the Collector would act as a mere link in the administrative hierarchy, writing and forwarding reports and statistics. Nor was he a believer in the impersonality of the administrative machine that later developed on the lines of the Weberian bureaucracy. Elphinstone in fact deemed it indispensable 'that the Collector should give audience for at least two hours every day to all ranks, receive revenue complains *viva voce,* and grant decisions and orders on [subordinate] *mamlatdars* as the cases require. If he confines himself to receiving petitions in writing, it is impossible that he should have time to become acquainted with the state of things in his district.'[41]

The Elphinstone papers makes it clear that, unlike Cornwallis who laid the foundation for a cumbrous and centralized bureaucracy to secure the protection of the property rights legally created, Elphinstone emphasized procedural simplicity and reduction of bureaucratic hierarchies to keep clear of the causes of litigation that flowed from a 'revolution in the state of property'.[42] He justified his emphasis on summary decision by European judges on the ground that his policy involved no such revolution in the structure of property;[43] no change, either real or apparent, in the laws; no dislocation of indigenous institutions, opinions and feelings that had kept the community together in the past.

As Commissioner of the Deccan Elpinstone did not have the opportunity of personally carrying out these principles laid, he was soon appointd Governor of Bombay. Even so, he used his influence as Governor to secure the execution of the plans formulated earlier.

Collector-Magistrate Level

The Bomaby Code of 1827, for instance, invested the Collector with powers to decide (1) all disputes regarding the rent of land, (2) all questions regarding the use of roads and water resources, and (3) boundary disputes, including disputes about crops, fisheries, trees and premises. These powers also extended to questions of exemption from the payment of land revenue, questions that arose in the process of settlement and called for immediate determination. They were exercisable even by subordinate revenue authorities, subject to an appeal to the Collector in the first instance. The Bombay Collector in fact enjoyed a much higher status and prestige than his Bengal counterpart. This was so not only because the districts in Bombay Presidency were much larger, but because his decisions or the decisions of a Sub-Collector lay in appeal to the Sadar Diwani Adalat at the provincial headquarters, not to the zillah judge in the district.

The Collector united in his office the function of District Magistrate under the Bombay Code of 1827. But here, as in Madras, the magistracy as a class exercised, under Regulation XII of 1827, revenue, police and judicial functions, a principle of district administration which applied even to all subordinate levels from Deputy Collectors through *mamlatdars* to village headmen. As in Madras, there was an intermediate office of covenanted criminal judges between the Magistrate and the sessions judge, who was invested with the full judicial powers exercisable by the Magistrate in Bengal. The judicial powers of the Bombay Magistrate as a criminal court of the first instance were, however, greater than those in Madras. The Collector-Magistrate in Bombay was far more powerful than others in the Regulation disticts of India.

And yet Bombay was the first to separate the police from the magistracy. The question of reforming the police had in fact engaged the attention of the Court of Directors as early as 1814, when in their despatch to Bengal they expressed themselves strongly against the ill-remunerated and corrupt *daroga* system imposed from above by Cornwallis in place of the zamindars in 1792. They wanted the Bengal Government to revive the old, socially remunerated village police to its original vigour and to unite in the office of the Collector the duties of the Magistrate and his control over the police. But since the Cornwallis Code continued to be viewed as sacrosanct by Bengal civilians, the magistracy remained tagged to the zillah judge. The Commissioners appointed in 1829 took over the control of the police within the limits of their jurisdiction, and a civilian Superintendent of Police had been appointed in 1808 and another in 1810 to supervise the work of Magistrates in the districts. But since these were all superior appointments in which the bureaucracy was immediately interested, the *darogas* for all practical purposes dominated at subordinate levels where corruption was rampant in the absence of effective control from above. Madras had taken steps to revert to the old system of village watchmen under Regulation V (1816), which united revenue, judicial and police functions at village, taluk and district levels. Bombay did the same under Regulation XII of 1827

The inadequate supervision by superior officers, however, did not cease. In 1837 the Court of Directors pressed for a change in the existing system. The Bengal Government appointed a Committee which, in its report submitted in 1838, emphasized uniformity of control to ensure coordination. In a separate Minute, Frederick Halliday, later the first Lieutenant-Governor of Bengal, made a number of proposals to improve the efficiency of police administration. These included a Superintendent and an Assistant Superintendent for each district, a Superintendent General of Police for the whole Province and four civilians as Deputies.

The bureaucracy in Bengal, however, withheld support to these proposals which tended to compromise the position of Magistrates in the districts and of Commissioners in the divisions. But Halliday's proposals to separate the police from the magistracy as a general plan was recognized by Sir Charles Napier in Sind where a separate and self-contained police force was first constituted in 1843.

Impressed by Napier's reforms, the Governor of Bombay, Sir George Clerk, introduced that model in the Presidency in 1853. Its main feature was the appointment of a Superintendent of Police who, though generally subordinate to the District Magistrate, was invested with exclusive control of the police force. At the taluk or tahsil level, provision was made for an Indian officer of the police whose relation to the *mamlatdar* or *tahsildar* was to be the same as that between the Superintendent and the Collector Magistrate. The supreme control over the police was transferred from the Sadar Faujdari Adalat to the Judicial Secretary to the Government whose police authority was, however, soon made over to a separate Police Commissioner appointed for the whole of the Presidency in 1855.

Mamlatdar/Tahsildar Level

The administrative unit below the district which Elphinstone reconstituted as Commissioner in the Deccan, was the taluk or subdivision of a collectorate. It was headed by a *kamvisdar* or *mamlatdar*, a revenue officer who, in addition, combined police and judicial functions. His business was to see that the several villages under his jurisdiction paid their instalments punctually, that village accounts were kept properly, that payments of revenue were duly receipted, that boundary marks of villages were kept in proper repair, and that village officers generally did their work properly. He was a subordinate magistrate, responsible for the maintenance of law and order as well as the proper functioning of the taluk treasury.

Village Patel Level

The *patel* (or *patil*) under Maratha rule was the village headman. He was chief revenue officer, chief police magistrate and even the chief judicial officer. According to Dr Surendranath Sen, he

> acted as an intermediary between the villagers and the Peshwa's Officer [*Mamlatdar*] and served as a link between the village and the suzerian state. In the village he had the advantage of acting as the exponent of the Peshwa's authority, and before the Kamavisdar or the Mamlatdar he appeared as the authorized representative of his village. As the officer responsible for

revenue collection he was consulted by the Kamavisdar at the time of assesment; if the assessment was too high, he had the right to protest, and in case the Kamavisdar still remained obstinate, the Patil could bring him to reason by leaving the village and making any collection whatever impossible.[44]

In his judicial capacity the *patel*'s function was to persuade the parties in a suit to come to an amicable settlement. But in case mutual agreement or arbitration failed, he appointed a panchayat. He inquired into cases of theft and robbery and had under him his village watchmen.

The *patel* was neither an elected officer nor appointed by the government. His role was hereditary and the office could even be sold and purchased. Though useful to the Peshwa's administration, he was not even paid by him. He was entitled to grant of lands, fees, and various little privileges and distinctions. The *patel* was assisted by the *kulkarni* who kept the numerous records and accounts of the village, including the general measurement and description of all the village lands, the list of fields with the names, sizes and quality of each, the terms on which they were held along with the names of the tenants and statements of the dues from each to the governmet.

As Commissioner in the Deccan, Elphinstone retained these main features of administration in the districts, subject to overall control by European Collectors. The Bombay Code also recognized the arrangements already made for taluk and village administration under the *mamlatdar* and the *patel* respectively. An attempt was however made to give the administration an official character. While the *mamlatdar* was, for instance, paid a regular salary, the *patel* and the *kulkarni* were allowed to hold a certain quantity or rent-free land or were remunerated by cash payment equivalent to a certain percentage of the collections. The watchman and other village servants like the carpenter, blacksmith, potter and barber also held land on more or less favourable terms as regards assessment and, in addition, received grain and other payment in kind from the villagers. For the purposes of both government and society the Bombay village community thus remained complete, and independent of the outer world. Indeed, Elphinstone took care to preserve the traditional influence of the village officers; for, unlike most Bengal civilians, he realized that the task of governing India down to the villages by a foreign government could not be accomplished properly except through indigenous personnel and communal self-government,[45] a form of district administration based on the principle of decentralization.

However, this was not democratic decentralization. A covenanted Assistant or Deputy Collector was appointed to look after the administration of the revenue covering, on an average, three taluks. He had to keep travelling during seven months of the year to see for himself through direct and personal inspection that the revenue work was being properly done. He nominated village officers; assessed the requirements of his taluks in respect of roads, wells, tree plantation and the like; heard appeals against the orders of *mamlatdars*; replied to references made by them, and generally supervized their proceedings, subject to the controlling authority of the Collector-Magistrate placed over the whole district and required to travel at least for four months in the year. No Board of Revenue was established at the Presidency headquarters in Bombay. It was the Divisional Commissioners who supervized the work of their district officers. They were constantly on the move in their respective divisions during the fair season and were the channel of communication with the Government.

Unlike in Bengal where the Cornwallis Code revolutionized the state of property and built up, on western lines, a judiciary-dominated system of administration to sustain it the Bombay pattern reflected more continuity than change from tradition. The Regulations which bear Ephinstone's name and embody his legislative and judicial reforms was, for instance, an attempt to ensure continuity by simplifying the laws of India. His rules were thus framed to reduce the written pleadings and to bring matters to a speedy issue. He realized that if justice was to be made available to the people, 'the language of the court must be the language of the district, and that the evidence of the witnesses must be taken in their own vernacular'.[46] He emphasized these principles because his own administrative success was in great measure due to his knowledge, not only of the local languages but also of the dialects which enabled him to make himself accesible to all classes and conditions of people. His regard for hereditary rights led him to give back jagirs to their owners on conditions of original grants. The most interesting evidence of continuity is, however, seen in Elphinstone's 'Minute on Education', where he warned the Christian missions against what he considered to be 'the dangerous path of proselytism in India'. This warning flowed not only from his recognition of Brahmins as the dominant caste in the Maratha country, but immediately from his fears of Brahmanic opposition to it. For, as he wrote, 'The only effect of introducing Christianity into our schools would be to sound the alarm, and to warn the Brahmins of the approaching danger. Even that warning might perhaps be neglected as long as no converts were made; but it is a sufficient argument that it can only be safe as long as it is ineffectual, and in this instance the danger involves not only failure of our plans of education, but the dissolution of our empire.'[47]

Regulation and Non-Regulation Provinces

Under the Company's rule a distinction was drawn between Regulation and Non-Regulation Provinces. The Regulation Provinces were, for instance, Bengal, Madras, Bombay proper and the North-Western Provinces (U.P.). The Non-Regulation Provinces, on the other hand, were the Punjab, the Central Provinces as well as the sub-provinces of Oudh in U.P., Assam in Bengal and Sind in Bombay. The latter were originally ruled by simpler codes and with greater centralization of functions in the hands of district officers, who were recruited not merely from the covenanted civil service, but also from the army and other sources. Instead of Collectors and Assistant or Deputy Collectors, they were termed Deputy and Assistant or Extra-Assistant Commissioners. There was no chartered High Court there. The principal court of criminal and civil jurisdiction was (except in Assam) a Chief Court or a Judicial Commissioner.

The necessity of a non-Regulation system arose mainly from considerations of protecting the person and property of the backward tribes and races. They were entirely distinct from the ordinary population in respect of their economy, culture and level of understanding. The system of government and administration established by the general regulations was in fact inapplicable to their circumstances. It worked to their great disadvantage and even destruction. Such were, for example, the tribes and hill dwellers of Bhagalpur, the Paharia community, whom Augustus Cleveland made special arrangements to reclaim before the introduction of the regular system. Provision was, therefore, made under Regulation X of 1822 to change the status of such territories as called for special protection by executive officers. The status of north-eastern frontier of Rungpur was accordingly de-charged under that Regulation. The existing rules for the administration of civil and criminal justice were suspended, and a Commissioner was appointed with full powers to conclude arrangements with tribal chiefs and conduct the entire administration of the tract, subject to the controlling authority of the Governor-General in Council. Regulation X of 1822 in fact marked the beginning of the earlier system of non-Regulation administration.[48]

Consistent with this principle, the Bengal districts came to be divided into three categories. The first category included districts subject to the general Regulations and Acts. The second comprised tracts known as Scheduled Districts. These were districts to which all the Regulations and the Acts were not to apply of their own force, but to which they might be extended at the discretion of the Government. The territories included in the third category consisted of independent tributary states which were either wholly or partly administered by British officers. Under the second head came the Santhal Parganas, the district of Angul in Orissa, the Hill Tracts of Chittagong, and the districts of Jalpaiguri, Darjeeling, Hazaribagh, Ranchi, Palamau, Manbhum and Singhbhum. These were originally subject to the general regulations but were later removed wholly or partly from their operation by special enactments. The third head consisted of the Tributary Mahals of Orissa and Chota Nagpur. The changes effected from time to time in the mode of administration for the second and the third categories of territories are summarized in the *Report of the Administration of Bengal 1901-1902*.[49] These changes took place in both directions. While a certain number of districts were de-regulationized, others were restored to their general regulation system. In 1895, for instance, as many as eight Deputy Commissionerships of the Non-Regulation districts were absorbed in the grades of District Magistrates and Collectors. Indeed, with the progress of education and economic change the old distinction between the Regulation and Non-Regulation tended gradually to disappear, and they began to be administered more or less on the same lines.

Special Departments

The 'special departments' of the Government were so called because they were intended to discharge functions of a specialized nature, separate and distinct from general administration which covered fiscal, executive and judicial functions. Speaking of these departments, the Royal Commission Upon Decentralization (1907-1909) thus said: 'Originally Collectors and their subordinates were responsible for almost all the administrative work of their districts, subject to the superintendence of Commissioners and Boards of Revenue. During the last 50 years, however, separate administrative departments have been gradually evolved, the most important of which are those dealing with Public Works, Education, Police, Forests, Medical administration, Sanitation, and Prisons. These departments have their own separate staffs and heads in each

Province'.[50] Though important, Agriculture remained tagged to Revenue and Commerce until 1905. These special departments thus dealt with subjects which were both 'normative' or regulatory and 'positive' or developmental in character.

It is clear then that the evolution of special departments as separate administrative units took place on the transfer of power to the Crown in 1858, not under the rule of the East Indian Company whose dominant consideration was economy and whose main source of finance was land revenue. Import and export trade grew considerably. Banking and joint-stock business showed a steady rise. But the pattern of the Company's financial system had hardly shown any sign of modernization.[51]

Public Works Department. In spite of the opening up of the Company's trade in 1813 and its complete abolition in 1833 a change in policy orientation hardly came about. Change was reflected in the rationalization of administration and the development of modern science and technology, a subject immediately related to the progress of public works connected with railways, irrigation, roads and buildings. These were all considered necessary not only in the promotion of agricultural products for the colonial economy, but also for industrial development in general.

The abolition of the Company's trade led to the progress of private European enterprise in India, particularly in indigo, jute, sugar, tea and coffee. But it was not until 1837 that Europeans were permitted to hold farms of their own. Then there was the question of security in the rural areas. No bank in Calcutta would agree to advance money for an indigo factory, for instance, except on very high interest. It was the civil servants of the East India Company who, through their local influence, supplied both security and capital for the promotion of the plantation industry. In the course of his evidence before the Parliamentary Select Committee on Colonization and Settlement in 1858, a European settler clearly acknowledged the capital contribution of civil service. The Company's civil servants were in fact the first capitalists to enter the industrial field and to take the lead in introducing even power-driven industrial plants during the administration of Bentinck. They were associated with certain business houses established in Calcutta and Madras.[52] Indeed, one of the important objects of the public works departments during these early years was to help in the mobilization of public resources and make them available to private entrepreneurs to facilitate the execution of industrial projects.

The construction of railways was initially an important instance of private enterprise. The parties who sought the cooperation of the Company's government included Messrs. White and Borret, Mr Stephenson, Chairman of the East India and China Association, as well as some others who submitted proposals for the construction of railroads in 1844. The opposition of the Court of Directors delayed the matter for a time. But the firmness and vigour with which Lord Dalhousie acted to promote private enterprise weakened the force of that opposition. Under its Railway Act of 1854 the Government of India entered into contract with a number of private European companies on the basis of what was known as the guarantee system, which provided for compensation against any loss of capital invested. This was the first tangible step towards industrialization and was significant not only in terms of social mobility and economic development, but also of defence capability and political stability.

Administratively, an immediate effect of this development was the establishment of a separate Department of Public Works at the centre in 1855. It was a civil department, replacing the old military boards which previously managed public works in the provinces, and under the Supreme Government. A department of public works run by a military board existed in each of the provinces, but the control of the Government of India was diffused and limited. It did not extend beyond a review of the projects referred to it from time to time. The execution of details vested in the Local Governments themselves. This procedure was altered in 1854. All projects beyond the authority of a Local Government were then required to be submitted to the consideration of the Government of India.[53] In the absence of a duly qualified separate civil agency at the centre, the projects so submitted had to be referred to the Home or Finance Department, or to the department concerned for approval. It was a patch-work system, lacking in technical competence and knowledge. On the recommendation of the Governor-General a separate office of Secretary to the Government of India in the Department of Public Works was, therefore, created. It was to be held by a highly qualified officer of the Corps of Engineers on a salary of Rs 3000 a month, with an Assistant Secretary belonging to the same Corps.[54] The officer so appointed as Secretary to Government in the Public Works Department was Colonel W.E. Baker of the Bengal Railways. Besides railways, he was to look after irrigation as well as roads and buildings.[55] The management of all the public works in the provinces came to be consequently centralized in the hands of the Secretary to the Government of India.

The superior staff of the Department for Buildings and Roads, Irrigation, and Railways were over the years recruited in England, mainly from the Royal Indian Engineering College at Cooper's Hill. It consisted of the chief, Superintending, Executive and Assistant Engineers, who formed the permanent Engineer Establishment of the Department. They were assisted by a considerable group of technical personnel, mostly Anglo-Indians and Eurasians, who were later organized into a subordinate or upper-subordinate service in a manner comparable to the recruitment of sub-deputy or Deputy Collectors and Magistrates in the civil service. They were the products of engineering schools meant for overseers and foremen, not for engineers who were recruited only from the engineering colleges. The Thomason College of Civil Engineering was the first of its kind when established in 1847 by the Government of the North-Western Provinces to meet the construction requirements of the Ganges Canal. An engineering class was opened at Elphinstone College in Bombay and a separate institution established for the purpose in 1856 at Writer's Building in Calcutta, although Dalhousie had in 1848 suggested that each Presidency town have an engineering college of its own to meet the growing needs of the Public Works Department. However, the progress made in this regard remained slow and tardy. For as late as Curzon's time the number of engineering college did not exceed four. These were the Civil Engineering College at Sibpur in Bengal, the College of Science at Poona, the College of Engineering in Madras, and the Thomason College of Civil Engineering at Roorke in U.P.

Doubtless the size of recruitment made in India from these Colleges increased over the years. But the Indians so recruited were classed merely as uncovenanted 'Provincial' engineers, a term finally accepted by the Government of India in 1892 in the light of the recommendations made by the Indian Public Service (Aitchison) Commission (1886-87). On the lines of the 'listed' posts reserved for Provincial Civil Service, the reorganization of the public services in 1892 provided for a number of guranteed appointments to the most distinguished students from the Indian Colleges, who could rise to the same positions as their 'Imperial' counterparts. This arrangement picked up especially after the abolition of Cooper's Hill College in 1904. Recruits were hereafter selected by the Secretary of State with the assistance of expert advisers who had obtained a degree, diploma, or other equivalent distinction at some approved institution for engineering education, and who had acquired some experience as assistants the preparation of the designs for, or in the execution of, some engineering work of importance. On promotion to the 'Imperial' category the Provincial Service recruits selected in India performed the same functions but drew a lower rate of pay in all grades except that of Chief Engineer.[56]

The structure of the engineering service in terms of its developmental significance is reviewed in the chapter dealing with the post-1858 period. It is, however, important to point out here that the promoters of the colonial economy which dictated the need for of irrigation as well as railways and road transport, were pioneers in the field of rural development, the development of commercial crops in the rural areas which called for the investment of capital and improvement of the soil. Equipped with money, manpower and material resources the zamindars could have promoted, but never did, an agricultural revolution. The Report of the Bengal and Orissa Famine Commission (1866) pointed out clearly that 'agricultural development' had 'never been generally recognized as a function of the superior landholder', a class of monied men of 'the older-settled and richer province of Bengal with whom the purchase of landed rights is the favourite form of investment', not the promotion of agriculture by an application of science to the soil. The purchasers were for the most part absentee landlords. Of the old and resident Oriya zamindars and their Bengali purchasers, the former constituted, on the whole, a better class in that they at least stored grain which was advanced to the raiyats, though at exorbitant interest. Though more accomplished and generally an 'educated class', the absentee Bengali proprietors remained unconcerned about agricultural improvement. They looked 'only to make the most of the rents as the returan for their money' and did significantly perform the functions of 'grain lenders' or 'patriarchal landholders'.[57] The Commission in fact noted with regret the absence of 'European settlers and merchants' in the interior of Orissa 'who might have seen the state of things and early drawn public attention to it'. There were no doubt Mission stations in Orissa. There was, in addition, the East India Irrigation Company at Cuttack. The Missionaries and the irrigation officers apprehended the danger of the imminent famine. But they first expressed their apprehension in correspondence with their home authorities and failed to press the matter directly with responsible officials. Even so, it was through them rather than zamindars that reports about the impending danger reached officers of the government.

The reports of the earlier famines of 1837-8 and 1861 presented a similar picture concering the problems of agricultural development. Famines and their repercussions on district administration in terms of rural development will be discussed separately in Chapter II. What is relevant to our immediate purpose is to emphasize that the exigencies of the colonial economy as well as the incidence of re-current famine dictated the need for rural development. Together, they called for such administrative changes as were needed to meet their respective demands.

Education. Educationally, however, the whole trend of the Company's Government under Bentinck and after acquired an urban orientation. The objectives of the policy decision based on Macaulay's Minute of 2 February 1835 have already been analysed in my *Indian Middle Classes*.[58] Here it is merely necessary to observe that this urban orientation flowed mainly from the immediate need to create for reasons of economy a loyal and subordinate class of government employees who might assist the Company's European civil servants in their revenue and judicial work according to the rules and regulations enacted in English. They were to be recruited from the affluent section of the upper and middle classes of urban society. In addition to institutions for higher education in the Presidency towns and the principal provincial stations, provision was therefore made for the establishment of a zillah school at the headquarters of every district. It was in fact a city-centred system of English education, intended for the dominant caste élites. They were to be used not only as a subordinate administrative agency, but also as a social base for imperialism. In Minute Macaulay said: 'We must at present do our best to form a class who may be interpreters between us and the millions whom we govern—a class of persons Indian in blood and colour, but English in tastes, in opinions, in morals and in intellect.'[59] It was 'by raising the standard of instruction among these classes' that the Government, as the Court of Directors had advised before, 'would eventually produce a much greater and more beneficial change in the ideas and feelings of the community than by acting on the more numerous class'.[60] For it was these classes, who belonged to the upper layers of urban society, who enjoyed the leisure for advanced study and seemed receptive to the western concept of moral and intellectual transformation. The complete neglect of elementary education for the mass of people did not form part of the policy, but it was financially impracticable. Even higher education in European literature, science and philosophy remained for financial reasons confined to the Presidancy towns and a few provincial headquarters.

The moral and intellectual influence of English education in its first phase was largely imitative. Indians who used the opportunities found neither adequate scope for their attainments, nor did their education fit them for the ordinary tasks and avocations of the society to which they belonged. According to Adam's *Report on Vernacular Education in Bengal and Behar* there emerged a communication gap between them and the common people. There was a similar gap between them and their foreign rulers who felt that educated Indians were being 'raised out of one class of society without having a recognized place in any other class'.[61] Even so, Adam's proposals to establish vernacular schools in Bengal and use the Indian languages as mediums of instruction in zillah schools found little favour with the Government. Lord Auckland made it the principal aim of his administration 'to communicate through the means of the English language a complete education in European literature, philosophy and science to the greatest number of students who may be found ready to accept it at our hands and for whose instruction our funds will admit of providing'.[62] The idea of vernacular schools was not given up altogether but was laid aside. The Government of India decided that its 'efforts should be at first concentrated to the chief towns . . .; in the expectation that through the agency of these scholars an educational reform will descend to the rural vernacular schools, and its benefits be rapidly transfused among all those excluded in the first instance by abject want from a participation in its advantages'.[63]

An analysis of the Company's educational records of the 1830s and onwards makes it clear that employment in the public services was the main inducement for the upper and middle classes in supporting the British Government and English education. While English education was recognized as the direct concern of the Government and meant for the upper layers of urban communities, rural education was to follow the progress of vernacular languages, a responsibility of the urban élites educated through the medium of English. Considering the financial limitations of the Government and the existing caste prejudices against education among the weaker sections of society, the Government used its limited resources on the education of those who best answered its administrative and political purposes. This policy continued more or less until the 1870s when, in addition to institutions under Government control, the scope of English education was extended to private enterprise, while vernacular education was transferred to rural boards.

Educational administration was of little concern to district officers before the establishment of zillah schools under the resolution of 1835. A General Committee of Public Instruction had been constituted in 1823 to administer the grant of Rs 100,000 sanctioned by the Charter Act of 1813. But while it was operationally confined to Calcutta, its immediate concern was limited to the promotion of Arabic and Sanskrit learning. Educational administration began to engage government attention when Bentinck's resolution of 7 March 1835 reiterated that all the funds appropriated for education would be best employed in the promotion of European knowledge,[64] and the Calcutta Committee determined on 11 April, 1835 to establish schools for the teaching of English literature and science through English as soon as funds and qualified masters were made available[65].

These were the policy developments that preceded the administrative reorganization of Lord Auckland, who succeeded Bentinck. In a Minute of 24 November 1839 Auckland first suggested the idea of having a single Superintendent of Government Zillah Schools with an establishment for inspectional purposes in place of the existing large Committee of Members that acted at intervals between other jobs. The Calcutta Committee of Public Instruction generally agreed with Auckland and made suggestions for the execution of his policy. The General Committee was abolished at the end of 1841 and a Council of Education constituted under Government orders in January 1842. The superintendence of the Council, it is true, was to remain confined to institutions in Calcutta. But the general and financial business of provincial institutions was brought under the control of the Government, except, in the North-Western Provinces, where control and management was transferred to the newly constituted Government of Agra in 1843. In 1844 this was followed by the appointment of an Inspector of Schools and Colleges for the Lower Regulation Provinces of Bengal and Bihar. An Inspector was also appointed for Assam.

The most important landmark in the history of educational policy and administration under the Company was the Court's Despatch of

1854 which encouraged the extension of education to the masses instead of confining it to the higher classes. This occurred with the introduction of the grant-in-aid system which imposed a budgetary limit on the state's expenditure and consequently encouraged private enterprise as a parallel agency for the promotion and advancement of European knowledge. A controversy did arise over the issue of Government participation in the promotion of education for the classes Macaulay had in mind when he wrote his famous Minute, but it settled down by 1859 when it was laid down that both Government and grants-in-aid institutions would continue to function side by side in the promotion of secular education.

The second important change that took place on the publication of the Despatch of 1854 was the establishment of a regular department of education on the dissolution of the Council of Education in 1855. William Gordon Young, a civil servant, was appointed the first Director of Public Instruction. In accordance with the instructions contained in the Despatch of 1854, steps were taken to organize separate departments of public instruction, and , between 1855 and 1865 a Director of Public Instruction, with a self-contained Education Department subordinate to him, including Inspectors of Schools, was appointed in every province.[66]

In terms of district administration, the establishment of a separate department of education in every province made no difference to the position of the district officer, except that it added to the chain of communication already existing between the district and the provincial headquarters. Before the appointment of an Inspector of Schools the Collector or a Divisional Commissioner reported on the functioning of educational institutions. As the officer responsible for overall administration of his district, the Collector also served as the common link for a special department like education, which, even after the establishment of a Directorate, had perhaps no local agency at the local level for purposes of departmental communication. But even otherwise, it was in fact the civil service that dominated the new department from its very beginning and for quite sometime thereafter. The Collector, a civil servant himself, was thus no exception. For, consistent with the despatch of 1854, the Court of Directors had already determined that the first heads of the department of education and some of the Inspectors should be members of the Indian Civil Service. As a subsequent educational despatch from the Secretary of State confirmed, the idea was 'both to show the importance attached to the subject of education and the estimation in which its was desired that the officers of the department should be held, and because among the members of that service the best qualified persons would be most likely to be met with'.[67] It was of course laid down that none of these superior appointments should be kept reserved for members of the covenanted service to the exclusion of others, who might be qualified for the job; but members of the Civil Service were in the first instance appointed Directors of Public Instruction in Bengal, the North-Western Provinces, Madras and Bombay. As regards Inspectors of Schools, several appointments were filled indiscriminately by civil servants, military and medical officers, and individuals unconnected with any of those services. In the Punjab the post of Director was filled by a person who was in the army at the time of nomination but who retired immediately after appointment.

The educational despatch of 1859, however, made it clear that the employment of civil servants in the Department of Education should be treated as a 'temporary arrangement'. Even so, no officer in the department was to be disturbed merely for this reason, for it was realized that difficulties might arise in finding qualified people unconnected with the regular services, civil or military.[68]

The three Universities of Calcutta, Madras and Bombay were in the meantime incorporated on the model of the University of London, with a Senate in each case invested with the control of examinations and affiliated colleges doing the teaching. A fourth University was later established at Lahore in 1882 and a fifth at Allahabad in 1887. Education thus kept expanding. But the educational service, like other public services, had yet to be reorganized on a footing that demonstrated administrative rationality. This was attempted largely after the recommendations of the Aitchison Commission (1886-7).[69]

Medical Service. From very early times, the Company's medical service was divided into European medical officers called 'Surgeons' and their uncovenanted Indian subordinates who functioned as assistants, later known as military or civil assistants, or sub-assistant surgeons. In Bengal these uncovenanted assistants were recruited from the trainees of the Calcutta Madrassa and Banaras Sanskrit College which provided for the study of indigenous systems of medicine. A separate school of medicine was opened at Calcutta in 1822 to make Indian assistants fit for employment under European medical officers.

The first tangible advance in medical studies for Indian assistants was made by Bentinck's Government. Guided by considerations of economy and the advantages arising from the extended employment of uncovenanted employees in the judicial and revenue branches, Bentinck appointed a committee to report on the ability or otherwise of Indians to submit to the conditions called for by higher medical education on European lines. The establishment of the Calcutta Medical College in 1835 was a result of the recommendation. The Bombay Government established Grant Medical College in 1845 with the same object in view.[70] Indians educated in India were not to be admitted to the Indian Medical Service which was primarily a military service recruited through competition in England.

Medical administration in India before 1896 corresponded to the old presidency army system under which each presidency had its own separate command and medical arrangement headed by an officer called the Surgeon-General. On the abolition of the presidency army system in 1896 all three armies were amalgamated and placed under the Commander-in-Chief and the Supreme Government. The Bengal, Madras and Bomaby medical services were simultaneously amalgamated into one Indian Medical Service, with a Director-General (formerly both Surgeon-General and Sanitary Commissioner with the Government of India) at its head, enjoying the rank of a Surgeon-General.

The principal medical advisers of Madras and Bombay retained the old title of Surgeon-General. Their appointment required the approval of the Government of India, not of the Director-General. In the other provinces, however, the appointment of the principal medical adviser, called the Inspector-General of Civil Hospitals (IGCH), was through nomination by the Government of India in consultation with the Director-General.

Medical administration in the districts formed part of the role of a district medical officer called the Civil Surgeon whose office had always been co-extensive with that of the Collector. Apart from giving free professional attendance to superior government officers and performing most of the medico-legal work of the district, he superintended medical institutions and, subject to the general authority of the District Officer, looked after matters connected with the health of the general population. He continued to functon independently of the changes effected in 1896, except that in the Bombay the Civil Surgeon was also occupied with the head-quarters' station, though he did some inspection too. It was the Surgeon-General who directly supervized rural hospitals and dispensaries. The sanitary side of medical administration which began to engage Government attention only from the 1860s onwards was looked after in Bombay by Deputy Sanitary Commissioners functioning under the direction of the provincial head in that department.[71]

As incentives to rural development in India flowed originally from the operatioin of the colonial economy, the realization of the importance of rural health proceeded from the sanitary needs of military cantonments. The report of the Commission appointed to inquire into the cholera epidemic of 1861 first stressed the point that the health of the army could not be separated from that of the sanitary conditions of the general population. 'If we desire to render the sanitary condition of our European soldiers really satisfactory', the Commission emphasized, 'we must not, when we come to practical measures of improvement, ignore, as we have hitherto done, the existence of the masses of native population in the midst of which our soldiers must generally live.[72]

Of course there had been cases when an active District Magistrate or a Commanding Officer took steps occasionally to ensure sanitary improvements. But these produced no lasting effect, for matters reverted to their original state under a successor who showed no interest. By Act XXVI of 1850 the Government had also sought to enable the inhabitants of district towns to provide 'for making repairing, cleaning, lighting, or watching any public streets, roads, drains, or tanks, or for the prevention of nuisances or for improving the said town or suburb in any other manner'. But the law could not accomplish its object on account of financial limitation and bureaucratic indifference. The report of the Cholera Commission, therefore, emphasized that 'until the importance of all questions which concern the Public Health be distinctly acknowledged by the Government, and measures be taken for establishing a properly organized system of Sanitary Administration upon uniform principles, we shall arrive at no satisfactory results'.[73]

The report of the Royal Army Sanitary Commission of 1863, however, gave initial impetus to the movement for improvements in the conservancy of towns and villages in India. Act XXII of 1864 gave full powers to the Government to make local Rules and Regulations. Measures were taken to enforce them for the protection of public health in all places included within the limits of military cantonments. This was followed by the appointment in 1866-7 of

Sanitary Commissioners in different provinces, where district Civil Surgeons were to act as their subordinates for sanitary work, except in Bombay where, as already noted, this was done by Deputy Sanitary Commissioners.

Forest Administration. For nearly a century of British rule in India the administration of forest resources did not seem to receive serious attention. Teak was considered the only timber of any account, and forests generally were treated as waste lands and appandages of the cultivated area, of consequence only for the miscellaneous addition they yielded to the regular land revenue.

In the earlier period there was no realization or knowledge of the fact that forests contribute to the preservation of physical features, to the prevention of floods and soil erosion, including the flow of sub-soil water and to the supply of a variety of forest products, such as timber, firewood, materials for making paper, honey, wax, soap-nut, horns, medicinal plants and the like. During the Company's rule the British were guided by an industrial bias inherent in a colonial economy, not by a desire to preserve the forests. The development of schemes for free hold and permanent settlements in fact created a situation where forests ran the risk ofbeing transferred to private hands for ever. Even though wiser opinion prevailed, the *laissez faire* land policy of the Government led with increasing tempo to the destruction of a considerable portion of timber forests in the country, especially with the expansion of agriculture, the construction of arterial roads and railways, and the consumption of large quantities of timber for the navy and other defence purposes. It was their inaccesibility and the unaided efforts of nature that saved forests from total destruction.

The first traces of forest administration appeared with the appointment in 1806 of a Conservator of Forests for the management of the teak forests of Malabar. Another Conservator was appointed for Bomaby in 1847 and for Madras in 1856. Lord Dalhousie in fact laid the foundation of modern scientific forestry in India. He invited Sir Dietrich Brandis from Burma to draw up plans for the conservation and scientific management of the vast and unexplored forests of Assam and Bengal. Matters were delayed till the re-establishment of settled government after the Mutiny, but it was about this time that the efforts of Brandis led the Government of India to realize the agricultural importance of forests. By 1861 it was realized that forestry was 'a thing valuable in itself, and in truth as essential to the community as wheat, sugar or cotton'.[74] It was about this time, again, that Conolly, the Collector of Malabar, started with the assistance of Chatnu Menon the famous Nilambur teak plantations.[75] The urgency of forest conservation was further reorganized when, by a Foreign Department Resolution of 1 November 1861 the Nagpur territory was joined with the Saugor and Narbada Territories and formed into a separate Chief Commissionership of the Central Provinces. For it brought under direct British administration a considerable expanse of forest-covered hills till then unknown to British officials. The work of forest conservation continued under the able guidance of Sir Richard Temple, the first Chief Commissioner of the Central Provinces and a great advocate of rural development, who later in a Minute of 6 December 1869, not only emphasized the need for a separate Department of agriculture for India, but also for civil servants equipped with the required knowledge.[76] Forest conservation had come to be recognized by him as related to agricultural development, although it took time for the principle to be fully translated into action. Immediate practical shape was, however, given to the idea by the creation of a separate Forest Department in 1864, of which Sir Dietrich Brandis was appointed the first Inspector-General.[77]

Certain Broad Conclusions

The foregoing summary of administrative developments during the first century of British rule, especially in the field of district administration, lends itself to certain conclusions which must be reviewed before proceeding to notice changes in the structure and function of district machinery as an instrument of rural development. The immediate and main concern of the Company's Government was, for instance, to reconstitute the administration of districts which, on the decline of the Mughals, had either disintegrated or become dysfunctional. It was natural that this reconstitution should have taken place in the first instance to ensure a due discharge of the state's regulatory functions, the functions of executive and judicial administration, with an emphasis on the collection of the public revenues and maintenance of law and order. Before the abolition of the Company's trade in 1833 the scope of district administration remained largely limited to these functions. The executive head of the district was the Collector-Magistrate, except in the permanently settled districts of Bengal where the Judge-Magistrate continued under the Cornwallis system to hold the first position in the district hierarchy for nearly forty years after 1793. The Collector-Magistrate, the District Judge and the Civil Surgeon were three superior officers who figured in the administration of the districts up to Lord Bentinck's period. Though predominantly rural in setting, district administration had no separate officer to take care of agriculture. It was the duty of the Collector to remain in touch with the raiyats, to induce them to bring waste areas into cultivation, and to take necessary measures to promote agriculture and protect peasants against the ravages of nature and the oppressions of landlords. Men like Elphinstone and Munro would not permit any agency to stand between the Collector and the people. Even the Famine Commission of 1880 emphasized that 'the Collector of a district should retain in his hands the supervision of every branch of civil executive business'. For, it was 'that general supervision which invests him in the eyes of the people with the position of the local head of the civil government'.[78]

Below the superior covenanted officers of district administration there was the subordinate native agency employed in the several departments for reasons of economy, especially under Bentinck. This class of subordinate public employees remained lumped together over the years without any defined rules governing qualifications, appointment, classification and promotion. There was in fact no system in the employment of Indians in the subordinate service of government, especially when the state of education was such that no rigid educational tests could be adopted for purposes of recruitment. Improvements occurred with the progress of higher education, but it was not before 1892 that this category was classed as 'subordinate' and 'provincial' services with prospects of promotion from one to the other. Their limited education and their traditionally undefined conditions of service were largely responsible for the inefficiency and corruption that later increased in their ranks in spite of structural improvement.

The opening of the Company's trade in 1813 and its abolition in 1833 provided incentives to free trade and colonization, not by a body of uneducated and ordinary Europeans, but by 'men of good education and steady habits' who were able to promote, direct and superintend 'agricultural and commercial undertakings'.[79] Educated public opinion in India as well as the bureaucracy encouraged Europeans to settle as capitalists and directors who could bring modern science, technology and capital to bear upon the development of India's internal resources. It was this class of colonizers who urged the Company's Government to improve India's communications and introduce railways to facilitate the movement of trade in commercial crops and agricultural produce. It was they who provided incentives to the establishment of 'special departments' to support the extension of free enterprise, especially in the rural areas where the exigencies of the colonial economy dictated the need not only of road and building construction, but also of irrigational, medical and public health facilities. They served as a primary instrument of rural development, though not in a positive sense.

The free traders of Britain liberated business enterprise from official control and restrictive barriers. They in fact emerged in course of time as an organized pressure group in India, influencing both its Central and Local Governments to enact measures, the economic benefits of which extended likewise to the affluent Indian landed and commercial classes. There developed in fact an identity of interest[80] between them and the emerging Indian middle classes in business and other fields that brought David Yule, the Chairman of the Bengal Chamber of Commerce, to preside over the annual session of the Indian National Congress in 1888.

Administratively, *laissez-faire* or free trade promoted liberalism, a rational principle based on the functional proliferation of administrative organizations as a means to ensure efficiency in the protection of person and private property. The complexities of the constitution of courts, their procedural sophistication and the codification of laws were all evidence of the concern which the Government of India felt for the promotion of that efficiency.[81] Accompanying these legal reforms, there was an agitation organized by the British Indian Association and the Indian Association, which represented the views of the aristocracy and the educated middle classes in various fields. They demanded the separation of the executive and judicial functions of the magistracy, a demand that continued to be voiced over a number of years. This doubtless had a political dimension in the imperial setting, but its social and economic signifiance was deeper. In their agitation, the affluent classes sought to preserve their dominance by obviating executive interference. The magistracy remained undivested of its criminal judicial powers. The protection of the lower orders of society, especially of lower castes and tribes, continued to form part of the duties of Collector-Magistrates. But the collaboration of European pressure groups with their Indian counterparts reinforced, with added rigour and complexity, the judicial system which Cornwallis had designed to ensure the protection of the rights of zamindars created by law in 1793.

The rational administrative principle of *laissez-faire* which called for functional specialization as a source of efficiency came to be applied to the Indian situation in 1837 when the Company's Government under Lord Auckland permitted Britain's free traders to hold farms of their own. It was thereafter that District Collectors began to be relieved gradually of their magisterial duties, especially in respect of policing in Bengal. Bombay and Madras took steps in quick succession to establish their separate department of police. The experience the Mutiny of course dictated the expediency of the Collector retaining his magisterial powers. Even so, the police in India was organized in each province into a separate department under Police act V (1861), the object being to provide a uniform and more effective security of person and property. This enactment was in great measure an expression of the views presented by the planter community before the Parliamentary Select Committee on Colonization and Settlement (India) in 1858. There were two other measures which the Government of India enacted about the same time in keeping with the views of the community. These were the Bengal Tenancy Act (1859) which facilitated mobility in the transfer of land, and the High Court of Judicature Act which rationalized the administration of justice in India on a uniform principle that promoted the growth of free enterprise without much of executive and bureaucratic interference.

The second phase of the Company's Government which started with the abolition of its trade thus marked the beginning of a new era in the history of district administration, an era of modernization which, in course of time, dictated the necessity of specialized departments being extended to the district level for rural development purposes.

II
RECURRENT FAMINES AND RURAL DEVELOPMENT 1858-1905

Rural development in the context of district administration in India mainly signifies the development of agriculture and such other elements as are of immediate relevance to the welfare of the rural population. The importance of agriculture as the mainstay of the rural economy and the direct responsibility of the state to promote it came to be specially realized as a result of a series of famines that occurred in different parts of India in the eighteenth and nineteenth centuries, famines which provided in due course a conceptual framework and set the tune for rural development.

The Report of the Famine Commission of 1880 gives an account of Indian famines from 1770 onwards and provides figures for the principal famines that occurred during the first seven decades of the nineteenth century.[1]

Taking all the 21 famines and scarcities as recorded in the last 109 years in any part of India, the production is 24 years of bad seasons to 85 years of good, or about two bad to seven good; in each case on an average one-twelfth of the population of the whole country, that is about 20 millions, may be approximately taken as the portion affected, so that the result might be said to be equivalent of a famine of scarcity over the whole country once in four years. Of these calamities, 8 may be classed as intense famines, 9 as famines, and 4 as severe scarcities.[2]

Even so, before the famine of 1860-1 in the North Western Provinces, no famine had ever formed 'the subject of a special inquiry'. It was only during the progress of the famine in the North-Western Provinces that Colonel Baird Smith was first 'deputed to examine into and report on the causes, area and intensity of the famine, the economic facts it disclosed, and the best measures to be adopted for its relief'.[3]

Apart from the terms of inquiry to ascertain the causes of famine and related matters, the measures of relief were specially significant in suggesting concepts of rural development, and, in fact, of development administration itself, that flowed from the experience gained through relief administration. The object of this chapter is to identify these concepts and to analyse the extent to which administrative action, though sought to be induced logically to meet conceptual expectations, lagged far behind in meeting the requirements of policy within the framework of district administration and its limitations.

Evolution of Concepts

Welfare

An important element in the concept of rural development was a humanitarian welfare approach to administration, not the stiff attitude of mind needed for the enforcement of penal laws. There was little or no trace of it in the famine policy of the East India Company after the opening of its trade and the emergence of free enterprise. The first 'very severe famine' of the nineteenth century was, for example, that of 1837-8 which affected the entire region between Allahabad and Delhi, more especially the districts lying between Kanpur and Agra. The Report of the Famine Commission (1880) points out that prices rose to about three times their ordinary rates, though seldom higher than 20 lbs of ordinary grain to a rupee. The famine which had been caused by an almost total failure of rain, led to 'violent agrarian disturbances and robberies of grain carts and grain stores'. Troops had in several cases to be called out to curb lawlessness. The loss of life due to the famine was estimated at more than 800,000. Even so, considerations of welfare formed no part of Government policy. 'The views then adopted were that the main duty of Government was to offer employment to those who could work, but that the relief of the helpless and infirm members of the population was the business of the charitable public . . . where the pressure on these charitable funds was exceptionally great, some assistance was given from the treasury, but not as a matter of right.'[4]

The famine of 1860-1, too, witnessed no change in the principle of relief administered in the North-Western Provinces, especially between Agra and Delhi, covering an area of 48,000 square miles and 19 million people, in addition to those in the adjoining states of Rajasthan. These principles were the same as had been adopted in 1837. It was reiterated that 'the duty of the state is to provide employment for those who can work, and the public to support by charitable assistance those who cannot'. The only difference was that both the principles were carried out in a more provident and thorough manner to make sure that relief works selected were of 'permanent utility' and executed with care under the supervision of professional engineers, not civil officers known for their laxity in 1837.

Consistent with these principles, it was emphasized that able-bodied labourers employed in relief works be paid 'at a low rate of daily wages, a fixed task of work being demanded in return'. And since welfare-based gratuity was no part of the concern of the Government, relief was 'carried on at the expense of the charitable public, aided by contributions from other parts of India and from England; it was generally distributed in the form of cooked food to persons who submitted to the condition of residence in an enclosed poor house'.[5] The poor-house idea was first introduced by Sir John Strachey, at the time Collector of Moradabad, who was perhaps influenced by the Christian Missionaries involved in famine relief.

The element of 'public' welfare was absent even in the Bengal and Orissa famine of 1866. According to a report of the Civil Surgeon at Cuttack, 'people died in the roads and fields all about; many died who never were seen; . . . In my opinion the cause of excessive mortality was that the people were gone too far before they came in; they all died from starvation, not from sickness in the ordinary sense'.[6] And yet the Government had long remained indifferent. Little or no care was taken to prevent loss of life. 'If the relief had been commenced two or three months earlier', the Civil Surgeon said, 'thousands of lives might have been saved, but no one seemed to appreciate the gravity of the situation'.[7]

However, a change soon became noticeable in the attitude of the Government. It had by now come to be universally recognized that excessive mortality flowed not merely from starvation, but also from violent epidemics of a number of diseases that followed in the wake of famines: diarrhoea, cholera, dysentery, fever, opthalmia, etc.[8] Indeed, the Cholera Commission of 1861 was the first to raise this question in order to invite the attention of the Government to it, and, as noted earlier, the Royal Army Sanitary Commission of 1863 viewed the health of European soldiers as ecologically connected with the health of the Indian population living in the surrounding areas. An act was accordingly passed in 1864 and rules framed under it to ensure the health of military cantonments, a development which led to the appointment of Sanitary Commissioners in 1867 to look after the conservancy of Indian towns and villages.

So when the Orissa famine of 1866 was followed by a failure of the rains in 1868-9 in the greater part of Western and North-Western India, including Rajasthan, the Central Provinces and several districts of U.P. and Punjab, some evidence of the concept of public welfare made its appearance. According to the Report of the Famine Commission (1880),

It was now laid down for the first time that the object of the Government was to save every life, and that district officers would be held responsible [for ensuring] that no preventible deaths should occur. It was found necessary to depart, in some degree, from the old principle, that it is the duty of the public to provide for the gratuitous relief of the infirm and weak, seeing that so large a proportion of these were foreigners and not the local poor; and the Government declared that it would supplement private subscriptions by whatever sum might be necessary for the support of persons incapable of work . . . Relief to the able-bodied was not confined, as in 1861, to large works of permanent utility under professional officers. There were indeed several of these, but there were also a large number of minor works under civil officers, which, in some cases, in the opinion of those officers, had the effect of attracting people who were not in immediate need of relief'.[9]

Obviously, the Government now aimed to improve the state of public health by an attempt to prevent loss of life from starvation and to check the outbreak of epidemic diseases resulting from the unhygenic conditions caused by famine. Apart from the immediate sanitary considerations for military cantonments, the credit for the welfare content of policy goes in no small measure to the efforts of Christian missions. They raised subscriptions from England and influenced the Government in India to make relief from such private sources available 'in the shape of cooked food'. The relief so rendered was of course to be 'conditional on residence in a poor-house',[10] where paupers hesitated to go for fear of a loss of caste. The element of welfare was nonetheless there.

The Bihar famine of 1873 was another occasion when the Government was guided by considerations of public welfare, not by profit designed to flow from large works of permanent utility accomplished by robust persons employed during famines on low wages. The Government reiterated its 'intention' of 'preventing loss of life at any cost, so far as practicable'. Tests and restrictions were, therefore, 'relaxed in respect of the wages, the amount of work done, and the character of the work offered'. Provision was instead made for sufficient money or grain to sustain 'all comers who were *prima facie* in want'. Cultivators were at the same time 'invited to take loans of money or rice repayable without interest'. The Government had in fact taken care to build up a sufficient reserve when the original purchase was effected, so that when the pressure passed this surplus was sold at a loss. It added not a little to the total cost of relief measures, 'which reached six and a half million sterling, or as much as the total expenditure on all past famines in all parts of India from the beginning of the century up to that time'. The inquiries specially made on the subject indicated that the object kept in view was duly fulfilled: there was no mortality due to famine, although people were obliged to return the value of the 'bountiful relief' given to them in their days of distress.[11]

This humanitarian approach to the concept of public welfare was, however, modified at the instance of Local Governments, especially Bengal, in the course of the famine relief operations of 1876-8. The principle was of course reaffirmed that the Government would spare no efforts 'to save the population of the distressed districts from starvation, or from an extremity of suffering dangerous to life', but they would not 'attempt the task of preventing all suffering and of giving general relief to the poorer classes of the commuity'. For, 'every one admits the evils of indiscriminate private charity, but the indiscriminate charity of a government is far worse'. The Government in fact felt that the task of saving life, irrespective of cost, was something beyond its power. All that it could do was to provide 'efficient assistance for the suffering people without incurring disastrous expenditure'. The Secretary of State for India, too, agreed to this modification in the famine policy of the Central Government, which he regarded as 'precautions' taken 'in the interests of the distressed population' as well as 'of the tax-payers generally'.[12]

An important reason for this reaction against the Government's relief measures of 1874 in Bihar was its interference with the free movement of trade. This came to light in an inquiry ordered by the Bengal Government at the instance of the Famine Commission in 1878.[13] The Magistrate and Collector of the district of Saran (C.J.S. Hodgkinson), for instance, reported in a spirit of disapprobation that in 1874 large quantities of grain were imported into Sarun by Government, and in my opinion very serious and unjustifiable interference with trade was caused by disposing of it in various ways at a rate considerably cheaper than the market rate. Not only was the power of trade greatly neutralized, but the people became demoralized and reckless, seeing the extraordinary exertions of Governmet, represented by its officials, to get rid, apparently, of as much grain as possible by some means or other.[14]

Hodgkinson was critical also of the manner in which advances were distributed 'recklessly' to the people. Many of them, he said, took them under 'the belief that a paternal Government would never demand repayment'. However, the bitterness among the people created by efforts to recover these advances led them to remark 'that they would sooner die of the famine than be induced to take advances from Government'. The discontent shook the confidence of the people in the Government, but what seemed worse to Hodgkinson was the attempt of the Government to interfere with free trade. 'I can conceive no condition', the Collector of Saran thus emphasized, 'which would justify the importation of grain by Government with a view to undersell the ordinary trader, if trade exists at all in the distressed district.'[15]

A complete disregard of the financial aspect of famine relief had of course its dangers. Cases occurred where money advanced even for land improvements or purchase of grain was diverted to other channels. The Sub-Divisional Officer of Sewan (Siwan), Mr Wright, pointed out in a report to his Collector at Saran, for instance, that 'a man who had taken some Rs 400 advances nominally for wells, had undoubtedly really borrowed it for a wedding in which the whole of it was spent'.[16] There was, therefore, a general consensus among officers that relief should be meant to help those who could make use of it to tide over the strains of famine, not to those who were helpless from the start. They were strongly opposed to the kind of indiscriminate charity given in 1874 to all and sundry. For, in the words of one of the Sub-Divisional Officers, relief work given to unskilled labourers, including women and children, was viewed 'as a wild phantasmagoria of laziness and wretchedness, of bad work and high wages'. The result was that the relief work executed in 1874 in the whole district of Saran, especially in the construction of roads, were, according to its District Engineer, 'one-fourth of what they cost'.[17]

There was, however, no change of policy in respect of the importation of grain by the Government and its distribution through the public agency. Unlike in Saran, where the recovery of advances had been a cause for bitterness, the Collector and Magistrate of Monghyr, C.F. Magrath, justified the supply and distribution of grain under official supervision. Speaking of his experience of 1874, he said: 'The grain was first sold at 10 seers, subsequently lowered to 12 seers, and then about the time the people went home to 14 to 15 seers per rupee. Petty trades were always allowed a margin for profit. The purchase of grain was done by the Government of India, and its transport by the Government of Bengal.' Money was doubtless given out as advances. But this was subsequently recovered. 'The only great loss which Government made was in selling off the surplus grain by auction', which could have been avoided if the grain so sold had either been held for a while or sent to Assam. But considering the profiteering of private importers, 'the principle adopted was held to be the best'. Magrath in fact emphasized that 'where there are no importers, or where they will not import, Government must step in, or starvation of the masses will ensue'.[18]

In response to the Famine Commission's Circular of June 1878, even H.E. Abbot, the Manager of the Jaintpore Indigo Factory in the district of Muzaffarpur, took a similar view of interference with private trade. He regarded such interference on the part of Government as 'a most necessary measure'. His argument was that it 'causes the local grain-holders, who would otherwise hoard their stores waiting for higher rates, to bring it into the market, enabling the district officers to obtain reliable statistics of the actual amount of grain in the country, and thus judge of the quantity necessary to import'.[19]

The policy of 1874 as modified in 1878 in terms of certain financial restrictions and a more selective approach to famine relief had the approval of the Famine Commission of 1880 which, in addition, also recognized the importance of suspensions and remissions of land revenue as a 'palliative' in times of famine. The Commission, however, introduced a new dimension in the concept of welfare by suggesting, besides suspensions and remissions of revenue, a number of other 'preventive' measures of constant application to counteract the recurrence of agricultural distress or to mitigate its severity in future. These measures, for instance, included provisions for irrigation and rural financing, advances of loans and agricultural statistics, tenurial improvements and agricultural administration. These suggestions were most significant in that the agricultural classes in India constituted the vast majority of its total population; their welfare lay in freedom from the periodical occurrence of famine and the appalling distress involved. The period that followed the Commission's report of 1880, was, therefore, characterized by efforts to apply both the palliative and preventive principles of public welfare. Our attention at this stage, however, will be confined to the former which attempted to combat famine directly during its prevalence.

The palliative measures of relief were put to test again in 1897 when India fell under the shadow of a great famine, the first of its kind since 1878. A commission was appointed under Sir James Lyall to look into the administration of relief and suggest improvements. It reported towards the end of 1898, and Lord Curzon on his arrival found the report upon his table awaiting orders. The report was no departure from the lines followed hitherto, except that it relaxed the financial discipline imposed earlier and recommended a scale of wages which experience showed to be too high for what was contemplated. The report's emphasis was both on procedural flexibility and financial generosity.

A second calamity, however, overtook the country within six months of the submission of Lyall's report. By August, 1899, the danger seemed to appear more terrible than ever before. It affected the United Provinces, the Central Provinces and Bombay. The Member of the Revenue and Agriculture Department in the Government of India toured the affected area in October and made a detailed statement regarding the character and extent of the approaching distress. By December it became clear that 'the severity of the distress had in certain provinces led to an exaggeration of the liberal policy advocated by the late Commission. The wages adopted upon famine works were in places so high as to exceed the market rates and to bring upon relief vast numbers of people who could well support themselves.'[20] However, the severity of the famine soon increased and reached its climax the following July, when the Viceroy himself had to visit the most smitten areas. Later, in a statement, he explained that the famine of 1899-1900 'was the greatest and most appalling that any Indian Government had ever had to face, and that it had been faced with an efficiency unprecedented in history. It had not been merely a failure of crops, but was accompanied also by a failure of fodder and in many tracts by an almost complete extermination of cattle'.[21] A comparative view of the two famines can be formed by figures given below:[22]

	1897-8	1899-1900
Population affected	10 per cent	18 per cent
Numbers on relief	4 million	6 million
Revenue remitted	2 crores	2 crores
Loans to cultivators	130 lakhs	238 lakhs
Direct expenditure on relief	7 crores	10 crores

In applying the principle of welfare in different tracts, however, conflicts arose, especially between the Central Provinces which had also experienced the disaster of 1897, and Gujarat, to which the famine of 1899-1900 was a calamity undreamt of before. The administration of the Central Provinces had been accused of being remiss in 1897. So when the subsequent disaster appeared, it hastened in 1900 'to throw open the doors of relief upon lenient terms, and the people [for the most part tribal], inured to the methods of famine and free from the self-respect induced by poverty, flocked in thousands to the sources of relief'. This was not the situation in Gujarat where the administration looked on famine as something 'inconceivable'. Delay naturally occurred in commencing and introducing 'the more liberal forms of relief'. With their standards of comfort and social position unbroken by the previous famine of 1897, the people themselves were induced with difficulty to accept the assistance offered as relief. It was no easy task for the Government of India, therefore, to steer a proper course in the midst of these two conflicting tendencies arising from two different circumstances.

The case of the Central Provinces was the first to engage the attention of the Government, which issued a Circular on 17 December 1899 cautioning Local Governments 'against excessive liberality'. As famine conditions deteriorated, the Government of Bombay was advised to support a more sympathetic and liberal system of relief. 'But although the drift of the orders in the two cases differed widely', it was explained, 'there was no inconsistency in the attitude of the Government of India'. For 'the two Provinces had each its own difficulties'. And if they had failed, they had failed 'in opposite directions'. The Government of India sought to ensure a middle course for safety. With this object in view 'the one was restrained, the other was to be urged', a policy that 'forestalled much unnecessary pauperization on the one hand and much avoidable mortality on the other'.[23]

There were in addition other questions of policy touching on the kind of reasons for giving relief and the level of wages payable. These were referred, in December 1900, to a special Commission under Sir A. MacDonnell as chairman. Consistent with its recommendations the Government of India by its Resolution of 21 March 1903 laid down instructions involving the introduction of such principles of welfare as did not permit a total disregard of financial considerations. Subject to certain reservations, the Local Governments were, therefore, advised to adopt a system which permitted the rejection from relief works of persons not in need of relief. The wages recommended in 1898 which had been found excessive, were sought to be reduced. And, subject to certain conditions and exceptions, it was laid down as a general rule that there should in future be no minimum wage for able-bodied workers. The lessons derived from the famine provided, on the one hand, against unpreparedness before undertaking relief and, on the other, against undue liberality in adminstering it. The first lesson was that from Gujarat, and the second from the Central Provinces. And on the basis of the principles so laid down it was hoped that the Government would meet any eventuality with increased efficiency and relieve the distress it might be confronted with.[24]

The palliative norm of welfare administration which was recognized broadly in 1878, thus formed an important guide in subsequent years. It was within the framework of free trade and capitalist enterprise, which had to be bent to provide for the alleviation of human suffering. Elements of planning and executive control, features antithetical to free enterprise, were introduced to a limited extent about the same period for the same reason. It was an important concept of development administration that found fuller recognition later through further experience.

Planning and Executive Control

Before the opening of the Company's monopoly trade there had been an attempt by the administration to control the price of grain in the famine-affected areas. In 1804, for instance, the failure of the rains in the North-Western Provinces and Bombay caused 'a very serious and widely extended famine'. The effects of drought were greatly enhanced by the ravages of the army of Jaswant Rao Holkar and the Pindaries in his train. To make relief available, therefore, the Company's Government brought grain into Bombay 'and sold at a fixed price to the public', exports being at the same time prohibited. The Report of the Famine Commission (1880) points out that 'public works and hospitals were started for the relief of those who flocked into the towns of Bombay and Surat'. In the North-Western Provinces, more especially in the severely affected ceded districts of Oudh, the measures taken to relieve distress consisted in the remissions of land revenue, advances of loans to the cultivators and a bounty on all grain imported into the afflicted areas.[25]

In the course of the Madras famine of 1807 (the first occasion with recorded evidence of a district in distress) 'the Government at the outset declared against any interference with private trade' which had already started gaining in strength, though not yet strong enough to effect a breach in the Company's monopoly. In view of the distress, the Government ultimately 'conceived it necessary to purchase, guaranteeing a minimum price to importers'. When the famine came to an end after plenty of rain in 1807, 'large stocks were left on hand, and had to be disposed of at a loss'.[26]

The position of the Company, however, had changed by 1812 when the Parliamentary Select Committee declared against the continuance of its monopoly and the Charter Act of 1813 soon left the Indian field open to Britain's private traders. And when famine came again in 1812-13, the policy of non-interference with trade was more firmly adopted. On this occasion the Governor of Madras 'refused to sanction the prohibition of export, or to import grain on Government account, declaring his belief that unassisted trade, if left to itself, could do more to relieve distress and to effect an equitable distribution of supply than Government could do with all its resources'.[27] This was the beginning of the freedom of private trade from bureaucratic control, an economic principle that encouraged unrestricted competition as the best means to ensure what Bentham called the greatest good of the greatest number. It took time to bring back that executive control as an effective instrument of relief against calamities. Even Mountstuart Elphinstone, who had earlier been an advocate of executive interference to control prices and export-import trade, fell in line with free traders when famine occurred in Madras and Bombay in 1824-5. He declared as the Governor of Bombay that 'it was wiser to adhere to the general principle of non-interference'.[28]

When the severe famines of 1837-8 and 1860-1 occurred the Government remained unconcerned about the control of prices or the supply of food grains. The hypocrisy of free traders, more especially of Indian dealers who had little or no scruple, came to surface in the course of the Bengal and Orissa famine of 1866. The report of the Commissioners appointed to inquire into this famine acknowledged without hesitation that 'increased demand' for Orissa rice for export to Calcutta and its outposts 'largely operated to enhance the price of grain, and in some degree to drain the country'. Emphasizing the fact of export trade as an important cause of the Bengal and Orissa famine, the Commissioners said: 'Not only have the countries round the Bay of Bengal become of late years more and more the source of supply of rice to Asia and Australasia, but within India recent movements have greatly tended to increase the drain on those same countries'.[29]

The findings of the Commissioners who obtained their figures of exports from the Board of Revenue, are clear from the following table which shows the prices and exports of the Lower Provinces of Bengal including Orissa:[30]

The official dependence on private trade as the only recognized agency of food supply and distribution led the Government to neglect its own duty to take early measures of relief. It did nothing to assess the situation in advance or to ascertain the magnitude of the calamity that was to overtake the province. The Commission regarded this neglect as a 'very serious question' and pointed out categorically that the 'only cause of increased suffering' was 'the delay which occurred in respect to measures of relief'.

An individual Collector here or there no doubt attempted to ward off the danger. The report of the 1866 Commission on the district of Nadia, for instance, shows that, in view of the relatively poor state of the rice crop of 1865, Lord Ulick Browne, the Collector of that district, had apprehensions of something like a famine. Moreover, grain merchants were beginning to raise prices by storing rice, with the result that it was not easy to buy even at the existing high prices. There was need for planning, need for executive direction to provide relief to the rural poor who complained to the Collector that they were without food and that he should do something for them. The fixing of the price of rice was suggested, but the Collector had to abstain from doing so. For, as he wrote to his Divisional Commissioner, 'it was an established principle of Government that commerce that is in force in England, shall be accepted in all her dependencies throughout the world, whatever may be their condition and circumstances, and that such a thing was quite out of the question'.[32]

Lower Provinces of Bengal

Quantity of Rice and Paddy Exported, in Maunds

	Calcutta		Out-ports		Total		Approx. average price of rice in Calcutta each year				
	Rice	Paddy	Rice	Paddy	Rice	Paddy					
1855- 6	89,11,500	2,705	5,64,137	20,734	94,75,637	23,439	Rs	1	2	3	p. md.
1856- 7	89,08,088	18,795	7,58,506	48,865	96,66,594	67,660	"	1	13	6	"
1867- 8	72,74,174	5,418	3,24,204	67,724	75,98,378	68,142	"	2	2	2	"
1858- 9	43,80,998	1,113	1,23,066	4,712	45,03,764	5,825	"	2	7	0	"
1859-60	47,34,715	10,756	7,01,771	5,00,408	54,36,486	5,11,164	"	2	13	0	"
1860- 1	75,27,556	4,412	5,08,939	3,51,497	80,36,495	3,55,908	"	2	3	2	"
1861- 2	1,06,86,378	18,447	7,60,555	2,25,701	1,14,46,933	2,44,148	"	2	0	9	"
1862- 3	1,14,87,707	6,518	11,02,566	2,28,566	1,25,90,273	2,35,447	"	2	2	0	"
1863- 4	1,52,47,048	20,906	11,76,430	2,80,414	1,64,23,478	3,01,320	"	2	4	0	"
1864- 5	1,75,55,250	23,710	16,31,272	2,41,150	1,91,86,522	2,64,860	"	2	15	10	"
1865- 6	86,46,497	1,405	8,43,721	1,71,929	94,90,218	1,73,334	"	3	8	7	"
1866- 7 up to February	46,37,147	3,685	6,01,880	39,645	52,39,027	43,330					
Up to 12 March for Calcutta only	1,92,950	-	-	-	1,92,950		"	4	7	7	"

N.B. The exports from out-ports are given up to February 1866-7. For Calcutta they have been entered up to the latest date to which the returns were made up, viz., 12 March 1867.

Theoretically, the principles of free trade were expected to encourage the movement of grain from sub-division of Kushtia, where it was selling at Rs 2-4-3 a maund, to Krishnagar, the district headquarters, where the price of grain of a similar quality was Rs 3-4, the cost of transit involved being hardly 4 annas a maund. But the grain dealers preferred not to move the grain lest prices fell at Krishnagar. In vain did the Collector endeavour to induce respectable people to bring in rice from Kushtia to Krishnagar at a cost very much below the price at which the dealers chose to sell; he toured the district and suggested publication of the prices at which rice was selling in different districts. But he would not himself transport the grain on behalf of the Government or organize anything in the nature of a public agency for distribution. Delays occurred in this manner and the weaker sections of society fell victim to the severity of famine that befell them in May-June 1866.

The behaviour of business interests became worse still when in July the rivers began to rise with unprecedented rapidity and caused serious injury to crops in the western part of Nadia, with the result that prices of grain rose to $6\frac{2}{3}$ seers to a rupee. Referring to Krishnagar, the headquarters of the district situated along the banks of the Bhagirathi river, the Collector wrote about the concerted efforts of private business to keep the prices up. He said:

> Numerous grain boats are passing down the river, but only a few stop here, and the occupants being unable to come to terms with the four dealers who have combined to keep up prices, while no one else will purchase wholesale, the boats have, in almost every instance, passed on. The first result, therefore, of the opening of the rivers, combined perhaps with apprehensions to the effect of inundation on the crops, has been a decided rise in prices in some places.[33]

The general tendency of the business communities was thus to exploit the sufferings of the people to amass wealth. The principles of free trade imported from England, a country where these principles had the conscious support of a free and comparatively educated society, proved harmful in Indian famine conditions. Reflecting on the state of Indian society, the Collector sorrowfully said:

> It is unfortunate that the principles of political economy do not work a little more freely and quickly in this country. If, for instance, seeing the great difference in price between grain in the boats passing by and in the bazar in Krishnagur, a cooperative society were formed among the Natives of the town not to deal in grain, but to supply themselves with it for the next two months, it would soon have an effect on the market here.[34]

The attempts of the Collector of Nadia to make popular pressure interfere with private trade were an exception to the general rule. The views of the civil service were as a whole regulated by the contemporary doctrine of *laissez faire*, a doctrine that was calculated to promote Britain's economic interest in collaboration with Indian traders who used it as a lever to secure freedom from bureaucratic control for their own profiteering purposes.

A civil service so ingrained with economic liberalism differed from the old school of officers in Orissa, who were intimately acquainted with the province and sincerely devoted to the people placed under their charge in the districts. The report of the Orissa Famine Commission (1866) made special mention of men like Sir Henry Ricketts and Mr Mill, of Mr E.T. Trevor and Mr Shore, who spent the best part of their lives in Orissa and acquired an intimate knowledge of the people and their living conditions in the course of their settlement work and revenue administration. But with the transfer of the Company's administration to the Crown officers began to lose touch with the people, for transfers and promotion became more rapid as the role of the administration expanded. The result, as the Commissioners reported, was that 'officers of the same standing and local experience are not now found in charge of districts, and appointments are made with greater regard to general than to local considerations. Under the influence of this change of system, the [old] Orissa school has ceased to exist', a school that 'made the most of the virtues' of the Oriyas 'and the least of their faults' and held 'in respect some rural virtues above the ordinary native standard' of the Bengalis living in Calcutta. At the time of Orissa famine in 1866, the seniormost civil officer with some extended local experience was a Mr Barlow with ten years' standing in the service, 'who had been four years Magistrate and Collector of Pooree'.[35]

The separation of the police from the magistracy in 1861 was yet another step that affected planning and executive control as an instrument of welfare administration. The Superintendent of Police was no doubt under the control of the Magistrate-Collector, but the personnel of his department was quite independent, being immediately under its own Superintendent. Thus the district officers were deprived of the only means at their disposal of obtaining information about the interior of their districts. Their complaint, as the Famine Commissioners pointed out, was that they 'are now obliged to look, if they look at all, vicariously with the eyes, and to hear with the ears of the District Superintendents of Police, some of whom are quite ignorant of the language and have very little experience of the people of the Lower Provinces'. Besides, considerations of policy demanded that the special department of the police be restricted to the performance of its specific duties of dealing with crime, and prevented from doing anything like 'making pretexts for interfering in matters beyond their proper province after the fashion of the old Police' which functioned as an integral part of the magistracy.[36]

There was in fact no planning to meet the drought that fell on Orissa in 1866 when nearly a third of the population or about a million people died of starvation and famine epidemics. According to the report of the Famine Commission (1880) 'no such calamity had occurred in the whole province for nearly a century'. In the absence of any plans to counteract it, 'it had to be dealt with by a body of officials necessarily ignorant of the signs of its approach, unprepared to expect it, and inexperienced in the administration of relief measures; nor were the native inhabitants of Orissa in any respect more aware of what was coming on them than the British officers'.[37]

As already pointed out, the drought of 1868 in the North-Western Provinces obliged the Government to introduce an element of welfare as a guiding principle of famine policy. It enabled the administration to foresee the danger and plan relief measures in good time to avoid death from starvation and disease. It was, however, the Bihar famine of 1873-4 that brought into relief the elements of planning and executive control as important instruments of rural welfare.

On the failure of rains in 1873 and the loss of the winter crop of rice the Government of Bengal instituted inquiries which established the inevitability of a severe famine involving the inhabitants of a large part of the province. It accordingly set about preparing vigorously for the required relief measures. The principles adopted by the Government were very different from those accepted on any former similar occasion: the operations of private trade would not be relied upon, and it was thus necessary to accept responsibility for providing the distressed districts with all the food likely to be required.[38]

The Secretary of State and the Government of India were both persuaded by the Government of Bengal to use executive interference with free trade as the only means of saving the masses from its deadly grip over the market. Approval was, therefore, accorded for the import of 480,000 tonnes of rice and its distribution to the several depots in the famine areas through the agency of Government officers.

The famine area was estimated at 40,000 square miles, and the affected population at 17 millions. Of these 735,000 were employed on works for nine months, 450,000 received gratuitous relief daily for six months, and 3,200,000 bought grain at low rates or received advances of grain or cash, a large part of which was repaid to the Government.[39]

As observed earlier, cases occurred where cash advances were misused and the stocks of grain left over were sold by public auction. The agitation of the business community against bureaucratic control was not without impact on the Government of Lord Lytton, more especially in terms of the expenditure involved in charity on public accounts. The conceptual principle of welfare was, therefore, modified so as to relate it to financial considerations. Even so, no departure was made from the principle that the Government should do all it can to save human life from the extremities of suffering during famines. This involved a responsibility which could not be enforced except by the executive officers of government.

Some other Concepts

There were, in addition, some other concepts that flowed from the recurrence of famines, concepts that were related not only to meeting distress but, more especially, to the positive aspects of rural development in terms of agricultural improvement on a continuous basis. These included central direction, statistical information and feedback, and specialization in developmental services involving the knowledge of science and technology. Famines in India not only provided a conceptual frame of reference, but also dictated the necessity of administrative action based on the concepts so developed. Ultimately, this promoted rural development, esepcially agriculture.

Positive Administrative Action

The first administrative measure in the direction of agricultural improvement was the creation of a special department to investigate the condition of agriculture in India, the need for which was brought into focus in 1866 by the Bengal and Orissa Famine Commission.

The question of agricultural inquiry received very full consideration under Lord Mayo's Government in 1870. The result of these deliberations was the formulation of a scheme for the constitution of both central and provincial departments of agriculture, meant respectively for coordination and execution. The object of Lord Mayo's scheme, as the Secretary of State later acknowledged in a despatch of 1875, was the establishment of a specific branch in the administration whose prime duty it would be to collect from village records such statistics and information as might throw light on questions of agriculture, including the economic resources of the country, and then to suggest measures for the development of agricultural industry.[40] Consistent with this object, the first step taken was the formation in 1871 of a new branch of the central secretariat to deal with the general scheme of agricultural development as part of the department or revenue and commerce.

The establishment of an agricultural branch was followed in 1875 by the creation of a provincial department of agriculture in the North-Western Provinces by Sir John Strachey who had, as a member of Lord Mayo's Government, taken a leading part in the formulation of the original programme. However, the state of financial crisis that developed on account of the famine and scarcity of 1876-8 stood in the way. It not only prevented new action in the provinces, but even led to the temporary suppression of the central department itself in 1879. It was determined that the separation which had been effected in 1871 between the Home Department on one hand and the Department of Revenue, Agriculture and Commerce on the other, should be done away with and that the two Departments be amalgamated under one Secretary with a combined office. The change introduced in 1879 did not abolish the agricultural branch. Under pressure of financial exigencies, it merely regulated afresh the agency for the conduct of its business by a transfer to the Finance Department.

The very famine which thus arrested the progress of further action brought about the resuscitation of Lord Mayo's scheme on a wider and firmer basis by attracting renewed emphasis on the improvement of agriculture.

The Famine Commission which was sent out to India in 1878 at the instance of the British Parliament submitted its report in 1880 after a prolonged tour of the country and a thorough study of its economy. The Commission doubtless suggested measures which were to be taken in a systematic manner on the actual occurrence of scarcity or famine in accordance with a famine code drawn up well in advance. But the greater part of its report dealt with recommendations for land reforms and administration, more especially for the promotion of agricultural improvement, emphasizing the necessity of extending railways and communications of enlarging the canal system, and of otherwise expanding the large protective works of the country. The basic idea was that 'agricultural prosperity in ordinary times was the best shield against the difficulties and trials of a season of drought'.[41] The Commisssion, therefore, insisted on the necessity of taking evey measure which might, on the one hand, prevent or minimize agricultural loss and distress, and, on the other, tend to increase and improve by an application of science to the soil, the produce of land. It was recommended that for dealing with these matters steps should be taken without delay to establish central and provincial departments of agriculture.

The Government of India realized the importance of the Commission's proposal and admitted that without some enlargement and reconstitution of the amalgamated Department of Home, Revenue and Agriculture full justice could not be done to the important task ahead. The amalgamation effected in 1879 was accordingly done away with, and a new Secretary to the Government of India was appointed in 1881 with direct and special charge of Revenue and Agriculture. The new Department so created was invested with three main functions:

First — A complete and systematic inquiry into vital agricultural and economic information for every part of India, in order that Government and its officers might always be in possession of an adequate knowledge of the actual condition of the country, its population, and its resources.

Secondly — The general improvement of Indian agriculture, with the view of increasing the food supply and general resources of the people.

Thirdly — A better and prompter organization of famine relief, whenever the actual approach of famine might be indicated by the statistical information available with the officers of government.[42]

Consistently with the decision so taken, the services of E.C. Buck, at the time Director of Agriculture and Commerce, North-Western Provinces and Oudh, were placed at the disposal of the Government of India in the Home Department. He subsequently took over as Secretary in the Department of Revenue and Agriculture.

Limiting Factors: Generalist-Specialist Controversies

For the attainment of its three objects, more especially of the first two in ordinary times, the Famine Commission made three other recommendations. These included the creation or expansion of a very elaborate local machinery functioning under the supervision and control of the provincial departments of agriculture, and, in the last resort, by a branch of the central secretariat; the inclusion of agricultural science and surveying among the subjects which could be taken up in the final examination by selected candidates for the Indian Civil Service, and, finally, the preparation of land records with reference to each individual field of an Indian village for purposes of statistical information. But there were limiting factors which in each case stood in the way.

Local Administrative Machinery. On the question of the local and provincial agency as well as of the adequacy of central supervision the Famine Commission held a very comprehensive view. Its argument was that success in agricultural inquiry would depend mainly on the completeness and accuracy with which the agricultural, vital and economic statistics to be dealt with were collected in each village, and compiled in each sub-division and district throughout the country. It was, therefore, considered necessary that the institution of village accountants be reformed and revived; that they be put under effective supervision, and that there should be in each district a special officer of the rank of Deputy Collector whose main or 'only duty would be to take charge of all matters connected with the economic condition and well-being of the people'. This special officer was to test and compile the agricultural returns, to examine the market prices and ascertain from these and other data the relative value of each year's crop, according to whether it was below or above the average.

From a continuous record of the harvests, it was believed, the special officer could obtain data for judging whether the landed classes were in a depressed or prosperous condition.

It would be his object to obtain similar information as to all sections of the population, and to learn what are the causes of depression, and what classes would be the first to succumb under the pressure of scarcity. The accurate registration of vital statistics and the investigation of the causes of any abnormal mortality would lie within his province, and he would be the agent of the health officer of the district for the purpose of scrutinizing the record of births and deaths. The extent of the food stocks, the ebb and flow of local trade, the current rates of interest charged on loans to different classes, the deficient or super-abundant supply of any kinds of labour, and the customary wages paid to each kind—these and other kindred topics, on which information is at present far from precise, would fall within the scope of his inquiries.[43]

As regards the relations of special officers with their Collector, they were to be 'generally subordinate to the District Officer'. They were, however, to function 'specially under the orders of the Agricultural Department' of their province as far as their returns were to be prepared and checked.

The local machinery recommended by the Famine Commission was an attempt to insert into the framework of 'general administration' a specialized element. Though subordinate to the head of district administration locally in terms of general disciplinary control, in technical matters it was to be guided by the provincial Department of Agriculture presided over by a Director of Agriculture who was to be its executive head. A corresponding officer was to be appointed to perform analogous duties under the Government of India in order to assist it in its dealings with the Local Governments in their Departments of Agriculture.[44]

However, the Collectors as a class were opposed to any division of their authority in the districts. They viewed the plan of a local agency as 'very extensive' and expressed themselves against it on the score of its being very expensive. The Government of India, a bureaucratic organization of civil servants, agreed with them. In its letter of 14 March 1881, it advised the Secretary of State to reject the Commission's plan for local machinery. The argument was that it would involve 'not only the creation of a separate Agricultural Department under a Director for each Province, but also the appointment to every district in India of a separate departmental agent', involving 'a departure from sound principles of district administration'. For, it was added, the role sought to be assigned to the special statistical officer was 'one of the highest and most essential functions of the chief district officer'. The comprehensive nature of the agricultural, vital and economic inquiries assigned to the special officer, it was further argued, had the risk of his being entitled to interfere in any department. Any idea of sharing with the District Officer in the totality of his executive control over administration was at the time considered wholly unpalatable. 'We certainly think', the letter emphasized, 'it would be hazardous either to transfer duties so vital from the hands of the more highly trained and responsible public servant to those of his official inferior, or to expose the working of the scheme to all the risks inherent in divided government'.[45]

Though not very keen to proceed immediately with the establishment of provincial departments of agriculture, the Government of India was not opposed to it either. Its opposition was basically directed towards the creation of the department in the districts. A

'Local Agricultural Department', the letter said, 'may hereafter be constituted at the headquarters of each province, somewhat on the model which has been very successfully adopted in the North-Western Provinces, and we are prepared to entertain favourably any such proposals; but we do not think that it would be advisable to go beyond this at present in the direction of the creation of a special local agency' in the districts.[46]

In pursuance of the Famine Commission's advice a central Department of Revenue and Agriculture was created in 1881. Under the instructions of the Secretary of State for India, it took steps to arrange with Local Governments the organization of similar provincial departments, which were invested with the tasks of agricultural inquiry, agricultural improvement and famine relief. The suggested famine codes were drawn up in 1882. The other measures suggested by the Commission were also placed for consideration before a conference at Calcutta where every province was represented by selected officials and experts connected with the administration of land or the conduct of agricultural departments. The Calcutta conference of 1882 determined the main principles on which future cadastral surveys, the basis of agricultural statistics, should be conducted. A second general conference, held again at Calcutta in 1883, prepared a scheme for the registration of inland trade statistics as well as the compilation and publication of agricultural and trade returns. A third conference was held at Delhi in 1888 and dealt with the important subject of agricultural education.

Agricultural Education for Civilians. The need for the agricultural education of civil servants was first felt in the context of the Bengal and Orissa famine of 1866, which affected not only the supply of food to the mass of people, but also the colonial economy dealing with the commercial export of agricultural products such as cotton, jute, tea, coffee, indigo, sugar, spices, cinchona, saltpeter, oil seeds, forest products as well as iron and coal. The attention of the Government towards the primitive state of Indian agriculture was first directed by the Manchester Cotton Supply Association which entered into correspondence with the Secretary of State in 1869 and urged him to take such measures as were considered necessary 'for the establishment of a Department of Agriculture in each of the several provinces of India, and the more active employment of Collectors of districts in matters connected with cotton cultivation'[47] with a view to improving its quality and supply.

The improvement and development of agriculture as well as commerce and industry in India, for which a separate department was sought to be established in 1859, were in fact functions which, as the Secretary of State pointed out in a despatch of 22 September 1870, already vested in the several Revenue Boards of Bengal, Madras and the North-Western Provinces. The Revenue Commissioners in Bombay, too, had been specially charged with these very duties. It was thus reiterated that 'although commercial interests have possibly not met with the [official] support which those connected with commerce demand, the Government of India and the subordinate Governments have been always forward in the promotion of schemes for the improvement of agriculture and the development of the resources of the Empire'. The Secretary of State in fact took pains to emphasize that with the exception of the permanently settled province of Bengal, the Government had shown 'direct and immediate interest in the improvement of agriculture which is possessed by no government in Europe'.[48]

However, the motive for the Government underlying all its measures of improvement was the increase of its revenue resources, a financial approach to land policy and administration. Even while accepting in principle the proposed establishment of a Department of Agriculture, the Secretary of State did not, therefore, omit to advise that land revenue must form part of the new department and that 'the application of measures for the improvement of agriculture must, in the last resort, be mainly kept to the Collectors of Districts',[49] and to no other agency.

What the Manchester Cotton Supply Association or the planting community generally wanted was the modernization of agriculture by an application of science to Indian agriculture, for contemporary experience in all parts of the world had proved conclusively that there was no branch of industry in which the effects produced by science were more certain or more remarkable. This view found expression in Lord Mayo's letter to the Secretary of State, recomending the establishment of a special Branch of the Home Department to deal separately with agriculture and commerce.[50] The letter admitted not only the 'primitive and backward condition' of Indian agriculture thanks to the non-existence of scientific knowledge, but also the fact that 'the Government has not done for its improvement all that it might have done'.[51] The development of agriculture, as the letter clearly suggested, involved the use of specialized scientific knowledge and increased government participation. In other words, it meant a process of planning and bureaucratic control involving interference with private enterprise.

Naturally, the choice was between continuity, which meant *laissez faire,* and change which involved some government control. In the history of rural development the Viceroyalty of Lord Mayo marked the first step towards change within the framework of continuity. Except under special circumstances, he observed that the Government

> cannot with advantage attempt to carry on any of the [commercial] operations of agriculture. In regard to this, as to other branches of industry, the State may do much to foster and encourage the efforts of private individuals, but it can do comparatively little through the direct agency of its own servants. Nevertheless, the exceptions to this rule will, in this country, be important, and we believe that it may often be the duty of the Government to act as the pioneer to private enterprise.[52]

With this end in view Agriculture and Commerce were in the first instance placed under a Director-General as a Branch of the Home Department. Under the instructions of the Secretary of State, Revenue was added to this Branch and the whole formed into a department which in 1871 came to be designated the 'Department of Revenue, Agriculture and Commerce' and placed under a Secretary to Government.[53]

This proposed role of the Government to assist individuals in the development of the stock and quality of the great staples of Indian agriculture as well as to act as 'the pioneer to private enterprise' required equipping its civil servants with a requisite knowledge of agricultural science.

The idea of training them had in fact occurred to the Government soon after the 1869 suggestion of the Manchester Cotton Association to establish a separate Department of Agriculture. In a Minute recorded by Sir Richard Temple on 6 December 1869, he emphasized the importance of establishing 'some agricultural training schools' and introducing such other measures as were 'partly scientific' and partly 'practical'. His view was that if Indians were to be taught to improve agriculture 'the real agency must be that of Local Governments' who must in each case appoint a trained public servant as 'a special officer, something like an Agricultural Commissioner, with some leisure to devote himself' to the development of agriculture. Considerations of economy, however, stood in the way and no such special officer could be appointed in any province except U.P. A civilian Director of Agriculture was appointed there in 1875 as a special case, with the result that Kanpur became the first centre of modern agricultural education in North India. The agricultural education of civilians was thus generally shelved for a number of years until the question was reopened in 1879 during the inquiry of the Famine Commission.

When the subject of agricultural training was considered by the Government of India in 1879, the Sir John Strachey recorded a Minute where he said:[54]

> There might be no great difficulty in carrying out the suggestion that a certain number of young civilians should, after passing their examinations in England, go through a course of instruction at some suitable place of agricultural education. I should like to ask the Famine Commission to consider this subject, in the hope that the practical experience of Mr. Caird [of the Commission], and the knowledge that he possesses of Indian and English agriculture, might teach us how the suggestion could be acted on.

In their Notes recorded on the same subject in 1879 itself, C.L. Tupper and E.C. Buck, both of the Indian Civil Service, independently expressed an opinion that it would be undesirable to require all civilians to undergo an agricultural training soon after passing their competitive examinations or even to select a certain number in England for that purpose. Both agreed that such a course would be expensive and prejudicial to a man's career, without being able to produce a valuable class of specialists.

But there were other reasons, too, to oppose the inclusion of agriculture as a subject either for the competitive examination or the special examination in such subjects as bore relevance to the requirements of the ordinary executive and administrative functions of a civil servant. The original object[55] of the competitive examination introduced on the recommendations of the Macaulay Committee (1854) was to ensure intellectual excellence and moral integrity that were deemed to go with the humanities. Higher mathematics was included in the test because it was recognized by Cambridge as an intellectual exercise. The whole emphasis of the competitive examination was on the cultivation of the mind as the mainspring of human action and the key to understanding behavioural motives in human affairs. The assumption was that a civilian so selected would be able to view any situation in its totality, and not merely from a single technical point of view. The generalist was thus recognized as superior to the specialist, and the proposed inclusion of agriculture as a subject for the competitive examination naturally clashed with this fundamental assumption.

The special examination of probationers, too, had its own relevance. It prepared them for their primary duties, executive, judicial and administrative. The course prescribed was so extensive as to occupy a candidate fully and it could not be curtailed without prejudice to the purpose for which it was designed. Besides certain languages, it included Indian laws, general jurisprudence, proceedings in English courts and the law of evidence, Indian history and geography and political economy. The addition of agricultural training to the existing training in England, was, therefore, considered not only costly but also prejudicial to the main purpose of the special examination.

In his Note Tupper therefore objected to young civilians being selected in England for agricultural instruction before their arrival in India. His ground for opposition was that the authorities there had no opportunity of picking suitable men for such instruction. And it was not every officer who, if he had the proper knowledge, would make good use of it in India: 'I fear he might become imbued with theories applicable only to English or European farming, and find, on reaching India, that he had an immense deal to unlearn'.[56] Tupper's own view, in these circumstances, was that so long as India did not have its own College of Agriculture, young civilians, say of five years' standing in India, might be deputed to Europe to go through a course of study in an Agricultural College on conditions somewhat similar to those under which officers of the Staff Corps and Indian Armies were allowed to enter the Staff College at Sandhurst.

Based on his experience of the Department of Agriculture in the North-Western Provinces, Buck's main complaint was that independent of whether it was a case of 'Civilian, Planter or Native', agricultural science was 'practically altogether wanting'. He pointed out that the situation could not improve merely by selecting a few young civilians unless the Government had 'at its side as adviser a man of really high scientific acquirements', with a number of suitably trained young civilians acting under his guidance in the Agricultural Departments of Local Governments. This could be done, he said, by importing from England scientific knowledge in the person of a trained agricultural chemist to serve at the centre and by sending home to England clever young civilians for training in agricultural science.[57]

The proposals were discussed in 1879 and all referred to the Famine Commission for opinion.[58] In its recommendations the Commission for the first time suggested, for developmental purposes, that 'more weight should be given to the natural and physical sciences in the open competitive examination'. It went to the extent of recommending that so far as the intermediate and final examinations of civil service probationers were concerned, agricultural and organic chemistry should even replace some of the compulsory subjects. It was added that candidates who distinguished themselves in these subjects in their written tests should be allowed to spend an additional year in England to enable them to study agriculture on two-thirds pay as an incentive, the officers so selected being preferably enlisted in the agricultural department after a period of normal service. Junior civil servants of five or six years' standing were, in addition, to be selected and sent to England for a year or more to study agriculture. The object of the Commission's recommendation was thus to provide for a theoretical training of probationers to be tested by examination, and then for a practical training of a few of these at an agricultural college at Government expense. These were to be in addition to the otherwise generally approved scheme of deputation, recommended by Tupper and Buck. It was an attempt to meet their points as well as those of Sir John Strachey.

The recommendations of the Famine Commission were given serious consideration by the Government of India.[59] Nobody agreed to make agriculture a subject for the competitive examination. It was considered 'practically useless' even as an optional subject during the probationary stage. Lord Ripon, the Viceroy, agreed with Buck and S.C. Bayley, who in their Notes were strongly opposed to any interference with the existing pattern of examination. If a knowledge of agriculture, surveying of any other technical subject was needed for developmental purposes, it might be added after a certain period of service and experience in India. In his Memorandum[60] Buck clearly explained this point which the Government of India literally lifted for acceptance by the Secretary of State.[61] Buck had said:

We want men to qualify themselves as executive and judicial officers. Everyone must make himself competent for that work. If a few can be found to superadd a knowledge of agriculture, their services will be much valued, but to attempt to give this knowledge during the preliminary stage of a civilian's career is hardly possible without knocking more useful subjects out of the curriculum, and, if acquired, it is not likely that its acquisition as a book subject would be attempted by the class of men least likely to make a practical use of it. Any way it would be incomplete, theoretical, and not specially adapted to Indian requirements. I would therefore prefer to adopt the idea of letting Local Governments select a very limited number of civilians from 5 to 12 years' service, and give men so selected special encouragement to study at Cirencester or some other agricultural college.

Consistent with Buck's opinion, the Government of India in its letter to the Secretary of State deprecated 'any attempt to give an agricultural training to civilians previous to their arrival in India'.

At the instance of Ilbert the Government agreed in principle that efforts should be made to arouse real interest in the subject among probationers, so that those with an aptitude for agriculture were encouraged. Though 'orderly and intelligent' and working hard to pass in their special examination subjects, the probationers, however, showed little or no enthusiasm about their future career. It was here that Ilbert suggested means to make them interested in the real facts of Indian life, their careers and the kinds of openings that would be available to those who showed a special aptitude for agricultural work. His suggestions included acquaintance with published manuals dealing with the revenue and land tenure systems of India, more especially interesting lectures and talks occasionally delivered by ex-civilians with considerable experience of settlements operation in 'khas' estates or an estate under the management of the Court of Wards. It was pointed out that the best raw material for a good settlement officer or officer of an agricultural department was probably to be found in a young man who was the son of an English country gentleman and who, from his boyhood, possessed a knowledge of and interest in, country life. But since most of the land in the vicinity of Oxford belonged to the various colleges, any probationer there might spend a holiday or two at a college farm, examine the condition of crops, soil and buildings, and participate in discussions about their improvement. Ilbert's view, with which the Government also agreed, was that nothing more than this could be attempted towards giving civilians an agricultural training before they left England. He was, however, 'disposed to think that agricultural chemistry might be admitted as an optional subject in the final examination by the side of botany, geology and zoology', already introduced by Regulations in June, 1881. The Government did not raise any objection.

As suggested by both Bayley and Buck, the Government of India also agreed to provide special inducements to those who chose to undergo the training in question during their furlough in England. The stipulation that furlough be restriced to officers who had served at least eight years in India, was, for this purpose, to be relaxed so as to allow a Local Government to select for the contemplated training any officer of not less than five years' active service. This relaxation would help ensure that specialized training was given at an early stage of an officer's career. The officer selected by a Local Government was to be sent on furlough to England on the usual furlough allowances and required to proceed to some suitable college and do a complete course of study in agriculture. As such courses usually lasted two years, the duration of furlough was to be of the same period even though this length of furlough might not have been due under the ordinary rules governing furlough. It was further laid down that an officer who succeeded in getting a diploma or certificate of competence was to be reimbursed to the extent of his college expenses and allowed to count one year of the course as service for purposes of his pension. The training so received would entitle that officer, at the discretion of a Local Government, to appointment as Director or Assistant Director of the Agricultural Department.[62]

As regards surveying, its importance was doubtless recognized for settlement officers, especially in the permanently settled districts of Bengal, which recommended its inclusion as a subject for the competitive examination. The proposal of the Bengal Government was, however, not accepted.

The report of the Famine Commission made an interesting recommendation with a view to making junior civilians fully conversant with the problems of agricultural development: it proposed that the existing rules prohibiting Government servants from engaging in private enterprise should, under certain restrictions, be so modified as to allow officers to lease land for farming up to a limit of 100 acres. However, after weighing arguments for and against the proposal, the Government of India decided against it. It was feared that once the arguments in favour of farming were accepted, these might with equal force be extended to other commercial enterprises. Sir Charles Wood when Secretary of State had declared in a despatch of 24 July 1860 that no civil or military servant should be permitted to engage in pursuits which would divert his time and attention from his proper functions[63] and in keeping with this principle, the recommendation was turned down.

The whole plan to provide facilities for a certain number of civilians to acquire a scientific knowledge of agriculture had its limitations, however. It was viewed by critics as 'an exotic importation transplanted fom England' to promote agricultural development in India where, in the absence of anything like a national or indigenous system of education in the field, the knowledge would not filter down to grassroot levels.[64] It is true that no progress was possible without a knowledge of agricultural science and technology. Rural poverty could not be fought with primitive weapons. And once the state undertook the developmental job as part of its welfare duty, the first agency to acquire that knowledge was bound to be its own public servants. But they had to educate the people and be ready to be educated in the process. It was here that the scheme was found wanting, mainly thanks to finacial considerations.

Civilians with agricultural training were the first to be appointed as Directors or Assistant Directors in the Departments of Agriculture in the Provinces which accepted the establishment of such departments after the central Department of Revenue and Agriculture (without Commerce) had been created in 1881. Some even took independent action and by 1884 every major province came to have its own department in some form under a Director, though financial exigencies still did not permit any large outlay on agricultural research and experiment. The attention of provincial departments remained mostly confined to the improvement of land records for the collection of agricultural statistics.

As regards agricultural improvement, it called for the appointment of an expert who, as Buck had suggested a couple of years before the resuscitation of the Agricultural Secretariat in 1881, might act as adviser to the Government of India. The proposal was first made in 1882 in connexion with a scheme for a National School of Agriculture at Kanpur, which was disallowed by the Secretary of State as being premature. The question was considered again between 1884 and 1887. It met with a similar fate again, on financial grounds. At the instance of Local Governments, however, the Government of India took a lead and asked the Secretary of State to sanction the employment of a first class expert. The outcome was the deputation of Dr J.A. Voelcker, Agricultural Chemist of the Royal Agricultural Society, who came out to India in 1890.

Land Records. The district analysis made by Dr Voelcker did for the purpose of rural development and agriculture will be discussed a little later. Here we shall take note of a further limiting factor, the preparation of land records, which, though necessary as the basic source of statistical information, delayed the progress of agricultural improvement.

One of the functions of the new departments created in the provinces on the model of the central Department of Revenue and Agriculture was to provide agricultural and economic facts and statistics for every part of India. The Government of India accepted the responsibility of widening under imperial direction the projected scheme of national investigation as a precondition of agricultural improvement. It was realized that the first requisite in any programme of agricultural inquiry was the efficiency of the Land record establishments from the village upwards. This meant that the provision and maintenance of correct village and field maps and records, upon which inquiry was to be based, must be the first stage in schemes of agricultural reform, especially in the permanently settled districts of Madras and Bengal in which village accountants (patwaris) had either disappeared or remained beyond official control. Generally, however, there had always been attached to a village or group of villages an accountant with a hereditary duty to provide annually for each field a correct record of area, occupancy, rent, crops and other facts and statistics called for by his official superiors.

Before British rule these villages were grouped into administrative circles, each containing about a hundred villages placed under a supervisor,[65] an official (usually a *kanungo*) whose main duty it was to collate the returns received from village accountants, and to obtain such information about the agricultural and financial condition of the circle as might be required for purposes of assessment and land revenue administration.

The inquiries made in connexion with the cadastral survey scheme, however, showed that the original functions of these hereditary offices had in most cases been forgotten, all other considerations being overriden except those of hereditary claims. The supervisor, not infrequently, was found so illiterate or incapable that he could not perform without assistance any official duties assigned to him. His traditional functions had in fact ceased to be operative.

While reforming the land record system as a basis of agricultural inquiry, care was taken to recognize the hereditary claims of the village and circle officers and to introduce efficiency by providing, wherever necessary, for their education and training. In most cases older men were allowed to appoint substitutes or educated relatives;

time was given to the younger to learn and acquire efficiency in the performance of their real duties; and only those of the latter who were hopelessly incompetent were finally ejected. The staff of the department was materially expanded to meet requirements arising from the extension of cultivated area, the growth of population, the demand for more elaborate statistics, and other causes which had doubled the load of work.

In fact, the emphasis of the new departments remained for a number of years after 1881 on the improvement of revenue more than agriculture. The argument was that since the efforts of the central and provincial departments of agriculture would for several years be confined to scientific experiments of an apparently unremunerative character, it was necessary to make every effort to meet hostile financial criticism by turning 'the first attention of the new departments to remunerative work', that of improving the figures of land revenue collection. The Finance Committee of 1886 which included among its members the writer of the Famine Commission Report of 1880, justified this move, in spite of his being fully cognizant of the important advantages of agricultural investigation, research and experiment. The Committee 'came to the definite conclusion that expenditure on agricultural departments could not, under existing circumstnaces, be justified unless it could be shown that they were or would be directly remunerative. The departments were subjected accordingly to this financial test'.[66] The provincial departments of agriculture managed to pass this test, except in the permanently settled areas where outlay exceeded income, or where the partial substitution of the village officer by a more expensive agency had in some cases led to excessive expenditure.

Influenced therefore by the fact that 'in almost every province the utilization of village establishments had been found remunerative, the Governor-General in Council did not impose any further condition on the maintenance of departments of land records and agriculture than to require . . .that the maximum use shall be made of the village officer under all circumstances in which his employment can lead to further economy. In this view the claim of the State to his efficiency must be held to be paramount over all other claims' [67]

The developments which took place in the couple of decades after 1870 lend themselves to certain conclusions which are significant in terms of development administration generally. The exigencies of recurrent famines and the consequent collapse of the rural economy, for instance, led the state to undertake developmental operations in agriculture as 'the pioneer to private enterprise'. This called for corresponding administrative changes. The structure and purpose of the competitive examination for the Indian Civil Service were sought to be modified by an attempt to include agriculture as a subject of examination, a suggestion which clashed with Macaulay's original objective. But since the main purpose of the civil service continued to be competence in the performance of executive and administrative functions, agriculture was not included, nor were probationers obliged to devote an additional year to study that subject. Its importance however was recognized. Agricultural departments were established in the provinces and their Governments allowed to select young civilians to study agriculture in England before being entitled to selection for the post of Director or Assistant Director of Agriculture. The principle was that a civil servant must, in the first instance, be well-equipped intellectually and trained administratively before he proceeded to add a knowledge of specialized or technical matters.

At the instance of the Famine Commission, the importance of science and technology was recognized as essential for development. The physical and biological sciences found place in the special examination of the Indian Civil Service. The importance of agricultural inquiry, research and experiment were also realized as necessary conditions for rural development. But considerations of economy led to the emphasis being put on revenue rather than statistical investigation and agricultural research. The question of agricultural education in India becoming a part of its total education system was doubtless raised, but it made no progress.

Voelcker's Analysis

Voelcker's analysis dealt mainly with the projected scheme of agricultural investigation urged by the Famine Commission. He agreed with the Famine Commissioners that 'the revenue system in the greater part of British India is such as to present unrivalled means of ascertaining in the fullest manner all necessary facts relating to agriculture, but that those means have nowhere been completely utilized or made as efficient as they might be'.[68] The creation of central and provincial departments of land records and agriculture in and after 1881 was designed to fulfil the object, but it remained largely unattained. What Voelcker did later was to work out in detail the whole scheme of investigation which was afterwards briefly designated 'district analysis', a scheme of agricultural inquiry as part of district administration and showing the indices of affluence or poverty as the case might be.

The principle on which Voelcker acted was more or less the same as that adopted by the Government in 1881. This was to localize every agricultural defect, then discover its cause, and, finally, to devise such protective arrangements as might remove or alleviate its injurious action. As part of this scheme an attempt was to be made, for example, to examine each agricultural tract in respect to its tendency to suffer from drought on one hand, or the extent to which it was or could be protected from drought, on the other. What went wrong earlier was that the desirability of mapping out such tracts was in some provinces misconceived. It was assumed that a general inquiry into the agricultural condition of each district was required to be done once for all. It was not clearly understood that the scheme of investigation was to be slowly and gradually worked out on the basis of every defect being closely analysed and studied with a view to the possible discovery of remedial action. The element of planning in Voelcker's concept of district analysis was earlier missed completely. The result was that 'while in many parts of India excellent reports, maps and atlases were published in illustration of the general condition of each district, no precise inquiry was set on foot as to the agricultural circumstances of each village or group of villages; as to the particular defect or defects which prevented each locality from reaching the highest standards of agricultural efficiency; or as to the possibility of remedial action in each case.'[69]

It was with respect to the question so left unanswered that Voelcker's district analysis sought to supply the answer. He pointed out that in spite of the hereditary knowledge and experience of the Indian cultivator, several defects did exist in almost every district which, if they could not altogether be removed, could be considerably lessened. At the agricultural conference of 1890 he thus emphasized the necessity of 'laborious investigation' to trace out the causes which had 'stimulated development in some parts of India and retarded it in others'. His report in fact went far to prove the existence of innumerable defects in agricultural conditions and practices, which, as he pointed out, called for intelligent analysis with reference to facts and statistics collected from village officers and their land-records.

The agricultural conferences held in 1893 and then again in 1895-

96 endorsed Voelcker's line of action. It was recognized that failure to reach the highest attainable standard might be (1) of occasional, (2) of gradual, or (3) of persistent character. The object of inquiry was, therefore, to be an attempt to minimize agricultural distress and loss in each class of cases; and the first step was to decide how far the machinery of land records could be utilized in the investigation under each head.

Voelcker's district analysis constituted in fact a scheme of agricultural inquiry on the basis of the material available with the land-records machinery concerning all three categories of agricultural circumstances. It applied especially to districts with temporary settlement, where conditions of land tenure and agricultural operations were subject to periodical revision and control by governmental agencies right from the village onwards. The land-records machinery of the permanently settled areas, of course, stood on a different footing. But there, too, attempts were being made through cadastral surveys to bring together such information as might be deemed necessary to satisfy the requirements of what Voelcker meant by district analysis, an indicator of agricultural affluence or poverty.

The occasional failure to reach the highest attainable standard of agricultural production was, for instance, explained as sudden distress arising from an unforseen calamity, such as the failure of rain, hailstorms, inundations and the like calling for immediate relief. This relief could be made available on the basis of the land records indicating to district officials the extent and character of the calamity. All that was required of the land-records department was to organize or improve the system under which the prompt and continuous information supplied by the records should be brought before the responsible authorities to enable the district officers to take suitable action.

A more important case, however, was that of gradual failure, a 'gradual deterioration due to ascertainable causes requiring early and special measures of prevention and relief'.[70] Considerable distress was known to have been caused by cattle murrains, by swamping due to interference in drainage by railway embankments or canals, by the growth of obnoxious weeds and by other causes which gradually reduced the value of land and affected agricultural prosperity. The records maintained in almost every province by village officers, though scattered in form, contained information indicating serious deterioration in agricultural tracts. What remained to be done was to reduce the information so available to a clear and statistical abstract in such form as might enable district officers to grasp the pertinent facts at a glance without much difficulty.

The agricultural conferences which reviewed Voeleker's report between 1890 and 1895 expressed themselves in favour of adopting this plan. It was laid down that in every part of India where land records were maintained,

a book is now to be kept up by each circle officer, in which will be entered in English figures under appropriate heads such statistics as are calculated to show at a glance the advance or decline in prosperity of every village; such, for instance, as the cultivated and irrigated area of the year, the arrears outstanding, the sales or mortgages of land, and so on. Half an hour's examination of a circle book thus kept will indicate at once whether a village or group of villages is declining in agricultural condition; and this fact known, the cause of failure can be ascertained and remedial action suggested.[71]

The Government of India recognized the importance of the recommendation and emphasized that the circle books should be periodically inspected by some responsible district official so that the condition of every village should, within very few years, come under intelligent review. It was further resolved that Directors of land records and agriculture be instructed to consider it one of their duties to make sure that circle books were punctually and intelligently examined in every district. District Officers were, on the other hand, required to communicate to the Director for entry in his office ledgers the proved existence of any serious agricultural deterioration that might have occurred in any part of a district.

As regards persistent failure to reach the highest attainable standard, it was viewed as proceeding from more or less persistent causes. These, for instance, included want of irrigational facilities, the frequent failure of rain, cattle diseases, plant diseases and blights, want of drainage, the prevalence of saline efforescence, proved imperfections in agricultural practices, the want of suitable manures, and so on.

It was such cases that chiefly engaged Voelcker's attention. Many of these persistent defects called for scientific inquiry by experts and experimental investigation of agricultural farms over periods of many years. Even so, he emphasized that the land records and land record establishments could often be utilized to provide a basis for detailed inquiry on such matters as the distribution of irrigation, the character of rainfall in each tract, the occurrence of particular cattle and plant diseases, the area affected by the outcrop of salts, agricultural practices, and other features connected with the problems of agricultural development.

It is not that Voelcker did not recognize the importance of higher agricultural education and detailed scientific inquiry for the broader aspects of what he considered to be persistent defects. But he emphasized the immediate concern for rural development through agriculture, which could not in turn be effected without regular communication and feedback between officers of the agricultural department on one hand and the circle and village officers on the other. Obviously, the object was to relate scientific inquiries to the facts or rural experience. That is why his report reiterated that regardless of the nature of defects 'the officers of the department of agriculture should, as a first step, consider how far the land records and the establishments maintaining them can be utilized to provide information necessary to the inquiry'.[72] Agricultural inquiry for rural development was not to be conducted in a vacuum, but it needed to be based on a well-organized system of the land-record machinery.

The keynote of this system was the division of the whole country into easily managed circles of 50 to 100 villages each, an arrangement that already existed in the temporary settled provinces with some 200,000 village officials who formed a well-trained and disciplined rank and file, commanded by a staff of 5,000 or 6,000 circle inspectors. The famine codes drawn up in 1882 laid down the duties of these circle officers who, in ordinary years, were to provide the fullest information and statistics regarding the crops and agricultural conditions of every village. In times of famine, on the other hand, their duty was to supervise the distribution of relief; to promote the employment of labour on agricultural operations; to invite applications for the construction of wells and other agricultural improvements, to report on the price of food, the state of the people and cattle, and water supply; and to bring to the notice of district officials any occurrence deserving attention. In the permanently settled areas, however, there was no established agency comparable to these circle officers. Only recently, after 1947, were village and circle officers appointed with the abolition of zamindaris. Their emphasis was on the collection of revenue. The circle officers were in some places later replaced by block development officers who combined developmental functions with revenue. In terms of rural development there had been steady progress in other ways in the policy indicated by the Famine Commission of 1880, a policy that viewed the protection of the tenant class as necessary in the prosperity of the country. This was sought to be fulfilled, firstly, by the introduction of necessary tenancy legislation, and, secondly, by the extension of the system of land surveys and records of rights.

Rural Development: Concrete Steps under Centralized Initiative 1898-1905

The Report of the Famine Commission (1880) and Voelcker's Report which was reviewed by a series of agricultural conferences during 1890-6, provided clear guidelines on rural development being the most important remedy for the recurrent failure of crops and the resultant loss of human life. The urgency of promoting rural development as a direct responsibility of the Department of Agriculture was clearly realized even before the arrival of Lord Curzon as Viceroy. But any plan for agricultural or rural development had to pass the financial test before it could be accepted for implementation: thus agriculture remained tagged to revenue, and financial considerations slowed its progress.

Moreover, as agriculture, the core of rural development, called for a knowledge of science and technology which in turn involved a corresponding change in the old pattern of recruitment and training of civil servants, it took time for the emergence of a clear policy. Action was in the meantime further delayed by Voelcker's inquiry which laid down essential principles of agricultural investigation as a pre condition precedent of development.

But as soon as the guidelines were finalized by the agricultural conferences that followed Voelcker's report, there occurred two serious famines, one in 1897-8, the other in 1899-1900. However, far from being subdued by the immensity of the problem of relief operations, Lord Curzon determined to combat the evil, firstly, by direct treatment of the famine during its prevalence, and, secondly, by adopting measures to improve the material condition of the agricultural classes so that they could face future calamities with greater strength. His approach in both cases accepted the principle of social welfare, and the means employed was bureaucratic centralism which ensured speed.

Direct Treatment of Famine

Before the arrival of Lord Curzon, India had fallen under the shadow of a severe famine, the first of its kind after the great famine of

1878. When the distress lessened a Commission under Sir James Lyall examined the administration of relief to suggest improvements. The Commission's report was ready towards the end of 1898 and awaited Lord Curzon on his arrival in India. The report maintained the general line of policy hitherto followed, but favoured greater flexibility of procedure to make relief easily available and greater liberality in the gratuitous relief which the previous codes had not contemplated. These points were at once taken up for consideration and, within a fortnight of his arrival, the new Viceroy forwarded them to the Local Governments for their opinion.

The signs of a second calamity, however, appeared before a new policy could be laid down or new codes framed. By August 1899 another famine, more severe than the last, had already hit the United Provinces, the Central Provinces and Bombay. Amended codes were none the less introduced in September and October to guide the course of relief operations. By December it was, however, noticed that the severity of the distress in certain provinces, especially in the Central Provinces, had led to an exaggeration of the liberal policy advocated earlier by the Lyall Commission. The result was that 'the wages adopted upon famine were in places so high as to exceed the market rates and to bring upon relief vast numbers of people who could well support themselves'. A note of warning issued on 17 December 1899 brought the situation immediately under control and, 'within a few weeks the Government of India had the satisfaction of finding considerable improvement in the famine administration'.[73] The vigilance exercised by the Viceroy himself was indeed the major factor in the efficiency of the bureaucratic agency. For when the severity of the distress continued to increase and reached its climax the following July, Lord Curzon proceeded personally to visit the most sorely smitten areas. He had earlier taken similar initiative to open a Famine Relief Fund at a large meeting held in the Town Hall at Calcutta, where he himself presided and appealed for help.

In a statement to his Legislative Council the Viceroy reviewed the famine of 1899-1900 as 'the greatest and most appalling' calamity that any Indian Government had ever had to face. 'It had not been merely a failure of crops, but was accompanied also by a failure of fodder and in many tracts by an almost complete extermination of cattle'. Even so, as the statement pointed out, the calamity had been faced 'with an efficiency unprecedented in history'.[74] The amount of revenue remitted was approximately Rs 2 crores. The loans to cultivators, which amounted to Rs 130 lakhs in 1897-8, reached Rs 238 lakhs in 1899-1900, the direct expenditure on famine relief rising, on the other hand, from Rs 7 crores in 1897-8 to Rs 10 crores in 1899-1900. The Viceregal statement, in fact, gives the impression that efficiency in the direct treatment of the famine flowed not only from governmental concern and the centralized action of the bureaucracy, but also from the experience which the study of Dr Voelcker had brought to bear upon the functioning of the Department of Revenue and Agriculture.

Cotroversy, however, arose on the quantum of relief as well as on the distribution of central grants to the provinces. These and many other difficult and technical problems were referred in December 1900 to a special commission under the presidency of Sir A. MacDonnell[75] who submitted his report in May 1901. Consistent with the recommendation of the Commission, the Local Governments were advised to defer relief measures till the signs of distress were clear and to adopt rural works of local importance rather than public works where even those who were able to support themselves got generally admitted to relief. By a Resolution of 21 March 1903 the Government of India also laid down instructions which involved the introduction of several new and important principles. These left no room for doubt as to the kind of persons to be admitted to relief. The provincial famine codes were accordingly revised and precise orders issued for the improvement and maintenance of programmes governing relief works. Lord Curzon, in fact, viewed efficiency not merely as a mechanical ordering of public affairs, but as an effective instrument of progress and social service.

Measures to Improve Material Conditions

These measures were intended to increase the gross produce of land by an application of science and to protect the peasantry by tenancy legislation as well as by providing suitable alternatives to rural financing and employment to reduce indebtedness and the growing pressure on land.

The necessity for agricultural improvement by experts, by research, by experimental farms and by technical teaching had in principle been recognized in 1881 when the Department of Revenue and Agriculture was first reconstituted. But, as noted earlier, it was the improvement of the land records that engaged the attention of the Department more than agriculture.

Lord Curzon's Viceroyalty definitely abandoned the earlier attitude, and proceeded straight off to provide for an expert agency that organized research, opened experimental farms, and initiated agricultural education. For it was recognized that each of these requisites was mutually dependent on the rest. Organizationally, the Pusa Institute of Agriculture established in Bihar in 1903, became a centre for the realization of the objective.

Action in the matter of experts had no doubt begun with Voelcker Mission and the consequent appointment of an Agricultural and an Asistant Agricultural Chemist that followed in 1892. But the appointments were temporary and expired in 1897. No alternative arrangement was made until the appointment of the Inspector-General of Agriculture in 1901.[76] It was also agreed that gradually an expert staff should be built up round the Inspector-General. Provision was therefore made immediately for a cryptogamic botanist and an entomologist in addition to an agricultural chemist. For the purposes of research a well-equipped laboratory was essential, and Henry Phipps, an American philanthropist, came forward with an offer of a donation of £20,000. Subsequently Phipps added a further £10,000 to his original contribution. The foundation stone of the laboratory was laid by Curzon himself in March 1905.

As regards experimental farms, most of the Local Governments had already made some beginning, though with varying results. The Imperial Research Institute at Pusa was to have its own farm to serve as a model and supplement the provincial farms already in existence. A vacant Government estate at Pusa was therefore selected as a site for the new farm and its attendant buildings. Some four hundred acres were thus devoted to experimental cultivation and the rest to the maintenance of cattle to supply breeding bulls to the adjacent areas of Bengal and the United Provinces.

The progress of agricultural education under Lord Curzon had a two-fold aspect, basic rural education and higher collegiate education of a technical nature. The concept of rural education was clarified in a Resolution of the Home Department in 1904 on the history and progress of education in India: the aim of rural schools was not to impart definite agricultural training, but to give children a preliminary training which would make them intelligent cultivators, trained observers and experimenters, and also protect them in business transactions with landlords and grain dealers.

Proper teachers were needed and, as a summary of Curzon's administration points out, 'special courses of training for rural schoolmasters have been organized in some Training Colleges, to each of which a small farm is attached for teaching methods of nature study; the lesson books of rural schools have been revised, so that they may deal with the familiar surroundings of the children; school gardens have been started'. For it was realized that these schools should serve as centres for 'the education of the cultivating masses' on such principles as might conduce to rural development.[77]

As for agricultural colleges, such institutions already existed in Poona and Saidapet, in addition to agricultural classes in the Engineering College at Sibpur and agricultural schools at Nagpur and Kanpur. But all suffered from inadequate teaching staff, want of facilities for practical work and lack of proper equipment. They were modified under the scheme of expansion which led to a fully equipped Agricultural College as part of the Imperial Institute of Agriculture at Pusa. The College provided for a postgraduate course in agriculture for those who had passed the three years' degree course at provincial colleges. Its staff included, besides the Director and the Agricultural Chemist, an Entomologist and Cryptogamic Botanist, and Agricultural Bacteriologist, an Agri-Horticulturist, and a Biological Botanist, with a suitable complement of assistants, a surveyor, a teacher of physics, mechanics and a veterinary graduate. The experts were to devote themselves to the investigation of special products, such as cotton tobacco, wheat, sugar and fruit.

Apart from teaching and research, an important function of the staff at Pusa was to coordinate the work done by provincial departments. This was done through a Board of Agriculture which assembled annually at Pusa under the presidency of the Inspector-General of Agriculture. The Board comprised all the members of the Agricultural Departments, heads of the Veterinary Department, the Botanical Survey of India and the Bengal Education Department. It was to exercise no executive control, but brought together scientific and practical experts of the departments to enable them to arrange a common course of action for agricultural improvement in the country as a whole. The first meeting of the Board was held in January 1905, when a number of resolutions were passed for the development and coordination of agricultural work in India.

Thus, while the appointment of the Inspector-General of Agriculture marked the establishment of a separate Department of Agriculture at the Centre, the Director of the Pusa Institute and the experts in various fields under the supervision of the Inspector-General, created conditions for research and a thorough agricultural education. A Government of India, Finance Department despatch of 1 July 1905 showed that, besides the Inspector General of Agriculture and his Deputy, all the experts at the Centre and Provinces formed part of the Imperial Agricultural Service created in 1905.[78]

The Government of India announced in the mean time the grant of Rs20 lakhs to supplement the resources of Local Governments and enable them to follow the lead of the Centre in the area of agricultural development. The Secretary of State was, therefore, asked to sanction the appointment of a separate Director of Agriculture for each large province,[79] and the officer so appointed was initially to be a member of the Indian Civil Service. He would organize an agricultural college and research station, equipped with laboratories and classrooms, with a farm attached. The staff of each college was for a start to be recruited in Europe, but it was expected that specialists would gradually become available for recruitment from within the country itself. The Secretary of State was thus asked therefore to set aside from 1906-7 a sum of Rs 30 lakhs annually for the agricultural and veterinary departments.[80]

The Civil Veterinary Department, which mainly dealt with cattle breeding and the prevention of cattle diseases may be said to date from 1892 when an Inspector-General was appointed, with provincial and local agencies established shortly afterwards. For military reasons its officers originally had to concentrate on the horse-breeding operations of the Government. Their obligations as regards cattle were generally neglected, but the military authorites also remained dissatisfied with their performance with horse-breeding. A Commission was thus appointed in 1900 to inquire into horse-breeding and mule-breeding in India: the horse-breeding duties were consequently removed in 1903 from the Civil Veterinary Department and confined to certain selected districts under the Army Remount Department.[81] The function of the Civil Veterinary Department thus turned to matters connected with cattle and such horse-breeding as was carried out by local bodies. Though serving for the most part under the control of Provincial Governments, the superior officers of the Department remained on the central list for purposes of transfer, leave and promotion. The cost of the subordinate agencies operating under these officers was largely defrayed by district boards.

The emphasis which Lord Curzon laid on the organization of

agricultural departments in the provinces, was not without significance. He realized that the goal of agricultural development could not be attained by a central institution, however well-equipped and efficient. 'For its complete attainment', he believed, 'each province must possess its own staff, its own institute for research and experiment, in fact a properly organized agricultural department'. And that alone was not good enough if its rural orientation was lacking. For, as he added, 'it is not sufficient merely to create a Government department for the study of agricultural problem; mens must also be provided for bringing the results of research to the knowledge of the cultivators of the country. The entire object of the movement is to bring the one class into direct relations with the other, and to utilize the discoveries of science or the results of education for the improvement of the position and prospects of the raiyat.'[82]

The improvement of agriculture which formed the nucleus of rural development, was thus for the first time under Curzon a part of a definite economic policy of the Government of India. Measures to promote agricultural development had doubtless been suggested in the past, but these mostly operated on an *ad hoc* basis. What Curzon did was to supply direction to that policy which emphasized the importance of the rural economy and primary education not only as an instrument of peasant welfare but also as conducive to political stability. For he treated the élitist elements of Indian society as mainly selfish, politically motivated and prone to exploite the rural masses. As we shall further see below, he thought of the interests of peasantry. However, he strongly believed that this interest would be best served by the bureaucracy alone, not by elected representatives or democratic decentralization.

Land Reforms and Rural Financing

Land reform and rural financing were two other aspects of rural development that received the attention they deserved under Curzon.

The problems of land reform under the British have been dealt with in some depth as part of land revenue administration in *The Central Administration of the East India Company (1773-1834)* and *The Administrative History of India (1834-1947)*. These problems have, in addition, been discussed at length in terms of rural financing and social change in *The Indian Middle Classes*.[83] Here we shall review the consequences that flowed from an application of free competition in the transfer of landed property created under British rule by a supersession of custom by law, a supersession that destroyed the custom-based corporateness of jointly held villages and village communities, the unifying bond that kept the traditional societies together on the principles of equity and status. While in the permanently settled districts the classes affected by open courts and free transfers of land were the zamindars, their under-proprietors and occupancy tenants, the people who suffered in the periodically settled areas were mostly the peasant proprietors (*mirasidars*) and a class of respectable tenure-holders (*inamdars*, including *deshmukhs* or *deshpandes*) who belonged to the upper layers of society in terms of caste. The new moneyed classes, commercial or professional with economic interests in land, begun to flourish and oppressed the cultivators more than the old zamindars, especially in Bengal where the literary and professional classes were interwoven with landed interests to a degree hardly attained in other provinces operating under the mahalwari or raiyatwari systems.

The agricultural inquiries made by the Department of Revenue and Agriculture showed that the cultivator in pre-British days was allowed as much of the produce as was needed for his subsistence. The State or its representatives absorbed the rest. As the State gradually moderated its demand and fixed by law in perpetuity or for a period of time its share of the total assessment of land, the landholder functioning in between the cultivator and the State became entitled to a larger and larger surplus arising from an extension of cultivation without a corresponding increase in the state's demand. His land became valuable property. The security so provided by law encouraged the landholder to borrow and the moneylender to buy. 'The more reckless the landholder became, the more usurious became the moneylender; and by degrees the land through large tracts of country passed on mortgage or sale from the old agricultural families to an entirely new class of men.'[84]

Brought up on the ideas of Bentham and Mill, the English administrators of that period viewed free transfers of land as a feature of progress calculated to benefit both the agriculturist and the moneylender, who were after all essential units involved in the process of agricultural production. They were not surprised to see that by open courts and free competition the land went to the economically strong, whom they considered the most deserving. They in fact acted on the assumption that 'if the economically weak were ground out of existence, this was an inevitable result of the process which works for progress.'[85]

But moneylenders in the Indian situation were not capitalist entrepreneurs, nor were the civil courts instruments of justice. The former indulged in the traditional chicanery practised in usury, and the latter in the cruel precision and technicality of law. The Government sought to find remedies by interfering with the strict laws of contract, by altering the strict rules of evidence, by insolvency proceedings, by conciliation, by reducing the revenue.

But it was found to be all in vain. The land continued to pass—in some areas steadily, in others with appalling rapidity—from its old owners to the moneylender, the townsman, the successful lawyer, the prosperous merchant. These men were out of sympathy with the agriculturist; land to them was a commercial asset and a tenant a rival to be rack-rented. They were always of a different class from the agriculturist; often of a different caste or nationality, and in many cases of a different religion. They were inferior in physique and inferior in moral calibre to the men whom they supplanted. Their accession to property in land entailed in all cases impoverishment, and, in many cases, social and political discontent among the dispossessed peasantry. And yet no effective steps were taken to combat the evil.

The relations of the moneylending and agricultural classes which led to the expropriation of the peasantry and the old landowners, came strongly to the notice of the Government as a result of the *Report of the Deccan Riot Commission (1875)*[86] which, apart from compiling evidence obtained on the spot, examined the records of the Revenue, Judicial, Registration and Police Departments.

As the *Report* pointed out, the first open hostility, began against a Marwari moneylender, which led finally to the Deccan riots. It started in Kardeh, a village in the Sirur Taluka of Poona district, at the end of 1874. A Deshmukh of good family and considerable influence had, in the course of his service as a district hereditary officer of Scindia, accumulated a fortune and settled in the village. Having spent his fortune, however, he fell deeply in debt to one of his *sowkars*, a Marwari moneylender named Kalooram who obtained decrees against him from the civil court at Talegaon and, in satisfaction of the decrees so obtained, put the Deshmukh's house for sale by a public auction and himself purchased it for a nominal sum of Rs 150. When in December 1874, the plaintiff began to pull down the house, the defendant requested him not to do so, for he promised to pay the debts at his convenience and agreed in the mean time to pay rent for the house during its occupancy. Ignoring the request, the Marwari plaintiff had his own way.

The defendant did not resort to violence but collected the village raiyats who unanimously resolved that, since the Marwaris had started ruining them, it would be better neither to borrow from them nor serve them or purchase anything from them in future. This non-violent non-cooperation yielded results: The Marwaris could not get servants and were completely ostracized. And when they loaded their carts with their goods to proceed to Sirur under police protection in January 1875, the villagers submitted a petition to local authorities saying that they had given grain to the Marwaris who should not be allowed to leave the village until the Government assessment had been paid by them.

The villagers, who initially combined to refuse service as water-carriers, barbers, domestic servants and the like, tended gradually to become violent. They threw the carcases of dogs and other filth into the houses of Marwaris and mounted a campaign of hate and contempt against them. The example set by the people of Kardeh soon spread to other villages. The Marwaris, who had retreated under police protection to Sirur, petitioned the local magistrate for necessary action. In these circumstances the first actual outbreak of violence occurred at Supa, a large village of the Bhimthari taluka of Poona, where the houses and shops of Gujarati moneylenders were gutted, though no physical violence to individuals was committed. It transpired from subsequent inquiries that the rioters at Supa had the sympathy of influential people in their village. Combustible elements were ready everywhere, and the contagion spread to the neighbouring districts of Indapur and Prandhar, which called for detachments of infantry to prevent loss of life and destruction of property.

The report of the Commission doubtless mentioned cases of murderous assault upon moneylenders. In a few instances, personal violence actually occurred, and in several areas stocks of produce belonging to moneylenders were burnt; 'but as a rule the disturbances were marked by the absence of serious crime. The object of the rioters was in every case to obtain and destroy the bonds, decrees, etc. in the possession of their creditors. When these were peaceably given up to the assembled mob, there was usually nothing further done. When the moneylender refused or shut himself up, violence was used to frighten him into a surrender or to get possession of the papers'.[87]

Even so, the Marwari moneylenders fled from many villages on the first news of outbreak. Cases occurred where they also opened negotiations with their debtors for a general reduction of their claims and, in some instances, propitiated their debtors by easy settlements. But, as the Commission pointed out, mostly 'the Marwari and Gujar *sowkars* were almost exclusively the victims of the riots, and in villages where *sowkars* of the Brahmin and other castes shared the moneylending business with Marwaris, it was usual to find that the latter only were molested.'[88]

The crisis arising from the peculiar relations of agricultural and moneylending classes tended to impart to the Deccan riots the character of an agrarian disturbance where the bulk of the ordinary peasantry, especially of the *Kunbi* and *Koli* classes, led the movement against their rural financiers and showed a hostility characteristic of the Santhal rebellion of 1855 or the Bhil unrest of 1845. A letter which Sir G. Wingate wrote to the Bombay Government in 1852[89] about a couple of murders in Gujarat and in Sholapur district was viewed as an attempt to reinforce the belief that these were not results of isolated oppression on the part of creditors, but examples of the general relations subsisting between money-lenders and the agricultural population.

However, the Deccan riots of 1874-5 do not appear to have acquired the character of general agrarian unrest and are marked by the moderation of the peasantry, perhaps this flowed from the fact that in many cases the movement was led by the heads of the community, the *patels* and others; their participation was doubtless a breach of law, for they were responsible for maintaining order but, even so, it contributed to moderation.

An interesting disclosure in the *Report of the Deccan Riot Commission* was about the technicality and want of equity in the functioning of the civil courts, especially after 1866 when new laws governing limitation, procedure and evidence were gradually enacted to modernize judicial operations on the principles of contract. In a memorandum of 23 May 1872, for instance, the Assistant Commissioner of Sind reported that before the introduction of the new acts civil disputes were decided by executive officers of the Government who were intimately acquainted with the people of the district, their customs, means and circumstances.. They administered justice in a rough and ready way without drawing up proceedings with the elaborate precision required in the regulation districts. Cases were heard and decided on merit, not on the pleadings or arguments of lawyers, and arrangements were made that enabled debtors to pay their dues by instalments, so that, while creditors got their money, the debtors recovered credit and retained their property.

But the new judges who replaced revenue officials in the administration of civil justice gave people 'the dry bones of law and procedure, instead of the life-giving meat of equity and justice'.[90] Since actions for debt were sought on the basis of a written bond or contract, the judge was a mere tool, a machine to be put in motion at the will of moneylenders. The unlettered cultivator in fact considered it a waste of money to dispute the amount of the least bond even after having paid double or treble the sum entered in the original agreement signed on stamped paper. He knew that if he admitted the bond, the proceedings would end, even if unfairly; but if he denied them, there would be prolonged litigation and heavy costs, with the *bania* playing as he wished and even extorting renewed bonds for fictitious amounts. The debtor was utterly helpless.

In these circumstances the majority of suits were decided *ex-parte*. For instance, in Bombay Presidency (excluding Sind) in 1869-70 there were as many as 127,419 original suits of which less than 110,884 were for debts on written contract, nearly all being decided *ex-parte* or on admission of the bond. The state in Sind was even worse. For a judge had no discretion in such cases. In a suit defended by a zamindar, all he did was to give the debtor the time and opportunity to satisfy it, 'instead of selling him up at once'.[91]

But the tribals suffered the most. In a report of 24 July 1870 the Collector of Khandesh, for example, regretted that it was 'utterly impossible' for any Bhil 'to obtain justice' in a civil court 'presided over by a native gentleman'. There the merits of the case were not only made subordinate to the strict letter of the law, but 'the very presence of a Bheel would be considered offensive to the Brahmin judge and vakils of the court'. It required 'certain ceremonies of purification to be performed'. Ashburner, who was Collector of the district, discussed the matter with a judge who, however, expressed his helplessnes.[92]

Commenting in 1874 on the functioning of the judiciary in terms of property relationships the Revenue Commissioner of the Northern Division of Bombay pointed out that the lands of the 'agricultural community' were 'passing out of their possession' and that they were 'only permitted to cultivate them on a rental barely sufficient to support life'. This change was 'ascribed to their improvidence, the high rate of interest and the action of the civil courts'. Both the Commissioner and his Collector doubted that education would correct the evils, for long before people could be educated and their habits of improvidence cured, 'the land will have passed into the hands of a rapacious middle class, who will rack-rent it, and reduce the cultivators to a state of slavery'.[93]

An extract from the revenue records of 1843 shows that there was hardly any change either in the habits of the people or the state of rural financing. Relying on the report of his area, the Revenue Commissioner of the Northern Division thus observed that there were few villages in which there was 'one ryot unburthened with debt, and scarcely a single village in which three persons could be found not involved for sums above Rs 100'. These debts, as one of his reports confirmed, 'are contracted on occasions of marriages and other rites, interest charged varying from 25 to 60 per cent'. On the basis of another source it was pointed out 'that the usurious character of the village *bania* is notorious', and greatly contributed to the poverty of the Deccan raiyats. Even so, Government officers could do little to help, for, in the absence of any better alternative, the peasantry considered the *bania* a necessary source of finance.[94]

As the Minutes recorded individually by members of the Commission pointed out, about 90 per cent of the raiyats in certain talukas were not merely in debt, but hopelessly so. This indebtedness flowed partly from the introduction of the revised assessment which 'undoubtedly added to embarrassments of the ryots',[95] for, as their entire lands were mortgaged, it was more difficult to pay the enhanced rent; thus forcing them to go to moneylenders who took advantage of their poverty to press for remissions. As the actual owners of the land happened to be the moneylenders themselves, they alone profited by remissions. By refusing advances to the raiyats they prevented the punctual realization of revenue with the intention of forcing the Government to grant large remissions, knowing that a whole taluka could not be sold up and that it was worth their while to let a few fields be sold and then await remissions on the rest.

However, the raiyats, who thought they owned the land already mortgaged, feared that their fields could be sold for non-payment and accordingly pressed the *sowkars* to pay the instalments. The refusal of the latter to do so led to the disturbances of 1875 in Poona district where the revised revenue settlement had nearly doubled in many cases. It was only after Poona that the disturbances spread to adjoining talukas in Ahmednagar district where the revised assessment had not been introduced. It was thus the circumstances of the Poona area rather than enhanced assessment or the general state of indebtedness that led to the Deccan riots. These were in fact the cumulative result of socio-economic developments resulting from the impingement of law on custom. It was deeper in the ryotwari and tribal areas with their legacy of Brahmanic influence dating back to the Peshwas in Poona.

A sub-committee of the bania-brahmin dominated *Sarvajanik Sabha* (1873) attributed the disturbances entirely to the enhancement of revenue by the British who had overthrown the Peshwas in 1818. The old rates which even the Sabha admitted to be 'conveniently low', had remained unaltered despite the gradual rise in prices between 1848 and 1866,[96] and revised only in 1870-1. The prices, however, showed a remarkable decline soon after revision. The revised rates were, therefore, kept within the limits of Poona and Sholapur districts and there, too, government officers were enjoined to lay down precise instructions as to the extent to which the old rates needed to be modified. The published reports on which revisions were sanctioned by the Government in 1874 showed that the revised rates were, on the whole moderate. This is clear from the abstract given below:[97]

Whatever the cause and character of the Deccan riots, they brought to the surface the seriousness of the problems of land reform and rural financing. As already noted, these problems were soon highlighted by the *Report of the Indian Famine Commission* (1880) which, in its appendices, incorporated enlightened and informative documents on the condition of the peasantry. No clear-cut land policy, however, flowed from its recommendations. There were two basic hurdles which stalled the emergence of any policy direction, both imperial and national in character, with the latter more responsible. While the immediate concern of the Imperial Government remained confined for some years to the improvement of its financial resources as suggested by the Indian Famine Commission. Indian middle class élites impeded legislation intended to benefit the peasantry. The Bengal Rent Bill, for example, was a special occasion for conflict, where the Indian members of the Imperial Council solidly opposed any extension of tenant rights, more especially the formation of land records through cadastral survey. As the educated and urban élites of society, moulded public opinion, the Council was compelled to make a number concessions and water down the Bill enacted three years later in 1885.

Interestingly, in the wake of the Bengal Rent Bill demands were raised for the freedom of the judiciary based on the separation of

Name of Taluka	No. of culturable acres under old assessment	No. of culturable acres under new assessment	Total old assessment	Total new assessment	Average per acre under old assessment	Average per acre under revised assessment	Percentage increase
			Rs.	Rs.	Rs. a. p.	Rs. a. p.	
Indapur	238,135	270,076	81,391	1,24,700	0 5 5	0 7 4	53
Sholapur	381,882	433,572	1,74,915	3,09,630	0 7 4	0 11 4	77
Madhe	--	--	1,00,580	1,78,050	---	0 9 4	77
Bhimthari	190,410	212,703	80,464	1,46,596	0 7 3	0 11 0	69
Pandharpur	84,273	90,798	36,048	63,979	0 6 10	0 11 3	77
Barsi	248,465	278,509	1,24,658	2,07,174	0 8 0	0 11 11	66
Haveli	127,610	146,745	80,965	1,34,768	0 10 2	0 14 7	66
Pabal	161,240	192,411	1,02,228	1,52,108	0 10 1	0 12 7	48
Supa (Petta)	147,244	159,227	59,926	78,788	0 6 6	0 7 11	36
Karmala	271.194	299,242	1,10,824	1,46,890	0 6 6	0 7 6	32

executive and judicial functions[98] as well as for the introduction of elective principles in the organization not only of rural and municipal boards, but also legislative councils.[99] The nationalism of the educated and business classes of India viewed both a free judiciary and legislative control as safeguards of their social and economic privilege.

The principle of a free judiciary which was later conceded in a modified and limited form was the result of A.C. Lyall's efforts. He had earlier pleaded that absolute executive control over the judiciary would set up an arbitrary will in the place of law, multiply the elements of chance in the trial and decision of cases, and finally destroy the very notion of fixed and sovereign law, which the British had sought to inculcate in the Indian people since 1793.[100]

The question of legislative control stood on a different plane. Besides being immediately prejudicial to imperial interests, the representation of educated élites was viewed as a barrier to progressive legislation in favour of the rural poor. In confidential letters to Lord Northbrook, for example, the Viceroy, Lord Dufferin, expressed his fears by saying:

> We have recently relaxed the law in relation to debtor and creditor, and contemplate a still further relaxation of the penalties of imprisonment for debt. On such a point probably we should not receive much help from Members who would naturally be connected with the money-lending classes . . . the Brahmins would do everything they could to prevent the lower castes sharing in its advantages, whereas we should wish to do the very opposite.[101]

After the establishment of the Indian National Congress in 1885, the expansion of the Legislative Councils had become the focal point of the demands of educated Indians who, prior to 1905, were landholders and professionals, belonging mostly to the higher echelons of Indian society. The Government, which planned to go ahead with land reform for agricultural development, viewed the demand as prejudicial to the interest of the masses. Writing to Northbrook on the subject of extended representation in the Legislative Councils, Dufferin thus said in a letter of 16 October 1886:

> If it could be done, of course it would be an excellent thing; but the more I see of these people the less sanguine I am of reaching a conclusion which will both work advantageously for the country at large and satisfy native aspirations . . . . All the efforts of the Government of India are principally directed towards the improvement of the condition of the masses. We should

be very apt to find ourselves thwarted and opposed by constituencies whose qualifications are simply wealth and education. For instance, all our recent legislation would have been carried with infinitely more difficulty, and against a heavier dead weight of opposition, if more natives had been present in the Council.[102]

But once the rule of law and the fixity of its procedure were recognized as a sovereign principle that must govern the conduct of government and administration, the middle–class demand for an extension of legislative control could not be stalled for ever. For the supremacy of law could not co–exist with bureaucratic absolutism. A free judiciary necessarily called for mild government which could only come about by being representative. A representative government was thus installed under the Indian Councils Act (1892); however, it represented not the masses, but the limited constituencies of wealth and education, the urbanized middle classes to whom the lands of the agricultural community were passing. It proved difficult for an Imperial Government to choose between the interests of the masses and the demands of the educated classes or to strike a balance between the two.This led to *ad hocism* in the formulation of a definite programme for rural development and continued till Lord Curzon decided in favour of centralized bureaucratic initiative to stop the transfers of land and provide rural credit on a cooperative basis as an institutional alternative to private moneylenders

The reduction of the right of transfer first began in the Punjab with the Punjab Land Alienation Act. Its main object was to restrict the sale or mortgage of lands, so that moneylenders might not have them transferred in satisfaction of court decress.

The Act was passed on 19 October 1900 and came into force in June 1901; it was to be of general application throughout the Province apart from the small district of Simla[103], the abode of Europeans.

As regards the definition of the classes whose rights of transfer were to be restricted, the Act dealt with the population of the Province under three categories. Those belonging to 'agricultural tribes' came first, for they were the people whom the Act was specially intended to protect. The second category was that of 'agriculturists', a more or less artificial class including those who, without being members of agricultural tribes, had long–settled interests in the land, with prescriptive claims which could not be ignored. The third head included the rest of the population, more especially the moneylenders from whom the peasants were sought to be protected. It was laid down that members of the second and third categories might sell or mortgage lands as they pleased; but the first category was rendered subject to restrictions. It was provided that if a member of an agricultural tribe wished to sell his land, he might (in the absence of special permission) do so only to an 'agriculturist' of the same village or to a member of the same tribe or group of tribes. In case he wished to mortgage, he was subject to no limitations if the mortgage happened to be a member of the same tribe or group: otherwise the mortgage might only be in one of three prescribed forms, which secured that either the mortgager would remain in cultivating possession at a reasonable rent, or that the mortgagee would hold possession for a reasonable time not exceeding twenty years, at the expiry of which the mortgage debt and interest thereon would be considered cancelled.

Another important provision of the Act was that the sale of the land of a member of an agricultural tribe in execution of a decree was absolutely forbidden. The insidious form of mortgage known as 'mortgage by way of conditional sale' was not only forbidden, but the terms of all such mortgages were to be modified so as to approximate to the ordinary forms of mortgage permitted by the Act. All these provisions were enacted despite the opposition of the Indian National Congress, which fought for the landowners and moneylenders.[104]

The Act practically put a stop to permanent alienations of land from the agricultural to the non-agricultural tribes. The measure was accepted with gratitude by the hereditary landowners also. Above all, it led to a reduction in extravagant expenditure and, as a subsequent Report said, it encouraged the financing of the poorer landowners by their richer breathren.[105]

The principle of restricting the alienation of agricultural land on the Punjab model was soon extended to Bundelkhand in the United Provinces, where measures were intially taken to revise revenue management by the introduction of a system of fluctuating assessment to free landowners from the growing burden of debt caused by the existing system of compulsory liquidation. An Act was then passed in 1903 to prevent free alienation of agricultural land. It differed from the Punjab enactment mainly in that no provision was made for the grouping of the agricultural tribes and the statutory agriculturist of the Punjab Act was not mentioned. The first report of a complete year's working of the Act came out in 1905, and its beneficial results seemed very similar to those in the Punjab. In view of the increasing rate at which agricultural land was changing hands in other districts, the Government of India asked the U.P. Lieutenant-Governor to other parts of the province.[106]

The Presidency of Bombay, where the alienation of agricultural land had first caused a series of disturbances, was still without a measure comparable to the Punjab Act. Thanks to local opposition reinforced by the strong Brahmanic tradition which lent support to the bania, the inquiries instituted on the subject in 1895 remained in a state of correspondence till 1899. In a letter of 7 October 1899 the Government of Bombay affirmed that 'the available statistics relating to the transfer of land from the agricultural to the trading and professional classes indicated a grave political danger which it was more easy to prevent than to cure'[107] and even advocated legislation of the Punjab type for eight districts. But Lord Sandhurst, the Governor, dissented on a plea that a proper record of rights was an essential preliminary to the enactment of the measure proposed.

The conditions created by the famine of 1901, however, soon called for a review of the earlier decision. The Famine Commission of that year found that 'at least one-fourth of the cultivators in the Bombay Presidency had lost possession of their lands, that [only] less than one-fifth were free from debt and that the remainder were indebted to a greater or less extent.'[108] The Commission therefore suggested immediate legislation to restrict the transfer of agricultural lands. While conceding that some legislation was necessary, the Bombay Government nevertheless discouraged a definite measure of the Punjab type. It was then that the Viceroy showed his firmness and directed that an Act on the Punjab model ought to be passed for Bombay Presidency and Sind and applied to select districts where agricultural indebtedness was rife, and a record of rights prepared with a regular mutation system already established. In arriving at this conclusion Curzon recognized that it might be violently assailed by vested interests, he believed it necessary 'to balance the disadvantages of such agitation against the disadvantages of allowing the Bombay cultivating classes to degenerate in the not remote future into rackrented serfs upon their [own] former land—a far easier prey and a much more fruitful for the political agitator of the future'.[109]

The problem of rural financing was even more complex. The supply of capital for rural development was beset with serious difficulties not only in terms of people's attitudes, but also of imperial policy. Even so, Curzon attempted to strike a balance through a legislative measure in 1904 for the establishment of Cooperative

Credit Societies as an alternative agency for the supply of capital on reasonable terms without involving too great a measure of state aid.

The history of official efforts at rural financing go back to 1882 and 1883 with Sir William Wederburn's plan to establish an agricultural bank at Poona. But the plans were dropped when the Secretary of State discouraged major financial involvement in the scheme. The Madras Government then took the initiative in 1892 and deputed Frederick Nicholson to explore the possibility of introducing a system of agricultural or land banks. A complete report was presented with elaborate recommendations, but no action taken.

A change, however, came about in 1899 when Nicholson's Report engaged the attention of the Government of India. A book was at the same time published by a civil servant who reflected on proposals to establish what he called 'People's Banks' in North India. The new scheme abandoned altogether ideas of land banks involving the state in heavy financial responsibilities. It suggested a system of Co-operative Credit Societies, based upon the principles enunciated in Europe by Schultz Delitzsch and Raffeisen and exemplified in Madras by the mutual loan associations called *Nidhis*. The Government of India at once seized this idea and had it examined in consultation with the Local Governments. A committee studied the matter further in 1901 and in the light of its recommendations the Government formulated proposals which eventually led to a Bill that was passed into law on 4 March 1940.[110]

The cooperative banks established under the Act did not require the financial intervention of the state, but the initiative of the people themselves. The legislation aimed to remove legal obstacles to the formation of mutual loan societies of the Raffeisen type, encouraging the agriculturist to invest his money and utilize the joint security of the members of his society to ensure a supply of loans on reasonable terms. The Act also conferred on such societies some small and reasonable privileges and made them subject to a suitable degree of official audit and supervision.

The mutual loan societies were to be both rural and urban, a restriction of membership by locality being provided in both cases to utilize the advantages of local knowledge and public opinion. Provisions were included which dealt with the liability of members, restrictions on loans and borrowing, the character of the security and the degree of Government control exercised through a Registrar of cooperative societies in each province.

As regards financial aid from the Government, it was decided that, the assistance actually given should be confined within definite limits: the amounts advanced by the Government were not to exceed the amounts subscribed or deposited by members, or Rs 2,000 per society. The principles of the Act were explained to the Local Governments and they were called upon to appoint suitable officers as Registrars to encourage and supervise the working of societies.

Irrigation

It has already been noted that under Lord Dalhousie, the Government of India established a Civil Public Works Department which dealt with matters relating to irrigation, buildings and roads. The office of Inspector-General of Irrigation was originally created in 1867, when the policy of developing irrigation works through borrowed money was initiated. Its functions were subsequently merged in those of the Public Works Secretary to the Government of India,[111] and only in 1906 a separate Inspector-General of Irrigation was appointed—for a period of three years at the outset. He was to assist the Government of India in dealing not only with remunerative, productive undertakings financed from loans, but also those constructed as 'protective' works against famine, from what was then known as the Famine Insurance Grant, the selection of undertakings in both cases and the distribution of money for them being vested in the Government of India, though their construction and up-keep were left to the Local Governments.

The appointment of a separate Inspector-General of Irrigation resulted from the initiative of Lord Curzon. Following the experience of the great famine of 1900, an Irrigation Commission was urgently appointed in the autumn of 1901[112] under the presidency of Sir Colin Scott Moncrieff. Its investigation extended over two winters and it finally reported in April 1903. The establishment of a separate office of Inspector-General of Irrigation proceeded from one of its recommendations. This was intended to enable the Inspector-General to tour in the provinces and supervise the numerous projects recently sanctioned, apart from recommending new projects. The appointment was offered to J. Benton, C.I.E., who had just retired as Irrigation Chief Engineer of the Punjab.

The Irrigation Commission generally propounded the need for a more generous outlay on both productive and protective works (Rs 44 crores) and advocated stronger encouragement to minor irrigtion works as well as to private efforts in the matter of wells and tanks. In fact, the recommendations of the Commission provided definite direction to irrigation policy, not only by providing a systematic frame of reference for measures hitherto generally dealt with in piecemeal and haphazard fashion, but also by giving definition and authority to principles which had so far been nebulous and half-considered. Its Report also clearly determined the limits within which action by the Government was desirable or possible. Speaking appreciatively of the general section of the Commission's Report, Lord Curzon in his Budget address to the Council in March 1904 observed:[113]

> I wonder how many of the Hon'ble Members whom I am addressing, and still more how many of the outside public have read their Report. To me the first part of it, which relates to general considerations, is infinitely more interesting than a novel, for it deals not with the hypothetical problems of human character, but with the positive agencies that affect the growth or decline of human life; and it bases conclusions, dramatic in their sweep, upon promises of scientific precision. By slow but sure degrees ever since, we have been assimilating and taking action upon that Report.

The Commission's recommendations to be dealt with by the Public Works Department covered major irrigation works, both productive and protective, the latter being undertaken in all provinces according to some definite schemes where Local Governments would be responsible for execution after they had been accepted by the Central Government. The remunerative productive works included such major undertakings as the Chenab Canal in the Punjab which had been completed before Lord Curzon's Viceroyalty, the Jhelum Canal completed under him, and the group of canals known as the Upper Chenab, the Upper Jhelum and the Lower Bari Doab undertaken by his Government. By 1904-5 the Government of India had spent in all Rs 46½ crores, or £ 31 million, on irrigation works which covered 50,000 miles of canals and distributaries, and irrigated 21½ million acres out of a total irrigated area in British India of about 47 million acres. The Government derived from its total outlay on productive works a net revenue of £ 2,700,000 per annum, or a net revenue on capital outlay of approximately 7 per cent.[114]

Taking an overall view of the irrigation policy for the country, the Irrigation Commission had recommended that the existing distinction between productive and protective works be done away with, both being included in the class of major works where all the capital outlay should be met from loan funds. While accepting its report, the Government of India realized that protective works presented a difficult problem as their construction protected only a section of the community at the cost of the general taxpayer, which partly explains why expenditure on such works under the existing arrangement had remained comparatively small. But even though the two famines during Lord Curzon's time called for increased expenditure on protective works the Commission's proposal to abolish the distinction between productive and protective works was not fully accepted by the Government of India, the proposal evidently hoped to secure larger and more continuous expenditure on irrigation works, irrespective of the financial return they might yield, and this was based on the assumption that the Government could increase its borrowings to any figure it chose. The Commission did not realize that the money spent on productive works was part of business enterprise: the expenditure incurred on loan funds was a profitable investment and justified by sizable returns. This was not so with protective works, which were justified by necessity.

Local Governments were nevertheless advised to pay attention to protective works and go ahead with the execution of those already approved. The Secretary of State, on the other hand, sanctioned an increase in the strength of the Public Works Department from 80 to 892 members, in addition to the recruitment of some officers to the permanent cadre and others for a period of time. Apart from strengthening the staff and recruitment to the establishment of the Royal and Civil Engineers, steps were taken to improve the organization and pay of the higer grades of Engineer establishments.[115]

An important change that affected the recruitment and establishment of engineers for the Public Works Department under Lord Curzon was the abolition in 1904 of the Royal Indian Engineering College in Coopers Hill.

This was done for several reasons on the instructions of the Secretary of State, who overruled the advice of the Government of India against abolition.[116] As regards action to be taken in the Department of Revenue and Agriculture, the most important matter falling to it was the question of improving and extending the system of State loans for agricultural purposes, called *takavi* advances. Consistent with the suggestions of the Irrigation Commission the Government of India took certain decisions intended to secure greater liberality, simplicity and elasticity in giving loans, without creating a forced and spurious demand for them at the same time. Encouragement was also given to hydraulic experiments and a systematic survey of subsoil water supplies. Improvements brought about in agricultural production by private wells, tanks and embankments enterprize were exempted from enhancement of land revenue.[117]

Lord Curzon's administration was a major landmark in every field of development but the stamp of his dynamic personality was most strongly reflected in his immediate concern for rural problems. His approach to reforms through the bureaucracy tended to isolate the élitist elements of Indian society, however, who resented his attempt to glorify the superiority of official authority. In the light of the foregoing analysis, the Montagu-Chelmsford Report on Indian Constitutional Reforms appears justified in stating:

> the administration of Lord Curzon had been marked by a great period of investigatory and constructive activity. Department after department, service after service, was overhauled and a new programme of work was laid down for it. Principles were enunciated and standards set. New deprtments or new authorities were created to relieve or to improve the existing machinery. All this tended to a marked concentration of authority in the hands of the Central Government against which natural reaction in due course occurred. In addition, Provincial Governments were beginning to chafe under financial and administrative restrictions, devised for a more primitive system, which fettered them in their plans of individual development. Complaints were heard also that the prevalent [political] unrest was due in part to loss of touch between officials and the people. The district officer was said to be too closely bound by rules and regulations; too much occupied in writing to his official superiors; too much of a machine and too little of a personality. These reasons led to the appointment of the Royal Commission on Decentralization which presented its report in 1909.[118]

III

DECENTRALIZATION AND DEVELOPMENT, 1905-35

Reaction against Centralization

The demand for decentralization at the start of the twentieth century was a result of conflict between two opposite, though related forces which, in the course of the nineteenth century, competed for recognition in the formulation of policy for social and economic development. These were the forces of private enterprise and imperial interest. While the former demanded absolutely no governmental interference with the free movement of trade, the latter for its own stability could not but intervene on the side of the community as a whole. As noted in the preceding chapter, considerations of general welfare obliged the Government to apply executive control and take positive administrative measures to prevent the recurrence of famines by means of agricultural improvement. Individual Collectors even went to the extent of controlling the market by resorting to public agencies in the distribution of foodgrains and other essential commodities. The dire conditions in fact called for bureaucratic intervention as the surest means of ensuring protection against profiteers.

It is true that the general trend of policy remained unrelaxed in favour of *laissez faire*. But the shift to centralized governmental direction which Curzon effected institutionally was, in the context of earlier tenancy reforms, viewed as an attempt to by-pass the middle classes who had been emerging in collaboration with European business. The downward filtration of education was, in addition, creating a class of unemployed malcontents, and raising social and political issues. Together these factors called for a change of policy in favour of decentralization which, in terms of both politics and administration, was considered necessary for purposes of development.

Conceptual Constraints

The terms 'decentralization' and 'development' are used in this Chapter in the context of modern India's historical development, not in any theoretical frame of reference. For our purposes, decentralization, for example, signifies a relaxation of control effected from time to time by the higher authorities through the downward filtration of power and gradual simplification of the administrative process. This work thus surveys relations over the years between the Government of India and the Provincial Governments, and between the latter and the district authorities subordinate to them.

In addition to financial and administrative matters, the relaxation of control had an important political dimension calling for a transfer of some authority to non-official agencies, elected or nominated as the case might be. It assumed in due course the form of democratic decentralization, a political mechanism which afforded opportunities for some share in power and patronage to those who, though not well educated or even forward-looking as a class, could not get into the superior Services of the Government, but claimed legitimacy on the ground of direct popular links. And as Indian society happened to be divided along caste lines, democratic decentralization boiled down to decentralization from the higher echelons of the caste order to members of lower castes. This kind of decentralization was based on financial considerations, the extent of non-official representation in local bodies and in the central and provincial legislatures.

Development signified both economic growth and social welfare, the former being reckoned in productive terms and the latter in terms of protection against natural calamities or provision for recognized standards of life. As the experiences of famines showed, the concept included planning as well as executive control.

Political Framework up to 1905: Centre-Province Relations

The political framework of the Government of India provided by the Charter Act of 1833 invested the Governor-General in Council with powers to supervise, direct and control the entire civil and military government of the British territories in India, including the revenues, and power to legislate for all persons and places.[1] The exigencies of this measure arose from the agitation of the free traders of Britain, an agitation which led to the abolition of the monopoly of the

East India Company. Under the Act the Company was obliged to surrender all its real and personal property in India in trust to the Crown in return for an annuity of £630,000, being the dividend then payable to its Proprietors. To ensure the regular payment of this annuity for a period of forty years the Government of India was invested with full powers in all fields, legislative, financial and administrative. The necessity of decentralization to promote development was recognized and even sought to be fulfilled. But the arrangement made under the Government of India Act and communicated to the Governor-General in Council under the Company's letter of 10 December, 1834 could not altogether be ignored.

The Government of India Act (1833) in fact created dichotomy which represented a compromise between the economics of monopoly and free trade, between continuity and change; the former required centralization and the latter development and decentralization; for no development was possible unless the provinces were equipped with their own financial resources and administrative agencies functioning under their immediate control. Despite the restrictions imposed by the Act, province asserted themselves in a manner which Lord Ellenborough recorded with annoyance in a Minute of 8 November 1843. He said:

> [We are] constantly in the habit of receiving applications . . .for augmentation of salaries and allowances, for the increase of establishments, for the creation of new officers to be held by Covenanted Servants, and for many other new things, all represented as necessary and expedient . . .In each particular case the charge may be small, and because it is so, it is frequently sanctioned . . .They come before us as charges already sanctioned subject to our confirmation, and there is always a disposition not to distrust that which is already done.'

Bitterly annoyed with the failure of his restrictive measure to plug loopholes, he wrote to the Duke of Wellington on 9 June 1844: 'Every idle man and every foolish, vain man wants to increase establishment, and to have more slaves bowing about him. There is a sad want of business-like habits every where'.[3]

This dichotomy continued until later compulsions cast their weight in favour of provincial decentralization as the only alternative for the promotion of development. These early compulsions included the obligations of the state to win over the peasantry involved in the Indian Mutiny, to implement the recommendations of the Cholera Commission appointed in 1861, and, finally, or organize relief operations to counteract the effects of the famine which occurred in the North-Western Provinces in 1861, and in Bengal and Orissa in 1866. Added to these were the recommendations of the Royal Army Sanitary Commission (1863), which viewed the health of the army as immediately connected with the general state of public health. In these circumstances, under Lord Mayo's Financial Resolution No. 3334 of 14 December 1870 the Government of India transferred to the Local Governments such heads of expenditure as related to jails, registration, police, education, medical services, printing, roads and civil buildings. And to provide for their management it also transferred the means, which consisted partly of the receipts, if any, under each of these heads and partly of a fixed consolidated allotment from the imperial revenues. In the fields so decentralized, the Government of India also declared its intention to divest itself of responsibility and control within certain limits, so that this transfer of responsibility might encourage local economy and lead to local development. This was the first real beginning of financial and administrative decentralization for development. Though still of minor importance, the establishment of Agriculture as part of a separate Department of Revenue and Commerce, plus the beginnings of municipal institutions and local bodies, marked the progress of trends in the same direction.

The principle of provincial finance recognized in 1870 was extended by Lord Lytton who wanted economy to lead to the abolition of import duties on cotton. His settlement of 1877 invested the Provincial Governments with responsibility over such additional services as were connected with general administration, land revenue, excise, stamps, law and justice. They were also given the revenues from law and justice, excise, stamps and licence tax, where any prospective increase was to be shared with the Government of India who might also meet any deficit. The system of fixed grants continued. But an important departure was made in 1879, when it was substituted by a share of the land revenue for fixed assignments. The Provincial Governments thus came to acquire a direct interest not only in the provincialized revenue, but also in important items of the imperial revenues raised within the provinces. This was a limited form of rationalization effected on the principle of *laissez faire* to promote development within the broad framework of imperial stability. It reserved certain heads of revenue as Imperial, with minute local exceptions; others were divided on a more or less equal basis, while the rest were made wholly provincial, with certain minor exceptions.[4] The system so established in 1882 became known as the periodical provincial contracts or the 'quinquennial settlements', which were revised in 1887, 1892 and 1897.

The system of periodical contracts had its limitations however. It was created not as a basis of claim to the growing scale of provincial expenditure, but only as a device to enforce economy. The Government of India was not bound under the contract to permit increases of expenditure merely because a Provincial Government had sanctioned it within the terms of its contract and the funds available at its disposal; it reserved the right of limiting the expenditure of any province with reference to the financial requirements of India as a whole.

The all-India view of financial control over provincial development was not without justification, but it also meant that the interests of backward provinces could be neglected by exclusive Imperial concern. On the expiry of the quinquennial agreement of 1897, therefore, Lord Curzon introduced in 1904 a new quasi-permanent settlement. The revenues assigned to a Provincial Government under this arrangement were not to be altered except in rare cases of grave imperial necessity, or in the event of experience proving the assignments made to be beyond the normal requirements of a province.

However, the old classification of revenue remained more or less unaltered. While the Government of India received all the revenue accruing from opium, salt, customs, the mint, railways, posts and telegraphs, and the tributes from Indian States, the Provincial Governments kept all receipts from registration as well as from the spending departments they managed, such as the police, education, law and justice, medical, minor irrigation and provincial civil works. The divided heads of revenue, on the other hand, included receipts from land revenue, excise, stamps, income tax, forests and major irrigation works.[5]

Curzon's attempt to define the limits of financial operations to promote development in the provinces did not fully succeed. For even though the Government of India theoretically hoped to confine itself to strategic control and avoid petty and vexatious interference with the details of provincial administration, it was extremely difficult in practice to distinguish between these details and the general principles of control and supervision. Decentralization did not originate locally or from the Provincial Governments; it was a gift of the Central, imperial force and conceded because developmental administration could not easily be carried on from a single headquarters in a vast sub-continent. The creation of a larger area of responsibility for provincial and local authorities was thus necessary to raise resources and promote development. As already noted, however, in the early phase of decentralization under Lord Curzon efficiency and uniformity were emphasized, rather than respect for local sentiments and traditions: Curzon had no alternative but to choose between virtual inaction and bureaucratic centralization, between *ad hocism* and a definite direction. To promote development he chose the latter. The choice no doubt had its limitations in that it neglected popular elements that might have been used as a go-between. But his administration nevertheless laid foundations in all fields of developmental activity. This was done by using the powers of the Government of India over the Provincial Governments, and of the latter over their subordinate authorities. The Centre exercised its control by means of financial rules and restrictions, or by particular checks of a purely administrative nature. It likewise called for preliminary scrutiny of proposed provincial legislations as well as the sanction of Acts passed in provincial legislatures. Other modes of control included general Resolutions on questions of policy, suggestions made in periodic departmental administration reports, the action taken on matters highlighted by the Inspectors-General, and the rights of appeal possessed by persons dissatisfied with the actions or orders of a Provincial Government.[6]

Administrative Framework for Developmental Services

The administrative framework established for development consisted of specialized services, separate and distinct from those meant for general executive or judicial administration. Organized on a similar principle, the highest or Superior Services were recruited in England, and the other two, the 'Provincial' and the 'Subordinate' recruited in India.

The specialized Superior Services recruited in England were comparable to the Covenanted Civil Service, while the services recruited in India corresponded to the 'uncovenanted', functioning on the executive and judicial side of general administration.[7] Under the recommendations of the Aitchison Commission the Superior Services were divided into the Central Services and the All-India Services.

The Central Services dealt *inter alia* with the Indian States, frontier affairs, the state railways, posts and telegraphs, customs, audit and accounts, as well as such technical departments as the Survey of India, Geological Survey and the Archaeological Department. The All-India Services, which the Aitchison Commission preferred to call 'Imperial', but which at the instance of the Secretary of State came to be designated as 'Indian', included, besides the Indian Civil Service and the Indian Police, a number of developmental services, such as the Indian Service of Engineers (Road and Building Branch as well as the Irrigation Branch), the Indian Education Service, the Indian Medical Service (Civil), the Indian Forest Service, the Indian Agricultural Service and the Indian Veterinary Service.

The Aitchison Commission had mainly studied the problem of reorganizing the civil service in a manner conducive to rationalization and extended Indian employment. The study of the specialized services did not form part of its principal task. This was entrusted to a sub-committee appointed by the Government of India on 8 March 1887. But the operation of the principles laid down by the Commission for the reorganization of the civil services into three classes, Superior, Provincial and Subordinate, extended to the specialized services also. The difference, however, was that while the decision taken by the Government on these principles under its Resolution of 21 April 1892 came into force immediately in so far as the civil service was concerned, the formation of the specialized services for developmental purposes was staggered between 1892 and 1905.

The Indian Service of Engineers. This Service was created in 1892 on the recommendation of the Aitchison Commission. The Superior class of the Service consisted of the Chief, Superintending, Executive and Assistant Engineers recruited mostly in England from the Royal Indian Engineering College at Cooper's Hill, a proportion of the Service being Royal Engineers officers. Engineers recruited in India from local colleges were classed as Provincial engineers. They were Indian citizens, including also domiciled Europeans and Eurasians. The subordinate or upper subordinate ranks, including overseers, were products of engineering schools. On the analogy of promotion to 'listed' posts on the civil service side, there were some guaranteed appointments in the Imperial branch of the Service which the most distinguished Provincial engineers could hope to be promoted to.

There were similar openings each year from the subordinate ranks to the Provincial.

Under the arrangement of 1892 the Government of India and each major province maintained a Civil Public Works Department headed by the Chief Engineer who also functioned as a Secretary to the Government, dealing with matters relating to irrigation, roads and buildings. In provinces such as Madras, Bombay, Bengal, U.P. and Burma there were two Chief Engineers, one for irrigation and the other for roads and buildings. The division of functions in most provinces between the Chief Engineers extended also to the districts in U.P. and Punjab, where the development of irrigation called for separate Executive Engineers for irrigation as well as for roads and buildings. Elsewhere the general practice was to use the same officers for both purposes.

Each province was divided into Public Works divisions comprising single civil districts, or portions or groups of districts, each such division being placed under an Executive Engineer. Executive Engineers had under them Assistant Engineers, who received a training for higher jobs, and a staff consisting of subordinate engineers, supervisors and overseers, holding charge either of part of the division or of particular works. Five or six such divisions were grouped into a 'Circle' and placed under a Superintending Engineer, whose primary duty was to scrutinize the estimates passed on to him by Executive Engineers, and to inspect the works and projects that went on in his circle.

The control of the Government of India over Public Works Departments in the provinces was exercised through accounting and auditing, its primary responsibility. For the Public Works Accounts branch was under the direct control of the Public Works Department of the Central Government. It also allocated funds for irrigation and other projects which were defrayed from current Imperial revenues or borrowed funds. The actual construction and up-keep of roads, buildings and irrigation, however, formed part of the responsibility of the Provincial Governments, subject to control by the Centre. through general financial regulation. Even the general organization of the provincial departments was regulated by the Centre in that the pay of different grades of officers, the general conditions of their service and their spheres of action were all laid down by it.[8] This control conduced to efficiency but irked the provinces in the execution of development projects and later led to measures of administrative decentralization.

The Indian Forest Service. As already noted, the constitution of a regularly organized Forest Department goes back to 1864.

Forest work had originally been dealt with by the Government of India in the Public Works Department. When the Secretary of State did not favour this arrangement, forests became a branch of the Revenue and Agriculture Department. It long remained a branch, though a specialized one, of the general land-revenue administration, which admitted the futility of imposing any rigid or uniform system. This was recognized by the Secretary of State who, in his Despatch No. 5 of 25 February 1863, took exception to forest work being placed under the Public Works Department of the Government of India and advised that it should be in the same hands as the ordinary land-revenue administration. And when the Resolution of the Government of India (No. 4, P.W., 2 March 1864) appointing an Inspector-General of Forests was passed, it was, on the same old advice of the Secretary of State, laid down that in Madras and Bombay as well as in the then three Lieutenant-Governorships of Bengal, the North-Western Provinces and the Punjab, forest administration should be entirely under the Provincial Governments, the Inspector-General being merely an inspecting and advisory functionary. It was only in lesser provinces that he was given any power of direct interference.[9] In spite of this original intention, however, the control of the Government of India later became much closer especially after the reorganization of 1892, which classified the Service into three categories on the same principles as applied to other services.

The Forest staff was controlled by the Local Governments and consisted of 'Imperial', 'Provincial' and 'Subordinate' branches. Recruited in England, the Imperial branch supplied most of the superior controlling staff comprising the Inspector-General, Chief Conservators (Burma and Central Provinces), Conservators,[10] Deputy and Assistant Conservators, the Assistant Inspector General and the Principal of the Forest College.

The Provincial service consisted of Indians, classified in various grades[11] as Extra-Deputy and Extra-Assistant Conservators. They were mostly from the Dehra Dun Forest College established in 1878 to provide the requisite training for higher officers recruited in India.[12] It was under the direct control of the Government of India who exercised it through the Inspector-General of Forests. The Provincial service men were in due course to take over, on the analogy of 'Listed' posts in the Civil Service, one-fifth[13] of the major forest charges formerly held by Imperial officers, and all the minor charges. Apart from direct recruitment made by the Local Governments, the officers of the Provincial service were also selected from the Subordinate service rangers of long experience and proved ability, irrespective of educational qualifications, as also from rangers who had passed from the Dehra Dun Forest College and served for a prescribed period. These appointments were made in accordance with the general qualifications laid down by the Government of India.

The Subordinate service included such situations as rangers, deputy rangers, foresters and forest guards. Their recruitment was practically left in the hands of Local Governments. Unlike the Provincial service officers who enjoyed uniform scales of pay throughout the provinces, the pay of the Subordinate service men varied in the different Provinces.

Administratively, the forest areas of each large provinces were divided into circles, divisions, sub-divisions or ranges, and beats. The circle was placed under a Conservator, and most important divisions were under officers of the Imperial service, the minor charges alone being headed by officers of the Provincial Service.

Forest administration in the earlier stages was carried on under executive rules. The first forest law was enacted in 1865, a year after the establishment of the department. It was intended for the whole of British India, except Madras and Bombay where the Local Governments were left free to apply it by notification. The Act was the first attempt to provide for punishment of forest offences. But it drew no distinction between 'reserved' and 'protected' forests. Moreover, Bombay remained without a forest law until 1878, and Madras until 1882, and central control over forest administration continued to be diffused and nominal. The Indian Forest Act of 1878, which applied also to Bombay, distinguished between 'reserved' and 'protected' forests and specified procedures for the settlement of rights and the exercise of control by the Government of India.

But the Inspector-General of Forests, who alone could exercise central control, discharged no more than an advisory function. Thus when the Government of India issued orders in 1870 intended to strengthen the Inspector-General's capacity to 'effectually inspect and supervise all forest operations and freely advise the administration in all matters relating to forest management', the Governments of Madras and Bombay protested. These were overruled by the Secretary of State, but that did not settle the matter. The action of the

Secretary of State was viewed as the work of the Bengal Civilians who dominated the Central Government and led to unsatisfactory results and friction. The orders were consequently withdrawn in February 1875. 'Fresh instructions were issued which restored Madras and Bombay to the independent position they occupied in 1864.'[14]

The position of the Government of India gained strength under Lord Lytton. The Indian Forest Act of 1878 was applied to Madras in 1882. However, only after the administrative reforms of 1892 was Central control in forest matters tightened under general financial rules. The permission of the Centre had to be sought for any establishment changes involving an expenditure of more than Rs. 25,000; for the creation, abolition or enhancement of remuneration of an individual post in excess of Rs 250; and for the creation, abolition or alteration of emoluments of any class or grade of officers.

The authority of the Government of India was further enhanced by a Resolution of 19 October 1894 which defined forest policy by classifying forest areas and prescribing procedure and agencies for preservation, management and protection.[15] Other means of promoting centralization included the use of the Inspector-General of Forests in the management of state forest property and scrutiny of periodical returns (except in Madras and Bombay); the appointment by the Government of India, if necessary, of Conservators and Chief Conservators of Forests outside Madras and Bombay; the use of the centrally-controlled College at Dehra Dun which trained Provincial Forest Service officers, and, finally, of certain provisions of the Indian Forest Act, which required sanction by the Government of India of rules governing deforestation, village and protected forests, and levies on timber or other forest produce. The forest code and the stringency of the forest audit system further rendered the provinces subject to central direction. Here, as in the case of the Public Works Department, decentralization was later considered necessary for the encouragement of provincial and local initiative to promote development.

The Indian Educational Service. The machinery of educational administration organized under Wood's Despatch of 1854 remained provincial until a Director-General of Education was appointed in 1901 to advise the Government of India in educational matters. Between 1855 and 1866 a Director of Public Instruction, with a self-contained Education Department subordinate to him, including Inspectors of Schools, was appointed in every province.

In February 1882 a Commission was appointed by the Government of India to report on the progress made and the extent to which the principles laid down in 1854 had been followed. To accelerate the pace of education without increasing the state's financial commitment the Commission emphasized private initiative, with official supervision to maintain standards, as well as the scale of fees determined by the Director of Public Instruction for the state-aided private schools. This policy led to the expansion of employment for educated Indians, for it increased the size of the inspecting staff needed at different levels. The policy also brought into focus the importance of rural education, which had thus far been neglected. The Commission advised that the management of indigenous elementary schools and the control over primary school expenditure be entrusted to municipal and local boards wherever they existed. The aim was to enable the state to concentrate on the elementary education of the masses.

On the principles laid down by the Government of India in 1892, the Indian Educational Service (IES) was created in 1896. The Service was divided into the usual three categories, namely, the Superior, the Provincial and the Subordinate Educational Services. The Superior was generally recruited in England on a scale of pay commencing at Rs 500 a month and rising up to a normal maximum of Rs 1,250 to Rs 1,500, excluding, of course, the Directorships of the Department usually held by members of the Indian Civil Service. The Provincial Educational Service included in its rank such functionaries as Indian Inspectors of Schools, Principals and Professors of Government Colleges and Headmasters of high schools. The lower grades on the administrative side or in teaching institutions were occupied by the Subordinate Service.

Subject to the general control of the Local Government, the Director of Public Instruction was invested with the entire management of education in all its branches. He prepared educational estimates, controlled the distribution of grants, and recommended appointments and transfers. He functioned in fact as an expert adviser of his Local Government and to local bodies to which the Home Department Resolution of 23 October 1884[16] had entrusted a role, especially of primary education.

The central control of education, however, began with the appointment of an Imperial Director-General of Education, an appointment recommended by the Directors of Public Instruction at a Conference held at Simla in 1901 at the instance of the Viceroy who presided. The function of the Director-General was to make periodical tours in the provinces, where he held meetings with educational officers and inspected institutions, and to advise the Government of India on all educational matters. Though not invested with powers to give any executive instructions to the provincial authorities, he served as an agency of central control in policy matters. For he also presided over a small educational bureau organized to collect information on the curricula, methods and organizational patterns of schools in India and abroad. The Local Governments and their officers made use of the information so collected and occasionally published reports for the guidance of educational officers. Though not directly involved in primary and secondary education, the Government of India thus provided a direction that ensured a degree of uniformity in standards.

In the field of higher education, however, the Government of India became directly involved. It appointed a Commission to examine the working of the Indian universities, namely, the Universities of Calcutta, Madras, Bombay, Allahabad and Punjab (Lahore). The result was the Universities Act of 1904, which remodelled their governing bodies, vested them with teaching functions and gave them powers to exercise greater control over affiliated colleges, both in terms of management and academic standards.

In fact, education in general became a subject of periodical review by the Government. Under its Home Department Resolution of 11 March 1904 the Government of India was to issue on such occasions a body of instructions considered necessary for future development. These were, of course, general principles designed to guide educational administration. But since the grant of liberal financial assistance to Provincial Governments went with the due observance of periodical general instructions, nothing could prevent the growth of a tendency towards uniformity, a tendency which was further encouraged by the Imperial Educational Service where even the temporary filling of vacancies required the sanction of the Secretary of State. The Government of India did not appear to have laid down rules governing the qualifications of officers to be appointed to the Provincial Educational Service. But even at the provincial level, Local Governments could not create appointments or alter emoluments except in accordance with the general financial rules laid down by the Centre.

The Indian Medical Service. Formed in 1896, this was primarily a military service recruited in England by open competition. Those selected had to undergo a four months' special course, and, after passing a second examination, joined the army in India. Except under special circumstances, they were required to perform two years' military service before becoming eligible for civil employment. The Service was open to Indians, but the number of Indians in it was small. The military duties of the Indian Medical Service were confined to the 'Native' army. Those who tended the European troops were officers of the British Royal Army Corps.

While the Chief Medical Officer and administrative head of the Indian Medical Department was Director-General, Indian Medical Service, with the rank of a Surgeon-General, the principal adviser of a Local Government, as said before, was an Inspector-General of Civil Hospitals[17] (Surgeon-General in Madras and Bombay) and a Sanitary Commissioner. In Madras and Bombay, the apointment of the provincial head of the Department required the approval of the Government of India. In other provinces, the head of the Department was actually nominated by the Government of India after considering the recommendations of the Director-General. However, apart from matters of appointment, medical and sanitary administration remained under the immediate control of the Local Government.

The medical and sanitary arrangements of each district, except in Bombay, were under the Civil Surgeon. Besides dealing with most of the medico-legal work of the district, his duties included the superintendence of medical institutions which were mostly maintained by the rural boards and municipalities. He assisted and advised these bodies in dealing with sanitary matters. Subject to the general authority of the Collector, he in fact dealt with all matters connected with the health of the population in the district. In Bombay the position of the Civil Surgeon was quite different. Here he was occupied mainly with the duties of the headquarters station, though he also did inspection work. The rural hospitals and dispensaries in that Presidency were supervised directly by the Surgeon-General, the administrative head of the medical department, while the sanitary work was committed to a number of Deputy Sanitary Commissioners who took their orders from the provincial Sanitary Commissioner. Deputy Sanitary Commissioners looked after the sanitation of the districts and towns within their Circle, inspected dispensaries, and advised district officers on matters affecting public health. They also dealt with vaccination and vital statistics which, before 1880, had formed part of the duties of 'Superintendents of Vaccination'. The local bodies, both rural and urban, were likewise entrusted with these jobs since 1884-5.

Below the rank of the Civil Surgeon were the upper subordinate officers of the Civil Medical and Sanitary Departments—mostly Civil Assistant Surgeons trained in Indian medical colleges. They held charge of minor hospitals and the principal dispensaries, but were also employed in the larger hospitals and other subordinate situations. Their services were lent likewise to municipalities and rural boards for work in the institutions maintained by them. A certain number of Civil Surgeon's posts which were originally held by officers of the Indian Medical Service, were, on the pattern of 'listed posts' in the Covenanted Civil Service, set apart in each province for Assistant Surgeons. Though belonging to a 'Subordinate' Service, they had in fact the same status as the Provincial Services in other departments.

The 'subordinates' in the medical field basically consisted of civil hospital assistants trained in local medical schools and employed in posts lower than Assistant Surgeons. Some military hospital assistants were, however, also placed at the disposal of the Local Governments for civil work.

Sanitation. As already pointed out, the *Report of the Royal Army Commission* (1863) led to the appointment of Sanitary Commissioners for different provinces in 1866-7.[18]

To raise the status of the Sanitary Commissioners so appointed, provisions were made under a Home (Military) Notification of 15 March 1880 for their promotion to the administrative rank of Deputy Surgeon-General on fulfilling 26 years' service.[19] This rule governing promotion continued until the limitations of the period of sevice imposed in 1880 were done away with in 1884 and provisions made for regular selection on merit and ability.[20]

The principle of uniting the offices of the Medical and Sanitary heads at the provincial level in 1880 applied to the Centre also. Between 1880 and 1904, the Director-General was also Sanitary Commissioner of the Government of India, and only in 1904 was a separate Imperial Sanitary Commissioner appointed. In a Resolution of 8 September 1904 the Government laid down that he would advise it not only upon sanitation but also on bacteriological questions which he was expected to discuss with Local Governments and their sanitary officers without encroaching on their administrative authority. He was, however, in direct charge of the Central Bacteriological Institute established in 1905 at Kasauli,[21] an Institute which was supplemented by similar provincial institutions at Guindy in Madras, and at Bombay, Calcutta, Agra and Rangoon.

In a letter to the Government of India on 14 August 1906 the Imperial Sanitary Commissioner suggested that sanitary administration throughout the country could be improved only by direct Central appointment of a provincial Sanitary Commissioners[22] and the creation of an imperial service of sanitary engineers. The existing character of the Indian Medical Service was maintained, and centralization continued in the medical department; but an imperial service of sanitary engineers was not created. To improve sanitary administration, however, provisions had been made in 1888 for the creation of a Sanitary Board in each province, with engineers to act as a central agency in guiding the local bodies. The precise constitution of these Boards and their relations with the administrative head of the provincial medical department varied in every province. The U.P. Sanitary Board, for example, included the Inspector-General of Civil Hospitals, the Sanitary Commissioner and the Sanitary Engineer, while in Bombay the Surgeon-General was not on the Board. But the functions of the Board in all cases were to advise the administrative heads of departments and to sanction and secure the execution of works undertaken by district boards and municipalities.

The Indian Agricultural Service. The importance of applying science to agriculture had begun to be realized since Voelcker's days. It led to the appointment of a considerable number of agricultural experts. But the immediate incentive to have more proceeded from the recommendation of the Famine Commission (1901) which, in paragraph 353, emphasized the necessity of a much stronger staff of experts as well as of agricultural research.

Consistent with this recommendation, Lord Curzon's administration established the Agricultural Research Institute at Pusa. Within four years of the appointment in 1901 of an Inspector-General as an expert to enlarge the scope of departmental operations and coordinate the work going on in the provinces on independent lines, it was not only the Imperial staff of experts that had increased and called for further increase, but even the provincial departments of agriculture. In 1901, for instance, a trained Deputy Director existed only in Madras, Bombay and the United Provinces, while the Economic Botanist in Madras was the only provincial representative of the more specialized branches of the subject. Since then expert Deputy Directors came to be sanctioned for Bengal, the Punjab and the Central Provinces which, in addition, was allowed an Agricultural Chemist. The United Provinces had in the meantime an Economic Botanist, and Bombay its own Professor of Agriculture and Agricultural Chemist.

The expansion was quicker on the Imperial side. In four years its expert staff of six had expanded to twenty-four appointments already sanctioned or recommended.[23] The extent of development so reached necessarily called for a policy of recruitment that might conduce to building a regular research and scientific cadre of experts, especially in view of the extent to which the Government had become financially committed not only to secure agricultural improvement but, more so, to promote agricultural research and experiment.[24]

In a despatch of 26 October 1905 the Government of India asked the Secretary of State to approve an extended plan of development which envisaged a much stronger staff of experts, particularly in the provincial departments which, in six large provinces, needed a whole-time civilian Director of Agriculture and a group of specialists to form a nucleus of administrative and scientific talent out of which a full-fledged organization could develop. Curzon also proposed the establishment in each important province of an agricultural college and research station. Apart from a demand for experts in such special crops as tobacco, wheat, sugar, fruit and cotton, emphasis was laid on the creation of additional posts of supernumerary chemists, botanists, mycologists and entomologists in order to build up an adequate reserve of officers.[25] The number of European experts in the Imperial and provincial departments increased from 6 to 34 in the course of four years.[26]

The task ot agricultural development through European experts had its own problems, however. The question of acquiring a knowledge of the local language presented a serious difficulty. Even officers already appointed were under an obligation to pass within two years such examinations as might be prescribed by the Government in one of the languages of India. Their passing was theoretically a condition for the renewal of their job after five years. But the Government tended to ignore this qualification in practice.

There was also the question of combining the scattered scientific appointments into one cadre for the purpose of pay and promotion, for each incumbent had, under the existing arrangement, his own rate of pay and conditions of service, which proved both expensive against ideas of a well regulated pay structure. Since the number of similarly qualified agricultural experts was steadily increasing it seemed reasonable to bring all into a single graded service that might offer a less expensive and settled prospect of promotion capable of attracting scientific talent for future development.

A graded service involved a settlement of pay, probation, pension and allowances, but these were sought to be settled on terms approved by the Secretary of State in his Despatch of 8 January 1904[27] for the recruitment of officers to the Indian Educational Service established under a Home Department Resolution of 23 July 1896.[28] It was unanimously agreed that regardless of whether the staff of experts were to be employed for research or teaching, or both, they should be first-class men with good university degrees and some special training in Britain. The candidates chosen were to be of the same high calibre required for the Indian Educational Service.[29]

The terms and conditions of the Indian Agricultural Service were laid down in a Finance Department Despatch of 14 September 1905. The appointments included the Deputy Director of Agriculture,[30] Superintendent of Government Farms, Agriculturist Chemist, Economic Botanist, Mycologist, Entomologist, Professors of Agriculture, Chemistry and Botany at Agricultural Colleges, and so on. Some were included in the Imperial Department of Agriculture directly under the control of the Centre, but the majority were to be in the departments of the several provinces. In some cases candidates were to be appointed as supernumeraries. They were to undergo further training in India before being appointed to posts on the regular establishment as vacancies occurred.

The proposed Indian Agricultural Service was soon approved by the India Office. There were certain modifications in regard to the posts which were sought to be included in the Service as also to the scale of initial salary assigned. But the general scheme of the appointments was accepted on the ground of the expansion and developent of both the Imperial and Provincial Departments of Agriculture.[31]

The Secretary of State also accepted the proposal of Curzon's Government to create six Directors of Agriculture, one in each of the larger provinces of Madras, Bombay, Bengal, U.P., Punjab and the

Central Provinces. As recommended by Curzon, the Secretary of State agreed that this post should be separated from that of Land Records, a measure that effected a shift of emphasis from revenue to agricultural development. The Secretary of State also agreed that in the first instance members of the Indian Civil Service might 'appropriately be appointed' as Directors of Agriculture; for the most important work of that office immediately after its establishment would be the organization of the department, a function that was best discharged by a Civilian. 'But', the Secretary of State added in the same breath, 'I am of the opinion that the question should be re-examined five years hence.'[32]

The plan of provincial colleges of agriculture was likewise approved. As regards Curzon's proposals to add four experts to the Imperial department for special crops, the Secretary of State sounded caution and expressed some doubts. The real objection was in fact financial. For the estimated annual provision of Rs 20 lakhs for distribution among Local Governments was found to have risen to Rs 34 lakhs according to provincial estimates which covered both agricultural and veterinary improvements. As the results of research and experiment could not but be uncertain for a time, the Secretary of State 'thought that a policy of cautious advance would be preferable, that departmental expansion should take place by degrees, that the staff of imported experts should for the present be closely restricted, and that the development of the Agricultural Departments, as they show signs of life, should be chiefly effected by means of an indigenous agency trained at the Central [Pusa] Institute.'[33]

The caution so advised by the Home Government meant a curtailment of the general scheme for expansion and development of the agricultural and veterinary departments. Convinced of the soundness of its larger proposals the Government of India did not take the decision of the Secretary of State lying down. In two letters of 26 July 1906,[34] it reiterated its case forcefully for the creation of the posts of additional experts already suggestd by Curzon's Government in 1905. The general effect of the recommendations made in these two letters would have been (1) to add twenty-one experts to the provincial Departments and ten more to the Imperial Department, besides, two more officers to the Civil Veterinary Department; (2) to increase the provincial financial allotment to Rs 25 lakhs, and (3) the Imperial reserve to Rs 5 lakhs.

The Secretary of State did not underrate the importance of the proposals made by the Government of India and shared the hopes entertained by Lord Minto's Administration that the monies and establishments that of late had been allotted to the creation of agricultural and veterinary departments would in time effect substantial progress. What, however, concerned him most was the political risk of appointing an increasing number of British officers. For, he said:

> The number of officers who have recently been added to the Agricultural Service by appointment in this country is already large, and the grants for this Service have rapidly increased. I find myself drawn to the conclusion that a stage of development has now been reached at which a halt in the expenditure and in the number of European experts is desirable. There is the further consideration that beyond a certain point every additional European expert in this branch of the public service is a bar to the policy of officering it as far as possible with natives of India.

While the Government of India felt that agricultural progress could not be attained without a full complement of European officers, Morley emphasized that with the new additions he proposed to sanction, the Central and Provincial Departments would amply suffice for training the additional Indians required. He, therefore, reiterated that the political risk of relying too much on recruitment in this country should be avoided from the outset.[35]

The Secretary of State thus took care to create only those posts which appeared to be most urgently required. He assented, for example, to the creation of seven posts of Superintendents of Farms allocated to the provinces, an Agricultural Chemist and an Agricultural Botanist for Eastern Bengal and Assam. But he turned down the posts of mycologists and entomologists for the provincial departments which were advised to rely on the resources of the Central Institute of Pusa. In view of the ten officers added to the Civil Veterinary Department in 1905, its request for two more officers was likewise rejected. As regards imported experts on the Imperial side, sanction was accorded for the appointment of four supernumeraries and a third entomologist, but the appointment of the four crop specialists remained in abeyance.

This controversy between the Government of India and the Secretary of State on the subject of importing specialists shows that the task of rural development, of which agriculture constituted the core, was beset with numerous difficulties. It called for a decentralization of authority to speed up decision-making, specially in financial matters.

But a more serious problem was the need for a competent and organized administrative agency of experts. In a situation where Indian expertise was for the most part absent, there was no alternative to dependence on imported know-how. But in view of the Western education being promoted in India as a matter of policy any attempt to prejudice the employment opportunities of indigenous talent was bound to raise political issues, as it actually did. Morely correctly apprehended this potential danger and advised caution to avoid it. Whatever the trend of subsequent development, personnel problems in administration for development got generally mixed with politics, a trend which necessitated continued centralization in terms of both political and administrative authority. The need for the various All-India Services to draw trained personnel from abroad for development pointed in the same direction: it also called for centralization as an absolute necessity.

Agencies of Central Control:
The Inspector-General

The Various departments of the Government of India which were invested with control and supervision of the areas primarily administered by Local Governments, were headed by a Secretary to the Government, whose position corresponds generally with that of a Permanent Under Secretary of State in Britain. He was assisted by an Inspector-General with expert knowledge and larger personal acquaintance with local conditions than the Secretariat staff could be expected to possess. An Inspector-General could be designated Director-General: in the Department of Education, for instance, he was actually known as such. But the difference of title did not signify any difference of function which, in both cases, happened to be advisory, not executive. We shall, therefore, refer to these officers generally as Imperial Inspectors-General. The primary function of the Inspectors-General was to act as advisory officers to the Government of India and the Local Governments. It was clearly understood that in their relations with the latter their appointment was not to involve administrative interference, although the Government of India could easily intervene on the basis of the expert advice given to it by them. An Imperial Inspector-General in fact served as a regular channel of information for the Centre about Local Governments and enabled the Government of India to discharge its own responsibilities to the Secretary of State, or to exercise its legitimate functions of control over the Local Governments.

Though Bombay expressed itself against Inspectors-General being permitted to visit the provinces or to correspond with provincial officers unless authorized to do so by the Local Government, their utility as advisers and Inspectors was generally recognized. The minutes of evidence recorded by the Royal Commission on Decentralization (1909) confirmed this view and pointed out that the Inspectors-General, by inspection and advice, improved the technical efficiency of the administrative departments of both the Government of India and Local Governments. Doubtless they contributed to centralization. But this flowed from specialization, a necessity in modern administration. Administratively, there was thus little or no loosening of central control over the provinces in the developmental field.

Demand for Democratic Decentralization

The demand for democratic decentralization came from the educated élite who wanted a share in the exercise of power and patronage. It was limited to local bodies and municipalities and based on the principle that local needs must be met by local taxation. This principle was incorporated by Lord Mayo in a Decentralization Scheme formulated by the Government in 1870, which made provision for local funds being raised locally by municipal and rural boards to meet their local requirements.

The main object of Lord Mayo's scheme was to relieve the Imperial finances of the management of local needs. Lord Ripon extended a decentralized system of finance by transferring from from the 'provincial' to 'local' activity such additional items of receipts and charges as might equalize local and municipal taxation to secure uniform progress in their development throughout the country.[36] He not only carried out but also developed the policy of his predecessors.[37]

Lord Ripon also added a political dimension to the erstwhile scheme of financial and administrative decentralization to promote local development projects. His famous Resolution of 18 May 1882 thus said: 'It is not plrimarily with a view to improvement in administration that this measure [local self-government] is put forward and approved. It is chiefly desirable as an instrument of political and popular education',[38] necessary for the acquisition of skill and experience required in the management of local affairs by the elected members of municipal and local boards. The elective element had existed even before Ripon. But it was only permissive. Ripon made it a rule and enforced it as an instrument for the political education of the elitist 'competitors', who were projecting themselves as a potential alternative to the bureaucracy in such fields of administration as were being decentralized for political reasons.

Ripon's local self-government policy thus seemed to attain a two-fold objective. The first was to build a provincially reinforced local fund in order to free Imperial finances from local functions such as the maintenance of certain kinds of roads, hospitals, dispensaries, drainage, water supply and sanitation, vaccination, education (chiefly primary), pounds and ferries, markets, rest houses and other minor public works. The second, on the other hand, was to reconstruct local bodies so as to provide additional avenues for educated employment and keep the politically motivated élites engaged in the exercise of a measure of power, influence and authority which, though of minor intrinsic importance, raised their social status and prospects of acquiring wealth.

Considering the variety in local circumstances, the Government of India resolution of 18 May 1882 recognized that uniformity was impossible of attainment either in regard to the delegation of powers to local bodies or the methods upon which local interests could best be represented on them. Even so, two main principles formed the basis of the policy then adopted in terms of governmental control. It was laid down that the proportion of officials appointed to local bodies should be limited, and the necessary control over their proceedings should be from without rather than from within.

Consistent with the character of the local population the Government of India resolved that the Provincial Governments be empowered to maintain and extend throughout the country, in every district where an intelligent non-official agency could be found, a network of local boards, to be charged with definite duties and entrusted with definite funds. It was recognized that since local interest and knowledge did not extend beyond a certain limit, the area proposed to be allotted to each was not to be too large. For experience had proved 'that district committees are, as a rule, very badly attended by members not actually residing in the vicinity of the headquarters station. Those who do attend have frequently no intimate acquaintance with the wants of the outlying parts of the district. The consequence is, either that undue attention is given to the requirements of the immediate neighbourhood of the central station, or that the business falls entirely into the hands of the district officer, the committee contenting itself with formally endorsing his proposals'.[39] To remedy this situation the Resoluton of 18 May 1882 determined to create smaller units of subdivisional and *taluka* boards and emphasized the importance of political and popular education to widen the basis of élitist loyalty for the attainment of both local and imperial ends. It was to ensure a larger voice of non-official members that the Resolution provided that in no case ought the official members be more than one-third of the whole. But what decided the issues was not the size of the non-official majority which hardly ever mattered; for the interest of elected members in the people as a whole and their knowledge of public affairs bore poor comparison with those of officials. There existed in fact little or no organized rural public opinion that might serve as a check on both élitist and bureaucratic elements in the local bodies. These were a mere gift of the Government and had not grown from below. Reduction in the area of a local board did not inject a qualitative change in the mode of their functioning, and the later failure of village panchayats confirmed this beyond any doubt.

As the control exercised by the Government was external the Government revised and checked the acts of local bodies, but could not dictate to them. This control was considered necessary for any sanction required in order to give validity to certain acts, such as the raising of loans, the imposition of taxes in a form other than already authorized, the alienation of municipal property, interference with matters involving religious questions or affecting the public peace and the like. The restrictions were indeed a denial of the original principle on which local bodies had been established — to manage local affairs with the resources raised locally — and involved both financial and administrative limitations in the exercise of discretion by local bodies. And yet they were not without justification in the peculiar context of caste hierarchies and religious divisions which obstructed the growth of a common loyalty to higher goals: local bodies did not function as effective decentralized units of administration for development in the rural areas.

The other control exercised by the Local Government was to set aside altogether the proceedings of a board in particular cases, or, in the event of gross and continued neglect of any important duty, to suspend the board temporarily by the appointment of persons to substitute for the board until the neglected duty had been satisfactorily performed. That being done, a regular board was then to be re-established after fresh election. The executive officers of the Government had, therefore, instructions to watch the proceedings of local boards and point out to them matters calling for consideration. They were to draw attention to neglect of duty and 'to check by official remonstrance' any attempt to exceed proper functional limits or to act illegally 'in an arbitrary or unreasonable manner.'[40] Though officially guided by a desire to reduce bureaucratic despotism, the authoritarian character of Indian society and imperial considerations left no room for any relaxation of official dominance. It continued in spite of Ripon's remonstrance against a rigid bureaucracy, indifferent or hostile to democratic decentralization. Though in law invested with the immediate responsibility for rural development, the local bodies were in fact not the directive force. It was the bureaucracy that provided the necessary direction.

However, the legislation which followed in 1883 and after, proceeded, with certain local variations, on the general principles formulated by Lord Ripon in 1882.[41] The Madras system was considered the most advanced, for large villages or groups of villages were organized there as 'Unions' empowered to levy a small house-tax. These were grouped into larger sub-divisions of *talukas*, functioning under the general control of the district boards which administred the entire local fund, with powers to make allotments to their subordinate units. The revenue sub-districts or *talukas* were, on the other hand, recognized as the smallest local boards in Bombay, where districts happened to be smaller. In Bengal the establishment of District Boards was made compulsory, while that of sub-divisional boards permissive. The Bengal Act also provided for the establishment of union committees, which came into existence in some places. The laws enacted for the United Provinces, the Punjab and North-West Frontier Provinces also contemplated the formation of sub-district boards. These, however, never came into existence in the North-West Frontier Provinces. The Punjab created these in some districts, while in U.P., after an experimental attempt, the plan was given up altogether in 1905. Provision was made in the Central Provinces for the organization of the district into 'Circles' of villages (the smallest unit) and 'groups' of circles (corresponding to the *taluka* board in Bombay), which were subordinate to the District Board. In Assam the sub-division itself was made the unit for local board administration.

Administrative Decentralization in the Districts for Development

Generally, administrative decentralization meant a devolution of decision-making authority from the Centre to the provinces, and, within a province, from the Secretariat to the districts. In the districts themselves it involved a readjustment in the relationship between the officers of general administration and the heads of special departments which had over the years been growing, though slowly, as a result of the state's developmental activity, a phenomenon which under Lord Curzon had acquired an importance unknown before.

The necessity of such a readjustment in the generalist-specialist relationship was felt all the more after the establishment of a number of all-India specialized services. The organization of the specialized functionaries into separate services and their respective hierarchies on principles comparable to those of the Civil Service was a sound step in terms of the discipline and efficiency of personnel administration. But it encouraged a separatist attitude for departmental autonomy, which meant reduction of Civilian dominance in the administration of the districts. Since specialists of the Imperial category were yet to be posted in the districts (apart from the Indian Medical Service and the Indian Service of Engineers), only members of the provincial and subordinate services were called upon to deal with officers of the Indian Civil Service. Low in status and standing, they could not but remian subject to the power and influence of the I.C.S. Collectors. Local administrative independence and decentralization in these circumstances was thus not possible.

Existing Position: Supremacy of the Collector

According to the Royal Commission on Decentralization (1909) British India contained more than 250 districts. Their number and size in the eight major Provinces were as follows:[42]

Province	Area (sq. miles)	Inhabitants (in millions)	Number of Districts
Madras	142	38	23
Bombay	123	19	25
Bengal	116	51	34
E. Bengal and Assam	99	30	27
U.P.	107	48	48
Punjab	97	20	29
Burma	170	9	37
C.P. (with Berar)	100	12	22

The average area of a district at the time of the Commission's report was 4,430 square miles, and the average population 931,000, but the actual districts varied greatly in both size and population. They were largest in Burma and Madras, and smallest in the United Provinces.

As in 1859 and thereafter each district was under a Collector who was also the District Magistrate. His responsibility as Collector not only covered the collection of most branches of the revenue, but also included the management of relations between the Government and the rural population, especially disputes between landlords and tenants as well as mutation, registration and partition of lands paying revenue directly to the Government. As pointed out in Chapter II, the Collector watched over the general circumstances of his district, especially in times of famine or severe agricultural distress and introduced measures of relief including the grant of agricultural loans, the control of prices and the movement of trade. These functions had a direct bearing on the economic interest of the people. It was with this end in view that the Collector was invested with the preparation of agricultural and other statistics as well as with the administration of forests in the district.

In working with municipalities, the Collector often functioned as the actual chairman or presiding officer of one or more of them. He also presided over the district board, which, with the aid of subordinate local boards, if any, maintained roads, schools and dispensaries, and dealt with vaccination and sanitary improvements in rural areas.

As District Magistrate, he continued to be responsible for all matters affecting the peace of the district, and exercised general supervision over local police officers. He was, in addition, invested with control over subordinate criminal courts, with the exercise of some original and appellate jurisdiction in the trial of criminal cases and the punishment of offences up to a maximum limit of two years of imprisonment.

Each district was split into a number of sub-divisions, constituting the charge either of junior officers of the Indian Civil Service, or officers of the Provincial Civil Service, called Deputy Collectors or Extra Assistant Commissioners. In Bengal the Collector himself held direct charge of the head-sub-division of a district, while there were only a few sub-divisions in the Punjab. The duties of Sub-divisional Officers, who were magistrates as well as revenue and executive officers, varied in different provinces. But these were highly developed in Madras and Bombay, where they exercised, within their own charge, most of the functions of a Collector, subject, no doubt, to supervision by, and appeal to, the latter.

Except in Bengal there were smaller sub-district units, known as *talukas* or *tahsils*. These were administered by *tahsildars* who belonged to the subordinate service. They were under the immediate control of the Sub-divisional Officer, where there was one, and were assisted by *naib tahsildars*, revenue inspectors and *kanungos* who all formed part of revenue establishments and had direct relations with the cultivators and village officials.

The revenue and general administration of the country which handled law and order as well as the manifold relations of the Government with the people, constituted the main responsibilities of the civil service which, according to the arrangement of 1892,[43] was divided into Imperial (Indian), Provincial and Subordinate categories, the last two being recruited in India. Members of the Indian Civil Service were mostly Commissioners, Collectors and Deputy Commissioners, District and Sessions Judges, and Secretaries to the Government. Its junior men, on the other hand, were in training for higher jobs, functioning generally as Assistants to Collectors or as Sub-divisional Officers. On first arrival in India they were assigned to different Provinces, but, as the Indian Civil Service formed a single service for the whole country, they could be borrowed by the Government of India or for temporary service in another Province.

Each province had its own Provincial and Subordinate Services. But while it had a free hand in the choice of the latter, the rules governing appointment to the former had to receive the approval of the Government of India. For, besides being responsible for the discharge of duties in their capacity as Deputy Collectors, Extra Assistant Commissioners and Sub-Judges, some were eligible for a certain number of 'listed' appointments, such as those of Collector or District Judge, ordinarily held by the I.C.S. Officers. As said before, similar distinctons were recognized in the Services concerned with special departments also.

Prior to 1855, when the Public Works Department (Civil) and the Directorate of Education were established, Collectors and their subordinates were responsible for all the administrative work of their districts, subject to the superintendence of Commissioners and Boards of Revenue. As said before, separate special departments came to be established in the course of nearly fify years after that. The important ones were those which dealt with Public Works, Educaton, Police, Forest, Medical Administration, Sanitation, Prisons and Agriculture. They had their own separate staffs and heads in each Province, who were generally styled as Inspectors-General or Directors. These departmental heads were in direct subordination to Local Governments. As already stated, the Chief Engineer of the Public Works Department in each Province was also Secretary to Government. The other heads of special departments addressed reports and letters to one or other of the Civilian Secretaries.

The districts, however, remained ill-equipped in so far as the staffing pattern of their special departments was concerned. For, as already stated, members of the all-India superior services in the field of development did not in most cases reach down to the district level. The jurisdiction of the principal local officers of the P.W.D., for instance, did not necessarily correspond with district or divisional limits. So was the case with Inspectors of Schools who belonged to the Indian Educational Service. The Collector was doubtless concerned with sanitation, medical relief and elementary education. But this was principally in his capacity as President of the District Board. There were, no doubt, other officers who worked in close co-operation with the ordinary district staff, but they were I.C.S. officers who did not form part of the district staff. They functioned under the Board of Revenue, or Financial Commissioner, where either existed. The supremacy of the Collector in the administration of his district remained unimpaired. The position assigned to him by the Law Member of the Government of India in 1872 and the Indian Famine Commission in 1880 continued without a break until Curzon. He acted for all practical purposes as 'the Government'. Despite the increasing load of business no attempt was sought to be made to withdraw from him 'that general control which invests him in the eyes of the people with the position of the local head of the Civil Government'.[44]

In all the major Provinces except Madras, the districts were grouped into divisions, with each division placed under the general superintendence of a Commissioner whose office had been created in 1829. In Bombay there was no Board of Revenue acting as an intermediate authority between Commissioners and the Local Government. In other Provinces a Board of Revenue or a single Financial Commissioner existed to control the revenue work of Commissioners and Collectors.[45]

General-Specialist Controversy

The situation which led to the emergence of the generalist-specialist controversy, proceeded from the growth of special departments and the organization of the several all-India services intended to man them. These departments and their administrative services were an expression of the growth of science and technology which tended to be reflected in the administrative rationalization of the second half of the nineteenth century.[46] They expanded and functioned with considerable vigour under the initiative and direction given to them by Lord Curzon.

If the country's economy and society were to be developed, specialization in administration was a necessity. Curzon realized this, and, as shown before, made frantic efforts to build the necessary expertise.

The agency employed to promote scientific research for rural development was the bureaucracy—generalist administrators on whom Curzon relied for the execution of his schemes. But in providing incentives for the growth of separate specialized hierarchies he was creating certain antithetical situations the implications of which were perhaps not very clear at the time. There was, for example, the grave risk of specialized departments pursuing their own course without reference to other departments, or their impact on the people as a whole, a risk which the generalist should, in fact, have sought to avoid. The problem was all the more obvious in a society notorious for an imbalance in the distribution of educational and economic benefits: the bulk of the people preferred a local officer whom they could approach with general grievances rather than a collection of specialized departments. The growth of administrative specialization in the midst of an unsophisticated and illiterate mass of people would not only serve the interest of a small élitist and monied minority, but could also obstruct an integrated approach to rural development. A local co-ordinating authority was in fact essential in the existing conditions of Indian society; it is true that one of the main functions of Provincial Governments was to provide this co-ordination and 'to check undue departmental zeal at the secretariat level'. But, as the Royal Commission on Decentralization rightly said: 'it cannot, we consider, do this thoroughly in respect of the district administration.'[47]

The need for co-ordination at the local level arose from a variety of reasons. The Public Works Department, for instance, was concerned with carrying out works on behalf of other departments for which the Chief Engineer and Superintending Engineers were invested with the allotment of funds. There was special need for co-ordination in the choice of works and their execution, but this was at times sadly wanting. Complaints occurred where Commissioners and Deputy Commissioners (Collectors) suggested the need for certain buildings and roads. But since the allotment of funds did not proceed from them, their advice was either not taken, or, even when they were consulted, they were not informed about the progress made. The Chief Commissioner of the Central Provinces thus remarked 'that it is often impossible for the Deputy Commissioner or Commissioner to say what works are in progress at any given time. He sometimes finds a building completed which he did not know was begun, and another work which he believed to be in progress not started, the money having been directed to some other purpose by some superior authority in the Public Works Department'.[48] In the matter of roads, however, the Collector exercised more or less full control in nearly every province as President of the District Board. In Madras, Bengal and eastern Bengal road operations fell almost entirely within the sphere of district and sub-divisional boards. In other provinces the more important roads were provincial, but the Collector was consulted even though the budget allotment for each district was prepared at the provincial headquarters.

Irrigation was another field where proper co-ordination was needed. In Madras, for instance, the Public Works Department was concerned with the distribution of water to a point just above that at which it reached the *raiyat's* fields, not with the supply of water to the fields or with assessments or remissions. The Madras Government's view was that the Public Works Department must be subordinate to the Collector in non-professional matters affecting the *raiyats*, and especially so in regard to the distribution of water and the repair of tanks. The general consensus was that, as the Collector was responsible for the realization of the revenue, he must also have a voice in the distribution of water, especially when the *raiyats* approached him and his Subdivisional Officer with grievances against Irrigation officers. In Bombay, too, appeals in certain matters connected with the supply of water lay from Irrigation Officers to the Collector. Engineering considerations alone do not govern the success of an irrigation work, for much depends on an intimate knowledge of traditional customs, prejudices and methods which a civil servant can better appreciate thanks to his wider experience of human affairs.

Similarly, measures which might commend themselves from the purely scientific angle of a forest expert, could cause grave discontent amongst hill tribes or the agricultural population in the plains. In

Madras, the District Forest Officer was therefore subordinate to the Collector in all matters affecting the people. The position was theoretically the same in other Provinces, but the subordination of the Forest Officer was neither complete nor well defined. The Royal Commission on Decentralization thus emphasized that 'in all matters which bring the forest administration into relations with the agricultural population, the District Forest Officer should be made definitely and clearly the assistant of the Collector' who should be entitled to give direct orders in regard to such matters'.[49]

The importance of a local co-ordinating authority was also underlined by the need to check fissiparous tendencies among specialists themselves. Antagonism between specialized departments was specially marked in the subordinate ranks, and needed to be halted on the spot to ensure their smooth functioning. On the strength of evidence, the Commission was convinced that this could only be done by reference to the Collector or the Commissioner.

But the increasing administrative rationalization and the ideological liberalism of an expanding capitalist economy under imperial restrictions that accompanied the growth of science and technology after 1858, was bound to change the old system of patriarchal rule by the Collector. The gradual emergence of special departments and the establishment of specialized superior services, which tended to weaken that system, were an inevitable accompaniment of new developments in the country's administration, economy and culture. Indeed, specialization was an historical necessity and bound to increase, as it did, as an instrument of economic and cultural development as well as administrative change.

However, specialization did not necessarily involve decentralization, and on the contrary, tended to result in centralization. The degree of centralization involved in technical advice led a number of Local Governments to express 'grave apprehension' and urge that they 'ought to be heard before the Government of India took any administrative decision upon the opinion of these [expert] officers'.[50]

The concern about centralization applied with equal, if not greater, force to the situation in the districts, where provincial expertise seemed to claim a similar pre-eminence in district affairs. Troubles were bound to arise when provincial experts crossed the limits of their advisory function and sought to claim primacy over the authority of the Collector in districts where respect for the Collector's authority had acquired the prescriptive sanction of history. In the field of district administration this respect for tradition and the Collector's overall responsibility reinforced a tendency towards restoring to the Collector, as the main instrument of rural welfare, some of the powers and prestige which the establishment of special departments and their own separate services had eroded.

The evidence taken before the Royal Commission on Decentralization shows that, while some officials were satisfied with the existing powers of Collectors, others held that larger powers would be undesirable. What was required according to them was 'not so much the bestowal of wider powers on Collectors as the grant of greater finality of decision in matters which they already deal with'. There was, however, a considerable body of opinion 'in favour of enhancing the position of Collectors'. This was especially mentioned to the Commission by the Punjab Government which suggested that 'action should be taken, *inter alia*, in the direction of restoring the influence of Collectors over the special departments, giving greater finality to their orders, and granting them larger financial powers'. Even Gokhale, the eminent Liberal leader, favoured the Punjab proposal, subject only to Collectors being in some way associated 'with the representatives of the people in the work of administration',[51] a condition which was sought to be taken care of to some extent in their relations with rural boards, if not to special departments.

The Collector and Special Departments

Problems in the relationship between the Collector and special departments arose, as said before, from the monolithic character of district administration being affected by the inevitable growth of specialization. To maintain the unity of district administration the Collector was recognized as its administrative head functioning under the Commissioner as the administrative head of his division. He was to be consulted and to have certain powers of control over the operations of special departments in so far as these tended to affect general administration or the welfare of the people, care being taken at the same time to avoid interference with technical details of a purely professional nature. The Royal Commission on Decentralization emphasized the observance of this principle as a guide to integrated development; for in view of the existence of separate service hierarchies the officers of special departments could not but otherwise remain independent of the Collector. They were in fact no subordinate to him in any departmental sense, except that he, like the

Commissioner, was entitled to call for information. They were, in addition, expected to give the fullest consideration to the Collector's views. The Commission felt that if this principle was recognized, the danger of the Collector's powers being unduly sapped by the specialized departments would be obviated and integration achieved in rural development.

But drawing a line between technical details and matters of general importance was not easy. Indeed, it was a Herculean task to achieve integrated growth under disintegrated patterns of politics and society. The Royal Commission on Decentralization was not wrong when it said that 'for harmonious working, we must trust in the last resort to common sense [though unsually uncommon], tact, and loyal co-operation as between the different servants of Government'.[52]

Advisory Councils for Collectors

The idea that Collectors should have Advisory Councils to assist them in their work was essentially non-official in origin. It was conceived as a device to enable district officers to know popular reactions to official measures. It was a Liberal reaction to revolutionary and agitational politics. When the idea was mooted and witnesses examined before the Royal Commission on Decentralization, Gokhale and non-official opinion was generally against them.[53]

Very few of those who advocated the Councils wanted them to be purely elected. Those who wanted them partly elected were in a majority, but others favoured their being altogether nominated. For these Councils were at the time being looked upon not so much as instruments of rural development as bodies for the recommendation of measures either to mitigate economic distress or satisfy certain interests through a reduction of rates. It was, for instance, suggested that Advisory Councils should be 'consulted about matters of general policy and proposed legislation, revenue settlements and the remission and suspension of revenue, famine and measures against epidemics, education, and religious and caste disputes'. To these were added for consideration such other questions as income tax, irrigation, liquor shops, police and management of estates by the Court of Wards.[54]

Opinion was fairly evenly divided on the question of whether the Councils should be purely advisory or vested with powers to see that their advice was made binding. The bulk of the non-official witnesses felt that where a Collector was at variance with the majority of the

Council, he should either accept its decision or refer the matter to higher authority. Some witnesses, including Gokhale, discriminated between matters in which a Collector or Commissioner might act on his own discretion, and matters in which he must accept or refer to the Council's recommendation. Risley, the Home Secretary, was in principle prepared to recognize a somewhat similar division of subjects, though at the outset he favoured purely advisory Councils.

The general argument in favour of associating representatives of the people with the actual work of administration was that it would not merely popularize the Government, but would also permit the delegation of powers to Collectors, to be exercised in the districts under some degree of popular restraint. Generally, however, Advisory Councils were being viewed as an arrangement that might enable Government officers, and the government itself, to acquire a clear insight into the people's feelings about policy and administrative matters.

There were also witnesses who saw in the proposed Councils the opportunity for non-officials to share the executive responsibilities of the Collector or Commissioner. R.C.Dutt, formerly of the Indian Civil Service and a Member of the Commission, for instance, held that an Advisory Council with such responsibilities would make district administration more efficient and popular. His argument was that the isolation of the existing district administration, which virtually constituted one-man rule, was 'the real cause of much discontent in India, and to invest the Collector with larger powers, as we recommend in this Report, without some provision to associate the people with him in his general work, would create discontent and dissatisfaction among the people'.[55] Thus, while European members of the Commission favoured the delegation of larger powers to the Collector as a local co-ordinating agency for integrated development, Dutt injected into it a political dimension and viewed the proposed Advisory Council as a popular agency to share the Collector's executive responsibilities.

The Commission finally agreed with those who spoke against a separate Advisory Council for the Collector. It accepted the alternative suggestion that the existing District Boards were convenient sources of advice for the Collector upon matters which, although not included in their administrative sphere, affected the district generally. The Commission noted that some Collectors had already begun making use of their District Boards which, besides leading officials, included representative non-officials. The Commission feared the potential danger of divided authority in district administration, a danger which might prejudice not only law and order, but also the progress of rural development; it therefore, agreed with those who expressed themselves against separate Advisory Councils for Collectors.

Separate Councils were also not recommended for Commissioners. To co-ordinate the work of various departments and to promote speed in decision-making the Commission suggested regular resort to the conferences of Commissioners and Collectors. The system of periodical conferences between Commissioners already existed in Bombay, and had developed more fully in Bengal under Sir Andrew Fraser, its Lieutenant-Governor. The Bengal system involved a conference every autumn for about a fortnight. It was attended not merely by Commissioners, but also members of the Board of Revenue, Secretaries to the Government and heads of provincial departments. Non-officials of standing, such as members of the Legislative Council, were also invited to attend certain discussions. The minutes of the conference were submitted to the Lieutenant-Governor who attended it before it dissolved and explained his personal views on important matters involved in the discussions.

The Commission recommended the extension to other provinces of a similar system. For, as it said, a 'Conference of this sort, bringing Commissioners into periodical touch with one another and with officials at headquarters, as also with non-official gentlemen of standing, gives great assistance in the disposal of matters which would otherwise take up much correspondence, and affords opportunity for full and friendly interchange of opinion.'[56] Likewise, the Commissioners of a province were to meet periodically. The result of their joint consultation was sought to be referred to the Local Government, especially on such questions as dealt with policy and administrative procedure.

In Bengal the annual provincial conference was preceded by Conferences of the Collectors meeting under the presidency of their Commissioners. The Commission's suggestion was that if, besides Collectors, these divisional conferences were to include 'the principal local officers' of the several departments which come into close touch with the people, with the admission of certain 'non-officials of standing from the different districts' during particular discussions, they should be of 'great service'. Together they would, it was believed, 'put the Commissioner in fuller possession of the views of the men with whom he has to work, would help to co-ordinate the work of the various departments, would bring the Collectors into touch with each other's views and difficulties, and would lead to closer contact with representative non-official opinion'.[57]

It is clear that by the time the Commission presented its *Report* on decentralization in 1909 the urgency of departmental co-ordination and the importance of closer non-official contact had both come to be realized. While the establishment of special departments was the first to impinge on the dominance of the Collector, the non-official pressure for a share in power came next but drove in the same direction. Together they cast their weight in favour of decentralization. But the exigencies of administrative co-ordination which called for unity of command, dictated otherwise. The co-ordinating authority of the Collector and the unity of his command were, therefore, sought to be protected against encroachment from both the specialists and the projected Advisory Councils.

As already noted, even the local boards which Lord Ripon created in 1882 remained pervaded with bureaucratic influence. According to the Decentralization Commission, public opinion went so far as to say that these boards had practically become a department of the Government administration'. The Commission recognized that such criticism regarding the actual functioning of rural boards contained 'a large element of truth'.[58] The Indian Civil Service had an exclusive control of district administration.

The Commission felt that as far as the work of rural development was concerned, the difficulty of European officers was that they were not 'sufficiently accessible' to the rural masses. Indian officers too were in most cases no exception, but the disabilities of European officers were especially marked because of their differences of race, creed, habits and upbringing. Apart from the question of contact with the people in general, the manner in which a non-official Indian was treated and received by district officers is indicated in one of the recommendations made by the Decentralization Commission with a view to cultivating good and friendly relations:[59]

Much may be done to promote more cordial relations by friendly gatherings at which Indian gentlemen can appear without detriment to caste rules, while district officers should, as far as possible, have regular times set apart for the reception of visitors, for whom suitable waiting rooms should be provided. Complaint has been made that the absence of these compels Indian gentlemen of position desiring to see a district official who may not be immediately at leisure, to wait in the sun, or in an open verandah, along with Government *Chaprasis* and other menials.

The Decentralization Commission recommended a series of measures aimed at the relaxation of control by the higher authorities, involving at the same time a simplification of certain administrative methods. Between 1910 and 1917 the desired relaxation of control was effected in a multitude of details. Much was done both to free local bodies from official interference as well as to delegate increased powers to the heads of departments both in the Government of India and Local Governments. But all these measures were taken within the framework of the Morley-Minto changes, a political framework based on 'constitutional autocracy' which supplied a requisite counterpoise' to the increasing influence of 'the educated and professional classes' by 'creating an additional electorate recruited from the landed and monied classes and from the Muhammadans',[60] with an official majority to prevent any change of government in the event of an adverse vote.[61]

Partial Provincial Autonomy (Dyarchy)

In so far as rural development was concerned, middle class Indian leadership stood opposed to legislation aimed to serve the rural poor. It wanted to control the legislative machinery of the Government to promote its own interest. The educated and professional élites constituted by far the most influential section of society and their demand for *swaraj* which the National Congress adopted in 1906 could be delayed but not altogether be ignored. Provincial autonomy on parliamentary principles, which constituted an important step in the direction of political decentralization for purposes of rural development, could not but be recognized as an immediate goal. The famous announcement made on behalf of the British Government on 20 August 1917[62] declared the goal to be 'that of increasing association of Indians in every branch of the administration and the general development of self-governing institutions with a view to the progressive realization of responsible government in India as an integral part of the British Empire', the time and manner of each successive advance being determined by the British Parliament itself.

The announcement was followed by the Montagu-Chelmsford Report which was published in July 1918. It recommended the grant of some measure of responsibility to popular representatives in the provinces on the basis of four principles, viz., (1) almost complete popular control over local bodies; (2) the beginning of some measure of responsible government in the provinces involving a great deal of legislative, administrative and financial decentralization from the

Government of India; (3) the continuance of the responsibility of the Government of India wholly to Parliament, pending experience of the effect of the changes to be introduced in the provinces, and (4) the proportionate relaxation of the control of Parliament and the Secretary of State over the Government of India and the Provincial Governments as the foregoing changes took effect. The Government of India Act 1919 was passed by Parliament broadly within the ambit of these principles.

The devolution of authority to Local Governments was effected under the Devolution Rules made under the Act. They applied to the legislative, administrative and financial spheres of nine major provinces which the Act called Governor's Provinces: Madras, Bombay, Bengal, the United Provinces, Punjab, Bihar and Orissa, the Central Provinces, Assam and Burma. In each of these the demarcation between the Central and Provincial fields was identical. In the subdivision of Provincial subjects into 'reserved' and 'transferred' categories, however, there were certain variations from one province to another.

The list of Provincial subjects included local self-government; medical administration and public health; education (with certain exceptions); public works and irrigation; agriculture and land revenue administration; forest and famine relief; police, prisons and the administration of justice; the civil veterinary department and co-operative societies; excise; registration of deeds and documents as well as of births and deaths; religious endowments; industries; local fund audit; fisheries and sources of provincial revenues.

The most important transferred subjects included local self-government; public health; sanitation; medical administration; education; public works; agriculture and fisheries; co-operative socities; industries; excise (alcoholic liquor and intoxicating drugs only); and forests (in Bombay and Burma only). The main reserved subjectes, on the other hand, were irrigation; land revenue administration; justice; police and prisons; factory inspection; labour disputes; industrial insurance; control of newspapers, books and printing presses; The reserved subjects were to be administered by the Governor and his Executive Council containing in practice two Indians out of a total of four members, and the transferred subjects by popular Ministers chosen by the Governor from the elected members of the Provincial Legislative Council. This distribution of executive powers between the Governor in Council and Governor acting with the advice of his

Ministers responsible to the Provincial Legislature was called dyarchy. The transferred subjects under Ministers were mainly of 'nation-building' character involving a positive welfare dimension of the State's activity.

Provisions existed within the 1919 Act itself for extended delegation of authority to the Government of India as well as the transfer of reserved subjects to the administration of the Governor acting with popular Ministers to promote the development of nation-building subjects. As regards the Civil Service, there was a general tendency to make it subject to legislative control.[63]

The provisions which had gone into the making of the Act were in fact recognition of the new social and economic forces emerging from conditions created by the Great War (1914-18). In a private letter of 2 May 1917 the Secretary of State, Sir Austen Chamberlain, clearly suggested to the Viceroy in India the importance of these conditions as a prelude to constitutional changes. 'After all', he said, 'we must take account of the changes produced by this war, of the constant emphasis laid upon the fact that the Allies are fighting for freedom and nationality, of the Revolution in Russia, and the way it has been hailed throughout Europe and America, and of the effect of all these things on Indian opinion and on our own attitude to Indian questions. What would have been a great advance a little time ago, would now satisfy no one, and we must, I think, be prepared for bold and radical measures.'[64] The manner in which the goal of British policy on Indian questions was formulated is indicated by Sir Austen's private papers themselves. It emerged from private consultations among Edwin Montagu, Sir Austen Chamberlain and Lord Curzon, whom the Cabinet recognized as the real spokesman on Indian affairs. The announcement of 20 August 1917 was a result of their joint consultation.

But the bureaucracy Curzon had reared when Viceroy became the real barrier to change within the Act. A couple of years after his Viceroyalty, Morley accused the bureaucracy of a 'professional contempt and suspicion against the inexpert outsider'.[65] Montagu who took over as Secretary of State after Sir Austen Chamberlain, held a similar view. Writing in his diary on 30 November, 1917, for instance, he noted: 'In my opinion the root cause of the whole problem is the profound distrust . . . shown by the Civil Servant of the Indian, and the Indian of the Civil Servant'.[66]

And yet the bureaucracy was not without a case of its own. As a body of organized and trained administrators it took into account the authoritarian and divisive character of Indian society which called for executive interposition to ensure peace and justice among the different classes of the country's population. It was strongly opposed to any step that Edwin Montagu, the Secretary of State, might take to divest himself of control over the executive authority in India, a control which the Civil Service was otherwise authorized to exercise independently of any legislature and subject only to the head of the executive government. In its opposition to such divestment the bureaucracy was helped by certain important developments in Indian politics leading to the non-cooperation movement, the arrest of Gandhi and the resignation of Montagu himself. The Swarajists who soon came out with a slogan to wreck the new constitution from within, lent additional justification to the bureaucracy's go-slow advice.

Developmental Task Politically Involved In Democracy-Bureaucracy Dichotomy

The refusal of the British Government at the instance of the bureaucracy in India to extend the list of transferred subjects and further constitutional reforms became not only the central issue in national politics, but also a bone of contention between Ministers and their Secretaries. Together these factors seriously impeded the progress of development in the transferred field. The emphasis shifted to power politics involving issues of law and order in the administration of the districts.

In the dichotomy that so developed the advantage remained on the side of nationalism and democracy, with the bureaucracy ill at ease though not without some initiative. The bureaucracy succeeded in intercepting further constitutional advance in the direction of responsible government, but had to await the recommendations of the Indian Statutory Commission and the Round Table Conference that followed. The scope for the exercise of power by Indian Ministers remained in effect limited to the transferred subjects in the provinces, and there too it did not extend to financial and disciplinary powrs, which continued to be exercised on behalf of the Secretary of State by the Governor-General and the Governors. And although the elected members of legislatures felt likewise cramped constitutionally, the bureaucracy could not but recognize the force of the continuing struggle for power ranging beyond the four walls of legislative chambers.

The legislative chambers in fact themselves became a common forum for propaganda against European predominance in the Indian Civil Service.[67] On 9 May 1921, when the non-co-operation movement was in progress, the Home Member of the Government of India recorded a Note, justifying a policy of reducing the number of Europeans employed not only in the Indian Civil Service but also in the other All India Imperial Services recruited in England. He was conscious of 'the efficiency and the integrity' of these Services being considerably affected, but none the less argued that 'political necessity' dictated the expediency of such a course.[68] These and other questions relating to the Imperial Services have been examined in some depth in *The Bureaucracy in India*. Politics led to a steady erosion in the morale and integrity of the Indian Civil Service which, on account of admission to it from the Provincial and other levels. had come to be 'a collection of separate services, by 1925 and ceased to be a compact body in terms of its original object based on competition alone.[69] Under the recommendations of the Lee Commission appointed in 1923 provisions were made not only for 20 per cent of the superior I.C.S. posts being filled with Provincial Service officers, but also for the provincialization of all those Imperial Services which functioned in the transferred field and administered development departments. These included the Indian Educational Service, the Indian Agricultural Service, the Indian Veterinary Service, the Indian Forest and the Indian Forest Engineering Services in Burma and Bombay, the Indian Medical Service (Civil) and the Roads and Buildings Branch of the Indian Service of Engineers. They were to cease being All-India Services from 1925 onwards and their recruitment and disciplinary powers came to be vested in the Local Governments. It meant an extension of the area of patronage which Ministers could use to their advantage. It also meant a material decline in the standards of recruitment and conditions of service. The only safeguard, though of a temporary duration, was that no change was to be made in the position of the existing members of these developmental services. They were to retain all the rights of officers of an All-India Service, and to receive such concessions in pay, pension, allowances and other matters as were sanctioned for corresponding All-India Services in the reserved field of administration. However, the cumulative effect of provincialization as a form of Indianizing these services was doubtless a loss of efficiency and their all-India standards of public conduct. Though administratively unsound and politically inexpedient in the long run, this provincial tendency was encouraged by Indian politicians as an easy means to acquire immediate control over the higher echelons of the bureaucracy as well as the technical services. In their haste and quest for power and patronage they little realized that the All-India Services not only kept the standard of recruitment high, but also preserved the political unity of the country.

State of Certain Special Departments Reviewed

The predominance of imported European expertise in special departments was a result of their unprecedented expansion under Lord Curzon whose administration was 'marked by a great period of investigatory and constructive activity'. But as this activity was not matched by a corresponding effort to produce indigenous talents to man specialized departments, exclusive dependence on trained Europeans from abroad was the only alternative if various schemes of development were to make any headway.

Agriculture. In the Department of Agriculture the increase of expert staff was specially marked between 1901 and 1905. Even so, the Secretary of State was requested to sanction further extension. John Morley, who had taken over as Secretary of State in December 1905, sounded caution. While, as noted earlier, he approved the appointment of Civilian Directors of Agriculture in the Provinces as a temporary expedient, with a suggestion that the Indian Agricultural Service should be able to provide its own chiefs, he warned that European experts should be 'closely restricted' and that the development of agriculture should be effected 'by means of an indigenous agency'.[70]

Despite this, the strength of experts from abroad went on increasing. For instance, only one Imperial Agricultural Chemist (Dr. J.W. Leather) had been appointed on a permanent basis in 1892. No further provision was made for any expert until J. Mollison was appointed Inspector-General of Agriculture on 14 October 1901. The total number of European experts appointed under Curzon between 1901 and 1905 rose to 17, including the Director of the Agricultural Research Institute and Principal of the Agricultural College at Pusa (B. Coventry) who was appointed on 1 April 1904. By 1910, the special appointments held by experts in the Imperial and Provincial Agricultural Departments reached a total of 58. Of these, 17 were in the Imperial Department of Agriculture (All European) and others in the Provinces, with only one Indian (Bhopal Chandra Ishan) holding the post of Deputy Director of Agriculture in Eastern Bengal and

Assam.[71] This total number excluded the Directors of Agriculture in the Provinces, posts which were invariably held by Civilians.

As regards the distribution of specialists among the Provinces, Madras was given the maximum number, while the North-West Frontier Province the minimum, as shown below:

Madras	8	experts
Bombay	5	"
United Provinces	5	"
Bengal	4	"
Punjab	4	"
Burma	4	"
Central Provinces	5	"
Eastern Bengal and Assam	5	"
North-West Frontier Province	1	"
Total	41	"

The Departments of Agriculture in the Provinces continued to be headed by Civilian Directors, although the Secretary of State had earlier expressed a view that the Indian Agricultural Service should itself supply the necessary requirements: When consulted by the Government of India the bureaucracy of Local Governments had expressed themselves generally in favour of continuing the existing arrangement, while in some provinces it was thought 'that a Civilian would always be preferable to an expert'.[72] The Government of India too agreed with the Local Governments and advised the Secretary of State to approve the existing practice. The Secretary of State was thus faced with a *fait accompli*, with no alternative but to accept it. But he continued to prefer specialists over Civilians and in a letter of 12 May 1911 refuted the contrary view by pointing out that those who held it, did not take 'account of the discouraging effect on a service of the exclusion of its members from the departmental headships'. It was regrettable, he averred, that it would even justify 'a much more extensive employment of Civilian control in all special departments of the administration than in practice is found to be necessary or expedient'. He expressed unhappiness over the recommendation of the Government of India itself, which he described as 'of a more restricted character', for it favoured the continuance of Civilian control 'without limitation of time'.

The Home authorities were thus seriously handicapped by the bureaucracy in India in the choice of an alternative. The Secretary of State agreed that in view of the Agricultural Departments being 'young and inexperienced Civilian Directors are necessary.' However, he added that 'full opportunity should be given to agricultural officers, as time goes on, of proving their fitness for the post; and that they should be tried as temporary vacancies occur'. The Government of India was advised to see that in authorizing the Loal Governments to appoint Civilian Directors it 'should instruct them to this effect', and so appoint them only 'so long as there is no agricultural officer in the province suitable for appointment'.[73]

In a general circular of 16 June 1911 the Local Governments were accordingly advised. But, surprisingly, about a month later followed an 'Order in Council' dated 21 July 1911 which said that 'the post of Inspector-General of Agriculture be abolished as a separate appointment', an order which also recommended the abolition of the posts of two other Inspectors-General belonging to the Veterinary Forest Departments. It was further ordered that the posts being abolished were to cease existing from 31 March 1912. The only condition attached to the 'Order in Council', was that 'a report be sent to the Secretary of State' and that 'the officers who are to lose their appointments be warned that this report has been made'.[74] Morley had by now quit the India Office and the Marquis of Crewe had taken over as Secretary of State, with Hardinge as Viceroy of India.

Finance Despatch No. 203, which the Government of India addressed to the Secretary of State on 17 August 1911, justified the abolition only partially on grounds of 'the urgent necessity for economy' arising from 'the approaching loss of our opium revenue'. But savings were not the determining factor, for the Government of India based its proposals 'on administrative rather than on purely financial considerations'.[75]

The despatch appreciated the 'theoretical efficiency', which the office of Inspector-General of Agriculture was supposed to have provided Local Governments through a uniform standard of technical advice acquired from a comparative study of other provincial systems. However,

> Advice to Local Governments tends to crystallize into instructions which may engender misunderstanding and resentment. The inclusion of technical knowledge into the Imperial Secretariat is a temptation to interference in detail at the risk of obscuring larger issues of policy. Efforts after uniformity deprive us of the lessons to be learnt from the variety of experiment for which India presents invaluable opportunities. And it has to be remembered that the very highest of efficiency, treated as an end in itself, is a luxury which India cannot afford. We have had, and still have, inspecting officers who have taken

a just and farsighted view of their duties. They have avoided the pitfalls to which Government by experts is liable, and have done much excellent work. Our experience, however, has been unequal and we are not satisfied that the balance of advantage, in most of the branches of our work, lies on the side of powerful expert control at headquarters. It certainly tends to friction with Local Governments, and has become one of their standing grievances. The fundamental demerit, however, of our system of expert inspecting officers lies deeper in the influence which it exercises on the Central Government; and it is mainly on this ground that we are convinced that the system calls for entire revision.[76]

Thus, what the bureaucracy objected to was the influence of the expert on the Government of India, an influence which affected the predominance of the I.C.S. officers, especially at the provincial headquarters, where the work of development departments was subject to inspection by the central experts. The I.C.S. were particularly keen to have the Inspector-General of Agriculture removed, because Departments of Agriculture in the provinces were invariably headed by Civilian Directors who had earlier been sought to be replaced by suitable agricultural experts. In this clash between generalists and specialists the former could win only by striking at the root and securing the abolition of Imperial Inspectors-General on the grounds of general administrative principle.

The Government of India did not impugn the policy which had led to the creation of Inspector-Generalships. 'The policy', it said, 'was admirable' and 'designed to raise the standard of work in the Government departments and to bring them into closer touch with modern requirements'. And yet the Government of India complained to the Secretary of State that 'the dangers' underlying the arrangement of 1901 'are now coming to the surface'. Elucidating the point, its despatch of 17 August 1911 thus pointed out:

The presence at headquarters of a number of experts, with no administrative duties and with all the specialist's zeal for promoting their own subjects, exercises a steady pressure on the Imperial Government. The work of Local Governments and their Departments is subjected to scrutiny in much technical detail . . . Inquiries are made from the provinces and suggestions offered, which multiply discussion and correspondence. Secretariat establishments have to be enlarged to cope with the extra work. The pursuit of perfection thus draws us gradually into a vicious circle of extra work and extra cost.[77]

The bureaucracy in the provinces wanted immunity from expert scrutiny by the Imperial Secretariat, a desire which the generalists at the Centre agreed with: 'We ought to resist every temptation to involve the Government of India in the minutiae of administration and to free Local Governments from all avoidable interference with duties which they are competent to perform'.[78]

Of the seven Inspectors-Generals whose posts were sought to be abolished, the Secretary of State agreed to the abolition of only three, namely the Cantonment Inspecting Officer on the military side and the Inspectors-General of Agriculture and Civil Veterinary Departments connected with rural development.[79] By a Resolution adopted on 16 March 1912 the Governor-General in Council thus decided 'with the approval of the Secretary of State' that 'with effect from April 1912, the post of Inspector-General of Agriculture in India shall cease to exist as a separate appointment', a decision which had already been taken by the Order in Council of 21 July 1911. Under this Resolution, the appointment was combined with that of the Director of the Research Institute and Principal of the Agricultural College at Pusa under the title of Agricultural Adviser to the Government of India and Director of the Agricultural Research Institute, Pusa. He was authorized to exercise the functions and powers previously exercised by the Inspector-General of Agriculture in India and by the Director of the Research Institute.[80] In practice, however, the functions of the erstwhile Inspector-General of Agriculture were sought to be 'considerably restricted under the new arrangement',[81] and the Agricultural Adviser was no longer to be an integral part of the Imperial Secretariat. The newly created post soon went to an I.C.S. officer to whom additional financial powers were delegated in 1919. He was succeeded, under the immediate effect of constitutional reforms, by S. Milligan a non-I.C.S. officer who effected economy and proposed a reduction in the annual budget of the Imperial Department of Agriculture from Rs 12,13,800 for 1920-1 to Rs 8,32,500 for 1921-2; the amount was finally raised to Rs 10,16,900 by the Government of India.[82]

To promote agricultural development the Government of India had effected some financial decentralization a few weeks before the famous Indian policy announcement of 20 August 1917. Under a Resolution of 1 August the Agricultural Adviser to the Government was given additional financial powers to meet the growing and varied requirements of agricultural development in such fields as cotton, indigo, pathological entomology, physiological chemistry and agricultural bacteriology.[83]

In January 1919 the Agricultural Adviser requested the Government of India for the delegation of powers in addition to those already permissible to him under Article 278 of the Civil Account Code, with regard to the creation or abolition of permanent appointments and the revision of permanent establishments. The Government sanctioned these additional powers to the Agricultural Adviser. They included the creation of temporary appointments for a specified period on monthly salaries not exceeding Rs 250, or for a limited period of six months if the pay and allowances of the appointment officer exceeded Rs 250 a month. He could also grant an officiating officer a higher salary than authorized by the Codes, subject to a maximum of Rs 100 a month and the condition that the salary did not exceed the pay of the officer for whom the officiating hand acted. The object of these additional financial powers was to enable the Adviser to manage his department in the interest of agricultural improvement and avoid administrative delays arising from reference to higher authorities.

The constitutional changes of 1919 had an important bearing on the development of agriculture and other transferred subjects. Under political pressure the division of subjects into Central and Provincial categories and, among the latter, into 'reserved' and 'transferred' groups had been rigidly done, more or less on the supposition that these could be administered independently of one another. A Home Department (Reforms Office) file (No.41/27-Special) in fact makes it clear that the Government of India took great care not to interfere with the administration of reserved subjects; although there was no provision in the Act for a relaxation of the control of the Governor-General over Provincial reserved subjects, he acted on a policy of non-intervention to allow Provinces the largest possible independence of the Government of India, except when inter-Provincial coordination or unifromity was required.

In the provincial field provision for joint deliberations between the reserved and the transferred sides was definitely enjoined by a Rule of Business made by the Governor-General under Section 49 of the Act. But it did not become a reality in practice for political reasons; it was feared that joint decision might 'insidiously' creep in. Besides, joint deliberation often became impossible in times of political disturbance when Ministers desired to stand aside.[84] But in a time of political unrest the problems of development administration increased. The Royal Commission on Agriculture in India appointed in 1926 reported, for instance, that in the absence of co-ordination between Central and Provincial agricultural departments agricultural research in the country, a vital condition for rural development, was 'still in its infancy.[85]

It was not the intention of the Commission to suggest changes in the Constitution which might restore to the Central Government its power of superintendence, direction and control over the administration of the transferred subjects, including agriculture. It no doubt indicated the manner in which the Government of India might assist provincial governments, for example, by the establishment of a Central Bureau of Information for Irrigation, by the use of central revenues to raise the quality of a selected provincial veterinary college as a training centre, and by a revival of a Central Bureau of Statistical Information. These and other suggestions of the Commisson raised some constitutional questions, but by far its most important recommendation was the establishment of an Imperial Council of Agricultural Research, where as it pointed out, constitutional objections based on the existing distribution of functions could be met by a suitable amendment of the Devolution Rules.[86]

In making this recommendation the Commission was guided by a desire to ensure co-ordination between the departments of agriculture at the centre and in the provinces, as also to create an agency which might involve the Government of India in terms of both finance and expertise for the promotion of agricultural development. For it was realized that such development was unlikely without central assistance and provincial participation.

Under the Devolution Rules agricultural research did not fall exclusively either in the Central or the Provincial field. Under item 33 of Schedule I 'central agencies and institutions for research and for professional or technical training or promotion of special studies' remained a Central subject. By virtue of this the Government of India administered the Agricultural Research Institute at Pusa. At the same time, under item 10 of Part II of Schedule II, agriculture, including research institutes, was classified as a Provincial subject, and agricultural research was conducted by or under the Agricultural Departments of the provincial governments. Agricultural research could thus be undertaken under the existing constitution by both the central and provincial governments, but the lines on which research was carried on remained unco-ordinated. The Commission sought to remedy this by the establishment of a central agency with powers to co-ordinate research and distribute funds derived from central revenues on research to be conducted in provincial institutions. The funds so distributed were not to be in the form of subventions paid to provincial governments, but to be used to finance particular lines of research, even by private agencies or officers employed in the government. The Commission suggested that the Imperial Council of Agricultural Research administer the Agricultural Research Fund, to be created out of a grant of Rs 50 lakhs from central revenues to which additions could be made from time to time as financial conditions permitted.

The Council was to stand in exactly the same relation to central as to provincial research stations, with no research stations directly under its control or its own staff of experts. It was for the Council, however, to decide whether particular researches were of all-India or local importance and, if the former, whether they could best be carried out at Imperial or provincial research institution or entirely outside such institutions, in a university, by private persons, or even abroad. It would then make funds available for the purpose. The recruitment of staff was not to be its function, and the central or the provincial governments concerned were to do this in the ordinary way. The Council was merely to determine the qualifications required of the staff, and the grant given only on condition that the staff with the prescribed qualifications was obtained. It was also expected to bring provincial veterinary colleges into closer relations with the Imperial Institute of Veterinary Research at Mukteswar.

The Chairman of the Council was to be an experienced administrator with a knowledge, if possible, of Indian conditions. He was to be assisted by two whole time members, one a scientist, the other representing the interests of animal husbandry. These three were to draw salaries from the funds of the Council which was to comprise 36 other members who were unpaid.

The Commission compared this Council 'in some respects with the Development Commission in England', which occupied 'a position distinct from government departments in the sense that it is free to report without reference to a Minister, that its recommendations are not subject to confirmation by Parliament, and that its status and procedure are laid down by statute'.[87] However, whereas in England grants were not made by the Development Commission itself but by the Treasury on the advice of the Commission, the Council for India was to distribute grants at its own discretion.

These and other recommendations made by the Royal Commission were in principle accepted by the Government of India, though some details were modified to suit administrative requirements.[88] Under its Resolution of 23 May 1929 the Centre acknowledged that 'There is a wide field open for the co-operation of the Government of India and of Provincial Governments in regard to agricultural research' and that it was its duty 'in the discharge of their ultimate responsibility for the welfare of the vast agricultural population of this country, to advance research in every way possible without encroaching upon the functions of Provincial Governments in that sphere'. The Government of India thus agreed to the establishment of the Imperial Council of Agricultural Research as a central co-ordinating authority.

As regards the structure of the Council, the Government accepted the Commission's proposal for three whole-time Members, one being an experienced administrator and functioning as Chairman. But it felt that a Council of 39 members would be too large to be effective and that the Legislative Assembly should not be deprived of its normal constitutional control over an activity which affected the staple industry of the country. To meet these objections the Government of India by its Resolution decided to change the structure of the Council as well as the method of financing it.

The central organization was divided into two parts, executive and advisory. The executive part, the Governing Body, managed all the affairs and funds of the Council, subject to certain limitations. Contrary to the recommendation of the Royal Commission, the Resolution provided that the Member in charge of agriculture in the Governor-General's Executive Council would be *ex-officio* Chairman of the Governing Body. The executive body consisted, in addition, of the Principal Administrative Officer appointed by the Government of India as the Council's *ex-officio* Vice-Chairman, one representative of the Council of State, two representatives of the Legislative Assembly, one representative each of the European Indian business communities, two representatives of the Advisory Board, and one representative nominated by each major province. These provincial representatives were to be Ministers following a conference in October 1928, where the provincial Ministers of Agriculture expressed the view that they themselves should represent their respective provinces on the Governing Body.

There were in all 18 members on the Governing Body, including the Chairman. The Principal Administrative Officer who was the Council's *ex-officio* Vice-Chairman received the pay and status of a Secretary to the Government and the two whole-time experts on the staff of the Council were each allowed a salary of Rs 2,500-125-2,750 plus overseas pay of £13-6-8. The tenure of all three appointments was ordinarily fixed at five years, and they were not pensionable unless held by officers already in government service. The officer appointed Secretary to the Council generally had eight to ten years' standing in the I.C.S. and received Rs 400 per month in addition to his normal salary. The Government accepted the recommendation of the Commission that the post of Agricultural Adviser should be abolished on the establishment of the Council.[89] The Commission's proposal in favour of a whole-time Director for Pusa was also accepted. He was allowed the same pay and status as sanctioned for the two whole-time experts of the Council.

The Commission's recommendation of a grant of Rs 50 lakhs underwent slight modification, for the Government decided on an initial grant of Rs 25 lakhs, of which Rs 15 lakhs were provided in the budget for 1929-30. From 1930-31 onwards the annual recurring grant was put at Rs 7.25 lakhs, of which Rs 5 lakhs were to be for the furtherance of the scientific objects of the Council, and the remaining amount for the cost of its staff and secretariat. The Council was allowed to have a free hand as regards the grants made to it for research purposes, subject to the condition that it incurred no liability over such matters as leave or pension contributions after the research had been completed. The Council's grant for staff and establishment expenses was to be treated like that of any other Department of the Government of India Secretariat.

The Council of State elected V. Ramadas Pantulu as its representative on the Governing Body while the representatives elected by the Legislative Assembly were Mian Muhammad Shah Nawaz and Chaudhri Mukhtar Singh. The two other representatives elected on the Governing Body were Sir Joseph Kay and Walchand Hirachand, the former representing the Associated Chambers of Commerce of India and Ceylon and the latter the Federation of Indian Chambers of Commerce and Industry. The Governing Body, which included provincial Ministers of Agriculture and elected representatives, was thus sought to be politically broad-based, although political considerations had hardly gone into the recommendations of the Royal Commission.

The Advisory Board, however, was a body of experts only. It consisted of all those whose inclusion in the Council was recommended by the Royal Commission. In consultation with provincial governments the scientific and university representation on the Board was naturally increased. It was, for example, composed of the Vice-Chairman of the Council, the two whole-time experts, the Directors of the Pusa Research Institute, the Imperial Institute of Veterinary Research at Mukteswar, the Indian Institute of Science at Bangalore the nine provincial Directors of Agriculture, the representatives of the Veterinary Departments of the nine major provinces, a representative each of the Dehar Dun Forest Research Institute and the Co-operative Movement. The elective elements represented the Inter-University Board,[90] the Indian Planters Association, the Tea Association and the Cotton Committee. Five non-official members were also, nominated by the Government of India on the basis of scientific knowledge and special qualification. The provincial governments were advised to take early steps to constitute provincial committees on the lines suggested by the Royal Commission. The Advisory Board was designed to examine all the scientific proposals which might be submitted to the Governing Body of the Council, to report on their feasibility and advise on any other questions that might be referred to it by the Governing Body.

This detailed analysis of the organizatin of the Indian Council of Agricultural Research is intended to highlight the Council as the first central organization of its kind to function at a national level in the promotion of agricultural research for rural development. Besides, at a much deeper if general level, it throws useful light on the limitations of decentralization as an instrument of development. A process of administrative decentralization had, for example, already started with the abolition of the post of Inspector-General of Agriculture. The Agricutural Adviser to the Government of India stationed at Pusa was given more powers to expedite decisions locally without reference to the Central Secretariat. The Government of India Act (1919) and the Devolution Rules that followed provided for an unprecedented measure of decentralization in the Provincial field at both political and administrative levels. And yet agricultural development had remained in a state of 'infancy'. The main reason for this was the lack of institutional and integrate co-operation between the centre and the provinces that was being seriously affected by political agitation. The Indian Council of Agricultural Research was a non-political device to bring the centre and the provinces together for the common cause of development.

The establishment of the Council was soon followed by a further delegation of authority on the lines of the erstwhile Agricultural Adviser to the Government of India, whose post was now abolished. The Directors of the Imperial Institutes of Agricultural Research, Pusa, and Veterinary Research, Mukteswar, were both authorized to confirm officers under their control in appointments where the maximum pay did not exceed Rs 250 a month. They were also given powers to fill substantively all non-gazetted posts under them, and to grant leave to certain classes of officers, with powers to make officiating arrangements in temporary vacancies. The object was to avoid delays involved in necessary and frequent reference to the Government of India.[91] This trend towards decentralization continued in the field of agricultural administration. The provincial autonomy introduced under the Government of India Act (1935) was another important landmark which encouraged that trend for developmental purposes. Wider powers were, for instance, delegated to the Vice-Chairman, Imperial Council of Agricultural Research; the Agricultural Marketing Adviser; and the Director, Imperial Institute of Sugar Technology.[92] The process of delegating financial and administrative powers in a planned way began soon after the establishment of the Imperial Council of Agricultural Research in 1929. The powers so delegated related, in addition, to the Director, Pusa Institute, which was transferred to Delhi after the Bihar earthquake of 1934; to the Director, Imperial Veterinary Institute, Muktesar; and to the Imperial Dairy Expert.[93] The Council, in fact, marked the real beginning of agricultural research and development.

The decision to transfer the Pusa Institute to a site near the imperial capital was announced in October, 1934, a decision taken not only from considerations of the irreparable damage caused to the Phipps Laboratory, its main building, but also of Pusa having proved very inconveninet for an all-India Institute. It was isolated and the staff was likely to get out of touch with the universities and scientific workers in provincial agricultural departments. Delhi, apart from being centrally situated was also the headquarters of the Imperial Council of Agricultural Research, which enabled periodical consultation between the centre and the provinces to take place. On 19 February, 1935, the Viceroy laid the foundation stone of the new premises of the Imperial Institute of Agricultural Research near Delhi.[94]

Public Health and Medical Administration. We have noted how the interest in public health began with concern for the army and in improving the sanitary conditions of the general population living around military contonments. Rural sanitation formed no part of immediate official concern, but since the frequency of epidemics affected the health of the urban and rural population alike, sanitary commissioners were expected to move about on tour throughout their respective provinces.

In the larger provinces the Sanitary Commissioner was aided by one or more Deputy Sanitary Commissioners who were officers of the Indian Medical Service, with a subordinate staff of inspectors, sub-inspectors and other supervising agents connected with the registration of vital statistics and vaccination. The duties of a Sanitary Commissioner in smaller provinces were combined with those of Inspector-General of Civil Hospitals, the head of medical administration, who, in Madras and Bombay, was designated the Surgeon-General. The function of the Sanitary and Vaccination Department was preventive, while that of the Medical Department curative. The Civil Surgeon at the district level united in his office both preventive and curative functions. This was the formal structure of the public health department in every province. The Imperial arrangement consisted of the Sanitary Commissioner of the Government of India and the Surgeon-General.

This organization did not work well as expected. A Home Department Resolution dated 29 September 1887, for instance, noted with regret 'that the Sanitary Commissioners had not invariably shown themselves as active in the performance of their duties as the Government had a right to expect of them'. They remained confined to the headquarters and were therefore requested to impress upon the Sanitary Commissioners 'the imperative necessity of exercising vigour and activity in the discharge of their functions particularly in the work of inspection'.[95] Indeed, the two sides of the public health organization did not work in co-operation. Sanitation was 'too much separated from the Civil Medical Department which [was] responsible for the distribution of medical relief'. A Home Department Resolution of 18 June 1894 admitted that these two departments, 'though working with the same aim in view, viz., the improvement of the health and conditions of life of the civil population, have not in the past been associated together in such a manner as most efficiently to further this aim'.[96] Separatism flowed from departmentalism which tended to block co-ordination. This was reflected especially at the subordinate levels of sanitary staff in the districts where the supervising agents engaged in vaccination and other public health operations received no special education in sanitary matters. The local medical officers, too, did little to impart that education.

In these circumstances Lord Dufferin's Government issued in 1888 a Resolution drawing the attention of 'local bodies and village unions' to their duties in the matter of sanitation. Sanitary boards were also formed at the same time in every province to improve the situation. By a Home Department Resolution dated 7 June 1888[97] it was also decided that junior officers with special qualifications should in future be appointed as Sanitary Commissioners for a term of seven years, the object being to ensure vigour and regularity in the work of local inspection.

In transferring sanitary duties to municipalities and local bodies the Government, however, little realized the general powerlessness of Civil Surgeons in sanitary matters. From a body of information collected in 1894 from Civil Surgeons on the subject of municipal sanitation, it became evident that real power in sanitary matters lay wholly with the municipalities. The Government expected the Civil Surgeon in an undefined way to act as an adviser on sanitation in his district, but had not invested him with real authority to enforce his recommendations, or to see that they were carried out. As a member of the board he might use his influence to get certain proposals approved if they did not involve much expense. But, as a general rule, a Civil Surgeon could not make himself active in sanitary matters, especially because of his preoccupations with medical duties.

The consequence of the delegation of power to local authorities in sanitary matters was even more paralyzing in the absence of an authoritative system of guidance and control. A decentralized system of local self-government called for a certain degree of expertise, administrative skill and social education. But while these requisites were found wanting in those invested with sanitary responsibilities, political considerations restrained the Government from attempting to provide an authoritative instrument of control. The result was portrayed in a paper read by Dr W.J. Simpson[98] at the Indian Medical Congress held at Calcutta in December 1894:

> From a sanitary point of view it is deplorable that the introduction of local self-government should have placed the sanitary administration of the country in such a position . . . . The defect which is the most patent and the

most injurious is the total absence of any machinery to carry on local-government sanitation. The transfer of power and of duties relating to public health to local authorities, totally unacquainted with the principles or practice of preventive medicine, and the omission to provide at the same time an efficient and strong local and central agency to guide and control these authorities, are the two important factors at work, bringing discredit on local self-government and impeding sanitary progress in this country as a whole.[99]

Dr Simpson recognized successes in the removal of unhealthy conditions. His paper noted 'the vast improvement in the health of the army' as well as the progress made by Sanitary Commissioners in recording the conditions of the civil population. in the collection of vital statistics, in the sanitation of large towns, more especially in water-supply, the spread of vaccination and the management of large fairs. In addition, Central Boards of Health in each province had helped co-ordinate work. Even so, as the sanitary figures of 1892 showed, in the European army there were 1,509 admissions and 376 deaths from enteric fever. In the civil population, on the other hand, out of over 7 million deaths recorded, more than ¾ million were ascribed to cholera and over 4½ millions to fevers. The unsafe health conditions of the country caused still more serious concern when a couple of years after 1892 calamity befell the East Lancashire Regiment stationed at Lucknow, where out of a total strength of 773 men 138 were attacked with cholera, of whom 92 died. Patients at the Sir Jamsetjee Jejeebhoy Hospital in Bombay, being treated for general disease, were similarly attacked with cholera. Out of 84 such attacks 66 died.[100] As Dr Simpson explained, though preventible, these epidemics had not been prevented for lack of an efficient sanitary service.

By a Resolution[101] passed in the Home Department on 26 October 1895 the Government of India recognized the need for the creation of a new machinery of health officers for both local and central purposes. The Government realized that 'if any tangible improvement is to be effected in sanitary work, particularly in rural areas, the quality of the supervizing [subordinate] agency must be improved'. This could not be done unless the local supervizors functioning under the control of Sanitary Commissioners were duly trained, especially in hygiene. The Resolution therefore suggested instituting a system of granting diplomas in public health on the basis of a regular course of teaching and examination. But since the change suggested involved considerations of time, money and the claims of existing incumbents, the duty of inspecting and checking the work of the vaccinators along with 'looking after village sanitation' was sought to be transferred to men who had gone through a course of hygiene and possessed sanitary qualifications. Influenced by Dr Simpson's recommendation, the Government of India was at the same time induced to extend the area of selection by planning to take officers for the Sanitary Department from the general body of Assistant Surgeons and Hospital Assistants. The Resolution clearly pointed out that 'men with medical qualifications employed in the Sanitary Department and provided with appropriate medicines and instruments for treating minor ailments, would be able not only to afford proper medical relief to many who do not obtain it, but also by this means to render their advice in sanitary matters more acceptable than it might otherwise be. They would also be extremely useful in outbreaks of epidemic diseases'. The men so selected were designated Health Officers and invested with such duties as the superintendence of vaccination, sanitation and the collection of vital statistics. The Resolution also suggested that 'each municipality or group of municipalities or local bodies should be required after a certain date to appoint a Health Officer'. In the absence of a sufficient supply of trained personnel it was felt that it might not be possible for the local bodies to appoint Health Officers before the beginning of 1900.[102]

However, the Resolution emphasized the necessity of taking some immediate steps to improve municipal sanitation. Candidates for certain municipal offices were, for instance, required to possess some qualification in hygiene. In large municipalities sanitary committees were sought to be appointed with a medical man, preferably the Civil Surgeon, as President to supervize the expenditure on sanitation often diverted to other heads. A health officer was also to work under the control of the Civil Surgeon.

It was laid down that the Civil Surgeon must without exception head the district organization in vaccination, sanitary and medical matters in every province. Although it was believed that his 'duties in regard to rural sanitation' had not yet 'in all cases been properly defined' the Resolution emphasized that steps should at once be taken to declare his authority and enforce his responsibility in all matters affecting public health in the district. It was even considered necessary that he should be furnished with an Assistant Surgeon of superior qualifications to relieve him of his multifarious duties at the headquarters.

As suggested by Dr Simpson, the Government of India had in the meantime taken steps to separate the sanitation of the army and of the military cantonments from that of the civil population.

Under Curzon the public health organization had been given a new direction which led to the creation of the post of Imperial Sanitary Commissioner. He was associated additionally with the conduct of bacteriological research to combat tropical diseases, such as plague, cholera, kala azar, malaria, goitre, diarrhoea and the like. As part of the promotion of research, the Central Bacteriological Institute was established at Kasauli in 1905.

The first cadre of the Bacteriological Department included thirteen appointments in the list forwarded by Lord Minto's Government on 21 June 1906. These were laboratory appointments, distributed as follows:[103] Central Research Institute, Kasauli, a Director and 3 Assistans; Bombay Bacteriological Laboratory, a Director and 2 Assistants; Madras King Institute of Preventive Medicine, a Director and an Assistant; Pasteur Institute, Kasauli, a Director and an Assistant; Pasteur Institute, Coonoor, a Director and an Assistant.

The staff so provided continued without addition until 1913. However, these institutions had in the meantime done useful work. The Central Institute, besides conducting general research in connexion with tropical diseases, prepared stores and dispatched vaccines and sera for use all over India. It was provided with four separate bureaus of epidemiology, protozoology and malaria, medical entomology, and of serum and vaccine therapy. The laboratory staff was, in addition, engaged in giving four courses of instructions annually in clinical bacteriology and in the new methods of diagnosis and treatment of tropical diseases and in conducting a couple of practical classes in anti-malarial work in the field. The result of the knowledge thus disseminated was the steady increase in the demand for vaccines and anti-sera manufactured at the Central Research Institute.

The Bombay Bacteriological Laboratory did the routine bacteriological work for Bombay Presidency and, in addition, prepared anti-plague vaccine for use throughout India. Its Director was a member of the Plague Research Commission and much of its work was done in his laboratory. The routine bacteriological work for the Presidency of Madras was done by the King Institute of Preventive Medicine, which also served as a depot for the manufacture of calf vaccine and for the training of vaccinators. The Pasteur Institutes at Kasauli and Coonoor, on the other hand, were centres for anti-rabic treatment in north and south India. The former was also the provincial bacteriological laboratory for the Punjab.

In a letter of 15 July 1913 the Director-General, Indian Medical Service, pressed the Government of India for an increase in the cadre of the Bacteriological Department. The Government of India agreed with the Director-General, especially in so far as his emphasis on bacteriological investigation was concerned. 'It is unnecessary to emphasize the fact,' it said to the Secretary of State in its despatch of 16 October 1913, 'that unless measures for the improvement of public health and the prevention of disease are based on facts ascertained and established by medical research, the result will be a wasteful expenditure of money on large and expensive schemes of doubtful utility.'

As recommended by the Government of India, the Secretary of State, in his letter of 30 January 1914, sanctioned the addition of fifteen appointments to the permanent cadre of the Bacteriological Department. Other proposals contained in the despatch of 16 October 1913 were also approved.[104] These new appointments were, for instance, not to be reserved to members of the Indian Medical Service, but were to be open to qualified officers available in India outside that Service. They were to be treated as cadre appointments only for so long as they were held by members of the Indian Medical Service. They would cease to be so treated in case they came to be held by otherwise specially qualified Indian officers who were not members of the Indian Medical Service. This trend was conducive to the development of the medical profession in specialized fields.

The trend towards the development of an independent medical profession first became perceptible in 1908, when Lord Morley was Secretary of State for India. It was then decided that about one-third of the civil appointments which, though held by the I.M.S., did not form part of the war reserve, could without prejudice to a military point of view, be transferred to medical men not belonging to that Service. Starting from that premise the Government of India concluded that, subject to certain specified conditions, a considerable number of appointments not included in the war reserve might gradually be transferred to non-I.M.S. medical men, a step which could open opportunities to indigenous talent for appointment to superior posts or for the growth of an independent medical profession. This policy was reiterated by the Government of India in its Home Department despatch of 17 November 1910. For, although Indians were in principle entitled to be admitted to the I.M.S. they formed no more than 5 per cent of the Service, which held all the superior posts in medical administration as well as in research and teaching institutions. Excluding plague and bacteriological appointments (all Europeans), the number of superior medical appointments in existence was 464. Of these, 354 were actually held by I.M.S. officers in the civil cadre (240 by officers belonging to the war reserve and 114 by officers in the civil employ outside the war reserve), while only 110 were held by or open to medical men recruited in India. Of these 110 posts, 35 were to be held by Civil Assistant Surgeons, 55 by Military Assistant Surgeons and 10 by private practitioners. The Military Assistant Surgeons who shared half the cake, were either Europeans or Eurasians who, by virtue of their education in India, were classed as indigenous practitioners. Even so, the medical men recruited locally in India were 23.7 per cent which compared well with the percentages fixed in respect of other services. The proportion of superior posts in the I.C.S. made available to local men was, for instance, 16.6 per cent, while it was 17 per cent in the P.W.D.[105]

Independently of the existing strength of Europeans in the superior medical appointments in the country, the Government of Lord Minto continued the policy of increasingly making those appointments open to men educated and recruited in India, care being taken to maintain the standards of recruitment as well as 'the reasonable claims' of the European servants of the Government residing in the interior of the country. The Government of India's despatch of 17 November 1910 recognized that although 'an independent medical profession trained on Western lines is steadily growing up in India . . .it has yet to overcome its universal rival in the form of the kaviraje, hakim, vaid, ojha and the like who are trained according to indigenous methods and in whom the population still trust'. The Government therefore proposed to the Secretary of State that, in order to overcome the existing obstacles to professional development, provision should be made for the establishment of more Government colleges and schools affiliated to the universities; for openings as house physicians and house surgeons in Government hospitals to be made available to the best students of each year; for the association of private practitioners with the staff of Government hospitals, and for consultation and use of the operating theatre. The Government colleges and schools to be so added to the existing number were no doubt to be manned mainly by officers of the I.M.S., but some professional posts could also be made available to the locally recruited men as encouragement.

These proposals had special relevance in the context of there being only 46 I.M.S. officers, for example, in U.P. with its 47 million people, 190 I.C.S. officers, 85 police officers and 60 P.W.D. officers recruited in England.[106] Obviously, public health had not thus far mattered as much as other administrative considerations.

The importance of the steps which the Government of India was taking to promote the growth of the medical profession as an effective instrument of public health was recognized universally. The appointment of the Plague Commission in 1898; the establishment in 1902 of a research institute at Guindy in Madras; the vigorous reorganization of the Sanitary Department by Lord Curzon in 1904 and the establishment of laboratories for the study of the problems of public health and bacteriological research in 1905; the arrangements made for the training of the superior sanitary staff and the appointment of public health officers for municipalities; the creation of a new department in 1910 to relieve the Home Department of its sanitary responsibilities; and the foundation of the Indian Research Fund Association in 1911, were all measures in tune with the recommendations adopted by the Government of India in 1895.

The foundation of the Indian Research Fund Association,[107] in fact, marked an important era in the history of sanitary progress. The control and management of the Association were vested in a Governing Body presided over by the Member in charge of the Education Department of the Government of India. The Governing Body was assisted by a scientific advisory board, of which not less than three members were on the Governing Body. They examined proposals for work connected with the scientific objects of the Association and reported on their importance and feasibility. Members of the advisory board were appointed for one year, but were eligible for re-election. They also had power to add to their number. Members in 1914 included the Director-General, I.M.S., the Sanitary Commissioner with the Government of India, the Director of the Central Research Institute, Kasauli, the officer-in-charge of the Central Malarial Bureau and Assistant Director-General, I.M.S. (Sanitary). Membership of the Association was open to non-officials. Every donor of Rs 5,000 was entitled to become a permanent member, while every subscriber of Rs 100 per annum could be a temporary member.

Members of the Association were entitled to attend and take part in its annual general meeting. Although the Fund had originally been financed solely by the Government of India, it was hoped that Indian philanthropists would in time contribute towards the expansion of the Association.

Since its incorporation in 1911 and up to the end of 1913 the Association had an income of Rs 15 lakhs. Out of this, I.M.S. officer was deputed in 1911 to study yellow fever and draw up proposals to protect India against the spread of the disease. Anti-malaria schemes were carried out on the results of preliminary surveys. Investigations were set in progress into problems connected with the prevalence of cholera, kala-azar, dysentery, leprosy and goitre. Inquiries were made into the pharmacology of cinchona derivatives, the use of hydrocyanic acid gas as a pulicide, and the fixation of chemical standards of purity for milk and milk products. Other investigations that proceeded under the auspices of Indian Research Fund Association, included bacteriological standards of purity for water supplies, the different anti-cholera vaccines and sera, the methods of water filtration and silt removal best suited to Indian conditions, the etiology of diabetese and the fevers of short duration, small-pox and tuberculosis. The research done was published in the *Indian Journal of Medical Research*, started by the Association itself. Besides financing investigations conducted by its own staff, the Association gave grants-in-aid to outside research on approved lines.

The investigations conducted by the staff of the Association represented work directly supervized by the Government of India, whose policy it was to keep the control of research under itself, but to decentralize other branches of sanitation to facilitate implementation. The creation of an Imperial Department of Sanitation was not therefore a departure from that policy. The Government of India made large grants to the provinces without any interference with their administration. While the general direction of a policy of public health remained with the Central Government, detailed control and executive action were left to Local Governments: 'The Sanitary Commissioner with the Government of India is a touring officer empowered to consult and confer informally with Local Governments and their officers upon matters connected with sanitation. He is not permitted to encroach upon the authority of Local Governments or the officers under their control'.[108]

The relationship of provincial Sanitary Commissioners towards the administrative heads of the medical department varied somewhat in different provinces. But the Government of India did not generally interfere with the arrangements which Local Governments might consider best suited to their needs. All that the Central Government did was to insist on the importance of defining the functions of sanitary and medical officers and securing to the Sanitary Commissioner the position of a responsible technical adviser to the Local Government in matters affecting public health. Functionally, the provinces thus exercised considerable freedom in the execution of details connected with sanitary admistration.

The Sanitary Boards established in the provinces served as a local agency in the promotion of public health. They were composed with varying powers, some being merely advisory, and others were invested with the sanction of schemes and allotment of funds. They consisted of officers belonging to the medical, sanitary, engineering and other branches of the civil services, with the addition of non-officials. To ensure a measure of uniformity in their functioning, however, the Government of India by a Resolution of 23 May 1914 favoured with 'confidence the devolution of financial authority and responsibility to these boards'. A salaried secretary to each such Board was sought to be appointed with a view to increasing efficiency.

The measures taken over the years for the improvement of public health were not without avail. They worked well, especially in so far as the health of army was concerned. This is clear from the figures given below (in percentages)[109]

Year	British Troops		Indian Troops	
	Constantly sick	Death Rate	Constantly sick	Death Rate
1875–9	62.40	20.37	44.04	19.93
1905–9	47.21	8.23	22.31	6.78
1912–13	28.90	4.62	20.10	4.42

The improvement so effected, however, did not apply to the civil population. In the case of the army the problem was concerned mainly with well-nourished adults living in sanitary surroundings under military discipline. For the civil population conditions were very different. Sanitary reform had to grope its way through a labyrinth of difficulties, such as the ignorance and prejudice of people, their social customs and habits, their dirty surroundings and poor financial means, their lack of co-operation and the diversity of their local conditions.

The Resolution of 23 May 1914 shows that the Government of India provided for a large increase in the number of Deputy Sanitary Commissioners and the appointment of Health Officers of the first class for larger municipalities and of the second class for smaller towns. Trained sanitary inspectors were appointed in large numbers and, in fact, urban sanitation received considerable attention for the improvement of drainage and water supply, especially in the larger towns.

But the rural population remained mostly neglected, except that the Civil Surgeon in every district was expected to superintend vaccination. 'Contaminated rites, polluted water-supply, badly constructed and insanitary dwellings, the habits and prejudices of the people' were believed to be important obstructions to progress, obstructions which in most provinces were still considered 'well-nigh insuperable'. The Government of India, therefore, advised the Local Governments to expend a portion of the grants for urban sanitation and on rural sanitation provided practical schemes for this purpose were forthcoming.[110] Special grants were not made unless schemes for rural sanitation were more generally advanced. Its importance was appreciated, but it was recognized that rural sanitation in India was still a subject for experiment and survey on such lines as might attract the co-operation of the people. The Government of India believed that, in the absence of adequate provision for rural education and people's co-operation, it would be dangerous to employ low-paid and imperfectly trained subordinates in matters so closely affecting village life. The result was that the urban population, more especially its élitist section, almost exclusively benefited from the progress made in the field of public health.

The position of rural health deteriorated even further when, under the recommendations of the Indian Retrenchment (Inchcape) Committee of 1922, the Government of India decided to suspend the annual contribution of Rs 5 lakhs to the Indian Research Fund Association, to postpone the scheme for establishing an Imperial Medical Research Institute at Delhi, and to keep in abeyance a number of bacteriological research appointments designed to counteract outbreaks of cholera, plague, malaria and other tropical

Statement of deaths in British India from various causes

Year	CHOLERA		SMALL-POX		PLAGUE		FEVERS		DYSENTERY AND DIARRHOEA		RESPIRATORY		ALL OTHER CAUSES		TOTAL	
	Total deaths	Ratio per 1,000	Total deaths	Ratio per 1,000	Total deaths	Ratio per 1,000	Total deaths	Ratio per 1,000	Total deaths	Ratio per 1,000	Total deaths	Ratio per 1,000	Total deaths	Ratio per 1,000	Total deaths	Ratio per 1,000
1918	560,802	2.35	93,076	.39	440,752	1.85	1,1134,441	46.60	276,648	1.16	430,935	1.81	1,959,147	2.21	14,895,801	62.46 (a)
1919	578,426	2.43	136.077	.57	74,284	.31	5,468,181	22.93	291.643	1.22	350,133	1.47	1,655,434	6.94	8,554,178	35.87 (a)
1920	130,140	.55	101,329	.43	99,368	.42	4,931,202	20.68	218,734	.92	333,669	1.40	1,541,212	6.46	7,355,654	30.84 (a)
1921	450,608	1.87	40,446	.17	69,682	.29	4,761,237	19.72	229,576	.95	334,103	1.38	1,499,460	6.21	7,385,112	30.59 (b)
1922	121,679	.50	40,836	.17	77,615	.32	3,689,086	15.28	177,852	.74	290.533	1.20	1,402,491	5.81	5,800,092	24.02 (b)

(a) Calculated on 1911 census.
(b) Calculated on 1921 census.
(c) At least 1/3 of the deaths from fevers are due to malaria.

diseases. The withdrawal of the financial support accorded by the Government since 1913-14, even though partial and temporary, attracted considerable public attention and unfavourable criticism both in India and Britain.

The matter was taken up at an All-India Conference of Medical Research Workers held in the Calcutta School of Tropical Medicine and Hygiene in October 1924. A priority list was drawn up of such researches as it considered necessary in the interests of public health.[111] Consistent with the recommendations of this Conference, the Scientific Advisory Board of the Indian Research Fund Association at its meeting held at the same venue on the following day, emphasized the urgent need for immediate restoration of the annual grant of Rs 5 lakhs previously given to the Indian Research Fund Association by the Government. To justify the demand for a restoration of grants to the Indian Research Fund Association a statistical chart of the impact of medical researches was supplied to the Finance Department to convince it that public health and medical research were areas where public money was employed with tangible results.[112]

In response, the Government decided to renew the Association's grant to the extent of Rs 3 lakhs per annum from 1925 onwards. Financed by the Government of India, the Association was later able to spend Rs 7–12 lakhs on public health research, especially on malaria and nutritional investigation. The Malaria Institute established under its auspices trained medical men in practical work and published papers of great value to India and the world. In 1936 the Government of India gave the Association a special grant of Rs 10 lakhs for anti-malaria work. The nutritional research of the Association was also recognized as being of special importance, and about Rs 1 lakh was spent on it annually.[113]

Another important organization maintained by the Government for research and training in public health was the All-India Institute of Hygiene. Originally included in the Calcutta School of Tropical Medicine and the Hospital for Tropical Diseases which owned their existence to the efforts of Sir Leonard Rogers, thanks to the generosity of the Rockefeller Foundation the All-India Institute of Hygiene was provided with separate accommodation in a fine building. It continued to work in close collaboration with the Tropical School of Medicine, which was financed by the Government of India.

Central Advisory Board of Health

In February 1937 the Government of India issued a Resolution establishing a Central Advisory Board of Health. It had been preceded by a Central Health Board set up in 1921 to advise the Central and Provincial Governments on technical matters which these governments might refer to it from time to time. However, no provision was made for consultation between those responsible for medical and sanitary policy. In the absence of such consultation the Board came to an end in 1923.

The Central Advisory Board of Health was established in 1937 to provide periodic consultation in the formulation of common policies and interchange of information. In fact, it was designed to act as a Central Information Bureau on all public health matters affecting India, and rendered advice on matters referred to it by the Central or Provincial Governments. It concentrated on three major items discussed at its inaugural meeting in June 1937: quinine supplies in India, the organization of provincial public health departments, and nutrition surveys. Provincial health units were soon established in Madras, U.P. and Delhi with the co-operation of the Rockefeller Foundation.

The Government of India was already aware of the problem of human nutrition and a Nutrition Advisory Committee was set up in May 1936. It recommended the creation of a liaison officer who might be a link between agricultural research and research in human nutrition. The Committee thought that each provincial Government should have at least one officer with special knowledge of human nutrition in relation to the findings of agricultural research. This was considered necessary because no co-ordination existed thus far between the medical and public health departments.

The Central Advisory Board of Health resolved in the meantime to promote the idea of nutrition, both human and animal, and recommended to provincial governments the necessity of conducting dietary surveys and instructing their medical, public health, agricultural and other departments to co-operate in the conduct of these surveys. It appointed in addition an *ad hoc* committee to investigate the whole problem of food adulteration in India, with special reference to legislation in force in the provinces. A certain number of medical men trained in accordance with the recommendations of the Nutrition Advisory Committee were in the meantime appointed to function as 'field workers'.[114]

A review of the functioning of developmental or special departments and services thus makes it clear that a decentralization of authority alone could not bring about rural development. A certain degree of central supervision, control and direction was necessary despite financial and administrative devolution. This necessity arose not only from considerations of efficiency, but more so from the advantage an individual province could gain from the total stock of scientific knowledge and experience that central institutions and agencies alone could afford to supply to the provinces.[115] In other words, only some kind of federal centralism could ensure what might be called a comparable pattern of rural development. It signified both financial and administrative decentralization within the framework of supervisory central authority. The soundness of this principle applied particularly to the functioning of local bodies as an agency of rural development, an agency that was in due course replaced largely by what came to be known as community development administration and national extension service.

IV

LOCAL BODIES AND RURAL DEVELOPMENT

The scope of this chapter does not extend to a discussion of municipal institutions but to rural boards, with special reference to their role in the promotion of rural development as units of local self-government. The policy objective of the rural boards organized at different levels in the districts was set out in some detail in the famous official Resolution of 18 May 1882. Its emphasis was mainly on the political and popular training of educated Indians through these local representative institutions. For the Resolution categorically stated that the measure was 'chiefly designed as an instrument of political and popular education', the education of the 'rapidly growing' class of 'intelligent' and 'public spirited men' whom it was considered to be 'bad policy' and 'sheer-waste of power' to ignore or not 'to utilize'.

This policy decision was taken in the context of recurrent famines which called for an improvement of the rural economy, as also of the continuing financial stringency that dictated the expediency of local services being managed with local resources. In addition to the old chaukidari police and pound, these services included famine relief and water-supply, education and health, village craft and sanitation, cattle improvement and communications. These were functions that the Government entrusted to local bodies under legislative enactments. They were not inherent in them as of right or grow out of the old and so-called village communities.

Hisorically, however, there was no functional vacuum. The improvement of the rural economy in India formed part of the responsibility of two main agencies in the pre-British days, the rule-based revenue administration of the government and the custom-based operation of the village community.

Prior to British rule in India, land revenue, as we know, constituted the mainstay of the Indian finances. Even in 1834, the land revenue of the East India Company was £13 million out of a gross revenue of £18.4 million. The position improved in 1858 when land revenue accounted for 50 per cent of the total revenue receipts.[1] Naturally, the promotion of the agrarian economy and the protection of the classes engaged in agriculture and its allied industries constituted the main concern of revenue administration. In his *raiyatwari* settlement of land revenue Sher Shah was, for example, guided chiefly by considerations of eliminating the intermediary zamindars who acted against the interest of cultivators. It was later known as 'Todar Mal's *bandobast*' and was prevalent in northern India throughout the Mughal period. In their revenue administration the British were guided by similar considerations of rural welfare when they brought care, precision and hard work to bear upon the preparation of their Settlement Reports of the North-Western Provinces, Oudh and Punjab, the Settlement Reports of the Central Provinces, the District Manuals of Southern India, the Survey Reports and Gazetteers of the Bombay Districts, and the several reports on the Punjab frontier tribes and their villages. The functions annexed to the rural boards by separate enactments were in fact not incomparable to those which revenue authorities in the districts looked after executively in the course of their laborious survey and settlement operation and revenue collection. As part of their immediate duties Collectors themselves were in most cases obliged to lead a camp life in rural areas for months on end in direct contact with the people.

As regards the role and constitution of the Indian village community, the accounts generally given are either vague and brief, or they represent an ideal rather than the actual. Sir Henry Maine's pioneering studies in *Village-Communities in the East and West* (1891) and *The Early History of Institutions* (1874) led him to the conclusion that consanguinity and private property in land held in coparcenary tenure constituted the primary basis of village communities in India, a basis that provided both social and economic ties for joint interest and action. In other words, Maine viewed these communities as patriarchal organizations, governed by custom and bound together by family relationships and common holdings of land.

These features of village communities were noticed in the North-Western Provinces where, like the Teutonic village communities, there was the arable mark in the village, divided into separate lots but cultivated according to minute customary rules governing individual shares, which were binding on all. There were, again, the reserved meadows as well as the waste or common land, out of which the arable mark had been cut, enjoyed as pasture by all the community *pro indiviso*. There was then the village, consisting of habitations, each ruled by a despotic pater-familias. There was, in addition, constantly 'a council of government to determine disputes as to custom', in accordance with 'multifarious rules governing the proceedings of the cultivators', their main object being 'to reconcile a common plan and order of cultivation on the parts of the whole brotherhood with the holding of distinct lots in the arable land by separate families'.[2]

In *The Early History of Institutions* Maine refers to 'the village-communities of the Aryan race' and compares what he calls 'the Hindoo village-community in India' with the Teutonic village-community in England'. He describes both as comparable to the primitive 'village council' of Europe, a council sometimes owning a responsibility to the entire body of villagers, sometimes disclaiming it, sometimes overshadowed by the authority of an hereditary chief, but 'never altogether obscured', the various shades of its power being in all cases indistinguishable. In other words, there was no clear 'difference between making a law, declaring a law, and punishing an offender against a law'.[3] Custom, the basic source of law, especially in the Indian situation, was recognized as all-comprehensive functionally.

India, however, had nothing like the Teutonic assembly of adult males, which later grew into a full-fledged separate legislative authority. According to Maine, India had only 'the *Council* of Village Elders', though even these were not universally found:

Villages frequently occur in which the affairs of the community are managed, its customs interpreted, and the disputes of its members decided by a single headman, whose office is sometimes admittedly hereditary but is sometimes described as elective; the choice being generally, however, in the last case confined in practice to the members of one particular family, with a strong preference for the eldest male of the kindred, if he is not especially disqualified. But I have good authority for saying that, in those parts of India in which the village-community is most perfect and in which there are the clearest signs of an original proprietary equality between all the families composing the group, the authority exercised elsewhere by the Headman is lodged with the Village

Council [of Elders]. It is always viewed as a representative body, and not as a body possessing inherent authority, and, whatever be its real number, it always bears a name which recalls its ancient constitution of Five [Panch] persons.[4]

Being a 'representative' and 'composite' body, there was always 'great pressure from all sections of the community to be represented' in the Village Council. There was of course nothing like a uniform mode of representation. Custom did not permit it. But there was general recognition 'that the members should be elderly men'.[5]

Another important feature of Indian village communities which impressed Maine was their self-sufficiency and organized management of all local affairs:

They, in fact, include a nearly complete establishment of occupations and trades for enabling them to continue their collective life without assistance from any person or body external to them. Besides the Head-man or Council exercising quasi-judicial, quasi-legislative, power, they contain a village police, now recognised and paid in certain provinces by the British Government. They include several Families of heriditary traders, the Blacksmith, the Harness-maker, the Shoemaker. The Brahmin is also found for the performance of ceremonies, and even the Dancing-Girl for attendance at festivities. There is invariably a Village-Accountant, an important personage among an unlettered population.[6]

The entire basis of representation on the Village Council was, however, governed by custom, not contract, a principle that went into the constitution of local bodies under the British. Further, the bond of cohesion for the village communities, as said before, was collective ownership and kinship, not the limited circle of one place with certain interests in common and possessing within that circle the means of local government for the satisfaction of needs without much reference to neighbouring villages, a feature that applied to *raiyatwari* areas, which Maine perhaps did not take into account in the absence of information which later became available. It was here that B.H. Baden Powell made his contribution to the study of the subject in the *Indian Village Community*, published in September 1896. Unlike Maine, he does not recognize the antiquity or universality of joint villages and blood relationships as the basis of village communities in India. He holds that the common-holding of land was traceable only among the superior tenures of the 'Hindu-Aryans' and that 'in very numerous cases' it was a small estate with an individual founder whose joint ownership depended solely on the existence of the joint family.

Baden Powell in fact does not deny the existence of communal or collective ownership. All that he says is that in India there existed, in addition to the joint village system, another type called the 'riyatwari' village, where 'there is no evidence that the holdings were ever otherwise than separate and independent'. And even in the joint type, he adds, 'it is equally important not to confuse the whole of the villages together, but to recognize the very different principles or bases of union which exist; the joint village on a tribal basis is very different from that which depends on accession of joint heirs to one individual founder, and that, again, is different from the group formed by families on no tribal and no aristocratic basis, or on voluntary association.'[7] His whole emphasis is on the need to recognize that the basis of village communities in India is not only the different brands of communal ownership, but also the separate and independent holdings of the *raiyatwari* tenure, where the bond of union is neither consanguinity nor common ancestry, but a community of interests binding a group of cultivators located in one place and governed by certain customs which, though comparables to those of neighbouring villages, call for the use of parochialism to satisfy those interests within the limits of that place.[8]

Both the premises of village communities were thus recognized as invested with a cohesive quality that kept them together in the performance of communal obligations to the village in respect of its local wants, centred mainly around agriculture and allied services. But the basic difference between the two arose from the fact that while Maine's concept flowed from the assumption of private property being the foundation of the 'Hindu-Aryan' system, Baden Powell's *raiyatwari* tenure was based on the theory and practice of rent which the British assumed to have inherited from their Muslim predecessors who had acted on the assumption that all the soil belonged in absolute property to the sovereign. The earliest experiments which they tried on the overthrow of Muslim viceroys in Bengal, were naturally based on the belief that the soil was theirs and that any land law would be of their exclusive creation. The Permanent Settlement created under that belief an aristocracy by conferring estates in fee simple, an aristocracy which, with certain exceptions, consisted of the 'assignees' who had served the erstwhile Muslim viceroy as tax-gatherers, a class of intermediaries called zamindars created between the state and the cultivating group.[9] Like the Khotes of Southern Konkan in the Presidency of Bombay, a body of land-holders, who had earlier been hereditary farmers of revenue with control over village for generations, the Bengal zamindars destroyed the village establishments and their ancient councils which had already disintegrated during later-Mughal times.

In Southern and Western India, however, Sir Thomas Munro set the norm. Recoiling from the error committed by Cornwallis in Bengal, he opposed intermediaries between the state and the cultivating community, recognizing the *raiyatwari* system as by far the best mode of settlement. This was in perfect harmony with the concept of the sovereign's absolute right to the soil, and did not involve interference with the self-acting institution of the village community or its hereditary headman, whose assistance was, in fact, enlisted on the side of the state. According to Baden Powell, the original chief of the tribal Dravidian village was even superseded by a sort of second Dravidian headman (*mahato*) because 'he was necessarily literate and could keep accounts'. In course of time both were 'officially recognized', though the second later became 'the prototype of our modern patwari' on whom the cultivators relied 'for a knowledge of official entries in the records, and the survey details of their holdings'. In fact, it was he who made out receipts for their payments and became responsible for village statistical returns, including the maintenance of documents such as bonds and land transfers. The traditional headman was supposed to be exercising small magisterial powers and doing various duties of police and protection, for which he was remunerated by a grant of the best land in the village, comparable to *watan* or hereditary and intimately valued family property granted to *patels* by earlier Muslim kings of the Deccan.[10] Similar holdings were enjoyed by the accountant, and on a smaller scale by artisans constituting the occupational groups representing the village community. The headman and the accountant were, however, the two principal officers and in large villages usually had deputies or assitants. There were other functionaries, like the village watchman and guardian of boundaries, and, in irrigated villages, an official to regulate the distribution of water.

The *raiyatwari* system in fact riveted the control of the Collector by creating a 'peasant-proprietary', with the village community directly enjoying the protection of the state and its guidance in the regulation of local affairs, a development which contributed to economic prosperity and social peace.

The efficiency of the Munro system perhaps induced the administration of the North-Western Provinces to try making revenue settlements with individual proprietors in the co-parcenary estates of that part of the country. In view of the abuses of early settlements made under Wellesley's declaration for a projected permanency after a certain period of time and the Company's preference for a *raiyatwari* system under Munro's influence, Holt Mackenzie had Regulation VII of 1822 enacted to ascertain in joint villages the extent of the interest of each individual and the nature of the title by which it was held.[11] It was in fact an attempt to destroy the corporate character of co-parcenary villages by admitting individual sharers to separate engagements.

In this context of continuing controversy between the *raiyatwari* and the proprietory basis of village communities Sir Charles Metcalfe recorded his historic view on the subject. In a Minute of 7 November 1830 he questioned the expediency of separate settlement with each individual cultivating proprietor; for he feared that this would sap the foundation of what is called 'little republics' in the form of 'village communities', conducive to the promotion of self-government and 'union for the pruposes of municipal economy'. Separate engagements, he reiterated, 'must tend to loosen, and ultimately dissolve the ties which bind the village communities together. Instead of all getting in union, with a common interest as regards government, and adjusting their own separate interests among themselves, according to established usage, each would have his separate arrangement directly with the government, and could hardly fail to be thereby less linked with his brethren.' But as the Lieutenant Governor of the N. W. Provinces, James Thomson, noted with regret in his Minute of 25 September 1848, the village survey and settlement operations started under Regulation 9 of 1833, led in practice 'to independent and separate engagements which, as Metcalfe had feared, tended to sap the foundations of village communities.

However, the scope for corporate or joint action by the community did not altogether disappear. Though mutually exclusive in terms of social status and relationship, the traditonal caste system supplied its own bond of union. For conformity to caste rules continued to be an essential condition for succession to property, a condition that embodied in social groups the elements of brotherhood and common landed interests.

Under these rules inheritance was made subject to the performance of caste obligations which were sought to be enforced with a vigour that tended to preserve the early character of Indian villages. The fear of loss of property acted as a serious deterrant against any violation.

In 1850 the Government enacted the Caste Disabilities Removal Act. It provided that no person should forfeit his or her right to property or inheritance 'by reason of his or her renouncing, or having being excluded from, the communion of any religion, or being deprived of caste'. One of its provisions also declared that the old rule of succession to property being dependent on the performance of caste obligations was not to be enforced as law in the courts within the territories 'subject to the Government of the East India Company'. The Act in fact re-enacted a provision of Regulation VII of 1832 which had remained inoperative. The measure so enacted in 1850, however, did not come into force on account of a fear of unrest.

The tradition-bound and caste-ridden village community which in the pre-British period functioned as an autonomous unit side by side with the revenue administration of any ruling power of the day, was on the whole left free by the Mughals whose interest in rural areas did not generally extend beyond the realization of their land revenue. But the situation started changing with the expansion of the Company's territories and the growth of British power in India under Lord Wellesley (1798-1805) who not only annexed most of Tipu's dominions and the Carnatic to the Presidency of Madras, but brought under the direct administration of his supreme government at Fort William in Bengal vast territories partly ceded by the Nawab of Oudh and partly conquered from the Marathas.[12] The change which affected the communal foundations of landed property and the corporateness of joint villages, proceeded more especially from the opening of the Company's trade in 1813 and its abolition in 1833, two important gains of the laissez fair movement of England, which accelerated the pace of modernization in terms of both economic and political developments in India. Economically, it contributed through records of rights to the growth of mobility in the transfers of land to a degree that induced investment for purpose of large-scale colonial and capitalist enterprise. Politically, on the other hand, it led to the evolution of a separate legislative authority that gradually superseded custom by law, a new development where the determination of rights to property came to be vested in courts which started making serious incursions into the erstwhile domain of custom-based village communities and caste panchayats.

Thus, the agency of modernization was that of Europeans, an

external agency of *entrepreneurs* or colonizers who not only applied to Indian conditions their experience of European science and technology, but also influenced the constitutional development of government in a manner responsive to their pressure within the framework of 'bureaucratic despotism'.[13] An effective step in this direction was first taken by Lord William Bentinck who lent his support to the whole body of land reforms which Holt Mackenzie recommended during 1821-31 on the model of the Munro system which Bentinck had earlier admired as the Governor of Madras (1803-7). He firmly believed that no modernization could take place in India except through Europeans, and that there was little room for change from within the infrastructure of indigenous institutions.

However, had attempts been made to expose village communities to a process of integrated primary education and rural development so that they could initiate change from within their infrastructure, the traditional social framework might have adjusted to new conditions without much dislocation. But the educational policy which the British introduced on the abolition of the Company's private trade did not aim to prepare the rural masses and the village community for local self-governments; rather it sought to produce through English education a middle class of élites and interpreters who might in subordinate positions assist the British in the administration of the country. Macaulay, who formulated the policy, had this class in view when in his Minute of 2 February 1835 he recommended the creation of a class of 'interpreters', who, though Indian in blood and colour, might be English in tastes, opinions, values and 'intellect'.[14] It was thus an urban and job-oriented educational policy, with exclusive emphasis on secondary and higher education.

Some rethinking, however, occurred on the transfer of the Company's government to the Crown in 1858. The experience of rural unrest during the Mutiny, which was followed by the outbreak of famines and epidemic diseases in the 1860's effected a shift of emphasis in favour of rural education. The home authorities issued orders that 'Government expenditure should be mainly directed to the provision of elementary education for the mass of the people'.[15] In the same year the government of Lord Mayo not only made additionl provisions for primary education but also took steps to secure agricultural improvement to fight recurrent famine. His policy was to transfer primary education to the local bodies gradually, and this was provided for by an Act of 1870. But the importance of primary education and local bodies came to be realized too late, for the implementation of policies was now through Western educated members of the middle class, an external agency of government, and not through those who were of the community and rooted in it as of old.

Local Funds for Rural Services

The administration of 'local funds' necessitated the creation of what came to be known as rural boards or local bodies in the districts. The funds formed part of land revenue in most cases, a source of income which the old village community once used for the promotion of protective and rural welfare services. The European Collectors who united in their office both executive and revenue functions, collected these funds executively in the traditional way and spent them to meet a number of local needs, the most important of which was initially the construction and repair of roads in the rural areas.

In 1853 the Collector of South Arcot proposed the establishment of a district road fund by surrendering for local expenditure a small portion of the land revenue assessment of that district. The Government accepted the proposal a couple of years later and the funds so raised in the Madras districts amounted to about Rs 400,000 by 1863. They consisted in some districts of revenue contributions, but also included ferry tolls, proceeds of cattle pounds and certain miscellaneous items. This arrangement continued until the local legislature enacted a measure in 1866 authorizing the government to levy a road cess of 3½ per cent on the annual receipts of rent from land, which helped raise the annual amount of local funds to Rs 26 lakhs. The semi voluntary funds which were once collected executively, thus became statutory.[16]

There was a system of voluntary associations that preceded the compulsory levy of tax in the Presidency of Bombay, a *raiyatwari* province where indigenous institutions had continued to operate under the benign influence of Elphinstone even after the fall of the Marathas in 1818. This involved taxation by consent of the people for local improvements.[17] There was hardly any trace of such a system of voluntary associations in Bengal where the personal influence of zamindars had superseded the corporate will of the community. The idea of raising local funds for local purpose had not occurred to the public or officials until Sir George Campbell took over as Lieutenant-Governor in 1871. Earlier, consultative committees for the management of schools, dispensaries and roads had existed, but the funds they controlled were very moderate proceeds from government estates, pounds and ferry tolls and the initiative taken was mainly that of officials.[18] The Mahalwari area of the North-Western Provinces too had lost its spirit of self-help on account of its periodical settlement aimed at the maximization of government revenue. There, too, use was made of consultative committees, nominated by Collectors to raise funds for local improvements. In the Punjab these committees were purely official and in the Central Provinces local rates were levied executively for roads and education which revenue officers collected along with land revenue. There was, in addition, a tax called *pandhri* on non-agricultural incomes, coming down from the Maratha times, which the British continued and applied for purposes of local improvement under executive authority.[19]

There was thus a continuous chain in the availability of some form of local resources for the fulfilment of local needs. The main source was a fraction of land revenue. But pounds, ferries and irrigation, were not excluded. The agency employed was either voluntary or imposed from outside a village by the government. There had existed a possibility of the old voluntary system being transformed voluntarily into autonomous units of local self-government from within itself. But while a general policy direction was found wanting, except in the individual cases of men like Sir Thomas Munro of Madras and Mountstuart Elphinstone of Bombay, considerations of British imperial interest dictated the necessity of bureaucratic dominance filtering down to remote villages. The rural boards which were set up to administer the existing local funds, functioned as an external agency to satisfy local requirements under the same dominance.

Period: 1860–1919

Mayo to Ripon (1870-85)

The rural boards set up under Lord Mayo's 'Decentralization Scheme' of 1870 to administer local funds differed from the earlier executively nominated consultative committees. They were each established under an Act on a principle which was partly elective, with provisions for the posts of presidents and vice-presidents, the officials being not more than half the strength of a board. As said before, it was the Presidencies of Madras and Bombay that led the way in respect of public spirit and voluntary service.

The history of the statutory panchayat system in Madras could in fact be traced to Regulation XXIX of 1802 which recognized and continued the indigenous institution of *karnam* (village headman). Regulation IV of 1816 declared him to be village *munsif* with powers to decide suits within a limit of Rs 10. He could, under another Regulation of the same year, assemble the village panchayat to decide cases of higher value and try petty criminal cases and award punishments. The panchayats later fell into disuse. But attempts were made in the 1880's to revive them.

Under its Local Funds Act VI of 1871 the Presidency of Madras was divided into local fund circles. A rural board was established in each circle with a president, a vice-president and three or more members, all of whom had to own land, or carry on business or reside in the circle. The Act, which vested a local government with powers of taxation, did not introduce any elective principle. It remained permissive, the Collector being authorized to exercise all discretion; for there was yet little or no opportunity for education in rural areas. Even so, the rural boards were established so that they might arrange, both financially and administratively, to meet the constantly growing needs arising from the expansion of state activity. Local bodies, as said before, actually provided means for both financial and administrative assistance to the Centre.

The elective principle was emphasized by the Government of India Resolution of 18 May 1882. The size of official membership was reduced and official interference from within prohibited. As pointed out earlier, the Madras Act of 1884 introduced a three-tier system, with the union board at the bottom, the district board on top, and the taluk board in the middle. A union was a group of villages under the control of a panchayat, comprising not less than five members of whom the village headman was to be one. The Madras Government's *Report of the Committee on Local Self-Government* (1882) took notice of the ancient village system and recommended the revival of village panchayats, with provision for their education in the management of village affairs. The Committee's recommendations were incorporated into the Local Boards Act of 1884 which raised the position of the village headman and provided for the establishment of union panchayats to handle village sanitation, the repairs of roads, tanks and walls, the construction of dispensaries and hospitals, and the diffusion of elementary education. These functions had earlier belonged to the village community and were now being assigned to village unions after the community had lost its identity. This was being done by an external official agency as a gift of government, not as something which had legitimately belonged to it as of right. For it was the Government that appointed union members and chairmen, although their appointment by election was permissive at the discretion of the executive government.

While the *taluk* board was to consist of a president and not less than twelve members, the board at the district level was to have a president and not less than twenty-four members. At least two-thirds of the members were to be non-official in the case of a *taluk* board, and three-fourths in the case of a district board. In both cases the president appointed was an officer of the government, the sub-divisional officer for the former and the Collector for the latter, although the Act had provided for the election of the president and vice-president in the same way as the election of members. Nomination continued in the beginning in spite of statutory provisions for election. Even so, a District Fund was constituted under the Act and the district officer authorized to levy taxes. No board was, however, to enforce taxation except with the approval of the executive government.

The voluntary associations or committees in Bombay received legal sanction under Act III of 1869, which created a 'local fund committee' in each district and a sub-committee' in each *taluk*, thus providing a two-tier legal system of local bodies. No elective principle was, however, introduced in 1869. The local fund committee was to consist of eight memebrs, with the Collector as *ex-officio* President and at least half the members being non-officials, all nominated by the Government. The Executive Engineer and Deputy Collector were among the officials on the committee, which levied a cess of one *anna* in the rupee on land revenue for services meant for the district as a whole. The *taluk* sub-committee assisted the district committee with advice and looked after the requirements of the *taluk*.

The Act of 1884 recognized this two-tier system and established two classes of rural boards—the district board and the *taluk* board. In addition, it introduced the elective principle which the Government of India had emphasized in its Resolution of 18 May 1882, although the principle so introduced was not without limitations.[20]

In Bengal the Road Cess Act passed in 1871 at the instance of Sir George Campbell was the first legal step towards local self-government. It established Road Cess Committees with permissive provisions for elective membership and a non-official majority. These committees were replaced by the Bengal Local Boards Act of 1885, which provided for the creation of a district board in each Bengal district, a local board in each of sub-division of advanced districts, and the establishment of unions of village committees on the lines of Madras. The difference, however, was that while the Madras Act itself created the unions, the Bengal Act merely inserted an enabling clause authorizing the executive government to create them as and when it thought fit. A union panchayat, when so created, was to be under the control of the local board of a sub-division.

Acts were passed in 1883 in both U.P. and Punjab to liberalize the functioning of local bodies under Lord Ripon's plan of 1882. As in Bombay, a two-tier system was introduced in both areas, with certain modifications to replace the statutory local committee established in 1871 to legalize local funds earlier collected executively.

As already noted, Lord Ripon's attempt to liberalize local bodies did not fully succeed. The *Report* of the Royal Commission on Decentralization made it clear that the intended relaxation of bureaucratic control had made little appreciable progress. Local bodies were doubtless situated in rural areas and invested with the discharge of rural functions, but the influence under which they operated was not only administratively bureaucratic, but also socially élitist. Local bodies functioned as a training ground for elected members who looked forward to seats in legislative councils. The attitudes of both officials and non-officials were mainly tradition-bound and power-based and rural development formed no part of their goal in ideological terms.

Bengal

Despite there being a provision for extensive use of elective principles and non-official Chairmen under the Bengal Local Self-Government Act III of 1885, the *Bengal Report of 1891-2*, for example, clearly pointed out that there were as before 38 district boards and 106 local boards and that 'all the District Boards were presided over by an official chairman, who is the Magistrate of the district'.[21] The elected members were in a minority: at the close of 1891–2, for instance, of the 790 members in the 38 districts of Bengal 168 were *ex-officio* members, 313 were nominated by the government, and 309 elected by local boards. Of the total, Indians numbered 593, the remaining 197 being Europeans and Eurasians. In the Local Boards, of the 1,248 members 40 were *ex-officio*, 739 nominated by the government, and only 469 elected. There were 154 official seats as against

1904 non-official and the number of Europeans and Eurasians was 105.[22]

Of the 790 members in the District Boards of Bengal in 1891–92, 31.5 per cent were government servants, 28.9 zamindars and *talukdars*, and 26.6 legal practioners. In the Local Boards, 47.7 per cent were zamindars, *talukdars* or their servants, 23.8 legal practitioners and 12.5 government servants. Government servants furnished the largest proportion in the District Boards partly because of the number of official chairmen. In Local Boards, on the other hand, the landed interest dominated. There were, in addition, other occupational groups that held seats—planters, missionaries and government pensioners—but their strength was imperceptible, although the weight of their influence was on the side of officials. The statement given overleaf illustrates the manner in which the District Boards were constituted in terms of occupational divisions.[23]

There was little or no change in the powers delegated to the Local Boards. In almost every district they continued to administer the grants made for village roads and to control pounds, but other powers varied a good deal in different districts. They extended to primary education in as many as seventeen districts and the control of ferries in twelve. In Bhagalpur all the dispensaries were under their charge, while in some other districts this control was only partial. The construction and maintenance of tanks and wells formed part of their duties in only four districts, while village sanitation and medical relief came under the Boards in such districts as Patna and Shahabad.[24]

An occupational analysis of the District Boards shows that zamindars and the legal practitioners together constituted the majority in all districts. They could have carried out plans of rural development, especially in the field of land reform and rural financing, but instead obstructed progress in both. The zamindars who dominated rural areas in Bihar became a united opposition of all land-owners against the introduction of the cadastral survey, a measure designed to improve agricultural production by an attempt to ensure the security of various occupancy and tenancy rights. The movement was led by the Maharaja of Darbhanga who presided over a meeting in November 1891 to protest against it officially. Several petitions were presented at different times, and, finally, in October 1892, a joint memorial was drawn up and submitted by the British Indian Association, the Bihar Landholders Association, the Zamindari Panchayat, and the Indian Property Association. The memorialists made several

Occupational Analysis of District Boards in Bengal, 1891–92

NAME OF DIVISION		Government servants		Zamindars, talukdars, & zamindars servants		Pleaders mukhtears		Planters		Missionaries		Government pensionars		Other Occupations		Total Number
		No.	Ratio per cent.	No.	Ratio per cent.	No.	Ratio per cent.	No.	Ratio per cent.	No.	Ratio per cent.	No.	Ratio per cent.	No.	Ratio per cent	of members.
1.		2	3	4	5	6	7	8	9	10	11	12	13	14	15	16
Burdwan Division	District Boards	33	30.	30	27.3	33	30.	5	4.5	1	.9	3	2.7	5	4.5	110
	Local Boards	35	14.5	103.	42.9	61	25.4	2	.8	..	..	7	2.9	32	13.3	240
Presidency Division	District Boards	36	33.	31	28.4	20	18.3	10	9.1	1	.9	3	2.7	8	7.3	109
	Local Boards	19	7.3	139	53.8	56	21.7	11	4.2	1	.4	5	1.9	27	10.4	258
Rajshahi Division	District Boards	36	33.0	32	29.4	20	18.4	7	6.4	..	..	1	.9	13	11.9	109
	Local Boards.	10	10.5	51	53.7	19	20.	1	1.1	..	..	..	..	14	14.7	95
Dacca Division	District Boards	31	29.8	25	24.0	40	38.4	..	..	..	..	3	2.8	5	4.8	104
	Local Boards	24	12.6	77	38.6	79	39.6	..	..	..	..	1	.5	17	8.7	198
Chittagong Division	District Boards	18.	35.3	16	31.4	12	23.6	4	7.8	..	..	..	..	1	1.9	51
	Local Board	5	18.5	14	5.9	8	29.6	..	..	..	..	..	..	..	..	27
Patna Division	District Boards	55	33.7	48.	29.4	25	15.3	30	18.4	..	..	..	..	5	.3	163
	Local Boards	33	14.7	119	53.3	35	15.7	27	12.1	..	..	..	..	9	.4	223
Bhagalpur Division	District Boards	19	20.21	36	38.29	19	20.21	14	14.89	..	..	1.	1.6	5	5.31	94
	Local Boards	10	7.75	62	48.6	24	18.6	11	8.52	1	.7	1	.77	20	15.5	29
Orrisa Division	Distric Boards	21	42.	11	22.	10	20.	..	..	2	.4	4	8.	2	4.	50
	Local Boards	19	24.3	31	39.7	17	21.7	..	..	2	2.5	4	5.1	5	6.4	78
GRAND TOTAL	District Boards	249	31.5	229	28.9	179	22.6	70	8.8	4	.5	15	1.9	44	5.5	790
	Local Boards	155	12.5	596	47.7	299	23.8	52	4.1	4	.3	18	1.5	124	9.9	1,248

objections to the proposed measure, but the Lieutenant-Governor remained firm and recorded a note that answered all the objections.[25] The scheme of cadastral survey went on until it accomplished the object of its institution.

The annual reports on administration in Bengal made it clear that in several districts the Indian members of local bodies little or no interest in attending the meetings. In fact, these had to be adjourned on a number of occasions for want of a quorum. A report of 1908–9, for instance, said: 'There Boards, those of Dhanbad and the Northern and Southern Zamindaries, Sambalpur, held only two meetings each, and out of 78 Local Boards, 32 failed to meet at least once a month. The Lieutenant-Governor trusts that the grant of travelling allowance which has now been sanctioned, will make it possible for outlying members to attend at meetings more regularly and frequently.'[26]

Both landowners and practitioners of law as a class betrayed a general lack of public spirit in the discharge of rural functions vested in local bodies. It was the governmental bureaucracy and the non-official European elements of District and Local Boards who imparted to these institutions a corporate character to serve as an agency of rural service.

The functioning of local bodies as an agency of rural development must therefore be assessed in the context of these limitations. Prior to the introduction of dyarchy in the Provinces under the Government of India Act, (1919), the work of District Boards in Bengal continued, with certain exceptions, under the official guidance of the Chairman, the District Magistrate, although the Royal Commission on Decentralization had discussed in the meantime the whole question of decentralization with special reference to village government. No action was taken on any general principle of policy, but village union committees were already established under bureaucratic initiative in the Burdwan and Presidency Divisions where public opinion happened to be far more advanced than in other parts of the province. The original intention of the government had been to recognize village unions as the working unit of local self-government. The Bengal Act III of 1885 was drafted on this basis. But a subsequent change made the District Board the actual unit of administration with Local Boards under it and Union Committees became of minor importance. The Government of India, however, willed otherwise and advised experimentally to introduce village unions in selected rural areas. It was then that the Lieutenant-Governor of Bengal introduced Union Committees in Burdwan and Presidency Divisions and in the Tipperah district.[27]

The administrative Report of 1907-8 referred to the extension of union committees to the Orissa Division also. They were, however, all weak and lifeless and their status and vitality can be judged by reference to the aggregate income of the entire 59 committees that existed towards the close of that year—a mere Rs 15,913.[28] The question of infusing life into these committees and extending their sphere of activity in fact led to the Bengal Local Self-Government (Amendment) Act V of 1908.

The Act effected a considerable delegation of powers to Commissioners of Divisions in respect of the appointment, removal and resignation of members as well as the election of Chairmen of Local Boards or the Vice-chairman of District Boards, and the sanctioning of various rules and bye-laws. The delegation of powers to Commissioners, however, did not signify any loosening of bureaucratic grip. In addition, powers were taken to levy tolls on bridges, and the diversion of the road cess to purposes other than those mentioned in the Cess Act (1880) was prohibited. The application of the District Fund was at the same time extended in various directions. Under the head of education, for instance, contributions did not remain confined to primary education under the control of a District Board. These were permitted to secondary and other schools under private management, and even towards the maintenance of hostels. In respect of medical work, authority was given to District Boards to train and employ compounders, midwives and veterinary practitioners. For the furtherance of sanitation, on the other hand, District Boards, unless specially exempted, were required to appoint sanitation committees and qualified sanitary inspectors. The scope of the expenditure permissible upon veterinary work was at the same time greatly extended. Under the Act changes were finally introduced with a hope to extend the sphere of action and usefulness of union committees as the best form of village government. It was provided that these committees should in future work in direct subordination to the District Board unless with the Commissioner's sanction a District Board desired that they be controlled by a Local Board.

The importance of a three-tier system of rural boards thus continued to be recognized as a separate local agency of social services in rural areas. The Act of 1908 not only provided for a measure of administrative decentration from the provincial secretariat to Divisional Commissioners, a step which helped reduce the arbitrarary proceedings, if any, of the Collector-Chairman, but it also extended the functional scope of District Boards and brought into focus the projected usefulness of union committees as an instrument of village development. It was within this framework that local bodies functioned until reconstituted in the 1920's under the Government of India Act (1919).

A report on local self-government in Bengal for 1908-9 shows that, while the total income of District Boards from all sources amounted to Rs 78,76,020 their total expenditure was over Rs 85,00,000, with civil works and education claiming relatively higher amounts, the former being nearly Rs 44 lakhs and the latter about Rs 13 lakhs. Expenditure on medical matters came next with a little over Rs 4 lakhs,[29] while that on administration was about Rs 2 lakhs only.

Apart from the revenues arising from different sources, more especially from the provincial rates, the main source, the provincial governments granted loans to District Boards for specific projects of development. In 1908-9, for instance, loans to local bodies from the government amounted to Rs 4,54,000 in all, of which Rs 3,50,000 represented the second instalment of a loan for the Magrahat drainage scheme in the 24-Parganas, while loans of Rs 54,000 and Rs 50,000 were taken by the District Boards of Murshidabad and Darbhanga for the construction of railway feeder roads and screw-pile bridges respectively.[30] Loans were also advanced to local bodies for the construction of primary schools, subject to one-third of the cost being raised locally.

The maintenance or aiding of upper and lower primary schools formed part of the general functions of local bodies. But certain District Boards like those of Saran, Darbhanga, Shahabad, Bhagalpur and Burdwan were also interested in maintaining or aiding technical or industrial schools as part of a programme to promote cottage industry in rural areas. The success attained varied greatly from one District Board to another, but it marked the beginnings of local organized effort in the direction of rural industry.

The number of dispensaries in the whole of Bengal, Bihar and Orissa were not many—in all, 158, of which 142 were aided. Eight new dispensaries were, however, opened by the Gaya District Board, while the management of the Arrah Hospital was taken over by the

Shahabad District Board. The experiment of a 'floating dispensary' was tried and given up in the Sundarbans tract of the 24-Parganas.

Village sanitation remained in a state of neglect. According to a report of 1908-9, the largest expenditure was incurred by the District Boards of Gaya (Rs 5,887), Patna (Rs 5,112), Midnapore (Rs 3,370) and Birbhum (Rs 2,530), but rural sanitation in most districts continued to be sporadic and very inadequate. All District Boards, however, incurred expenditure in improving the local breed of cattle. Famine relief like-wise formed part of the concern of local bodies, though it was mostly limited to charitable relief.

Water supply and water works did not generally extend beyond the construction of wells and tanks in rural areas. Successful experiments were, however, made in the use of well-boring plant at Muzaffarpur in Bihar, and plans were set afoot for other local bodies to emulate this example. Difficulties were encountered, but the results were generally most encouraging.

The civil works of District Boards were mainly concerned with 'communications— original works'. Public works under the head 'Famine' were also included. Railway feeder roads received in fact a large amount of attention from nearly all District Boards, while bridge-building was chiefly confined to the districts of Bihar. There was in the course of the year not only no falling off in the amount spent on the repair of roads, but the total mileage of roads maintained by District Boards increased by 432.[31]

In addition to civil works, District Boards maintained several railway and tramway lines which continued to work as before. The Antpur-Champadanga extension of the Howrah Amta Light Railway was opened for traffic on 24 August 1908. The extension of the Barasat-Basirhat Light Railway in the 24-Parganas to Hashnabad was also completed. In Patna, the extension of the Bakhtiyarpur Bihar Light Railway to Silas was under construction. Messrs Martin and Company of Calcutta were collecting information for the construction of a tramway from Gaya to Sherghati. A survey for the light railway from Arrah to Sasaram was being completed with an agreement drawn between the Shahabad District Board and Martin Company. In Saran district, the Chapra-Masarak extension was in progress, and survey operations on the Thawe-Tewaripathi extension of the Bengal North-Western Railway were completed. The construction of these and other branch lines was doubtless the immediate concern of a railway company, but District Boards were not without interest in them. They applied for loans and permission from the government to undertake their completion in case delays occurred. The four guaranteed lines in the provinces continued to work satisfactorily, with the Boards' shares in the surplus profits in 1908 being as follows:[32]

	Rs.
Howrah (Howrah-Amta line)	38,678
Hooghly (Howrah-Sheakhala line)	2,987
24-Parganas (Barasat-Basirhat line)	5,944
Patna (Bakhtiarpur-Bihar line)	1,914

There were some other functions attached to local bodies in respect of rural services. These included the organization of agricultural shows and exhibitions; experimental cultivation of various kinds of crops like jute, cotton, flax, sugarcane, potato and rice; aboriculture as well as sericulture. Not all District Boards took equal interest in the promotion of these and other measures of rural development, but the fact stands out clearly that, in the course of nearly fifty years from 1869, the statutory recognition of local funds as a means to promote rural services became the *sine qua non* in the functioning of local bodies as an agency, distinct from the normal executive apparatus, of district administration.

Other Provinces

The best record in the functioning of local bodies was in Madras, where Grant Duff in his legislation of 1884 incorporated the ideas of Lord Ripon by emphasizing the importance of union panchayats, the grass-root unit of local self-government. The Madras *taluk* boards too were no mere echoes of District Boards but had separate financial allocations of their own. The establishment of union panchayats and *taluk* boards was in line with Lord Ripon's emphasis on the need to raise the superstructure of local self-government upon the foundations of village communities, although it was little realized that the *raiyatwari* system and its tenancy legislation were destroying their corporate character, thus, the rural boards so created in a state of disintegration of the old village system were treated as impositions from above, without the village being able to influence this new development.

The establishment of union panchayats in Madras was of course an attempt to revive the village system. But, as said before, it was a measure that did not apply to all provinces alike. Its failure was specially marked in Bengal where villages had become subservient to farmers of land revenue and major landholders. It is true that it was not entirely so in Bombay, in the North-Western Provinces, in Madras, or even in the Punjab, where villages continued to be held jointly for a time by the members of a particular kin known variously in different parts of the country. But they were all proprietors of villages bound together in most cases by kinship or other ties, though not by considerations of a legal compact. The lower castes that formed the various occupational groups rendered service to them in a subservient relationship imposed by social and economic compulsions. With the downward filtration of imperial authority, the village proprietors were either divested of their erstwhile public functions or their village headmen recognized as part of the government's official apparatus. In both cases they were reduced to subservience to an external governmental authority. As pointed out earlier, while law reduced dependence on village consensus, education and economic development created an alternative agency of middle-class leadership, especially of lawyers and bureaucratic officials, who supplanted the power and influence of the chief proprietors of villages. The neglect of the primary units of union boards doubtless prejudiced the restoration of the old village system. But the infiltration of urban-based middle-class influence in local bodies obstructed the emergence of rural leadership. The status-bound chief proprietors of villages who had served under the Mughals as a link with the people, lived in their midst as part of a rural community. But they were being supplanted under the British by a middle-class of rule-bound professionals who claimed to serve rural interests from their urban centres. The British could not bye-pass them in their endeavour to promote rural development through local bodies.

Doubtless the local bodies were deemed to have inherited the erstwhile functions which the village communities were supposed to have discharged before. The basis of such thinking was the continuance of local funds and their collection by officers of the government before the local bodies came to be invested with their administration. But, as said before, no trace of the ancient village system had survived the impingement of a central bureaucracy and capitalist enterprise. The Royal Commission on Decentralization did not in fact think it possible to restore the old system. It wanted to create new types of village governments in the new legal context of administrative and social development. On the pattern of Madras, it recommended a uniform three-tier system for all provinces. Unlike the old, indigenous village panchayats which were free from government control, the new ones were, however, to be constituted as a local agency of the government to secure popular participation in the guided functions of local bodies.

The non-existence of the old corporate village system was confirmed by the census report of 1911. Even so, grants were made to provinces in 1912 for distribution among selected villages as might be considered fit to be developed into new primary units of local self-government.[33] The *Report of the Bengal Administration Committee* (1915) even went to the point of recommending that village panchayats be invested with the control of village *chaukidars*. Two of its chapters were devoted to plans for the reconstitution of local bodies on the principle of indirect election from the village upwards. But nothing came of this until the transfer of the local self-government department to popular ministers appointed under the reforms of 1919. An important change, however, had taken place in the course of fifty years when local funds came to be first recognized as statutory. The local bodies were at the outset looked upon as a mere agency for the collection of these funds. But from Lord Ripon onwards emphasis on political education for rural development started increasing despite the continuance of the old bureaucratic grip. And since in course of time a gradual increase occurred in the functions of local bodies, the need arose for a well-organized system of local finance to promote further development. Local bodies were invested with powers to raise their own financial resources, although they were generally loath to incur the odium of levying and collecting taxes.

Period: Post 1919

The principle of decentralization introduced under the 1919 reforms and its relevance to the process of rural development have already been discussed at some length. In the field of local self-government its immediate effect was the democratization of local bodies and the attendant influence of national, communal and caste politics that crept into their inner recesses and affected their potency as instruments of rural development on sound administrative principles.

Rural Boards in Madras

No official could become a member of any rural board by virtue of his office. Under the Local Boards Act of 1920 no official except a village headman could contest an election. The non-official presidents of all *taluk* boards became *ex-officio* members of District Boards, where nomination to the extent of one-fourth of their total number was sought to be retained to secure the representation of the minorities and women. The remaining three-fourths of the members were to be elected. The administration Report of Madras Presidency for 1922-3 indicates that all the 24 District Boards except that of the Nilgiris were presided over by non-officials, two being elected. At the end of that year there were in all 924 members, of whom 125 were *ex-officio*, 200 nominated by the government and the remaining 599 elected by *taluk* boards, the total number of which was 125. The presidents of 111 of these *taluk* boards were non-officials elected by the *taluk* boards concerned, and of the remainder all except one were presided over by non-officials. The actual number of members at the end of 1922-3 in the entire Presidency was 2,404, of whom only two were *ex-officio*, 692 nominated and 1,710 elected. This was a marked improvement over the earlier position. For the members of *taluk* boards were all nominated until provision was made in 1909 for the election of one-third of their number, which increased to three-fourths under the Local Boards Act of 1920.

The *taluk* boards were abolished in 1934, but the importance of village panchayats was reinforced. The Madras Village Panchayats Act of 1920 incorporated the recommendations of the Decentralization Commission in favour of all panchayat members being elected directly by rate-payers, an arrangement which continued until the Madras Village Panchayats Act of 1950 revised the earlier enactment.

In 1930 the system of nomination to District Boards was given up, but it was revived in 1934 to satisfy the demands of national politics. For purposes of nomination seats were reserved for such minority communities as Muslims, Indian Christians, Scheduled Castes, Europeans, Anglo-Indians and women. The problems of rural development, which were mainly social and economic, thus came to be treated in terms of politics and the élitist game of power.

The Government of Madras was, however, keen to see that rural interest was duly safeguarded. District Economic Councils were established in 1935 'for the improvement of rural tracts' and these 'came into being in almost all the districts'.[34] Out of the Government of India grant of Rs 15 lakhs 'for rural reconstruction', Rs 12 lakhs were sought to be distributed among districts for the improvement of 'water-supply, rural sanitation and village communications and also for the encouragement and development of loan and sale co-operative societies.'[35] These functions lay within the scope of local bodies also.

The District Economic Councils were abolished in November 1936 and Collectors were thereafter required 'to convene periodical conference of important gazetted officers of the district, the Presidents of all District Boards and all elected Members of the Provincial Legislature belonging to the district, at least once in three months and lay before the conference for notice all matters in which they used to consult the District Economic Councils'. The sum of Rs 12 lakhs distributed to the Collectors was earmarked for the purposes already specified.

The Madras Government enacted two other measures to improve the economic condition of the agricultural classes. A scheme for the grant of loans was introduced in 1935 to provide relief against indebtedness. The relief so provided in the course of a year, however, amounted to over Rs 24 lakhs only, for the scheme did not apply to all the districts. Under the Madras Debt Conciliation Act of 1836, Debt Conciliation Boards were established to relieve agriculturists of a substantial share of their debt burden. Of the two measures the scheme of long-term loans was more popular.

Functionally, the Local Boards Act of 1920 continued to provide for the services ordinarily annexed to local bodies. These included, for instance, communications (roads), education, railways, public health, with vaccination, sanitation, etc. On the introduction of a complete District Health Scheme under the Act the Vaccination Department was gradually merged with the wider Public Health Department. The Deputy Inspectors of Vaccination who previously supervised only vaccination work were made responsible for all branches of public health administration. They became known as Health Inspectors, while District Medical and Sanitary Officers were styled District Medical Officers. There was thus a certain amount of rationalization in the administration of the institutions functioning under local bodies.

Financially, the Local Boards Act of 1920 provided for the obligatory levy of land cess at one anna in the rupee of the annual rent value. An additional cess up to a maximum of 3 pies was authorized by the

Act for District Boards and a similar cess for the *taluk* board. Provision was made under the Act for the levy of 'profession and companies' taxes also. Tolls upon carriages, carts and animals were, in addition, collected in all the districts. House-tax, on the other hand, was collected in all unions. The Elementary Education Act, 1920, authorized the levy of a tax for the expansion of elementary education. A number of *taluk* boards made use of the power so given and total receipts for 1922-3 amounted to Rs 329.40 lakhs. The grants received from provincial funds aggregated Rs 82.26 lakhs and were specially assigned to aid the general resources of local boards for trunk roads, education and hospitals. There was in fact a considerable increase in the amount of local finance in Madras under the new Act of 1920.

The Report for 1936-7 shows that the number of District Boards had by that time risen to 39 as a result of division and that all were functioned under elected non-official presidents. There were as many as 437 ex-union panchayat boards and 5,723 non-union panchayat boards at the end of that year.

Under the provisions of the Madras Local Boards Act of 1920 land cess continued to be levied during 1936-7 at the rate of one and a half annas in the rupee of the annual rental value of all occupied lands. Two-thirds of the entire land cess collected were credited to District Boards and one-third to panchayat boards, and the former were credited with the amounts where there were no panchayat boards. The total annual receipts had by now risen to Rs 453.31 lakhs, while the grants given by the government amounted to Rs 144.60 lakhs. Out of the income so raised the local boards constructed 308 miles of new roads during the year and the total length of roads maintained by the local boards at the close of the year was 52,459 miles, of which 3,087 miles were trunk roads.

In the field of education, on the other hand, the local boards maintained 201 secondary schools and 16,893 elementary schools, of which 2,760 were for girls. The total expenditure on education was Rs 137.60 lakhs, to which the government contributed Rs 79.15 lakhs, while the income from fees and other sources amounted to Rs 28.96 lakhs.

Though not an integral part of the general administration of the districts, local boards were thus functioning as a separate non-official agency of welfare services in rural areas. They ran as many as 66 hospitals and 1,072 dispensaries, including 214 using the indigenous system which now began to develop thanks to the recognition extended by the rural boards from considerations of economy. Much of the credit for what Madras was able to do in the field of rural development was due to the constructive genius of C. Rajagopalachari who headed its Congress Ministry in 1936–7. He was rated by Lord Linlithgow as 'much the most capable of the new Chief Ministers; a person whom his Governor, Erskinc, assessed as a leader of "exceptionally high quality".

The railways owned by District Boards, according to the administration's Report of 1936-7, were at work in six districts of the Presidency. These included the Tenali-Repalle Railway (21 miles), the Podanur-Pollachi Railway (25 miles), the Bezwada-Masulipatam Railway (52 miles) in the Kistna and Bezwada districts, and the Tinnevelly-Tiruchendur Railway (38 miles). They served as the mainspring of rural development in its early stages.

Bombay

In the Presidency of Bombay provision was made by the Local Boards Act of 1921 for a two-thirds elected majority in most of the District and *taluk* boards. The District Boards reconstituted under the District and Local Boards Act of 1923 further advanced elective principles, at least three-fourths of the members of District Boards being elected directly, not indirectly as hitherto by *taluk* boards. The government was empowered to use nomination in order to secure the representation of Depressed Classes. The electoral franchise was reduced and separate representation conceded to Muslims as part of a national policy, for the usual voting returned in most cases members of the dominant caste, Brahmins.

Functionally, too, there was considerable accession to the status of District Boards. They became corporate administrative bodies invested with powers to appoint their chief officer, engineer, health officer and administrative officer for education. Primary education came almost completely under their control, and they levied an additional one anna cess to improve the state of education. The élites' desire for status, power and patronage was thus sought to be met at local levels in the districts. But since the operational area of control in terms of power and patronage remained limited, the government's attempt to raise through additional taxation the financial resources of local bodies served nationalist politics. The elected anti-imperialist elements of local bodies in fact supported nationalist aims.

As in Madras, steps were taken in Bombay to ensure economic

development, especially in the field of agriculture. With the introduction of the 1920 Reforms a Development Directorate was created to further agricultural improvements, with special emphasis on increasing the yield and variety of such commercial products as cotton and sugarcane.

The Development Directorate in fact was an extension of the department of agriculture first established in 1883 to supervise the functioning of the land records staff for the supply of improved agricultural statistics as part of a sound famine policy. It was only in 1905 that land records and registration were separated from the department of agriculture proper, which concentrated now on agricultural education and research, demonstration forms and experiments.

The Report of the Administration of the Presidency of Bombay for 1922-3 shows that the Presidency was divided into five divisions, each under a Deputy Director who had under him a Divisional Superintendent. These officers were to examine the working of the several farms and disseminate amongst cultivators the results of experiments in the various branches of the department. The agricultural farms and stations, which served as the main centres of departmental activity and extension, were mostly part-managed by undergraduate superintendents who were trained at the Agricultural College at Poona. They were assisted by a number of field men who had also generally received a short training in agricultural science and technology at the College. The work done at these stations consisted generally in the selection of varieties of crops suitable for different localities, selection of seeds, hybridization of different varieties so as to obtain a strain of superior quality, and experiments with different kinds of manure as well as demonstrations of improved agricultural implements of all kinds. Another form of aid to the cultivator was the introduction of foreign, high class seeds for commercial crops including wheat, groundnuts, potatoes, etc. Their popularity was proved by the continuously increasing demand from agriculturists.

The Directorate of Development, in addition, attended to such allied branches of agriculture as agricultural engineering, animal breeding, horticulture and soil physics, which were all placed under the control of separate officers. Agricultural engineering was particularly important in well-boring and the selection of such machinery as pumping plants, iron ploughs and other implements.

However, agriculture suffered in the absence of any scheme for rural employment. Field labourers in all the districts of the Presidency were increasingly migrating to towns and cities where employment was available in cotton mills, cotton ginning and pressing factories and other industrial concerns. The cost of agricultural production increased due to the comparatively high wages paid to field labourers, a natural consequence of the growth of big business without any provision for small-scale cottage industries as part of rural development. The *laissez-faire* policy of the government did not permit such development and in this context Gandhi's emphasis on constructive programmes appears radical.

Rural development sufferd in the absence of a cumulative economic policy covering both agricultural and industrial sectors. Like constitutional development under the Government of India Act (1919), economic policy, too, was treated piecemeal in separate segments. An integrated approach to rural development was lacking and steps taken to promote agricultural improvements failed to produce the desired result due to rising costs and the scarcity of agricultural labour, as indicated in the tables given below![36]

	Daily average wages of field labour								
	1913			1921			1922		
Political Division—	Rs.	a.	p.	Rs.	a.	p.	Rs.	a.	p.
Northern Division	0	4	9	0	9	9	0	10	3
Central Division	0	5	0	0	7	9	0	8	3
Southern Division	0	4	0	0	7	6	0	8	9
Economic Circles									
Gujarat Circle	0	4	6	0	9	3	0	9	9
Deccan Circle	0	4	6	0	7	6	0	8	3
Konkan Circle	0	5	3	0	9	6	0	10	3
Presidency Proper	0	4	9	0	8	3	0	19	9
Sind	0	7	9	0	12	9	0	12	6
Whole Presidency	0	4	9	0	8	6	0	9	0

	Daily average wages of unskilled labour								
	1913			1921			1922		
Political Divisions	Rs	a.	p.	Rs.	a.	p.	Rs.	a.	p.
Northern Division	0	5	3	0	12	6	0	13	3
Central Division	0	5	9	0	8	6	0	9	3
Southern Division	0	5	9	0	8	9	0	9	9
Economic Circle—									
Gujrat Circle	0	5	3	0	11	6	0	12	6
Deccan Circle	0	5	9	0	8.	9	0	9	3
Konkan Circle	0	6	3	0	10	9	0	12	0
Presidency Proper	0	5	9	0	9	6	0	10	6
Sind	0	8	0	0	1	0	1	0	0
Whole Presidency	0	6	3	0	11	6	0	12	0

The wages of skilled labour increased even more rapidly, especially in the Northern Division. *The Review of the Administration of the Presidency Bombay* for 1922-3 shows that the demand for skilled labourers as fast increasing in all centres, which further accentuated the migration of labour from rural areas. The following table indicates the daily average wages of this class![37]

	Daily average wages of skilled labour								
	1913			1921			1922		
Political Division—	Rs.	a.	p.	Rs.	a.	p.	Rs.	a.	p.
Northern Division	0	13	9	1	14	0	2	3	6
Central Division	0	13	0	1	4	9	1	5	9
Southern Division	0	10	0	1	1	9	1	1	-9
Economic Circles—									
Gujarat Circle	0	13	6	1	12	6	2	2	6
Deccan Circle	0	11	9	1	3	6	1	4	0
Konkan Circle	0	13	9	1	9	9	1	10	9
Presidency Proper	0	12	6	1	6	9	1	8	9
Sind	1	4	6	2	3	0	2	4	0
Whole Presidency	0	13	9	1	8	9	1	10	9

However advances were given to cultivators in the districts to maintain agricultural progress. The following table reveals the advances given under the Land Improvement Loans Act and the Agriculturists' Loans Act during two years. [38]

District	1919-20 For purchase of seed and cattle	1919-20 For permanent improvements	1920-1 For purchase of seed and cattle	1920-1 For permanent improvements
	Rs.	Rs.	Rs.	Rs.
Ahmedabad	21,604	860	2,68,173	43,785
Kaira	20,437	16,559	2,67,029	1,07,034
Panch Mahals	59,512	7,711	1,11625	28,414
Broach	49,440	4,400	5,49,235	7,000
Surat	5,001	1,775	12,235	2,600
West Khandesh	94,148	4,800	1,89,457	74,619
East Khandesh	23,282	10,750	1,71,160	2,24,775
Nasik	64,070	9,260	8,67,672	5,66,155
Ahmednagar	5,91,644	27,057	17,18,106	4,44,396
Poona	22,650	45,165	1,08,001	1,97,865
Sholapur	7,063	11,800	1,20,002	2,77,614
Satara	5,610	13,750	23,576	1,57,933
Belgaum	22,322	7,215	1,84,830	3,44,700
Bijapur	1,28,595	56,406	4,35,386	7,34,915
Dharwar	50,966	29,680	44,493	27,462
Thana	9,915	3,150	8,595	9,680
Kolaba	2,790	5,500	7,840	2,700
Ratnagiri	6,242	300	2,404	Nil
Kanara	31,612	3,988	17,609	6,450
Bombay	Suburban	—	—	—
Total for the presidency proper.	12,16,903	2,60,126	51,07,870	32,58,070

—

District	1919-20 For purchase of seed and cattle	1919-20 For permanent improvements	1920-1 For purchase of seed and cattle	1920-1 For permanent improvements
Karachi	1,73,859	54,082	1,35,266	62,945
Hyderabad	1,13,158	54,441	1,30,991	77,222
Sakkur	1,72,407	1,05,983	1,65,980	1,05,710
Upper Sind Frontier	72,485	74,430	87,134	1,18,350
Larkana	4,149	1,926	1,285	1,004
Thar Parkar	1,95,323	74,459	5,69,274	1,04,411
Nawabshah	2,87,070	63,115	3,05,575	1,55,885
Total for Sind	10,18,451	4,28,436	13,95,505	6,25,527
Grand Total	22,35,354	6,88,562	65,03,375	38,83,604

Bengal

The non-official chairmen of District Boards in the wake of the reformed Constitution of 1919, although a report of the Commissioner of the Presidency Division for 1919-20 shows that in some districts non-official chairman had come to be appointed even before 1919.[39] By the close of 1920 all the District Boards had come under non-official chairmen. Dyarchy in fact led to considerable increase in the elective elements of District Boards, which greatly reduced official influence. Writing in 1895, for example, the Commissioner of the Presidency Division, Westmacott, observed: 'District Boards are of some use as consultative bodies, but the work is really done by the Magistrate of the district as Chairman, and the quality of the executive work depends upon the character of the District Engineer and his loyalty to the Magistrate and Chairman. Had it not been for these officers, everything would have collapsed.'[40] The Commissioner of the Burdwan Division, an Indian Civilian, also admitted 'that the duties of the Board are consultative and not executive'. But he considered it 'a distinct gain in the cause of good government to secure the cooperation of representative non-official gentlemen in our administrative work'. He added that 'the real advantage of the system lies, not in better administration, but in the practical education in the management of local affairs which affords to those who share in the work'. This view was similar to that suggested by Gokhale at the turn of the century who favoured some kind of non-official 'advisory council' to assist Collectors in the discharge of their executive duties.[41]

The results of the change in favour of democratization were not immediately perceptible. The Chairman of the Dacca District Board, however, reported that the people appreciated 'the new change of things' which gave them opportunities to 'freely mix with the Chairman and inform him about their wants more unreservedly than what they could do to an official Chairman'.[42] What became generally apparent through the reports of Divisional Commissioners was indeed a repetition of old experience.[43]

Functionally, the contribution of District Boards, especially in the East Bengal districts, lay in the removal of water-hyacinth which had become a general pest of rivers in the whole province. Besides being a danger to crops and communications, the pest was believed to be injurious to public health. The accumulation of the weeds sometimes blocked the natural flow of water in rivers, obstructing the water-way connecting one place with another. The welfare service of water-supply, though related to water-hyacinth, was for the most part confined to the construction or repair of wells and the re-excavation or cleaning of tanks for irrigation. Local bodies also organized and rendered relief on the failure of crops and undertook, for instance, the sale of Burma rice at cost price under famine conditions.

On the medical side, the old system of charitable dispensaries continued in rural areas and their number increased under democratic management. Apart from medical officers being maintained by some District Boards as a 'permanent reserve to deal with epidemic', all District Boards of the Presidency Division were on advise by the government 'to consider the desirability of subsidizing medical practioners with a view to affording relief in the rural areas on the lines adopted by the Jessore District Board'. The idea was to encourage qualified doctors to settle in rural areas. A couple of centres were accordingly selected by the District Board of the 24-Parganas as an experimental measure and a sum of Rs 1000 sanctioned for the purpose in 1920.[44] This idea later found expression in a recommendation of the Royal Commissioners on Agriculture.[45] But outside Jessore where as many as ten subsidized centres functioned in 1920 itself, the scheme did not take practical shape in the absence of suitable doctors, although in a letter of 5 May 1938 the Government of Bihar, for instance, reported to the Government of India that 'the District Boards have been asked to adopt the scheme for subsidizing medical practitioners in rural areas'.[46]

In the field of education the emphasis of District Boards was generally on primary education, including middle schools. Their strength kept on increasing, though not their quality. Local bodies maintained in addition technical and industrial schools to promote such rural crafts as carpentry, brass casting, weaving, cane and bamboo work, smithy and fitter's work. They also continued to support scholarships to Veterinary, Weaving, Engineering, Art, Agricultural, Industrial, Medical, Blind and Deaf and Dumb Institutes. The scholarships so provided by the District Boards of the Presidency Division were as follows:[47]

District	Name of institution at which scholarship is tenable	No. of scholar-ships	Monthly amount of scholar-ship per pupil
			Rs. a
24-Parganas	Bengal Veterinary College, Belgachia	2	10 0
	Sibpur Civil Engineering College	1	10 0
	Government Weaving School, Serampur	2	6 0
	Calcutta Deaf and Dumb School	5	5 0
	Calcutta Blind School	1	8 0
	Government School of Arts, Calcutta	1	5 0
Nadia	Industrial Branch of the C.M.S. Middle School, Kachrapara	7	3 8
	Calcutta Blind School	1	8 0
	Bengal Veterinary College, Belgatchia	2	15 0
Jessore	Bengal Veterinary College, Belgatchia	1	12 0
	Calcutta School of Arts	1	10 0
	Weaving School at Serampur	1	10 0
	Calcutta Deaf and Dumb School	2	10 0
	Sabour Agricultura College	1	10 0
Khulna	Bengal Veterinary College, Belgatichia	1	12 0
	Calcutta School of Arts	1	10 0

The scholarship or stipends paid by the District Boards of the Dacca Division to promote technical education in rural areas were more extensive in their scope and value. The statement given below is an indication of the assistance made available during 1923.[48]

The District Board of Dacca gave grants-in-aid to 21 Sanskrit *tols* and 6 junior madrasahs at a cost of Rs 2,520. The Mymensingh District Board aided 34 *tols* and madrasahs and 37 night schools. The Faridpur District Board spent Rs 1,052 in aid of 15 *tols*. The Bakarganj District Board aided 6 *tols* and 4 madrasahs at a cost of Rs 1,314.

An important change was a shift of emphasis in favour of village unions. The Bengal Village Self-Government Act of 1919 provided for the conversion of union committees into union boards invested with powers to raise their own tax resources as corporate bodies. Several union committees in each district were superseded by union boards. But the process was gradual and no committee could be superseded except with the prior sanction of the provincial government. Only 13 union boards were, for example, established in the districts of Dacca during 1919–20. The district of Faridpur applied for the establish-

District Boards	Name of institution	Number of scholar-ships	Rate per month or the total amount paid dur-ing the year
			Rs.
Dacca	Serampur Weaving Institute	2	6 each.
	Calcutta Blind School	1	10
	Dacca Deaf and Dumb School	2	10 each
	Calcutta Deaf and Dumb School	1	12
	Dacca School of Engineering	4	12
	Veterinary College, Belgatchia	1	11½
	Agricultural Institute, Dacca	1	10
	Sabour Agricultural College	1	10
Mymensingh	Shibpur Engineering College	1	10
	Dacca School of Engineering	3	10 each
	Sabour Agricultural College	1	15
	Government Weaving School, Serampur	3	6 each
	Ditto ditto	1	12
	Ditto ditto	1	15
	Calcutta Blind School	1	10
	Calcutta Deaf and Dumb School	1	12
	Dacca Deaf and Dumb School	1	10
	Ditto ditto	1	12
	Mining School, Nudkhurkhi (dist. Mahbhum)	1	15
	Government School of Arts	1	12
	Indian Art School	1	15
	Dacca Midwifery School	2	12 each
	Calcutta Medical College	1	20
	Ditto ditto	1	25
	Dacca Medical College	5	10 each
	Veterinary College, Belgatchia	4	13 each
Faridpur	Faridpur Baptist Mission Industrial School	9	588 during the year
	Calcutta Deaf and Dumb School	3	676 during the year
	Faridpur Deaf and Dumb School	4	

District Boards	Name of institution	Number of scholarships	Rate per month or the total amount paid during the year
	Calcutta Art School	1	182 during the year
	Serampur Weaving Institute	3	227 during
	Faridpur Weaving Institute	4	the year
Bakarganj	Barisal Deaf and Dumb School	3	7 each
	Dacca School of Engineering	1	10
	Calcutta School of Arts	1	5
	Ditto ditto	1	8
	Bengal Veterinary College	1	12
	Shibpur Engineering College (Artisan class)	1	13
	Dacca Medical School (for training a Muhammadan)	1	15
	Calcutta College (for a blind student)	1	50
	Serampur Weaving Institute–		
	Lower standard	2	6 each
	Upper standard (to supplement Government stipends)	2	5 each
	Weaving Institute, Zorahganj (Chittagong)	1	8

ment of 35 union boards but did not get the sanction until about the close of the year, the total income of union committees in the whole of Dacca Division amounted in 1919—20 to Rs 93,109, of which Rs 42,577 was contributed by District Boards. The total expenditure incurred, on the other hand, amounted to Rs 81,264, of which Rs 31,832 was spent on roads, Rs 15,081 on sanitation and conservancy, and Rs 20,431 on water-supply.[49]

The establishment of union boards was in fact described by a District Magistrate as by far 'the most important part' of the development that followed the democratization of local bodies under the reformed Constitution of 1919. For in several districts these village authorities took 'intelligent interest in local affairs' and could 'get the work done more cheaply' than either the government or District Boards. They could pay even extra taxes 'so long as they see money spent for their benefit'. It was, however, suggested that the money spent on digging expensive wells and large tanks, on which the village authorities devoted great attention, did not bring a due return because of neglect. This was especially so because the supervision and control exercised over local bodies after 1919 was suddenly relaxed for political reasons. In the words of P. H. Waddell, the District Magistrate of Bakarganj:

> The time is near at hand when local bodies will have much the same freedom as they have in England but, although I am no opponent of this policy, I trust that all the control existing in England will be exercised. Especially as regards audit, England has reached its present stage of development in local self-government after many years and India is only beginning. If control is still necessary in England, it is much more necessary in India for the public benefit.[50]

But the legislation enacted after 1919 clashed with the principle of control so suggested, more especially with reference to expenditure and audit. It introduced direct elections and removed District Boards from the supervision and control of local officers of the government, no salaried servants being allowed to be chairmen or vice-chairmen even when the Board failed to elect one. An appointment had to be made by the government. Officers were likewise debarred from voting at elections for these posts. The union boards were invested with certain administration powers to be exercised subject to the control only of District Boards in respect of such subjects as schools, sanitation and some other matters. In order to supply union boards with funds, clauses were inserted making contributions from District Boards compulsory. In all such cases, care was taken to see that the local government officers were not permitted to interfere with the proceedings of local bodies. This removal of official control also involved the withdrawal of the assistance of the revenue and other staff who earlier did a good deal of work for local bodies.

In this context, local bodies became subject to the influence of politics, the politics of the non-cooperation movement which in its wake, gave rise to the politics of communalism in different forms. With the removal of official interference there emerged a tendency on the part of local bodies to make appointments on communal grounds only, irrespective of the merits of candidates. This encouraged corruption due to slack supervision and reluctance to punish defaulters who might be of the same caste or creed as the majority of the executive council. In spite of the new powers given to local bodies, political consideraions weakened their ability to face the unpopularity involved in imposing new taxes, or strictly to collect those already imposed, or to enforce the law impartially in dealing with cases of appeal for remission. Moreover, certain non-cooperators who had managed to capture some of the District Boards, in Bihar and Orissa, for example, managed in the absence of bureaucratic control to misuse local funds for political purposes.

All these developments were taken note of in the *Reports of Local Government on the Working of the Reformed Constitution*, issued in 1923[51] and 1924[52]; the *Report of the Reforms Inquiry Committe* of 1924,[53] and the *Views of Local Governments on the Working of the Reforms*, 1927. Normal conditions tended to return after the failure of the non-cooperation movement, but since the Collector had practically been excluded from the affairs of local self-government, the clock could not be put back completely. The Indian National Congress, which spearheaded the non-cooperation movement, viewed local bodies as mere instruments of new taxation, although before long its leaders proceeded to capture control of these bodies as part of their own power games.

A Resolution of the Government of Bengal dated 25 January 1923 pointed out that, in view of the non-cooperation movement, there had been a serious setback specially to village self-government. The Bengal Village Self-Government Act had to be withdrawn from some districts and union boards replaced by *chaukidari* panchayats. In other districts the introduction of the Act had to be postponed. The result was that at the close of 1922 the number of union boards did not exceed 1,089. Even so, many of these boards in the Muslim-majority districts did useful work despite political opposition. Some new dispensaries were founded, several wells were constructed and tanks cleared of water-hyacinth. Some even distributed free medicines to the poor. Several union benches and courts were established for local trial of cases according to the Village Panchayat Act. The Minister for Local Self-Government in fact congratulated these infant institutions for the manner in which they had 'weathered the storm', and, while it was considered inadvisable to force the pace by too rapid an extension of the Village Self-Government Act, it was firmly believed that these primary units of local bodies would in due course play an important role in the whole scheme of local self-government.[54]

A fair number of union committees, however, remained unconverted and continued in their old form. These were a kind of half-way house between the *chaukidari* panchayat and the union board, which covered an area ranging between two to nine miles, a wide variation indeed. The annual total income of a union committee did not, on an average, exceed Rs 700 and in some cases it was even as low as Rs 300. A committee administering this paltry sum over so large an area and for a population ranging between 5,000 to 10,000 could not be expected to bring much interest or enthusiasm to bear upon its task. Even so, more than two-thirds of the committees' resources in 1922 were expended mainly on roads, sanitation and water-supply.[55]

Water-supply, as said before, was in fact the gravest problem confronting the District Boards in Bengal, where a large proportion of wells went dry in April and May. It was realized that there could be no permanent solution except by a resort to loans from the government and local taxation by union boards. For the District Boards, even with some accession of revenue and loans, found it impossible to bring adequate water-supply within the reach of the vast masses. It was argued that they could guide, stimulate and subsidize the union boards, but the union boards themselves must be responsible for the water-supply of each village, for the District Boards were too large a unit of administration to do so. It was here that political co-operation was most needed to enable local bodies to function as an agency of rural development, and it was here that that co-operation was for the most part denied.

A Resolution on the working of District Boards during 1923–4, however, shows that the creation of new union boards as part of village self-government was still not being pressed. 'The bogey of new taxation' had not yet been 'allowed'. It was only when the people were assured that taxation was not obligatory that proposals for the creation of new boards matured in a number of places, especially after the failure of the non-cooperation movement and the formation of the Swaraj Party in 1923. By the end of that year, 2,157 union boards were sanctioned, of which nearly 1,300 were in working order.[56]

The union boards showed increased interest in the construction of roads. Some established their own dispensaries and distributed indigenous medicines, others introduced free primary education and paid attention to the improvement of water-supply through re-excavation of tanks and the sinking of masonry and tube wells. But their resources remained inadequate. As the report of review for 1923–4 said, 'Reliance is mainly placed on the District Boards and other external sources of finance and the powers given by section 37 (b) of the Bengal Village Self-Government Act to increase their resources were not much used by Union Boards.' Local finance remained in a sad state.

A few District Boards helped out, but this was more the exception than a general rule.

The shortage of funds, following the increase in prices and functional expansion without control, continued to be the chief problem with all the District Boards in Bengal. Their resources were sought to be improved by taxing carriages as well as *melas* and markets, but these were petty taxes which could not augment income to any appreciable extent. The expansion of the system of union boards was therefore recognized as the main dependable source of local tax and an effective and cheap way to meet local needs; the District Boards were left with their own problems which might be solved by them from existing resources, including an increase in the rate at which cesses were levied under the Bengal Cess Act.

In the situation that followed the Reforms of 1919 there emerged in fact a dichotomy between the officially patronized feudal elements of local bodies and the rising bourgeois elements of 'non-cooperators', who bid for positions of control in the government and administration. This situation was specially marked in Bengal, where the Permanent Settlement led to feudal continuity, and the spread of Western education led to emergence of a power-motivated intelligentsia that contributed to the radical and revolutionary nationalism of Bengal. The dichotomy, which was latent in the pre-1919 period, came to the surface with the democratization of local bodies in the period that followed. While most members of District Boards came to be elected, the chairman, who succeeded Civilian Collectors, mostly remained either loyal members of the aristocracy or title-holders.[57] The intelligentsia used the removal of official control to seek mass contact and captured rural boards and their finances as a test of power and influence. In this extension of popular control and the consequent power struggles, the work of local bodies as an instrument of rural development in Bengal was impaired.

Bihar and Orissa

The Bihar and Orissa Village Administration Act of 1922 and the Bihar and Orissa Local Self-Government (Amendment) Act of 1923 were two important measures intended to improve upon the system introduced after the Reforms of 1919. The first provided for the formation in village of union boards of exercise, subject to the control of District Boards, certain administrative powers connected with schools, sanitation and other matters; for the constitution of village panchayats with powers to decide certain civil and criminal disputes;

and for the transfer to the union boards of the duties and powers of the *chaukidari* panchayats in relation to the village police. There used to be, in addition, union committees as part of village administration, committees mainly confined to the maintenance of roads, sanitation, pounds and water-supply. Under certain conditions these were converted into union boards constituted under the Bihar and Orissa Village Administration Act and intended to enable the rural population to manage their purely local affairs through an agency elected by themselves. The committees and the boards were not co-existent. Later, as the Administration Report of Bihar for 1936–7 points out, further progress in the conversion of the union committees into union boards was gradually checked, a development which tended to reduce the number of these boards. The second Act, which dealt with local and District Boards, reduced the number of nominated members from one-fourth to one-fifth and introduced direct election to District Boards. The representation of minorities and special interest was secured, as in other provinces, by nomination made by the Government of Bihar and Orissa. The Act, in addition, removed all district officers of the government and made it impossible for its employees to be chairmen or vice-chairmen even when a board failed to elect one.

Prior to the enactment of 1923 this emphasis on the elective principle did not exist. Doubtless there were in 1921–2 non-official chairmen in Purnea, Puri, Balasore, Shahabad, Patna, Gaya, Bhagalpur and Cuttack, which was a noticeable step in the development of local self-government in the province;[58] but the Act of 1923 nevertheless emphasized the elective principle for the first time.

A report of Divisional Commissioners on the working of District Boards during 1921–2 shows that though union committees were functioning in the district of Bihar and Orissa, prior to the Act of 1922 their number did not exceed sixty. Despite several proposals received from local officers for the creation of new unions, they were not carried into effect by the government, for it was considered desirable to await the enactment which finally provided for the establishment of union boards with enhanced powers and resources.

Even so, some of the union committees gave a good account of themselves and the credit for this flowed not from their character as a corporate body, but from the enthusiasm and public spirit of certain non-official chairmen who imparted life and vigour to the committees over which they presided. The Khujwa union committee in the districts of Saran, which functioned under a non-official chairman, was, for example, reported to have considerably improved its conservancy arrangements and to have taken keen interest in adopting measures against cholera. The Dalsingsarai and Jayanagar unions, on the other hand, had undertaken street lighting. These were all popular measures. But the cost, instead of being met by residents, was borne out of the funds provided by the District Boards concerned. Cases occurred where the assessees refused to pay tax. In many districts unions regarded themselves as a mere 'agency for spending District Board money' and were 'unwilling to adopt taxation for local improvement'. It was the character of individual chairman, official or non-official, that produced results.

In between the District Boards and union committees there were local boards in several districts. But not all were invested with large powers. Some District Boards, however, followed the example of that in Monghyr by decentralizing their powers and delegating them to local boards, a system that seemed to work well. In the district of Saran the local boards had in addition been entrusted with the control and management of primary schools and ferries in 1921–2, while the Siwan local board had also been given the control of veterinary work. A similar plan for the devaluation of powers had been sanctioned for the Samastipur local board. Prior to the enactment of 1923, it was being realized that the system of regulated 'decentralization' should be suitably adopted on a general principle; for local boards were deemed to be in a better position than the central District Board to know the needs of a subdivision, to decide questions of detail such as the site of a school or the need for the improvement of a road, and to control the work.

Sources of Finance

The mainstay of the income of District Boards was the provincial rate or cess levied under statutory provisions. It showed an increase of over Rs 7 lakhs between 1920–1 and 1921–2. The receipts of two District Boards, such as Manbhum and Hazaribagh, deriving income from the cess on mines had increased since 1913–14 by nearly Rs 8 lakhs, while the total increase in the cess income of the remaining District Boards had in the same period been only Rs 13.32 lakhs.

The income derived by District Boards from pounds, on the contrary, showed a considerable decrease. In Purnea it fell by nearly 50 per cent. As the report of Divisional Commissioners pointed out, 'the main reason given is the non-cooperation movement, the local representatives of which prevented the settlement of pounds, partly no doubt in pursuance of their general policy of hampering the administration wherever possible, and partly, as was undoubtedly the case in pounds, with a view to collecting funds by the establishment of unauthorized pounds'.[59]

The increase of income under 'law and justice' represented fines imposed for that infringement of District Board bye-laws. The bye-law under which prosecutions were most frequently instituted and fines imposed was the prohibiting bullock carts from travelling in the centre or metalled portion of roads, side tracks being duly provided for them. Questions were raised in the Legislative Council against what were deemed to be heavy fines in the Tirhut Division, but inquiries proved that, while the damage caused to roads by bullock carts was considerable, the repeal of the bye-law demanded by legislators was not desirable. Even so, District Boards were advised to modify the bye-law by reducing the maximum penalty and allowing carts to use metalled portions of roads during the rainy season.

Receipts under the head 'Education' showed a decrease. This was attributed chiefly to the abolition of fees in the primary schools of the Saran District Board and the falling-off in the number of students in Tirhut Division on account of the non-cooperation agitation of the Indian National Congress. The income derived from 'Medical', on the other hand, showed an increase which was due to the large grants given by the government to meet the capital cost involved in the establishment of dispensaries. Local rates or taxes which enabled District Boards to maintain hospitals and dispensaries in rural areas were inadequate for providing medical relief on a standard comparable to that in other countries, where medical institutions were, as a rule, supported directly by the government, not by local bodies. In India voluntary contributions were required to supplement the receipts derived from local rates. But as the regular collection of subscriptions presented serious difficulties, Divisional Commissioners in their report of 1921–2 advised District Boards and dispensaries to collect lump sum donations to form endowment funds for the maintenance of their hospitals and dispensaries.

The increase of income under 'Civil Works' was also due to large contributions from the government. A portion of the grant under this head was distributed in 1921–2 to District Boards for the construction of bridges, the most important being the bridge over the Phalgoo river in Gaya which had been destroyed by flood, as also that over the Damodar river in Manbhum, which linked Dhanbad with Purulia.

About half the cost in each case was met by the District Board concerned.

The report of the Divisional Commissioners for 1921–2 made it clear that, although the cess income of District Boards had recorded a regular rise during the earlier five years, it was subject to a couple of limitations. In the first place, this increase was confined to only a few District Boards, notably Gaya, Manbhum and Hazaribagh, and, to a lesser degree, to Champaran and Darbhanga. Secondly, the increase was to a large extent 'discounted by a decrease in the purchasing power of the rupee' as well as a 'rise in the cost of material and in wages'. The report therefore suggested that 'the question of finding new sources of revenue is an urgent one, especially in view of the urgent demand for the development of primary education and the expansion of medical relief'.[60] The report did not suggest any remedy except the usual resort to loans for meeting the capital cost of heavy civil works in the case of bridges, as also an imposition of tolls to meet part of that cost. The gradual rise of Indian capitalism[61] which began in the wake of the First World War and gained in momentum in the 1920's posed some new problems for local bodies not only in terms of financial resources, but more so in their administrative and technological capabilities to handle problems of rural development. Local bodies remained invested with the old functions of rural development, although the necessity of provincialization and some degree of central participation was being gradually realized.

The financial pattern of local bodies thus remained more or less unchanged. While the cess income continued to be their mainstay, they devoted the lion's share of their resources to the construction of metalled roads and some bridges, especially in the districts of Manbhum and Hazaribagh where industrial developments dictated the necessity of keeping communications in good trim. With a view to improving the state of local finances the Local Self-Government Act was sought to be amended in 1923 to make local bodies more representative of wider interests so that they might more easily increase the local rates[62] or introduce new taxes to achieve their goals.

The following tables compare the income and expenditure under the main heads of account in 1912–13 (the first year in which the public works cess was made over to District Boards) and during 1920–1 and 1921–2.

An important feature of Bihar and Orissa was that while the Ministry of Local Self-Government openly objected to any interfer-

EXPENDITURE

Heads	1912–13 Amount (Rs)	1912–13 Percentage of total income	1920–1 Amount (Rs)	1920–1 Percentage of total income	1921–2 Amount (Rs)	1921–2 Percentage of total income
Interest	11,843	0.2	13,756	0.13	22,245	.2
Administration	1,38,550	2.8	3,20,311	3.03	3,59,908	3.24
Police (Pounds)	14,228	0.3	16,447	.155	20,181	.18
Education	8,55,818	17.1	17,95,537	17.94	20,60,000	18.56
Medical	3,36,492	6.7	9,39,833	8,89	11,71,982	10.56
Scientific & other minor departments	55,377	1.3	1,69,158	1.6	1,95,946	1.76
Superanution allowance and pension	60,394	1.2	80,523	.76	95,661	.86
Stationery & Printing	31,634	0.6	74.965	.75	79,398	.71
Miscellaneous	15,199	0.3	42,254	.04	41,151	.31
Famine Relief	141	0.003	4,009	.03	2,81,687	2.53
Railways	3,876	0.08	2,375	.002	—	—
Civil works	28,48,435	57.2	58,31,609	55.2	56,99,388	51.35
Repayment of loans	91,297	1.8	34,449	.32	52,584	.47
Deposits and advances	5,22,611	1.5	11,34,933	10.74	10,16,835	.16
Total	49,95,535	—	1,05,60,159	—	1,10,96,996	—

INCOME

Heads	1912–13 Amount (Rs)	1912–13 Percentage of local income	1920–1 Amount (Rs)	1920–1 Percentage of total income	1921–2 Amount (Rs)	1921–2 Percentage of total income
Land Revenue	156	.003	13,964	.12	826	.007
Provincial rates	23,56,721	47.2	62,86,701	56.34	70.20,011	60.8
Interest	20,919	0.4	1,07,686	.96	88,943	.77
Law and Justice	16,105	0.3	20,978	.18	26,223	.22
Police (Pounds)	2,18,968	4.4	1,92,743	1.72	1,52,694	1.32
Education	4,85,602	9.7	11,61,294	10.40	11,55,195	10.01
Medical	53,939	1.1	2,85,662	2.56	2,89,498	2.51
Scientific and other minor departments	11,974	.02	27,822	.24	19,883	.17
Receipts in aid of compassionate allowance.	—	—	223	.002	233	.002
Stationery	3,946	0.07	3,227	.029	2,518	.02
Miscellaneous	1,47,896	2.9	3,82,836	3.43	35,143	.3
Railways	4,827	0.1	5,872	.052	65,640	.56
Civil works including ferries	10,47,586	20.9	10,96,366	9.82	12,41,880	9.9
Loans	—	—	3,10,000	2.77	2,55,000	2.21
Deposits and advances	6,30,315	12.7	12,62,119	11.31	12,76,847	11.07
	49,98,953	—	1,11,57,503	—	1,15,30,534	—

ence by officers of the government in proceedings of local bodies, the Minister himself wanted their elected office-bearers brought to the headquarters for necessary guidance. For the Bihar and Orissa Council 'desired that all supervizing authority should be exercised from headquarters by the Minister or, preferably by themselves', which accounted for the establishment of a Local Self-Government Board: a majority in it consist of Members of the Legislative Council who were anxious to arrogate to themselves a right to inspect all rural boards and to interfere with the discretion of a local body in 'matters of purely local interest'.[63] The democratization of local bodies thus did not signify any local autonomy exercisable by District Boards. It meant a politico-administrative alternative which democratization provided for the exercise of a regulatory authority in place of the erstwhile bureaucratic hierarchy. Democracy did not necessarily imply decentralization in Bihar.

The United Provinces

The United Provinces District Boards Act of 1922 was modelled on the U.P. Municipal Act of 1916. But while municipal boards were to function as advisory bodies working through an executive, the District Boards were to be corporate units of direct administration.[64]

In its original form the Bill had made no provision for separate communal representation. To meet the demands of Muslim and official opposition the Minister for Local Self-Government was obliged to introduce an amendment providing separate representation for Muslims and, in addition, giving them due weightage. The passage of the Bill was naturally delayed and the elections which in the normal course would have been held in March 1922, had to be postponed in order that they might be held under the Act so amended in 1922.

The reviews of Divisional Commissioners on the working of District Boards prior to 1922, however, show a general lack of interest on the part of non-official members. The limited degree of democratization which had taken place before the Act of 1922 in its amended form, brought little or no improvement in their attendance. The lack of vitality from which the District Boards constituted under the District Boards Act of 1906 had suffered, seemed to continue despite considerable increase in the elected representatives. The tahsil committees or boards, too, were hardly an exception. This was attributed to 'lack of definite responsibilities' and 'opportunities for initiative' in respect of both administrative and financial matters controlled by the bureaucracy. They had no responsibility or local autonomy.[65]

However, the departmental sub-committees, especially of education and public works, stood on a different footing and their mode of functioning more encouraging. According to the reviews of Divisional Commissioners, a departmental sub-committee 'enjoys several advantage over the tahsil committee. It tends to be recruited from among the more zealous members of the board, and it is concerned with a definite sphere of activity. It affords opportunity for more exhaustive and at the same time more informal discussion than is possible in meetings of the full board'.[66] Through the free discussion and close interchange of views which a departmental sub-committee often permitted, the non-official members of boards tended to develop a sense of responsibility.

The aggregate income for 1921–2 rose from Rs 152.81 lakhs to Rs 172.52 lakhs and the expenditure from Rs 152.12 lakhs to Rs 184.65 lakhs. The rise in income proceeded entirely from an increase in government grants for education, which entailed an even greater increase in expenditure, thus producing no relief to the finances of District Boards. Since they had started surviving on the balances accumulated during bureaucratic regimes, the services other than education could not receive the attention they deserved. There was, once again, a large decrease in the income derived from pounds on account of the non-cooperation movement, from interest due to redemption of the War loan, and the sale of securities by several District Boards.[67] As already suggested, post-War developments not only posed local bodies with the problem of reviewing the old structure of local finance, but also called for an assessment of their capacity in terms of administrative and technological resources being made locally available.

Financially, government grants were made available for specific purposes. The government, however, recognized that it was not within the power of Boards to fulfil the liabilities which they, in accepting the grants, undertook to use them specifically for the purpose for which they were granted. It was therefore decided to resume the balances of grants and, instead of treating them lapsed, to redistribute them as additions to the general revenues of boards. This process was intended to relieve District Boards of their immediate difficulties. But the government believed that no permanent solution could be found except in the use of the powers of taxation with which the Boards had come to be invested under the new District Boards Act, powers which by and large remained unused for fear of popular clamour. The administration of local bodies naturally deteriorated and most of the services languished.

The position of District Boards in the United Provinces showed no marked improvement even after franchise was extended under the Act of 1922. According to a report on their working during 1923–4, the franchise had become as wide as that of the Legislative Council. It created bodies of electors differing widely in number and character from the restricted electorate of the old boards. Simultaneously, official chairmen were replaced by those elected by the Boards. Members nominated by the government were limited to two on each Board, and none could be a government servant. Another important change was the carving out of single-member constituencies in each district, an arrangement designed to secure representation for every part of the district. The number of seats was at the same time raised from 1,084 to 1,451.[68]

Even so, the progressive deterioration of the roads maintained by District Boards was not arrested and democratization could not deliver the goods. The government, as the report for 1923–4 points out, appointed a committee for the reorganization of the Public Works Department, which hitherto maintained the metalled roads on behalf of the Boards. The committee recommended that the maintenance of roads should be transferred to the direct management of the Boards. But instead of spending adequate sums on maintenance, the Boards spent rather more on metalling new roads, which resulted in existing roads falling to pieces in most districts.

As regards public health, there was nothing worthy of mention except the three districts of the Gorakhpur Division, where the district health scheme was in operation. The District Boards had no powers under the Village Sanitation Act, nor did they control village panchayats for purposes of rural sanitation. The only hope of improving the health of the rural public was the maintenance of an organized staff comparable to that provided in Gorakhpur Division. But having no specific agency through which to work, the activities of District Boards remained confined to sporadic efforts to construct or repair wells and drains and to fit the former with pumps. The work done under such measures was, unfortunately, always 'inappreciable'.[69]

Inspection was a problem of fundamental importance for the District Boards established under the Act, 1922. Earlier inspection was mainly performed by government officials and, except in the case of schools, mainly by the revenue staff. The government was guided by two main consideration. It wanted information regarding the manner in which the Boards acquitted themselves; and the Boards themselves might need information to ensure the maintenance of efficient standards. It was recognized that inspection of the latter kind was of a routine nature and that it was entirely a matter for individual Boards to undertake. But since this function had not previously been discharged by the Boards, except by a few of their more zealous members, no organized agency was available immediately for inspection and it continued to be done by the revenue staff of the government.

The progress of Boards in this direction remained in fact most uneven. Some made no attempt whatsoever to evolve a system of inspection.[70] The difficulty was that no Board could afford to maintain a special inspecting staff; and so far as individual members were concerned, it was doubtful whether they could bring to the task the qualities needed for its due performance. Even the chairman and secretary were unable to do all or nearly all the inspections. The tahsil committee doubtless offered the nucleus of an organization, but it was not used. There was thus no effective, organized alternative to the regular official agency of inspection. Indeed, the mode of functioning of the new Boards marked little or no departure from that of their predecessors, and since their finances too showed no improvement, all the services except education remained inadequate. Commenting on the manner in which the Boards functioned under the Act of 1922, a Resolution of the Local Self-Government Department observed:

> Interference in matters of details were frequent; this was often the outcome of a healthy interests in the Boards' work but tended none the less to undermine the authority of the Board's executive as well as to waste the Board's time. Much of all this can be summed up in the remark that Boards were still finding their feet.[71]

Punjab

The Punjab situation was less politically oriented than that in other areas. The urban classes of lawyers and businessmen, for the most part Hindu, no doubt guided by political considerations, but the agriculturists, who were largely Muslims, constituted a counterforce. Beneficiaries of the great schemes of irrigation in the couple of decades before the Reforms of 1919 as well as by the Land Alienation Act of 1900, they were more interested immediately in fresh initiative of the executive administration for economic and agricultural improvement rather than political involvements. They were also apprehensive of the moneyed and urban interests of Hindus. The influence of the executive administration was thus relatively more sustained in the Punjab than in other provinces and the first couple of years after the Reforms continued to be under official guidance. The mode of appointment or election of members was determined by rules made by the Local Government. Most of the District Boards constituted even in 1922 did not have an elected majority of more than two-thirds, while some had only one-third. And it was only in 1925 that they were given the choice of electing non-official presidents. Even so, no more than two Boards made the change in the 1920's and two more in the 1930's.[72] The electorate introduced for this level was based on separate communal representation, but it did not extend to village panchayats.

Under the Reforms of 1919 the Boards were all reconstituted in keeping with the new electoral rules providing for an extension of franchise. The Administration Report of the Punjab for 1919–20, however, said that the innovation so introduced exercized no marked stimulus on the electorate; for only about 20 per cent of the voters went to the polls in the greatly increased number of elections.[73] Nominations were made in districts where the elective system was not yet in force. It was believed that public interest might be stimulated by a further reduction of the official element on Boards, by the appointment of non-official chairmen and the grant of wider powers of taxation. But reluctance to undertake executive duties to enforce rules and payment of taxes continued in rural boards. It was not so in municipalties, where the policy of withdrawing official control was welcomed and quickened the interest of citizens in municipal affairs.

The Punjab District Boards maintained their diverse spheres of activity, which included the maintenance of roads and water-supply, of veterinary dispensaries and demonstration farms, the supply of well-bred bulls and rams for cattle and sheep breeding, experiments in sericulture and the promotion of aboriculture. A decided step forward to improve hygiene and sanitation was taken with the appointment of district health in certain areas. Primary and agricultural education as well as civil works and certain scientific services formed part of the Board's sphere of activity in the Punjab.

Financially, however, the Boards suffered from serious limitations. The continuing rise in prices, the increasing demand for education and communications, and the necessity of raising the salaries of District Board employees added considerably to the expenses of administration. A general difficulty in the matter of finance was the continued opposition by members of Boards to any increase in direct taxation. The result was that, while expenditure increased with the rise in prices, income remained relatively inelastic.

Even so, District Boards undertook schemes of expansion in education, medical relief and, in a few cases, communications. This they did without considering how the recurring expenditure involved would be met. Encouraged by the grants which the government made for capital expenditure on schools, hospitals or roads, they hoped that the government would come to their rescue and no Board cared to observe any economy.[74]

Apart from government grants, the main source of income was the local rate. Until 1921–2 this was limited to a maximum of 20 pies per rupee of land revenue. A legislative measure of that year raised the maximum to two annas and the minimum to 20 pies. An attempt had in the meantime been made by some Boards to broaden the basis of taxation by imposing a status (*haisiyat*) tax on those who did not pay land revenue.

The assessment and collection of the profession-tax, however, involved serious difficulties. The removal of the erstwhile *tahsildars* from membership of District Boards left these bodies with no agency to do the job. But more serious was the organized opposition of middle-class professionals who were members of District Congress Committees. The affluent amongst them benefitted from District Board roads but would not pay towards their maintenance. The grievance of *haisiyat* payers was that they were being taxed without representation on District Boards: the government removed this grievance by granting them franchise. Even so, when the profession-tax was inaugurated in the district of Ambala, the local Congress Committee organized an agitation not only for the repeal of the tax but also against the collection. The situation was met by administrative firmness and timely recognition of the principle that those assessed to this tax deserved registration as electors to District Boards.[75]

The service which suffered most from want of financial support was the maintenance of roads, which involved increased costs of materials, enhanced wages and freight charges. The increased wear and tear of the roads, however, proceeded in the post-War period from heavy motor traffic which called for the use of the stone metal in their construction instead of *kankar*. Under the new provincial 'Motor Vehicles Plying for Hire Rules' the government provided for the sale of road certificates. But only a part of their proceeds were credited to District Boards.[76] Besides, not all motor vehicles were taxed and only those on hire were called upon to pay—an arrangement which had its loop-holes.

The Central Provinces

In the Central Provinces the relevant institutions were called District Councils, with the local bodies below them known as Local Boards. The Local Self-Government Act of 1920 authorized the government to regulate the mode of election or selection of members of District Councils, but made no provision for separate electorates of the reservation of seats for Muslims or other minorities.

The Local Boards included a certain number of 'Zamindari local boards', with both official and non-official members whose attendance was difficult to secure as they were widely scattered. It was considered expedient to have unimportant business distributed among them individually, subjected of course to their reports and decisions being confirmed by the Board or the Council, as the case might be.

Under the Primary Education Act passed after the Reforms of 1919, primary education was to be made compulsory in the districts. But according to a report of 1921–2 very few local bodies took steps to introduce it. The Act had also provided for improving the state of rural literacy and it was hoped that local bodies would assist by opening village libraries. District Councils were at the same time expected to take steps to organize village panchayats and use them for purposes of education, rural sanitation and inspection of roads. But no progress was made in these fields in the absence of local enthusiasm. In Berar, where a special school-rate was levied, its was reported that 'complaints have been made that neither the panchayats in villages under the Sanitation Act nor the village officials in other villages are willing to help in the collection of the tax but preer that the odium of collection should fall on government'.[77]

As in other provinces, education and communications formed part of the services rendered by District Councils. The cost of school buildings and the maintenance of roads was partly met by government contributions. The expenditure on communications was significant, 55 per cent of the toal expenditure. Another important feature was the government's contribution for the maintenance of roads and buildings was sought to be transferred from the Public Works Department to District Councils.

The extent of devolution to local bodies in the Central Provinces was on the whole very limited. The position of their employees was far from secure, and there was a general aversion to serving under them, which retarded the efforts of the government to effect complete devolution. The Self-Government Department therefore advised under a Resolution of 1923 that appointments, dismissals and suspensions must be governed by definite rules and that powers must remain in the hands of a responsible committee of the local body, not in the hands of individual members.

As in other provinces, the political overtones of some District Councils and Local Boards discouraged devolution. Local leaders were actively interested in matters that did not fall within the sphere of local bodies, namely, the closure of liquor shops, enforcing the wearing of *khaddar* by their employees and schools boys, etc. In some cases, even school teachers were 'ordered to undertake Congress propaganda' at the cost of their normal work. Educational institutions naturally tended to become dysfunctional.

Reports on Agricultural Improvements

Though vitally related to the task of rural development, the improvement of agriculture did not form an immediate or direct statutory obligation of local bodies, but belonged to the Department of Agriculture. However, local bodies conducted a number of rural welfare services which had relevance to agricultural improvement also, and the Royal Commission on Agriculture not only recognized this but integrated it into its recommendations. These services were, for example, primary education, co-operatives, medical relief, water supply, irrigation, road communications and cattle-breading. It was natural to expect that any improvement made by local bodies in one or other of these services as part of their own immediate responsibility would be a contribution to agricultural improvement also.

In response to communications of the Government of India, the Provincial Governments submitted periodic reports on the progress made in giving effect to the recommendations of the Royal Commission. The sixth report, submitted for 1936 and 1937, contained useful references to the steps which local bodies were said to have taken to give effect to those recommendations within their own limited spheres.

Bihar[78]

The report which the Government of Bihar sent pointed out that the number of 'trained teachers' for the primary schools of local bodies was increasing and that 'adult education' was being 'imparted through the organization of night schools', the total number of night schools being 919 at the end of 1937. They were 'maintained partly by local contributions and partly by local bodies'. Some middle schools even offered a course in agriculture. There was a growing demand for more girls' schools, but the 'paucity of funds' at the disposal of local bodies and the 'dearth of qualified trained mistresses' militated against the spread of female education.

For medical aid to villages, District Boards had been asked to subsidize medical practitioners in rural areas, but no progress seems to have been made in this direction. In the veterinary field, however, as many as eleven new institutions were established by local bodies. In addition there were field veterinary dispensaries at different centres in out-lying rural areas which afforded facilities for the treatment of live-stock.

The Royal Commission on Agriculture had recommended the formation of irrigation panchayats for the management of irrigation and distribution from village channels. This recommendation was not acceptable to the Bihar Government which argued that, although the question was considered in 1916, the establishment of panchayats or irrigation boards was turned down 'owing to lack of communal spirit in irrigating villages'. Water therefore continued to be supplied under a 'personal agreement between government and each individual cultivation'.

As regards the general welfare service of water-supply as part of the function of District Boards, the government had already been making annual grants for wells and tanks, although it was recognized that the construction of ordinary wells was essentially a matter of private enterprise. The owners of these wells were assisted by means of 'test borings' for the construction of new wells, by the supply and fitting of 'Rahat' bullock pumps suitable to various sizes of masonry wells, and by sinking open tubes through the foundation clay to enable a better water-bearing sand to be tapped. Well irrigation, however, had started losing importance, although it was not abandoned. There was noticeable progress in work on small tube wells, though it was still limited to co-operate societies.

Co-operation did not seem to have made any headway with District

Boards, especially with reference to improvement in the amenities of village life. Uplift work and the rural community movement formed part of the responsibility of the 'Development Department' of the government, which had introduced the Bihar Village Welfare Scheme in November 1936, with four selected centres, one in each division. The sanctioned staff for each such centre consisted of a 'rural welfare officer', a 'village guide', an 'agricultural *kamdar*' and a *dai* for midwifery. The declared objectives of the government included agricultural improvement, cottage industry, better village sanitation, provision for good drinking water, primary education and the introdution of social amenities such as village sports, libraries, reading rooms, etc.

Bombay[79]

The sixth report shows that the progress made in the Presidency in implementing recommendations of the Royal Commission was the best. 'All local bodies like the taluka development associations and co-operative credit societies' were associated with 'arranging propaganda' for the improvement of agriculture in the same way as done by several other offical and non-official agencies. There were as many as 'thirty taluka development associations and four unregistered associations in the North Central Division which continued to supplement the work of the department'. These local bodies were 'guided and controlled by the Divisional Board'. Their function was to 'keep seed and manure depots'. They also stocked 'insecticides, fungicides, spray pumps, etc.' and give them out 'for use to cultivators'. Three 'taluka development associations', of Jalgaon, Jamner and Shirpur, were in addition running 'cattle breeding farms'. Local bodies took increasing interest in cattle shows and applied to villages the Livestock Improvement Act of 1933 which was intended to protect pure cows against breeding with undesirable bulls.

Irrigation panchayats were tried in certain parts of the province, but they were not very successful. Even so, the experiments were not discontinued. Use was at the same time made of pumping and bording operations and tube wells. To improve communications in irrigated tracts of the Deccan, the Bombay Local Boards Act of 1923 was utilized to set apart one-third of the cess on water rates of the improvement of such local board communications.

The importance of medical aid to cultivators was empahsized as relevant to agricultral imporvement. Instead of merely asking District Boards to introduces schemes of subsidized medical aid for the rural population, as Bihar had done, the Government of Bombay actually adopted in 1936 'the scheme of giving monthly subsidy to qualified [allopathic] medical practitioners to induce them to settle in small towns or villages'. Under this scheme each medical practitioner was to be in charges of three or four villages easily accessible by road or rail, and he was expected to visit them on definite days of the week. Four-fifths of the cost of maintaining subsidized medical centres were to be borne by the government and the rest 'met by the District Local Board concerned'. It was laid down that 'Ayurvedic and unani medical practitioners are also eligible for employment as subsidized medical practitioners, due regard being paid as far as possible to the wishes of the local population'. The scheme also provided an increase in the number of qualified nurses and midwives in local board dispensaries.

As regards village water-supply, the Bombay Government reported that prior to 1937 'about a lakh of rupees every year was spent on giving grants-in-aid to local boards'. In 1937–8 and 1938–9 an annual provision of Rs 10 lakhs was made 'for providing wells, etc., in villages'. This was followed by a provision of Rs 8.55 lakhs for 1939–40. It was added that 'prior to 1937–8 the local boards and villages were required to find one-third of the cost of a well, the remaining two-thirds being provided by Government. Since 1937–8, however, the entire expenditure was borne by the Government'. Local bodies like taluka development associations participated actively with the 'rural uplift' movement organized by the Department of Agriculture throughout the province. They took advantage of the movement in respect of 'seed and implement supply', land development and crop protection work.

The Bombay report appreciated the efforts of local authorities in spreading literacy. Their efforts in respect of female education, too, were applauded. 'The inspecting staff, the local school committees and other members interested in the education of girls held conferences in villages to promote the cause of the education of girls', with the result that the number of girls' schools started steadily increasing. Some local authorities (both municipalities and district local boards) had even introduced compulsory primary education.

While no co-operative society had been formed for adult education, additional night schools were opened in some places 'out of the Government of India grant for village uplift'. Some adult education classes had also been started with the help of grants-in-aid from the provincial Government.

The Central Provinces and Berar.[80]

The report of the Government of C. P. and Berar did not specifically deal with the contribution of local bodies to agricultural improvement. The Medical Department had introduced subsidies to encourage medical practitioners to settle in important villages in the interior, but no progress was made after the failure of the scheme. Some District Councils had doubtless introduced compulsory primary education, but in the absence of cooperation from parents and the distance which pupils were obliged to cover from the central school the scheme made little or no headway. Financial stringency, on the other hand, stood in the way of schools for adult education. Liberal grants were, however, made to District Councils for improvement of water-supply in rural development.

Other Provinces

Reports from other provinces[81] either were sketchy or discussed the measures taken by government departments to give effect to the recommendations of the Royal Commission. The contributions of District Boards did not specially figure in these reports, except in some matters of minor importance.

However, District Boards were associated with the action taken from time to time to relieve agricultural distress. In Rajputana, for instance, when tanks went dry and wells held little or no water in 1938, works were sought to be opened 'by the Public Works Department and the District Boards with the object of helping villagers in distress to earn a livelihood'.[82] Another case on record, of a District Board being actively involved in providing relief against agricultural distress was in Bakerganj in Bengal, where a cyclone had caused serious damage in October 1937. The distress was accentuated by a partial failure of crops caused by pests and a temporary contraction of rural credit. In a communication of 21 February 1938 the Government of Bengal reported the action taken and the role played by the District Board of Bakerganj. 'To relieve distress', as the communication pointed out, 'agricultural loans amounting to Rs 1,92,500 were distributed, a sum of Rs 10,000 was allotted for gratuitous relief, and test works were opened at 14 centres, through the agency of the District Board'. Similar action and the agency of local bodies employed to relieve agricultural distress were extended to other districts that suffered in October 1937.[83] Steps were in addition taken to control the wholesale prices of essential agricultural produce as well as to pass the Bengal Famine Insurance Fund Bill (1937) which provided for the establishment and maintenance of a separate fund to meet expenditure on famine relief and distress caused by such natural calamities as drought, flood, and earthquakes.

Welfare measures were likewise taken by Madras to provide relief against agricultural distress arising from natural disasters. They included provision for relief works, suspension and remission of rent, agricultural loans and gratuitous relief, supply of fodder and free grazing in village forests. But in Madras it was the Collector who led the way. The District Economic Council which had been constituted in all the districts for the improvement of rural areas, were dissolved, and District Boards acted as one of the agencies for mere consultation. Collectors were, however, required 'to convene periodical conference of important gazetted officers of the districts, presidents of District Boards and all elected members of the provincial legislature belonging to the district at intervals of not more than 3 months'. It was 'open to Collectors to lay before the conference for advice all matters on which they used to consult District Economic Councils in the past and also other matters of general importance pertaining to the welfare and administration of the district.'[84]

On the pattern of Bombay, rural medical relief as an aid to agricultural improvement was provided also by Madras through subsidized medical practitioners in charge of local dispensaries. The subsidized system of medical relief in rural areas was introduced in U.P. too during the Congress rule in 1937–8. The operation of this principle was extended to the Punjab as well as C.P., where a trial was given to 'travelling dispensaries'. The subsidized system operated generally at the dispensaries maintained by District and Local Boards. But a scheme for the appointment of subsidized medical practitioners in rural areas not served by any dispensary was also adopted in certain places. No scheme of medical relief through subsidized medical practitioners had yet been adopted in Bengal.[85]

Period: 1937–47

General Background to 1937. The beginning of 1937 saw the end of the dyarchic system which had effected the democratization of local bodies in varying degrees under the Government of India Act (1919). The new constitutional structure introduced in the provinces under the Government of India Act (1935) was founded on the principle of provincial autonomy, involving transference of the administration of all provincial subjects (including law and order), with certain safeguards, from the control of the bureaucracy to ministers responsible to legislatures. While the executive authority of a province was to run in the name of the Governor, he was to exercise that authority on the advice of his ministers.

Politically, the non-cooperation movement and the politics of the Swaraj Party had lost much of their force by 1926. The Administration Report of Bihar and Orissa for 1926–7, for instance, pointed out that during the year 'most of the boards showed less inclination to indulge in political activities'. As a result of elections held, 'the number of District and Municipal Boards with a definite Swarajist majority was substantially reduced'.[86] The success of a candidate was more a result of his own exertions and attainments than the strength and influence of a political party. As a consequence of the decline in political activity the practical work of administration received more attention and was better done. The relations of most Boards with local officials improved, although there were a few exceptions where official advice was uncompromisingly resisted.

A marked change that proceeded from the democratization of local bodies under the dyarchic system was the coming into focus of power politics. There was nothing unusual about this and Lord Ripon's policy itself had envisaged it. However, local bodies had been prevented from excessive political activity by their limited franchise and bureaucratic control over their functioning. These two factors together mainly accounted for their being usefully directed as instruments of rural development. The element of political and administrative education which Ripon had in mind was not absent and the services annexed to local bodies provided the necessary field for training. Their initial membership, however, remained mostly confined to the landed classes interested immediately in the development of the rural services of District Boards. Their interests were affected by increasing democratization, which brought into dominance the middle-class professional elements of local bodies, a dominance that shifted emphasis from rural socio-economic interests to urban political interests which misused the powers of local bodies for political propaganda and canvassing for candidates seeking election to Legislative Councils. This was specially so in Bihar and Orissa.[87]

Socially, too, dyarchy left its own impact on the functioning of local bodies. However limited, the element of democracy unsettled the privileged classes who had hitherto exercized the monopoly of social and political power. Apart from the emergence of Hindu-Muslim tension on religious and political grounds in the wake of the non-cooperation movement, caste feelings among the Hindus themselves tended to become a regular feature of public life, more especially in Bihar and Orissa where it filtered down even to the levels of all the local bodies. Speaking of 'caste movements' in the province, the administration report of 1926 thus said:[88]

> Caste associations are multiplying fast, and in many centres caste meetings of one kind or another follow on each other's heels with bewildering frequency. This activity is to be found among the upper ranks of the Sudra castes, who for some years have been striving to improve their social status. Vows of temperance, efforts after educational progress, assumption of the sacred thread, and determined opposition to the system of *begari* [forced labour], coupled with a general revolt against the performance of menial offices for the higher castes—these are among the subjects which fiigure most prominently in their deliberations.

Serious disturbances occurred between Goalas and Rajputs, between Goalas and Brahmins, and generally between higher and lower castes. Caste loyalties became in fact a regular and noticeable feature in the general election to the Legislative Council, a feature 'which held good in the elections of local bodies'. According to the report, 'it has become the practice for candidates to claim boldly the votes of their fellow-castemen, irrespective of any political or other considerations; and generally they are not disappointed. This development, unfortunately, tends to paralyse still further the conduct of public affairs by promoting the formation of those cliques and factions which already figure so prominently in self-governing institutions.'[89]

This state of politics and society continued until local self-government institutions were caught in the whirlwind of the civil disobedience movement. Even so, most of the rural services remained attached to local bodies, and although cases of maladministration were not found wanting, the local bodies conducted themselves fairly well. However, the Union Boards, which constituted the statutory base for the local administration of villages, tended gradually to languish in the eastern provinces of India. The relations between them and District Boards were far from encouraging. While Union Boards avoided incurring popular displeasure by the imposition of the necessary union-tax, District Boards took little or no interest in the affairs of Union Boards.

The dyarchic democracy interacting with growth of capitalist enterpise, science and technology, had in fact begun to reflect an urban bias and gravitate towards urban interests and culture. As local bodies were by themselves unable to employ science and technology to reorganize their rural services, the only course left was a trend towards provincialization. While the Boards had in the past been largely dependent on government grants and failed to build up a sound system of their own local finances for development, the provincial governments under dyarchy were cautious for political reasons and took little or no care to improve for purposes of rural development the age old machinery of local bodies.

Change under Provincial Autonomy

Bihar

A change came about when popular ministries took over power under provincial autonomy. A Development Department was, for instance, established in Bihar under a minister who was also in charge of education. It provided for a small sum of Rs 80,000 in order to make a beginning 'with a rural development scheme' for the entire province. It was to be worked out by a chief organizer and assistants appointed to open 'model centres of rural welfare work' in each Division, where 'efforts will be concentrated to improve village life in all its aspects' through stipendaries trained as 'village organizers and district inspectors'. The declared goal of this Department was 'rural uplift work', the basic units of the whole organization being village panchayats. It was to be 'a five-year plan of economic recovery of the villages.'[90]

Whether the proposed scheme of rural development produced results or failed is not of much importance for our purpose, especially as the Congress Ministry which took over in July 1937 did not stay long in power. It is important from a number of other points of view: first, rural development came to be recognized for the first time as a centralized, direct responsibility of the provincial government, not of the decentralized local bodies which did not possess the necessary human and material resources. They were left with the administration of certain traditional services like education, medical relief, public health and civil works. But there, too, their dependence, for example, on indigenous systems of medical relief and health services was for the most part inevitable. They could not afford to meet the cost involved in providing the specialized medical aid necessary for the treatment of new diseases resulting from the growth of industrialization. Secondly, the integrated concept of the goal of rural reconstruction and the necessity of planning to achieve that goal were both implicit in the declared policy which led to the establishment of the Development Department in 1937. Finally, the administrative arangement which was sought to be introduced, envisaged a separate hierarchy of its own from the provincial headquarters to the village panchayat level.

Consistent with the principles of this policy, an attempt was made by the Government to encourage a mass literacy campaign to remove adult illiteracy and to spread enlightenment among the masses in both rural and industrial areas. Emphasis was laid specially on the education of girls and local bodies were asked to spend a greater proportion of their income on this and primary education, for which additional training schools were opened.

The position of local bodies in Bihar under the Congress Government was sought to be liberalized, friendly advice in the first instance being preferred to the use of legal powers to put local bodies on the right course with the minimum of interference. A notable feature was the revision of the election rules for all District Boards in order to make a near approach to adult suffrage. It was laid down that every person assessed for *chaukidari* tax of any amount whatsoever was qualified to be a voter and eligible for election. But since the new rules were not put into effect, the old Congress-dominated Boards continued in office beyond the statutory period of five years. Though ideologically radical in its public utterances, the popular government of Bihar did hardly anything tangible in the field of rural development.

The United Provinces.

As in Bihar, 'rural development' in U.P. formed part of a separate official hierarchy annexed to the Department of Development. It was administered from the provincial headquarters in the same way as the departments of education, public health, communications, agriculture, co-operative societies, and the like. In other words, the importance of local bodies, which earlier shared the responsibilities for these and other social services in the rural areas, seemed to be on the decline. Their role was sought to be superseded by an alternative provincialized arrangement that was conceptually integrated in its approach and favoured unified control to facilitate co-ordination in the districts.

And since provincial control could best be exercized through the agency of district officers, the work of rural development became the executive charge of Collectors. They were authorized to make appointments to the district rural staff in consultation with the chairmen of District Rural Development Associations.[91] With the Collector placed in charge of rural development, the development units of his district became subject to frequent inspections by his revenue officers. An Assistant Rural Development Inspector was sanctioned for each district, to assist the Inspector. This is what the Congress claimed was 'decentralization' to promote rural development.

According to the arrangement made in U.P., each rural development village was to have either a 'Better Living Society' or a *'Gram Sudhar Panchayat'*, which remained in charge of development activities in the village. Steps were taken to see that such of the existing societies and panchayats as happened to be representive of village as a whole, were invested with powers provided under the United Provinces Village Panchayat Act, 1920. The Rover Scout (*Gram Sewak*) Movement which had been intended to inculcate a spirit of self-reliance to keep up the morale of villagers, proved useful, especially in connection with the protection of communications and government property in rural areas, particularly during the August disturbances of 1942. In the light of its proved usefulness the organization was to add '150 new Rural Development units', which were to be concentrated in the eastern part of the province along the main roads and railway lines.[92]

The other activities, which rural development covered in the districts, included the improvement of communications and water-supply, the supply of improved seeds and agricultural implements, the organization of 'Better Farming Societies,' and intensive cultivation in selected areas as part of the 'Grow More Food Campaign' started in 1942.

The U.P. Government provided for a regular refresher course of training for the entire Rural Development field staff of inspectors and organizers, the latter being also selected as Scoutmasters and trained to discharge the functions of *gram sewaks*. There were, in addition, auditor-organizers who were trained at the Co-operative Training Institute, Partabgarh. The organization was reinforced ideologically by the monthly magazine *Hal,* which was intended to further educate all the participants. Its message was supplemented by publicity vans which disseminated relevant news on rural development.

The functioning of local self-governing institutions remained mostly under the influence of national politics, which cared little for the progress or upkeep of the services that in the past had contributed to rural development under official control. It was only with the removal of that control after the Reforms of 1919 that the developmental functions of local bodies began gradually to be relegated to the background, for at frequent intervals they would be subjected to the disruptive political activities of those who represented diverse shades of opinion. The measure of success of such politics governed the extent to which local bodies were disorganized and their staff demoralized. This was especially so in the period that followed the resignation of the Congress Ministries in 1939. In fact, events in the country as a whole were moving in the direction of provincialization, which involved a considerable transfer of powers from local bodies to district officials under ministerial control at the provincial headquarters.

Bengal

The problems of rural development in Bengal were in no way different from those in other parts of India. They involved questions of policy and priority, of co-ordination and personnel management, of procedural techniques and planned integration, which called for no separate rural reconstruction staff or any separate agency like that of the Agricultural Development Department. As already noted, Bihar and U.P. tried to have a separate hierarchy for rural development. But there, too, it was the Collector who held charge of the department in the district, an arrangement which the Rowlands Committee on the administration of Bengal recommended in 1944–5.

In terms of rural development Bengal suffered from certain handicaps which did not generally exist elsewhere. Unlike the provinces where land was not permanently settled, for a century and a half Bengal could not establish direct contact with the masses in the absence of revenue staff. In the periodically settled provinces, the staff provided a representative of the government right down to the villages, with a hierarchy of staff from *kanungoes, naib tahsildars* and *tahsildars,* right up to the district headquarters. Though established primarily for revenue purposes, they served as a source of information as well as a means of carrying out executive orders for all branches of the government in rural areas. This lack in Bengal was sought to be remedied by the appointment of circle officers on the recommendation of the Bengal Administrative Committee, 1913–14; but their jurisdiction was so large that they could not fully accomplish the object of their institution.

The compulsions of democracy imposed by the provincial autonomy of the period were yet another factor that tended to kill bureaucratic enterprize and initiative. For, as all the actions of government servants were now open to criticism by the legislature, they tended to play for safety, to go slow and rely on precedent and past rules for guidance, although the exigencies of rural development called for fresh approaches.

The Rowlands Committee noted the virtual absence of anything like a 'coherent, consistent or continuing *plan* as distinct from general objectives, in the districts.'[93] If a district officer happened to be energetic, he might push through particular aspects of government policy in which he was immediately interested, whether it be water-supply, co-operative marketing or agricultural improvement. But otherwise he would take little or no interest in any of the development plans, treating these as the function of the representatives of the 'nation-building' departments in his district. Schemes of development in these circumstances could not take firm roots unless pushed vigorously and in a sustained manner.

Moreover, the relationship of the district officer with the heads of technical departments in the district remained vague and undefined. In the words of the Rowlands Committee, 'the lot of the District Officer, like that of the comic opera policeman, is not a happy one. He is expected to see that nothing goes wrong in his district, but he has little power outside the Magistrate and Collector field to see that things go right. He is supposed, to quote from an official publication, "to compose difference between other officers", but he has no power to impose his will upon the recalcitrant. He can cajole and persuade: he cannot compel'.[94]

In view of the increasing activities of the government in rural areas as part of its post-war reconstruction plans, practically every department had in addition started thinking in terms of a 'Provincialized Service', making 'little attempt to disguise its determination to go ahead with its own plans without reference to any other part of government'.[95] This trend owed its origin to the growth of specialization as well as departmentalism, a problem which, as noted earlier, had started emerging even as early as the administration of Lord Curzon.

As the main emphasis in government policy was steadily moving from its regulatory to developmental functions, the Committee advised a resort to planned priorities within the limits imposed by financial resources, and declared that the time had come 'in Bengal and we do not doubt in other provinces as well, to co-ordinate all the District Development activities under a single administrative head'. The Committee added: 'When the objective in a geographical area like a District is the welfare of its people, separate activities are merely means to a single end and each cannot be considered in isolation from the rest'.[96]

To ensure proper co-ordination the Committee therefore recommended that the district officer must be the 'undisputed Head of all other Government agencies in his District except as regards the internal administration and technical methods of those agencies'. Technical officers could of course correspond direct with the heads of their technical departments on technical matters. But they were to be prevented from pursuing 'their own whims at the expense of the whole'. They were in fact to be 'direct subordinates'. There was not to be any 'test of strength between the District Officer and the technical officer, backed up by his Department'.[97]

It was to ensure the direct subordination of the technical staff to the district officer that the Rowlands Committee recommended the abolition of 'rural development' as a separate department. For, as the Committee argued, rural reconstruction was

> the end result of the activities of the several 'National Building' Departments. In our judgement, it is unsound [therefore] to have a Director of Rural Reconstruction, with a separate staff, parallel to, but with no control over, the representatives of the technical departments, and indeed, almost wholly independent of the District Officer. With such a set-up there have been, as there was bound to be, friction and conflicts of jurisdiction and action. In the scheme which we have put forward there is no place of a separate rural reconstruction staff.[98]

In other words, the technical officers of the various departments in the district were themselves to be responsible for rural reconstruction or development under the Collector's co-ordination.

To reinforce the district officer's development goal the Rowlands Committee suggested that the number of circle officers be increased by reducing the area of their jurisdiction in each case and that the activities of Union Boards be strengthened and expanded.

It was recommended that there should be a circle officer appointed to each *thana*. His main function was to draw up a detailed plan of development for his circle and co-ordinate the activities of any technical offiicer operating within his jurisdiction. Local technical officers were, in other words, to be in the same relationship with circle officers as their district superiors were with the district officer. But as for some time to come the technical officers at the circle level were bound to be few and far between, the main task of a circle officer, besides guiding and helping Union Boards, was to achieve the targets set for him by the district in respect of such development activities as primary schools, dispensaries, minor irrigation schemes, tank improvement, debt settlement and rural co-operative or credit. He was in fact to act as an alternative agency to local self-governing institutions. These functions, however, were to be in addition to the collection of government dues and certain magisterial duties involved in the trial of petty cases. This combination of regulatory and developmental functions was based on considerations of economy, but it tended in effect to be destructive of the principle of homogeneity. It was therefore emphasized that the circle officer should not be burdened with duties that might seriously interfere with his prime task of pursuing and co-ordinating development activities.

As for the role of Union Boards, it was realized that they had failed to accomplish their objectives, largely because they lacked supervision and financial support. The Committee recognized their importance as effective instruments of rural development and pointed out that they could serve not only as a most useful agency for the promotion of local services, but also as schools for the political and administrative training of villagers.

Under the Village Self-Government Act of 1919 the Union Boards had been invested with the discharge of several duties connected with the improvement of villages. It was, however, laid down that a Union Board should, to the extent required by the district officer and within the limits of available funds, carry out such duties as the district officer might from time to time require them to perform.

In addition to the district officer and his staff, the Union Board looked traditionally to the District Board for advice and financial assistance. It was thus suggested that the Union Board should remain attached through the circle officer to the District Board rather than the district officer. But this suggestion was turned down by the Committee which, from considerations of afficiency, did not approve of Union Boards, being transferred to the sole authority of District Boards or made dependent on their charity even for any supplementary income.

District Boards Languish

With the gradual shift of emphasis on rural development under the direct administrative control of provincial governments, Union Boards or the primary units of village self-government started gaining in importance, while District Boards began losing vitality. As said before, the growth of science and technology called for the modernization of rural services and their extension on a scale which the limited financial and administrative resources of District Boards did not permit. The cesses upon which they relied for the major part of their income were inelastic, and there arose from national politics an added difficulty of collection.

Administratively, District Boards were already being divested of many of their old functions. As the Rowlands Committee said:

> We learn that the provincialization of the public health services will not long be delayed; and we understand that already many hospitals are being administered by Government. The road work of the vast post-War schemes will be carried out under the Communications, Transport and Buildings Ministry, while the Education Ministry expects that the Primary Education Act will soon have been introduced throughout the province. If the administration of health, of roads and education is taken from the District Boards, what will be left to them? In such circumstances, it would seem to us that the Boards will become *'functus officio'*, for they would be shorn of most of their activities.[99]

But there was no way out. In the given context of India's authoritarian society and government the centre of power under provincial autonomy had shifted to the provincial headquarters, to be there wielded by ministries subject to legislative control. And since that power could best be exercized locally through the agency of district officials the District Boards were bound to become, as they did, what the Rowlands Committee described as *functus officio*. A democratic attitude of mind and respect for decentralization could have created a sense of sympathy with those who believed that local interest, supervision and care could be best served by proper use of the local knowledge and experience of District Boards. But in the absence of both, history took its own course: the power-seeking of policy makers tended to divest District Boards functionally and bring their primary units directly under the thumb of the bureaucracy.

Conditions had clearly changed since the formation of district committees under the Viceroyalty of Lord Mayo. In the context of provincial autonomy it was no longer considered necessary to arrange 'exercizes in local self-government'. The provincialization of health and other essential services was taken recourse to as a means to attain uniformity of standards within the limited resources of a province. The construction of a network of roads had to be approached from a provincial and even national point of view rather than a district viewpoint. The management of the operational techniques of development had changed beyond the capacity of local authorities. The development plans of government in the changed circumstances could better be achieved under a system of provincialization with central assistance.

Even so, there was a case for District Boards which the ideological obsessions of the rising wave of indigenous authoritarianism failed to notice. Even the Rowlands Committee had expressed itself in favour of continuing expenditure on local services according to 'the wishes and needs of the locality'. But should that prove impossible, the Committee suggested an alternative to safeguard local interest:

> Should the time come when the District Boards are so bereft of functions as to render their continuance in their present form meaningless, we would advise that there be created in their stead a District Advisory Board, with members elected . . . which would meet for discussion of local problems and for the ventilation of local grievances. This Advisory Board would elect its own chairman, and its representatives would be freely invited to attend meetings of the District Officer, for we attach great importance to the close association of government's executive officers with non-official local advisers.[100]

With the extension of development activities in the district, the Committee doubtless visualized the expediency of having separate district development officers. But it never thought in terms of doing away altogether with a representative body of non-official advisers to district officials. An important consideration against District Boards, however, was that with their erstwhile statutory powers invested in them they in fact did not fit in with bureaucratic convenience. They had ceased to function as 'Advisory Councils' of Collectors ever since the Reforms of 1919.

Increasing Importance of Village Panchayats

While the status of District Boards was being steadily diluted and their function taken over by the rural development agency operating directly under the government in districts, the importance of Union Boards or village panchayats rose steadily as they gained freedom from the control of District Boards financially and administratively. The tendency was for Union Boards to get organically linked with the regular official machinery of rural development emerging as part of the post-war reconstruction plans of the British Government in India. In keeping with this trend provincial governments introduced on the transfer of power their separate legislative enactments for the establishment of village panchayats.[101] Article 40 of the Constitution of India itself laid down in a Directive Principle of State Policy that the State should take steps to organize village panchayats and endow them with the powers and authority to function as units of self-government.

Interestly, while the Rowlands Committee stressed the importance of Union Boards as convenient units of local self-government for rural development with special reference to Bengal, the India Office was suggesting the expediency of retaining the panchayat system as a primary unit for purpose of constitutional reform in the Indian States. A letter dated 17 February 1944 from the India Office to Sir Francis Wylie, Political Adviser to the Crown Representative, indicates that the idea proceeded from Sir Atul Chatterjee, a member of the I.C.S., who advised the government that, in view of the vast majority of men and women in India being illiterate, 'village panchayat or assembly might be utilized as the primary unit for franchise purposes', a suggestion made in support of indirect election from village panchayats upwards. The advice given to the Rulers to introduce panchayats in their States was that of Lord Linlithgow who believed in the soundness of these institutions as units of rural administration. According to Wylie these panchayats were working 'fairly effectively and satisfactorily in quite a number of States', but he did not fail to make it clear that 'encouragement of panchayats very often cloaks a desire to retard the political development of this country. The Political Department under him in fact viewed the 'pressure' about panchayats as 'an old India Office game'. In a note of 6 March 1945 V.P. Menon of the same department agreed with Sir Francis and said:

> The Working of the Panchayat System was last reviewed by the Statutory Commission whose observations contained in para 347 of Vol.I. of their Report are of interest. The proposal made by Sir Atul Chatterji is not a new one. The proposal that an indirect system of election by means of local groups should be substituted for direct election by territorial constitutencies was carefully considered by the Lothian Committee, but for practical reasons we had to give up the idea and adopt the system of direct elections instead.[102]

As pointed out in the next chapter, the question of indirect elections was raised again by Dr Rajendra Prasad who insisted that village panchayats be recognized as primary units for constitutional purposes. The inclusion of Article 40 as part of the Directive Principles of State Policy was, thus, a result of compromise.

Democratized Local Bodies at Work

Despite the pious wishes of Lord Ripon, prior to the reformed Constitution of 1919 local bodies had remained a virtual preserve of the bureaucracy who, after the recommendations of Dr Voelekar in 1890, started using them for the promotion of rural services, rather than as a mere instrument of political education. The sudden democratization that followed dyarchy caused a sense of imbalance which led popular legislatures to enact measures excluding government officers from the exercise of effectual control. In its anxiety to promote development in what came to be known as 'nation-building' departments, the Madras Council, for example, completely revised in 1920 the old Local Boards Act and the District Municipalities Act. It introduced at the same time new legislation relating to village panchayats, primary educationand town-planning. The result was a large increase in the number of local bodies and their removal 'official control which also involved depriving them o some extent of the assistance of the revenue and other staffs who had carried out a good deal of their work for them when revenue officers were presidents'[103] This effect of de-officialization was equally experienced in almost all the provinces.

Much of the success of a local body, however, depended on a quality of its non-official chairman. In case he happened to be an active head, dedicated to public service, honest and hard-working, he could well command obedience and supervize the functioning of his board. His limitations, however, proceeded from the fickle nature of members and constitutents whose only guiding principle might be either self-interest or the interest of their relations, caste or community. The most difficult task of the newly elected chairman was in fact to secure a majority for his policy and programme, a task which only a few could accomplish without compromise. The administration reports of the several provinces make it clear that in spite of their administrative difficulties and inadequate resources there were some chairmen whose ability, competence and public spirit imparted to their boards a degree of success that won the administration of their Divisions' Commissioners. But such cases were few and far between: in the absence of statutory provision for a new administrative machinery for local bodies under dyarchy the whole board itself continued to be recognized as the effective governing body, without provision for managerial staff being available in most cases. The chairman even of a democratized board had in fact to continue as its hinge, though without the assistance his official predecessor commanded.

Another major cause for inefficiency in the functioning of democratized local bodies was an inherent contradiction between their elective system and the structure of Indian society. The elective system introduced under the reformed Constitution of 1919 was territorial in nature, formal and based on law. The indigenous society, on the contrary, consisted of mutually exclusive religious and caste groups, tradition-bound and custom-oriented. A clash between the two caused confusion as well as insecurity in those who, because of their social and economic backwardness, could not compete with members of the advanced sections of society. And since success in elections carried with it a prospect of economic gains and the benefits of patronage, however limited, it was natural that backward classes, including religious and other minorities, should press for due recognition of their separate claims.[104] The provision of communal and separate representation in local bodies was in fact an attempt to readjust the elective system to the peculiar structure of Indian society, a politically viable attempt which implicitly justified the use of influence and power as an instrument to improve social and economic status. Consierations of ability and honesty did not necessarily go into the choice of candidates for nomination to reserved seats.

Likewise, the result of direct voting on a territorial basis was not conducive to clean administration. In Bombay, for example, it led to the dominance of upper castes. In a letter addressed to the Government of India the Chief Secretary of Bombay pointed out in 1927 that

> during the past three years the growth of Brahmin and Non-Brahmin strife in the Deccan and Karnatic Districts and of Hindu-Muhammadan tension in certain parts of Sind has had a serious effect on the administration of the local self-government Bodies. It has resulted in the loss of efficiency owing to (1) the tendency to make appointments on communal grounds only, irrespective of the merits of the candidates; (2) increase of corruption among the establishment due to slack supervision and reluctance to dismiss or prosecute defaulters who may be of the same caste or creed as the majority of the Councillors; (3) hostility of the leaders of the same caste due to personal rivalry; (4) efforts to secure special consideration for one section of the public only.[105]

This comment applied in principle to all provinces.[106] It was a case of non-Brahmins *versus* Brahmins in Madras, Hindus versus Muslims in Bengal and Punjab, and inter-caste as well as personal animosities everywhere. The *Reports of the Local Governments on the Working of the Reformed Constitution* (1924) make it quite clear that the new democratized boards contained more 'discordant and aggressive elements' than the old ones. Local questions were generally approached not from a public point of view, but in a spirit of caste and communal strife. Doubtless ministers became acquainted with the practical difficulties of administration, and so did the non-official chairmen of District Boards. But none of the fundamental ideas underlying a democratic system had taken firm roots; nor was any attempt made by any party to educate the constituents in their duties and responsibilities. A report of the U.P. Government, for example, said that, despite efforts of the Congress to achieve Hindu-Muslim unity in the course of the non-cooperation movement, 'the relations between the two communities are ... decidedly worse than they were 25 or even five years ago; and the explanation is not far to seek. As self-government has drawn nearer, each community has become more conscious of its own position, and more suspicious of the motives and intentions of the other'.[107]

The prospect of self-government not only intensified caste and communal awareness but also brought to light the inherent *class* approach to the conflict of interests between the feudal and the bourgeois elements of society, a new trend resulting from the growth of middle classes in modern times. Considerations of power as a means of individual advancement or a limited group of supporters, rather than the promotion of the general public interest, influenced both categories. The gains derived from democracy in local bodies thus generally happened to be more personal then institutional.

Financially too, the handicaps of local bodies were considerable. As said before, economy had been the overriding consideration underlying the creation of local bodies after 1958. The object was to shift some of the burden from imperial finances to local resources, which were mostly inelastic. The bulk of the income flowed from the land revenue cess which was usually passed on by landlords to their tenants. Tolls on ferries, taxes on animals and vehicles for road maintenance and cattle pounds were additional sources of income. But these too provided little scope for expansion. The old emphasis naturally continued, but it was harnessed from Curzon's time and after to a concern for the welfare of Indian society. The prevailing opinion in contemporary English liberalism and the Congress under Gokhale's leadership reinforced the importance of government-sponsored social services in rural areas, more especially for primary education and public health development, which received special grants between 1909 and 1915.

Considerations of economy continued under dyarchy, and demands for increasing expenditure for 'nation building' departments created a state of financial stringency which had already been assuming serious proportions on account of rises in prices and the no-tax campaigns organized from time to time by Congress leaders. They 'resisted the placing of additional burdens upon the property owning or income-tax-paying classes, and managed to shift a large share of the onus of local taxation upon the general public—that is, the lower classes.'[108] Their emphasis was in fact on such indirect taxation as market-fees and, above all, on octroi; or on such fixed levies as the pilgrim tax, tolls and vehicle tax. In U.P., a tax on *haisiyat* as well as on professions and trades was sought to be levied, but it was largely a failure for, in addition to the resistance of vocal sections of the public, the Boards feared unpopularity and lacked the staff to ascertain the degree of taxability. The financial problems of local bodies thus remained unresolved except in the case of a few District Boards which were situated either in prosperous industrial belts or in places of agricultural prosperity.

The *Reports of Local-Government on the Working of the Reformed Constitution* (1924) point out that with the introduction of dyarchy expenditure started rising steeply not only because of extended 'nation-building' projects, but also because the popular legislatures were unable to exercize the financial control earlier ensured by the government of India. Moreover, the formation of a large number of committees in various departmens of the government became a recognized mode of distributing patronage. There was a large increase in expenditure not only in the offices of legislative councils, but also on the travelling allowances of members of these committees.[109] Government 'by the people' was becoming more expensive than government 'for the people'. In pre-dyarchic days the officers who presided at rural boards used the resurces of their revenue departments for local inspection and financial checks. The mechanism of control was less expensive and more effective. The drawback, however, was that it did not provide for the partition of 'elected majorities', which in reality meant the educated and urbanized middle classes who were acquiring a new legitimacy in their own interest to represent the 'people'. This legitimacy found expression in the attempts of individual members to interfere 'with the postings and transfers of the staff'. which led to 'administrative deterioration'. Such a view was held, for example, by a Committee of the U.P. Legislative Council which, while commenting on the financial situation of local bodies, added 'The Boards cannot as a whole be said to have fully exploited their own sources of income . . . Little regard to economy has been paid by some Boards. It must be confessed that the keeping of accounts and observance of rules shared deterioration in common with many other aspects of the Boards administration.'[110]

Though in their public statements ministers of local self-government often expressed themselves in favour of local bodies continuing to retain powers to make decisions locally, in practice they would have those decisions generally made by themselves at provincial headquarters. Instead of the Government of India, it was now provincial governments (and therefore their Ministers of Local Self-Government) that came to be invested under dyarchy with powers to sanction loans or grants to local bodies. The provincialization of financial administration under the Government of India Act (1919), even though subject to some central control, provided leverage for ministers to reduce local bodies to subservience. The provincial autonomy that came in 1937 carried this trend to its logical conclusion. The powers and functions of District Boards began steadily to be transferred to a separate administrative agency for 'rural development', operating directly under the government with the Collector as its head in the district.

V

ALTERNATIVES TO LOCAL BODIES AND RURAL DEVELOPMENT

Though designed by Lord Ripon primarily as an instrument of political education, the local bodies which developed in the context of India's recurrent famines and agricultural crises were of necessity invested with the discharge of functions of a socio-economic character, logically justified even as relief to the government and its bureaucracy in the management of local affairs. The preceding chapter which deals with this subject has already shown how the local bodies were called upon to engage in a number of welfare functions which contributed to the progress of rural development under a three-tier system, with the District Board on top, the village panchayat or the Union Board at the bottom and the local or the taluka board in the middle.

The new arrangements that came to be introduced a few years after the transfer of power in 1947, were, technically speaking, no alternative to local bodies which also continued side by side. In reality, however, they did operate as alternatives, especially after 1958. For they not only took over most of the functions which the local bodies performed earlier, but added new ones of their own. Like the local bodies, the alternatives were in principle to be also based on a three-tier system in the districts. These were the *zila parishad*, comparable to the District Board and the block or *panchayat samiti*, parallel to the taluka or local board. There was practically no change in the designation of the village panchayat, except that its importance increased. What was, however, entirely new to the whole range of the erstwhile self-governing institutions in terms of both concept and approach, was the introduction of what came to be known as Community Projects Administration, which covered the administration of the Community Development Programme and the National Extension Service inaugurated respectively in 1952 and 1953.

Need for Alternatives to Local Bodies: the War and New Approach to Rural Development

The search for a new approach to rural development proceeded in the 1940's from three main considerations, the emphasis underlying each consideration being on the production of more and more food. The exigencies arising from a pressing demand to Grow More Food created a situation which local bodies could not by any stretch of imagination ever claim to meet in terms of both obligations and resources. Alternatives had to be found to supply a remedy. The seriousness of the situation was such that nothing less than a resort to government resources alone could save it.

The first consideration was the need to increase 'the food and fodder supplies of India', a consideration that had 'assumed greatly increased importance owing to the exigencies of the war situation'. In a letter of 10 March 1942[1] the Government of India invited the attention of the provincial governments to the seriousness of the problem and suggested steps to improve the supplies of food and fodder. These included, for instance, the supply of free seed, subsidies for the construction of wells and embankments, the supply of manure, the remission of rent and revenue, the fixation of a minimum price for grains, a guarantee by the government to purchase the surplus crop, a reduction in the areas under sugarcane, cotton, jute and groundnuts. In view of the difficulties arising from poor maintenance of road transport under the control of local bodies, the whole arrangement was in fact sought to be made on 'a regional basis' and on the principle of 'improved local self-sufficiency', so that supplies could be ensured locally for military purposes independently of transport difficulties.

Consistently with the advice contained in the Government of India's letter of 10 March 1942, a Food Conference was held at New Delhi on 6 April 1942, with N. R. Sarkar, Member in Charge of Education, Health and Lands, as Chairman. It was this conference that initiated the 'Grow More Food' campaign and recommended detailed programmes of work for it. The steps suggested in the letter for increasing food production were reiterated and it was further added that, with a view to improving 'the nutrition of the people all available lands adjoining homesteads should be used for the production of vegetables and quick growing fruits, such as papayas, bananas and melons and green fodder crops for increased production of milk'. The campaign so initiated was sought to be carried out through the press and platform in association with existing non-official agencies, such as co-operative societies, farmers' associations, 'rural development associations', village panchayats, and so forth. The conference went a step further and recommended the establishment of a Central Food Advisory Council which was to function as a co-ordinating body under the Government of India. The functions assigned to it included dissemination of all available information on the subject of food production, the planning on an all-India basis of a food and fodder production programme for different regions, and advice to the authorities concerned about the equitable distribution of the available food stocks.[2]

The second factor that aggravated the situation and called for added emphasis on the importance of the Grow More Food campaign was the calamitous famine of 1943 and its continued ravages borne for the most part by the province of Bengal, with a considerable loss of life caused in the country as a whole. Before the Japanese occupation of Burma its surplus rice used to be exported for consumption in Bengal. But with the fall of Rangoon, the supply of rice from Burma was cut off, and in the existing state of political uncertainty in the country the British Government of the day, though unable immediately to find substitute sources of supply, determined to intensify the Grow More Food campaign with a view to mobilizing internal resources to meet the catastrophe.

Appeals were made to farmers and landholders, the latter being especially persuaded to help their tenants in respect of irrigational and other facilities considered necessary for increased food production. The result of the campaign was fairly encouraging in such provinces as Punjab, Bengal and, to an extent, in U.P. and Madras also. But the public in Bihar were found to be 'woefully and blissfully ignorant' of the Grow More Food campaign. The Bihar Landholders' Association, though overtly in sympathy with the main objective of the campaign, expressed its helplessness on the ground that the tenancy 'laws of the land have crippled our power and we are not now in such a fortunate position as we were'.[3]

The weakness of the Grow More Food campaign in fact proceeded mainly from two sources, especially in the permanently settled provinces where the revenue staff of the government did not operate at the lower levels of administration. The first of these sources was the self-complacency of the bureaucracy at the seats of power and authority, a slow-moving bureaucracy that failed to realize the imperatives of the campaign and the magnitude of the problem it was designed to resolve. It could not enlist the support and co-operation of non-official organizations as an effective agency of publicity. The second source of weakness was the political opposition of the Indian National Congress, more especially of the 'Quit India' movement started under the leadership of Gandhi in August 1942, hardly four months after the initiation of the Grow More Food campaign. The Japanese advance in south-east Asia was perhaps viewed as a lever and handle for the seizure of power. But the firmness used by the government of the time belied the hopes of nationalist leaders. The movement was suppressed, but the popular co-operation sought for the Grow More Food campaign remained largely a dream, although the soundness of its aim could not be denied or disputed.

Also, the local bodies invested with the discharge of certain welfare functions were of little or no help. They suffered from serious handicaps. Food and agriculture, for instance, formed no part of their immediate statutory obligations. They possessed no infrastructure to enable them to establish links with families in rural areas. And, above all, they too were not free from the influences of national and local politics, a result of democracy operating within the broad imperial power structure and the mutually exclusive indigenous social system. Even food, a non-political subject of common interest, became invested with politics as a ground for withholding support to the Grow More Food campaign. The efforts of the government, however, continued unabated.

A third incentive to promote increased food production emerged from a policy of planned development, a policy that abandoned the use of *ad hoc* measures and envisaged planning for a period of three years to start with. The object of this policy was not merely to satisfy the requirements of the army, but to enable work under the Grow More Food campaign to 'merge into that of post-War reconstruction'[4]—a planned endeavour to supply the needs of the civil population.

In a letter of 22 June 1944 the Government of India made it clear to all Provincial Governments and Local Administrations that the Grow More Food campaign had, in spite of public criticism, achieved a great deal of success. About 4 million acres of land had, for example, been diverted from cotton to food crops and an additional 3 million acres had been brought under cultivation. The results so achieved were not regarded as negligible. But it was none the less recognized that the campaign could not do more because of the *ad hoc* nature of its organization: it was actually started 'on a short term basis' in 1942 and it naturally took up in the first instance the work that seemed to it 'most promising'. It could not take a long-range view of the problem of food production. But, as the letter said, 'the Government of India have now decided that the Grow More Food campaign should be on a three year basis', a basis that would give 'an opportunity for taking up the work on more systematic lines'.[5]

Consistently with the new policy of planned development, a new organizational arrangement was sought to be introduced to ensure popular co-operation. It was proposed that suitable agricultural associations should be set up in each district, *tahsil, kounty* (*kanungoe* circle) or *firka* (Union Board circle). The local agricultural staff was to be obliged to explain their plans to these non-official associations which could be organized by 'the co-operative or rural development department'. It was, however, emphasized that agricultural officers themselves must help and take up the organization themselves, where necessary, and see that these organizations included 'the people who really have some contributions to make and not merely yes-men'. It was added that while the work of organization in the districts was going on, provincial (agricultural) staff should fix provisional production targets for each district. The district agricultural officer should then break this down for each *tahsil* and again for each *kounty* or *firka*. The *kounty* or *firka* officer should then break it down for each village in his circle. A regular infrastructure from the provincial down to the village level was thus proposed to be established as part of a three-year plan for the production of food.

To enlist the co-operation of villagers it was then suggested that the target for each village should be revised in the light of local conditions, indicating in the form of a statement the area of cultiveable land as well as waste and fallow areas, the reasons for certain lands being not cultivated and the steps needed to bring them under cultivation. The statement to be so drawn up for each village was in fact to be indicative of the felt needs of cultivators in respect of wells, tanks and other sources of irrigation; embankments and drainage, supply of improved seed and green manure; of agricultural implements, bullocks and power. The Provincial Governments were asked to find out the extent to which production would be increased if these facilities were provided.

The Government of India wanted that, on the basis of this information collected from each village, 'a plan for the provision of the necessary facilities can be drawn up for the *kounty* or the *firka*. These would then be consolidated into the district plan, those facilities which are likely to give the maximum time receiving priority. Certain items which concern more than one *kounty* or *firka* (e.g. anti-erosion works, dams, etc.) would have to be added. The same process would be repeated in preparing the provincial plans'.[6] The whole idea underlying rural development in terms of food production was thus based on the principle of planning from below, from the village upwards through the district to the province. The agency involved in the collection of data and planning was, however, official, comprising officers of the department of agriculture, who, if necessary, worked in collaboration with the revenue staff, *amins* and village *patwaris*.

The collection of information along these lines was considered necessary, for, as the letter pointed out, 'it is not enough to tell cultivators to grow more food; this has to be supplemented by providing the necessary facilities for each village to enable it to do so', not only as part of an immediate programme to produce the maximum quantity, but of a regular post-War development plan. The Provincial Governments were, therefore, asked to issue necessary instructions to give effect to the plan so suggested and to provide the staff required for the purpose, a staff that was to include not only 'subordinate and inferior' categories of 'the various departments concerned but also the secretarial staff to ensure that there is no delay' in the execution of the plan.[7] The Grow More Food plan was thus being proposed to be worked out in collaboration with the various departments concerned but under one co-ordinating agency of the department of agriculture. The principle of an integrated approach was being slowly recognized and evolved, a task which no District Board could ever hope to accomplish.

The year 1944 was in fact the beginning of a planned approach to rural development with its main, though for a time exclusive, thrust on food and agriculture. The Government of Bihar, for instance, had its 'Post-War Reconstruction Board' and the first meeting of the

Board's Agricultural Committee was held on 21 January 1944, with the 'Adviser, Development', as Chairman who explained at some length 'the plan to be followed in preparing and carrying out the post-War development schemes and the procedure contemplated for ensuring co-ordination with the Centre'.[8] Commenting on the relationship with the Centre, the Chairman made it clear that the Government of India 'would lay down certain common economic policies to be followed by all provinces. They would also co-ordinate the schemes initiated by the provinces. Beyond this the Central Government would not interfere and each province would be left to make and execute its own plans'. He emphasized that there should be no cause for concern on financial grounds. 'Substantial funds', he said, 'were likely to be available from the Centre to supplement the Provincial Reconstruction Funds, particularly for schemes which gave a return and could be financed by productive borrowing'.[9]

In the course of discussion on the development of agriculture the Committee laid special stress on the extension of the activities of the Provincial Co-operative Bank 'on the lines of the Credit Agricole of Egypt',[10] the object being 'to provide a machinery for the distribution of improved seeds, implements and manures on a large scale, and giving advances against stocks, not only to members of co-operative societies but also to non-members', who formed part of the general body of cultivators.

Another equally important matter which the Committee emphasized for the development of agriculture was 'the need for trained men' who might be available 'in sufficient number' within a period of 'three to four years' before senior officers of the department of agriculture retired. This emphasis on the need for trained staff for development was a new trend which marked the beginning of a departure from the old law and order approach to district administration. It is not that much progress was made in this direction, but it was a beginning.

However, a Government of India Finance Department letter dated 4 May 1945 and a Planning and Development Department letter dated 11 May 1945 confirmed that, as already indicated, the development proposals made in the course of 1944 were 'special preparatory measures', 'anti-deflationary' and 'incidental to resettlement' in the projected post-War perspective. They had followed immediately in the wake of the Grow More Food campaign and were in fact the result of various decisions taken from time to time even before Germany had fallen and the early collapse of Japan had not yet been envisaged. A Government of India Finance Department letter dated 24 November 1945 thus clarified the previous policy by saying that 'general development with Central assistance was not contemplated before 1947'. A new situation, however, had arisen after the fall of Germany. The letter said: 'The sudden termination of the war, the early commencement of demobilization, the contraction of war expenditure and the unlikelihood of any appreciable expansion of industrial employment in the near future necessitate a reconsideration of that policy.'[11]

In view of the conditions that emerged from the termination of the War, the Government of India decided that it was 'no longer necessary to adhere to the 1st of April 1947'. The 'general development' projected in the meantime on a five-year basis could not be taken up. There were, however, certain preliminaries which were sought to be completed before the general plans could be adopted for execution. For the emphasis so far had mostly been on a regional basis to meet the exigencies arising from the shortage of food, not on an all-India basis to satisfy general requirements. As the letter of 24 November 1945 pointed out, 'the Central and provincial 5 year plans' had not yet been examined 'with a view to their co-ordination with all-India planning, subject by subject or with the object of ensuring that development planning, as a whole, is properly balanced between subjects. The examination is in hand but will take some time to complete. The object is to complete it in readiness for the budget for 1947–8, so that in that year fully co-ordinated development may begin throughout the country'.[12] It began with the establishment of the Planning Commission in 1951.

The British Government of the day proceeded in the meantime to 'embark forthwith on schemes selected out of the five-year plans with the special object of counteracting deflation and unemployment'. Their selection was to be determined by considerations of employment potentialities and the costs involved, as well as by the fact that for the success of planned development emphasis had to be laid in the earlier years on productive and such other schemes as would increase national income. Efforts were therefore sought to be concentrated on two categories of schemes. The first included 'productive self-financing schemes' which, on completion and the lapse of the necessary time for their full operation, were expected to yield adequate revenue to cover the interest on the capital, working expenses, maintenance and depreciation charges. The second category of schemes were of economic importance, such as minor irrigation, roads, anti-erosion, agricultural measures, forests, etc. These might not be self-financing but were considered conducive to the growth of national income. They were to be supplemented by such other schemes as were related to public health, especially anti-malaria measures, water-supply and drainage schemes which, besides being productive, were also regarded as being of economic value in terms of increasing the efficiency of the people. The expansion of education and medical facilities were considered to be of the same category.

To obviate purely financial considerations from standing in the way of adequate measures being taken, the Government of India decided to offer reasonable assistance to Provincial Governments. This was in the form of loans to the extent necessary for financing such projects as Provincial Governments might themselves decide to loan money. All self-financing projects were in fact sought to be so debited. The letter of 24 November 1945 made it clear that 'pending a decision on the methods to be adopted for the distribution of Central grants for the Provincial Government plans' payments were to be made by the Government of India 'to the extent desired by the Provincial Government during the years 1945–6 and 1946–7 for the execution of schemes selected from the provincial plans and approved generally by the Central Government, but not exceeding the expenditure actually incurred up to and inclusive of 1946–7, which may be regarded as unproductive' in the sense of their not being 'self-financing'. The payments so decided to be made were to be quarterly or 'half-yearly, as might be convenient to the Provincial Government concerned, on the basis of the expenditure incurred in the previous quarter or half year. 'They were to be treated as advances made to Provincial Government, not recoverable but subject to being adjusted against the scheme of grants for post-War development as a whole'.

The principle of planned development on a five-year basis and the necessity of central involvement to promote it were thus both recognized and envisaged a couple of years before the transfer of power. The main emphasis, however, still remained on the Grow More Food campaign, to which were added technical training, education, employment and the re-settlement of ex-servicemen. It was in this context of continuing urgency and importance of food production as part of post-War plan that a 'Grow More Food Inquiry Committee' was appointed by the Government of India under a Ministry of Food and Agriculture Resolution of 8 February 1952, with

V.T. Krishnamachari as chairman. The Congress Government of 1946 had in the meantime continued the campaign for another period of five years till 1951.[13] It was obliged now to recognize the soundness of the policy the British had been pursuing to promote the food production campaign, which the Congress had declined to support when not in power. On the attainment of Independence the scope of the post-War schemes of both the two broad categories was in fact revised and enlarged to form part of the general post-War Reconstruction Plan already formulated before the transfer of power.[14]

Administrative Arrangements for Development Work—Bengal Suggested the Norms in 1944–45

Apart from the 'nation building' or development departments of the government, the work of rural development, as said before, was assigned to local bodies with certain limitations. Of the two agencies of development, the latter never came anywhere near the former in terms either of statutory obligations, personnel qualities or material resources. They functioned more or less as a subordinate agency, subject to being superseded at the discretion of the government. Their performance, too, had been generally disappointing, while the experiences gained in the course of the War proved beyond doubt their incapacity to handle any of the developmental functions connected either with military objectives or civil supplies. They allowed themselves to become politically involved, conduct which appears misguided in a state of famine and food scarcity. Financially, too, they were no better. The crisis which flowed from the inelastic character of income derived from cesses worsened because of the added difficulty of collection and the counter claims of the primary education cess.

In these circumstances, it was thus well nigh impossible for local bodies to cope with the post-War reconstruction plan and the schemes of development that emerged from it. The road work of the vast post-War schemes was sought to be carried out by the Communications and Transport Department of the government. Education and Public Health, which had earlier formed part of the administration of local bodies, were likewise being put on the road to provincialization. The exigencies of planned development in fact dictated the expediency of provincialized administrative and financial control, a new trend of development which forced District Boards to become *functus officio*.

Confronted with the immediate problem of reorganizing government and administration for development purposes, the Government of Bengal took the initiative and set up under a Resolution dated 5 December 1944 a Committee, with Sir Archibald Rowlands as chairman, to recommend measures necessary not only for effective co-ordination, but also the extent to which local bodies could be utilized as an efficient adjunct to the administration, with special reference to welfare services. Consistent with its terms of reference in regard to local self-governing institutions, the Committee expressed itself in favour of provincializing some of the welfare services earlier administered by District Boards. It said:

> Times have changed since the District Committees were established in 1871; and we agree that, with the coming of provincial autonomy, it is no longer necessary to arrange 'exercizes in local self-government'. We appreciated that the provincialization of the health services will enable the limited resources of the Province to be used to secure uniform standards of health services; we recognize that the construction of a network of roads is a task which must be approached from a provincial rather than a district view-point; and we realize that many duties were entrusted to the District Boards prematurely, before the correct techniques were worked out. Though, therefore, questions of policy are outside the terms of reference, we can understand that Government's development plans may be better advanced under a system of provincialization.[15]

However, the Committee did not completely ignore the development of democratic institutions functioning as advisory bodies; for it said: 'If the Boards' functions are provincialized, and if, in place of the Boards, it should be found necessary to create advisory bodies, no one who believes in the development of democratic institutions could fail to regard such an arrangement as historically retrograde, if the arrangement were intended to be *permanent*. In good time, when the road system has been built, and when the health services have been established, public opinion will doubtless press government to hand back to local bodies the functions of which they have been temporarily relieved.'[16]

But once the principle of provincialization was recognized and carried into effect, there was little or no chance left to local bodies to get fully reinstated. Democratic alternatives were doubtless created. They came to be designated as Panchayati Raj Institutions (PRI). But the alternatives so created could not act as independently as local bodies once did. Provincialization made its influence felt through financial pipeline and administrative channels, though in principle they were said to be acting as adjuncts to the democratic institutions set up in the districts at different levels.

As regards the element of co-ordination, the existing administrative arrangements were found sadly wanting. The *Report of the Bengal Administration Inquiry Committee* showed that even the post-War reconstruction plans were being 'drawn up in separate compartments without any attempts to relate them to the schemes of other departments.'[17] Though well-organized and directed to improve rural areas, these departments did not function in a coherent way. They worked independently of one another and followed their own programme without a common goal. Each of the Departments of Agriculture, Animal Husbandry, Irrigation, Education, Health and Sanitation, etc. approached the village through its own hierarchy and the weakest link in all was usually the last official who had to be in touch with the villager, an official who, in most cases, happened to be poorly trained and incapable of providing guidance to the village folk who hardly felt his presence because of the large area of his administrative jurisdiction. The revenue officers who were traditionally known for their direct touch with villagers at many points of contact, remained unrelated to development departments. Even 'the Local Bodies which under the law were responsible for welfare services in the rural areas, like communications and water-supplies', remained without any link whatsoever with the 'nation-building' departments of the government,[18] departments which, on the basis of their specialized knowledge and skill, had a separate axe to grind against the generalist executive officers who claimed primacy in all administrative decisions, general or technical.

The existing development departments were thus found wanting in many ways. Departmentalism and the absence of an infrastructure required for close linkage with rural families were two serious impediments to the promotion of rural development, which, instead of water-tight compartments, called for a single-line approach to affect synthesis and co-ordination in all matters of development, from the Centre down to the grass roots. The Provincial Governments, which stood in-between, were likewise required to modify their age-old isolationist behaviour and to subject themselves to an all-India perspective for rural development, an integrated approach for concerted action, not a mere departmental concern.

Since agriculture was recognized as the key to rural development, increasing emphasis continued to be laid on its improvement, especially since the time of Curzon's administration. It was, however, the Royal Commission on Agriculture that brought to light the practical problems of organizing the Department of Agriculture and its personnel in promoting development at the grass-root level. The Indian Council of Agricultural Research was of course the most important result of its recommandations. But it was again this Commission that, for the first time, suggested the necessity of an extension service which might carry to rural families the fruits of research carried on in laboratories and displayed in demonstration farms. It recommended the appointment of Village Guides for the purpose. No progress was, however, made in this direction until the importance of direct contact with villages began to be increasingly recognized as part of the Grow More Food campaign and the post-War reconstruction plans that began to take shape in its wake in 1944-5. F.L. Brayne worked out a plan of extension service on a limited scale of experiments in the district of Gurgaon in Punjab. Its usefulness was confirmed in the course of several other experiments in extension carried on elsewhere in Punjab, Madras, Cochin, and U.P. These indicated a new direction both in terms of approach and method, their object being not merely to bridge the gap between research and practice, but also to secure people's full participation in government-sponsored programmes of development, with special emphasis on Grow More Food.

The Bengal Administration Inquiry Committee realized that 'the organizational structures and methods which were suitable enough when the activities of Government were confined to the regulatory, policing and revenue fields, are quite inadequate to handle the advance on the economic and social fronts which have increasingly become the major concern of governments in progressive countries.'[19] It made a number of suggestions, including changes in the basic objectives of the government and regrouping portfolios. But the most important thing it did was to emphasize for purposes of development activities the immediate need for co-ordination at both policy and executive levels.

The Committee recommended that for close and constant co-ordination in the field of development the structure of the headquarter's machine should consist of a Cabinet Development Committee composed of ministers in charge of development departments and presided over by the Chief Minister as co-ordinator of the machinery of government[20] as well as the activities of departments operating in the economic and social field. The cabinet committee was to be assisted by a Development Board consisting of the Secretaries of development departments with the Chief Secretary as President. The business of the Board was to prepare for the Cabinet Development Committee an integrated Provincial Development Plan in consultation with individual development departments, and to transform the functional plans of departments into a territorial plan for each district. The Board functioned more or less as a planning body which was to be assisted by scientific advisers to co-ordinate research activities, in addition to economic and engineering advisers. The newly created Statistics Bureau was also to be attached to the Development Board. There was, in fact, to be a technical inter-departmental committee to discuss certain technical questions between heads of departments, with the Secretary of the Development Board as Chairman. The object was to facilitate the work of the Board as the Board itself hammered out alternatives to facilitate the work of the Cabinet.

The Bengal Committee suggested, in addition, the creation of what it called Advisory Bodies representing the wishes of the people whom the official machinery of government was to serve. The object was 'to retain public confidence' and to make available the knowledge and experience of all sections of the community'.[21] The basic objective was to see that in the sphere of development activities the official and non-official bodies functioned side by side as adjuncts to each other. This principle was later sought to be applied to district administration under the recommendations of the Balvantray Mehta Committee Report.[22]

As regards the machinery of development at the district level, the Bengal Administration Inquiry Committee suggested the division of the district into three tiers with the district headquarter's machine on top, the Union Board at the bottom and a new small jurisdiction of circle officers in the middle, a jurisdiction comparable in size to what came to be known later as a block, the object being to see that the Union Boards remained under the close and constant supervision of an officer.

Of the local self-governing institutions, the Union Boards were considered by the Committee to be 'by far the most promising'. It visualized these Boards 'as becoming definitely a more active agent in the development work' in terms of both the activities they undertook and their influence on village life. It was therefore proposed to strengthen them as 'the basic unit of administration'[23] and to provide them a full-time government-paid clerk, a 'Jack of all Trades' and the last officer in the chain of development in rural areas. The Panchayat Raj Acts later actually provided for such an officer, called a 'secretary', for each *gram panchayat* consisting of a number of villages.

The Committee recommended that the strength of Circle Officers should be increased to the extent of one per *thana*. 'Their main function', as the Committee suggested, 'will consist in planning in detail the development work of their circle, and in co-ordinating directly the activities of any technical officer operating within the area. Local technical officers will be in the same relation to Circle Officers as their district supervisors will be to their District Officers'.[24] Besides guiding and helping Union Boards, a Circle Officer was to be invested with the preparation of a plan for his *region* to facilitate achieving the various targets assigned to him as part of the total district plan. It might be possible for him to bypass for the Subdivisional Office and correspond directly with the District Officer if this was likely to more effective it was on this principle that the Committee recommended the abolition of the post of Divisional Commissioner, the Collector himself being directly under the Development Board at the provincial headquarters.

On the pattern recommended for the structure of the provincial headquarters the Committee suggested a plan for co-ordination in the development activities of the districts also. It said: 'We are satisfied that the time has come in Bengal, and we do not doubt in other Provinces as well, to co-ordinate all the District Development activities under a single administrative head', the District Officer. For, as the main objective was the welfare of the people in the district, 'separate activities are merely means to a single end and each cannot be considered in isolation from the rest', especially in a situation where every specialized department had started thinking in terms of a separate provincialized service. The District Officer was of course functioning as the head of district administration and expected 'to see that nothing goes wrong in his district'. But, as the Committee observed, 'he has little power outside the Magistrate and Collector field to see that things go right'. He was expected to compose differences, could 'cajole and persuade', but not 'compel'.[25]

The Committee, therefore, emphasized that the relations of

technical officers to District Officers must be re-adjusted to strengthen co-ordination for development: 'Instead of a vague, undefined relationship which either allows officers to pursue their own whims at the expense of the whole or leads to a test of strength between the District Officer and the technical officer, backed up by his Department, the District Officer will be the undisputed head of all other Government agencies in his district except as regards the internal administration and technical methods of those agencies.' In other words, the technical officers were to be 'the direct subordinates of the District Officer for what they are to do, and for actually getting it done'.[26] The position proposed had in addition the sanction of the history-based prestige of the Collector.

Increasing Importance of Village Panchayats After 1947

The importance of village panchayats which had already been rising in the course of the War and the Grow More Food campaign was reinforced by a constitutional provision in favour of panchayats under Article 40 of the Directive Principles of State Policy at the instance of Dr Rajendra Prasad, who initially wanted the Constitution to begin with the village and go up to the Centre[27] His decentralized concept of democracy was turned down and the centralized parliamentary system finally adopted on the model of the Government of India Act, 1935. But the inclusion of the Article, even as part of the non-justiciable Directive Principles of State Policy, was recognition of village panchayats as an essential 'form of local self-government, as schools of democracy, as instruments of village uplift'.

In fact, village panchayats were not the creation of the Indian Constitution. The Draft Constitution did not even mention panchayats. These were incorporated into the Directive Principles of State Policy after a great deal of wrangling, and there, too, as a thing merely to be desired. Village panchayats in their statutory form had already come into being under British rule, more especially after 1919. The inclusion of an Article in the Constitution, however, represented an emphasis and a reminder of both policy objectives and a *modus operandi*. The idea was that every state should organize village panchayats as primary units of local administration, deriving their authority from local communities and attending to their needs to the maximum extent possible. This approach to the organization of village panchayts differed but little in principle from that under British rule, more especially because it remained tagged to the Department of Health, where it formed only a part of the subject of local self-government until 1958, when it was transferred to the Ministry of Community Development.[28]

The integration of village panchayats with the community development programme and the national extension service made a difference in the post-Independence period. The socio-economic aims which in the past had formed part of the obligations of the higher echelons of local bodies, were after this integration shifted to village panchayats which were now expected to function 'not only as units of decentralized administration, but, almost simultaneously, as units of decentralized economy, in the sense that the rural social order should be receptive to industrialization and should so adjust itself that its economy does not get paralysed with the impact of industrialization'[29]. The idea was to do away with the age-old notion of rural self-sufficiency and to link Indian village organically with the outside world.

The goal of community development in relation to village panchayats was not merely to make them an effective instrument of rural economy and employment, but also to extend to them the principle of a corporate organization invested with the exercize of civil functions comparable to those of municipalities.[30] The declared intention of policy makers was in fact to see that village panchayats should begin to function as primary units for both social and economic development, with powers to administer their own affairs and to command such resources as would be considered sufficient for their purpose. Community development in relation to villages was in principle to be 'both an educational and organizational process' providing requisite 'attitude and practices' for 'social and economic improvement'.[31]

Concept of Community Development

It was recognized that a programme of community development could not succeed if it became integrated or closely related to the existing structure of administration at the local, intermediate or national level. The declared goal of the programme was to secure the participation of the community, willing and spontaneous, with a realization that all the activities of community development, conceptually cumulative and organizationally integrated, were to be the people's own concern and that the government's concern was only to assist the people where such assistance was considered necessary. The task of community development was in fact to carry conviction with the people that the programme was essentially a people's programme and that it was precisely with this end in view that it was planning to develop such institutions as panchayats and co-operatives, so that a much larger participation of the people in the planning and implementation of its programme might be ensured. In other words, the intention was 'that the government programme with people's participation should be changed over to a people's programme with government participation'.[32]

Community Projects Administration

Origin and Early History

As already noted, the integrated concept of rural development was a result of a number of experiments conducted even before India attained independence in 1947. These were tried out not only by the government in its effort to promote rural reconstruction, especially as part of its Grow More Food campaign, but also by workers associated with Gandhi and Rabindranath Tagore. Of equal importance as the forerunners of nation-wide programmes of community development were a number of other projects organized on a limited scale in Madras, Baroda, Kerala and Punjab. Experiments were subsequently also made with considerable success in the Pilot Projects of Etawah, Gorakhpur and Nilokheri. These experiments as well as the experiences of the government established beyond doubt a principle that the various aspects of rural life were inter-related and that no lasting result could be achieved if these were sought to be handled in isolation. The community development programme that came to be organized under the auspices of the Community Projects Administration, was thus an apogee of the accumulated experience of rural work in India during the previous couple of decades.

For administrative purposes, the Community Projects Administration was linked with the Community Development Programme which formed part of the Technical Co-operation Programme Agreement the Government of India made with the United States of America on 5 January 1952. In fact, the Community Project Administration owed its origin to this Indo-US Technical Agreement and started functioning with effect from 31 March 1952.[33]

The Agreement provided that the programme should in the beginning be confined to approximately 55 projects, each embracing nearly 300 villages with a population of about 200,000 people. A project area was to be divided into three development blocks, each comprising about 100 villages and a population of about 65,000 people. The projects initially proposed were to be of the rural development type, including irrigation, fertilizer application, agricultural extension, health measures and education. For, increasing food production and rural development were given first priority in India's five-year plan for economic development. Six of the 55 projects, however, were to be of the opposite type including, in addition to the foregoing activities, small and medium scale industries, township planning and development. The Agreement contained full details and break-ups of programmes relating to agriculture, communications, education, health training, social welfare, supplementary employment, housing and organizational matters.[34]

Consistent with the terms of the Technical Co-operation Agreement, increasing food production and rural development were given first priority in India's First Five Year Plan. The Government of India also considered it necessary to lay a proper foundation for the industrial and general economic development of the country. It, therefore, adopted the Community Development Programmes, so that the benefits arising from both agricultural and industrial development should reach as large a section of India's population as possible. The programme was undertaken by the Government of India in consultation with the appropriate authorities of the various State Governments, the object being to make the best use of the assistance provided by the U.S.A. for developmental purposes.

Organizationally, the Government of India acted in pursuance of Paragraph I of Article IV of the Technical Cooperation Programme Agreement of 5 January 1952. It designated the Planning Commission as the Central Committee to lay down broad policies and provide general supervision for the agreed programme. The implementation of policies was earlier left to the Ministry administratively concerned, but since Community Projects were in principle not relatable to the sphere of any particular Ministry, their implementation was vested in the Central Committee itself for overall implementation, perhaps on the model already suggested by the Bengal Administration Inquiry Committee. The Committee for that purpose appointed its own Administrator, S.K.Dey, who had earlier served in the Ministry of Rehabilitation in May 1950. He was now given the powers of a Head of a Department in so far as the administration of Community Projects was concerned.

The Administrator was responsible for planning, directing and co-ordinating the Community Projects throughout India under the general supervision of the Central Committee and in consultation with the appropriate authorities in the various states. He was to be assisted by a body of qualified staff to advise him on administration, finance, personnel (training), community planning and other matters, including operating divisions in the fields of agriculture, irrigation, health, education, industries, housing, community facilities, and similar other matters connected with project administration. He had in fact under him a central organization called the Community Projects Administration for carrying on the day-to-day work. Up to 31 March 1952 the expenditure was met from the budget grant of the Planning Commission as directed by the Ministry of Finance.[35]

However, the Community Projects Administration was soon allowed a separate secretariat from that of the Planning Commission and a subhead was created for it and its secretariat formed in August 1952.[36] Financial powers were in the meantime delegated to its Director under a resolution of the Planning Commission which, besides ordinary routine matters, authorized him to create new posts in the subordinate services for a specified period of a year at a time and to sanction miscellaneous recurring expenditure up to Rs 500 a year and Rs 2500 non-recurring.[37] An estimated amount of Rs 5,57,000 was in adition sanctioned to enable him to pay the salaries of officers and to meet the cost of establishment, allowances and other charges.[38] He became free to build up his own sphere of influence and patronage.

Growth and Development

The staffing pattern of the Community Projects Administration went on increasing in size and variety until it was transformed into a separate Ministry, the Ministry of Community Development, with effect from 20 September 1956.[39] The Community Projects Administration grew by stages in the course of the First Plan. The first stage was the establishment of fifteen pilot development projects sponsored by the Ford Foundation in fifteen different states. The second was the 55 Community Projects which the government inaugurated on 2 October 1952 under the terms of the Operational Agreement of 5 January of the same year. The third, on the other hand, was the launching of a countrywide National Extension Service Programme a year later, on 2 October 1953. Each of the Ford Foundation pilot projects consisted of a block of about 100 villages containing about

50,000 people. Their object was primarily to test the feasibility of the Foundation's intensive development scheme as well as to determine the suitability of the extension method and organization necessary for a country-wide development programme.

As a first step in its programme of intensive development, the Government of India made a beginning with its stipulated 55 community projects located in certain selected areas. Each of these projects covered nearly 300 villages with an area of about 450–500 square miles and a population of 2.9 lakhs. Each project was divided into three development blocks which covered all aspects of village life. As the immediate objective was increased agricultural production, selection was guided by the existence of irrigational facilities or assured rainfall. While the schematic budget for a project provided by the government amounted to Rs 65 lakhs for a period of three years, the assistance provided by the U.S. Government consisted of equipment, such as jeeps, audio-visual equipment,, artificial insemination equipment for cattle, road rollers, tractors, etc. The first 55 development projects were spread out evenly in 81 areas covering all the States. This opened a new chapter in the life of rural India. For, only six of these were composite projects which were sanctioned for West Bengal, the remaining 49 being purely rural.

Another 110 areas had necessarily to be added to the original 55 in the course of hardly six months. The response of the people became so overwhelming that it was well nigh impossible to resist pressing demands from all quarters for an expansion of the programme. But since the country's resources in terms of both finance and suitably trained personnel were limited, the planners started thinking in terms of a less intensive programme which could be accommodated within the available resources. A new scheme had, therefore, to be evolved. It was called National Extension Service, and envisaged some conucleus funds and the same staffing pattern consisting of a coordinating officer called the Block Development Officer who covered about 100 villages with 60,000 to 80,000 people. He was supported by a group of Extension Officers representing agriculture, animal husbandry, rural engineering, public health, co-operation, social education, women's and children's programmes as well as rural crafts and industries. Like the Community Development programme, the National Extension Service, too, envisaged for every Block a certain number of Village Level Workers with a basic high school education in addition to some training in extension methods. In the words of

S.K.Dey, the National Extension Service was a 'more diluted version of the [Community Development] programme'.[40] It was inaugurated a year later, on 2 October 1953.

The pattern of staffing of the National Extension Service, as of the Community Development Programme, was essentially the result of the recommendations made by the Grow More Food Inquiry Committee which reported to the Government of India in June 1952, a Committee appointed with V.T.Krishnamachari as Chairman. It examined the economic aspects of village life in great detail and observed that since these aspects were all inter-related, 'no lasting results could be achieved if individual aspects of it were dealt with in isolation'. The Committee also recognized that the cultivators would never readily respond to the government's appeal to grow more food unless the government on its part took the initiative and first helped people meet such 'felt needs' as education, public health facilities and regular water-supply for irrigational and drinking purposes. The Committee, therefore, recommended that, like the Community Development Programme, the National Extension Service should be organized to cover all aspects of rural life in the country within a period of seven or eight years. Secondly, it worked out the pattern of official and non-official organization at all levels—the state, district, *taluka* or *tehsil* and village; and thirdly, it recommended central aid to the establishment of the service in all states.[41]

It was under the recommendations of the Grow More Food Inquiry Committee that the lowest administrative unit of *taluk*, *tehsil* or circle with 100 to 120 villages came to constitute a convenient development block under a Block Development Officer heading as co-ordinator the extension organization of technical experts. The organization was expected to function as a team constantly consulting one another and exchanging experience. And as its main emphasis had flowed immediately from Grow More Food considerations, the extension organization was directed to establish 'the closest contacts with agriculturists and be their friend and guide'.[42]

The Planning Commission accepted in principle the recommendations of the Grow More Food Inquiry Committee. But that acceptance was not without opposition. Since the erstwhile Grow More Food campaign had been sponsored by the Ministry of Food and Agriculture and the concept of Community Development itself was an outgrowth of that campaign, the claim of the Ministry was that the entire Community Development Programme with the rural extension service should continue to be administered by itself. But both Jawaharlal Nehru and V.T.Krishnamachari asserted that a national community development programme which, as they believed, would one day reach out and involve all of India's thousands of villages, could not be the exclusive concern of a single ministry. Therefore, the Planning Commission itself was to function as a Central Committee with the Prime Minister as Chairman and the Minister of Food and Agriculture as one of its members. All the 'nation-building' ministries were directed to collaborate with the Community Projects Administration established for the purpose. The Planning Commission so reorganized for the execution of the Programme at the policy-making level, treated Community Development as the method and Rural Extension as the agency through which the Five-Year Plan would seek to transform the social and economic life of villages. [43]

The administrative arrangement made at the state level followed the pattern established at the centre. It had its State Development Committee with the Chief Minister as co-ordinator and Chairman and ministers of the 'nation-building' departments as members. It was like the Cabinet Committee for Development which the Rowlands had recommended for Bengal in 1945. The State Development Committee had under it a competent officer called Development Commissioner co-ordinating at the administrative level the development programme of the state as a whole. At the district level the Collector was to function as Chief Co-ordinator and give the lead through a District Development Committee consisting of the district officials representing the various nation-building or development departments as well as non-official members belonging to the state legislature and Parliament hailing from the district as well as prominent social workers. The Block level too had its own Committee. In the course of the First Five-Year Plan it represented a similar pattern of organization, with the Subdivisional Officer acting as the head of the team for supervisory guidance on behalf of the Collector and the District Development Committee. With the rapid expansion of the programme during the very First Plan a new set of functionaries was injected as Block Development Officers. They were recruited from the department of revenue. Functioning in the manner of a traditional bureaucracy, they remained preoccupied largely with the attainment of targets rather than the education of people to help themselves through the agency of rural extension.

N.E.S.–C.D. Stages

Organizationally, there was, as said before, no marked difference between the C.D. Programmes and the National Extension Service. In both, the work of agricultural extension was also a common factor. In the Community Development Blocks, however, the works programme was more comprehensive. A Development Block under an extension programme could subsequently be selected in the light of its performance for intensive development under the C.D.Programme. Ultimately, a Development Block of each variety which was supposed to have passed through an intensive stage, was expected to revert to what was called the post-intensive phase after a scheduled period of operation. It was the third phase of development in which people and their own local institutions were expected to have greater responsibility in order to maintain the tempo of work started with government initiative, its main objective being to bring about a stage of development where the change from the government's programme to a people's programme might become possible with the help of a permanent extension agency locally available, as the Grow More Food Committee had earlier visualized.

In order to enable the N.E.S. and C.D. programmes to constitute a nucleus to which funds could be added by the development departments in the states the Government of India decided to provide Rs 4½ lakhs for an N.E.S. Block and Rs 15 lakhs for a C.D. Block for a period of three years. Each development block of either type was to cover a population of 60,000 spread over an area of 100 square miles and 100 villages.[44]

Assistance from the U.S. Government

The Government of the U.S.A. offered assistance to the Community Development Programme in the matter of supply of various items of equipment considered essential for the programme and not manufactured in the country. The aid so given was under the U.S. Government Technical Co-operation Mission Programme in the form of funds which covered the cost, freight and other charges involved in the import of equipment procured from abroad. The 'rupee' cost on the import of the equipment like customs duty was borne by the Government of India. The total aid made available to the Community Development Programme under the Technical Agreement was about 14 million collars,[45] the rest being in the form of grants. No further allotment of funds was made for the Community Development Programme under the Agreement.

All the equipment indented for under the Agreement was duly received and supplied to the various states in India. It was agreed that there would not be any more import of equipment for the Community Development Programme under U.S. Dollar Aid and such aid was altogether discontinued from 1957. It was in fact laid down that all requirements of equipment for the programme must in future be purchased by the State Governments themselves in rupee from indigenous manufacturers and stocks in the country itself. The State Governments were, however, advised to ensure the proper maintenance and full utilization of the equipment supplied to them by the Government of India for the Community Development Programme. They were to utilize the resources in their respective departments, which expected to be responsible for their servicing and full utilization.

Training of Development Personnel

In view of the escalating expansion of the extension services and the existing shortage of expertise and inputs, the importance of training suitable personnel was being fast recognized in the interest of the entire Community Projects Administration. Considerations of speed naturally did not call for quality and depth in the content of training. All that the programme required was a large number of persons who should be given some modicum of training in the subjects concerned, with an orientation for public and community service in rural areas, an orientation which could hardly be measured qualitatively through training courses.

Before Community Development was started in 1952 there were no institutions in existence for the training of Block Development Officers, Village Level Workers and Social Education Organizers, a set of new categories of employees. It was necessary to set up institutions for the training of such personnel. For other categories the existing institutions were sought to be strengthened and increased in number. The concerned ministries at the Centre lent full co-operation to the states in the organization of training centres for Extension Officers, for Village Level Workers as well as for Health Personnel.

Block Development Officers. This category of the project personnel was drawn generally from the existing state services. There was no provision for any training in the beginning, when they were selected as revenue officers. The training later given was of a purely formal nature, stretching over three weeks of orientation lectures. There were in all three training centres which were first set up in April 1954. These were located at Nilokheri (Punjab), Himayatsagar (Hyderabad) and Ranchi (Bihar). A fourth was later established near Lucknow. While the first three centres were government institutions run directly by the Ministry of Community Development, the fourth was run by the U.P. Government with a hundred per cent grant-in-aid from the centre. Together they conducted five courses in a year, their total capacity per course being not more than 200. The total number of Block Development Officers so trained up to the end of December 1957 was said to be 1,811.[46]

Social Education Organizers. The number of social education training centres established in Aplril 1953 was only five. These were situated at Nilokheri, Allahabad, Santiniketan, Hyderabad and Gandhigram, with a training capacity of forty in each course at each centre, the period of training being limited to five months. The fact that the training capacity was doubled in January 1955 was an indication of the speed with which community projects were expanding. It was also decided to open some more training centres to meet the increasing demand for Social Education Organizers. As many as eight more centres (three in 1955–6 and five in 1957–8) were established at Udaipur, Belurmath, Baroda, Indore, Gargoti, Coimbatore, Gopalpur-on-Sea and Bakshi-ka-Talab. Except Nilokheri, which was a government institution under the Ministry of Community Development, all the other training centres were either private institutions or run by State Governments with grant-in-aid from the Government of India.

In October 1955 a training centre was opened at Ranchi. The object was to impart a three months' specialized supplementary training to those of the Social Education Organizers who had already received the five months' usual training and who were either required to work in tribal areas or already engaged in such work. This centre was directly administered by the Ministry of Community Development.

Village Level Workers. Gram Sevaks were the first category of village level workers. As many as thirty-four Extension Training Centres were set up for them in 1953 by the Ministry of Food and Agriculture, the parent source of the National Extension Service. The object was to impart to village level workers a six months' extension training in basic agriculture. But since the training given proved to be insufficient, it was decided to open Basic Agricultural Schools/Wings for that purpose. There the period of training was extended to eighteen months, one year at the Basic Agriculture Schools/Wings followed by six months at the Extension Training Centre. The number of such schools functioning at the end of December 1957 was 78, and that of extension centres, 63.[47]

Two Gram Sevikas, women village level workers, were assigned to each C.D. Block. As on 31 December 1957, there were as many as 25 Home Science Wings attached to the Extension Training centres as well as to two other centres run under the auspices of the Shivaji Education Society, Amravati, and the Kasturba Trust, Indore. The training at these centres was of a year's duration, with a capacity of 30 trainees per course at each institution.

Group Level Workers. This category of extension officers operated in the field of Agriculture Husbandry under the auspices of the Ministry of Food and Agriculture, which had established eighteen training centres which conducted orientation courses of two months' duration. This was later sought to be substituted by a common course which was to be taken along with other functionaries of a Block for orientation purposes.

Extension Officers (Industries). In 1955 arrangements for the training of these officers were made by the Ministry of Commerce and Industry four of its small industries service institutes situated in Delhi, Bombay, Calcutta and Madras. They were required to do a course of six months' duration. Under a subsequent arrangement they were to have their training at one of the five Khadi Board Mahavidyalayas which ran a year's course. This decision was soon modified by the Central Committee which struck a compromise requiring industrial extension officers to spend four months at their service institutes and the remaining eight months at Khadi Mahavidyalayas.

Extension Officers (Co-operation). Provision was made for eight training centres established in 1955 with a total capacity for 800. The duration of the course was initially ten months, which was subsequently raised to eleven months.

Health Personnel. The various categories of health personnel were drawn from institutions run by the Ministry of Health in collaboration with State Governments. It was, however, felt necessary that the personnel appointed should be given a short-term orientation training to bring them in tune with the basic objective of service to the rural community which for social and historical reasons had for ages remained in a state of neglect. For this purpose three centres were established in 1954 at Poonamalles, Singur and Najafgarh, where training of two months' duration was imparted to this category of functonaries.

Central Institute of Study and Research. A Central Institute of Study and Research in Community Development was established at Mussoorie in May 1958. The object was 'to stimulate thinking in key personnel, both administrative and technical, engaged in the Community Development Programme with a view to creating in them a better understanding of the objectives of the programme, approaches, techniques, etc. through orientation courses at the Institute'. It was in fact to function as a 'Brains Trust' of the Ministry of Community Development in all policy matters as well as in providing technical data resulting from different studies and researches carried out either directly or through the various training centres or universities. The principal of the Institute was a senior I.C.S. Officer of the rank of a Joint Secretary.[48]

The categories of officers who were brought to the Central Institute to attend an orientation course of training of five weeks' duration included Collectors, Heads of Technical Departments, Development Commissioners and their Deputies, Secretaries and other senior officers of development departments. The emphasis in the course of training was supposed to be not only on the objectives and growing techniques of Community Development, but also on its philosophy, rural sociology and public administration.

Reorganization of Training Programmes. The Central Institute at Mussoorie was in fact a result of the recommendations made by the Expert Committee on Training and the Study Team on Community Development which extended its scope so as to embrace all categories of development personnel from the Development Commissioners on top to the village level worker at the bottom. The new pattern of training envisaged a number of changes. All block extension officers, including the Block Development Officer, were, for example, expected to receive orientation training together at common centres. Job training for each category of personnel, on the other hand, was to be arranged in specialized training institutions run by the concerned ministries. Provision was sought to be made for refresher training to each category of Block functionaries as well as to district heads of technical departments engaged in the work of Community Development. Even officers holding key positions were not to be exempted. Special facilities were to be made available to Collectors, Heads of Departments and Development Commissioners for short-term study on Community Development. Provision was sought to be made for separate training facilities for women extension workers.[49]

The Central Institute of Study and Research established in May 1958 at Mussoorie started in 1960 a regular research wing and academic supervision of training centres for Community Development personnel. In 1962, the Institute for Instruction, which had been established at Rajpur, was merged with the central wing of study and research, together formed into the National Institute of Community Development. The National Institute so formed was shifted in 1964 from Mussoorie to Hyderabad. It became a registered society on 1 November 1965, with a general council, consisting of both official and non-official members, enjoying autonomous status. This flexibility in its constitution was designed to enable the National Institute to acquire an academic reputation to secure co-operation from universities.[50]

The emphasis of the National Institute of Community Development was, however, mainly on the conduct of orientation courses for key personnel in the Community Development programme, such as Development Commissioners and their immediate deputies, heads of technical departments as also Secretaries, Joint Secretaries, Deputy Secretaries and Under Secretaries of various departments. The list of key personnel, in addition, included Collectors, District Planning Officers, Chief Executive Officers of *Zila Parishads*, Members of Parliament and State Legislatures. Certain selected Pradhans of panchayat samities and other officers of the rank of Deputy Collectors and Subdivisional Officers also attended these orientation courses.

When the Orientation Training Centres started functioning from October 1958 under the direct administrative control of the Government of India, they replaced the old Block Development Officers' training centres. In these centrally controlled training centres even training for supervisory personnel at the block level was provided through a common course; orientation to extension officers was similarly arranged through regular courses. This in fact was a coming together of extension and other workers from the field, and arrangement which was considered necessary for integration in Community Development at the block level.

Composit training centres were reorganized from April 1967 for training at the middle level. There was to be roughly one such training centre maintained by each of the State Governments.

Periodical Review

Since programmes were expanding on a gigantic scale supposedly to build up the rural economy and to effect social change, the need arose for a careful review and assessment of the results. This by itself called for another organization, supposed to be 'independent' and unbiased in its review. Thus the Programme Evaluation Organization was established in 1952 itself to review annually and report on the programmes.

However, the Programme Evaluation Organization was itself a sizeable unit. An Estimates Committee report of 1 December 1956 points out that the Organization was headed by a Director at the headquarters where he was assisted by two Deputy Directors, eight Research Officers and other staff. There were in addition three Regional Evaluation Officers, stationed at Calcutta for the eastern zone, at Bombay for the southern zone and at Delhi for the northern zone. Each had their own separate staff. They had under them twenty Project Evaluation Officers, one for each of the twenty evaluation centres chosen by the Community Projects and the Pilot Extension Projects, two of the principal type of the rural development projects, existing at the time.

A Project Evaluation Officer was selected through the Union Public Service Commission. These officers were expected to keep themselves informed of developments in the Community Projects or N.E.S. Blocks in which they were posted. A more important part of their duty was to conduct with the help of research officers rural surveys, both statistical and non-statistical. The object was to record the economic and social changes taking place in rural areas as a result of the Community Development Programme. They were officers of standing, appointed on the grounds that the work of measuring the impact of the Programme could not be 'entrusted to less qualified or lowly placed staff.[51]

The Director took charge of his post in October 1952, while the Project Evaluation Officers joined in April 1953. Even so, the existing evaluation effort, according to the Committee's report of 1 December 1956, remained far from being adequate. For in the course of his evidence before the Estimates Committee, the Director, instead of throwing light on the results of evaluation, emphasized the need to further strengthen his organization by involving universities in the task of evaluation and asking Community Projects Administration to draft a manual of rules for the guidance of village and block workers, so that records of performance might properly be kept for a survey by social scientists. The Director in fact made it clear 'that the Organization needed strengthening on the sociological side, specially because the social changes which were occurring in the country were extremely important and it was necessary that the Evaluation Organization charged with the task should provide more information of what was happening'.[52] He added that since the universities were not interested in the kind of work expected, there was no alternative to adding further personnel. He made no comment on the attainments, if any, of the Project Evaluation Officers earlier appointed precisely to do the same job! Even so, the Estimates Committee recognized the demand for further expansion, suggesting, however, that efforts should at the same time continue to be made to enlist the support of universities and other institutions.[53]

Committee on Plan Projects (COPP)

This committee recommended the appointment of a Study Team on Community Development and National Extension Service. The team so appointed *inter alia* recommended that transfer of authority to the people and people's institutions should be effected for formulating and implementing the programme on the principle of democratic decentralization. Another of its important recommendations was to rephase the C.D. and N.E.S. Programme during the Second Plan as well as to abolish the distinction existing between the C.D. and N.E.S. stages.

Both these recommendations were accepted with slight modifications. The State Governments proceeded to take suitable measures to give effect to the first recommendation consistent with the demands of local conditions and needs. The rephasing of the C.D. and N.E.S. programme and the abolition of their distinction were also accepted. The old distinction between C.D. and N.E.S. which was based on differences in their respective degrees of development and viewed as discriminatory in terms of resource allocation was sought to be abolished, especially when the 'post-intensive' stage involving a change to people's initiative in planning remained unfulfilled for all practical purposes and without reducing the financial responsibility of the Centre. It was therefore decided that Blocks as the basic units of planning, were to be given Rs 12 lakhs each for five years in Stage I at the end of which they would enter Stage II with a budget of Rs 5 lakhs. This important feature of the revised arrangement which came into effect on 1 April 1958 laid down that at the second phase development departments in the states were required to make increased block-wise allotments of funds in their charge. The object was not only to maintain with state resources the tempo of progress, but also to achieve progressively increased development in the area. However, this development was measured for the most part in terms of inputs and on the basis of statistical data supposed to be prepared under the supervision of the Ministry's Administrative Intelligence unit. The National Extensive Service which had owed its origin to the recommendations of the Grow More Food Inquiry Committee, was, however, able to prove its worth as a 'permanent agency' in the promotion of agriculture, the original object of its institution, although here, too, Norman Borlaug, the eminent food specialist, described the so-called surplus of gains in India as 'artificial', because 'millions were still hungry'.[54]

Legislative Enactments on Panchayats

The old village panchayats in India which Sir Charles Metcalfe described as little village republics were not based on legislative enactments but were custom-based and tradition-bound institutions sustained by a reciprocity of interests between landowners bound together by ties of kinship and principles of pre-emption on one hand, and the farm labourers and tillers of the soil on the other. It was a status-governed, static arrangement where mobility hardly existed. There was a prevailing sense of an equity-based consensus of local opinion, but no contract-based rule of law, the foundation of modern democracy. The land legislation enacted under British rule was in recognition of this principle of contract which tended to free individuals from the exercise of communal obligations and rendered them subject to law which recognized the right to property in their individual capacity. The rule of law encouraged individualism and increased litigation which, in effect, sapped the foundations of the old village communities.

The Royal Commission on Decentralization realized the danger of disintegration in rural communities and recommended that every village should have a local body with certain judicial powers as well as powers to manage primary education, sanitation, cattle ponds and fodder reserves. It was in keeping with this recommendation that laws governing village panchayats were enacted in different provinces under the Reforms of 1919. The legislation so enacted, however, took only a partial view of things. It did not take into consideration the peculiar structure of land tenure and the caste system which in the past had preserved village communities as custom-based corporate institutions. The new laws of property, which destroyed the erstwhile corporate character of villages, were wishfully sought to be conceived as pillars of community living in rural areas. The legislators of the post-Independence period followed in principle the same line of thinking. Constitutionally and functionally, however, the legislative enactments of this period marked a considerable advance towards modernization.

U.P.

Village panchayats in U.P. were governed by the United Provinces Panchayat Raj Act, 1947, which was later amended from time to time to meet new requirements. Panchayats and *panchayati adalats* were, for instance, inaugurated on 15 August 1949 after the first general election. The Act had provided for the establishment of a *gaon sabha*, comprising in the beginning a population of 1,000 covered in one or a group of villages. It was designed to be a general supervizory body without any executive powers which vested in the *gram panchayats* although the Pradhan (President) and the Up-Pradhan (Vice President) were to be the same person for both. The Pradhan and members of *gram panchayats* were to be elected directly by the *gaon sabha*, each comprising a population with a minimum as small as 250, a change which led to considerable increase in their number.

The number of members to be allotted to a *gram panchayat* in addition to the Pradhan was as follows:

1.	*Gram sabhas*	with a population of	1,000	15	members
2.	”	”	” 1,000 up to 2,000	20	”
3.	”	”	” 2,000 up to 3,000	25	”
4.	”	”	” 3,000 up to 4,000	30	”

Seats for schedule castes were reserved in proportion to their population in *gram panchayats* only.

The Pradhan and members of *gram panchayats* were elected by *gaon sabha* members by a show of hands, while the Up-Pradhan was to be indirectly elected by members of *gram panchayats* from amongst themselves. If seats in *gram panchayats* remained vacant despite two bye-elections, the District Magistrate could nominate members to them.

There was to be under the Act a *Nyaya Panchayat* to make cheap justice available to villagers. It was to consist of 5 to 8 members of the *gram panchayats*, with powers to determine simple civil and criminal cases. Its jurisdiction extended to suits up to a value of Rs 500, while in criminal cases it could impose fines up to Rs 100.

The Act indicated certain items for purposes of taxation and sources of income for panchayats. The field of taxation included land revenue, trade, callings and professions, pack animals, the sale of goods in local markets, registration of animals, slaughter houses and water rates if the *gram sabha* arranged water supply. In actual practice their income flowed from a certain percentage of tax contributions, donation, grants-in-aid, a part of *Nyaya Panchayat* income and other sums ordered by the State Governments from the sale proceeds of compost, rents, etc.

Administratively speaking, the Panchayati Raj Department was under the Ministry of Local Self-Government, with a Director and some Deputies to assist the Secretary of the Department. At the district level, the District Planning Officer was *ex-officio* District Panchayat Officer looking after panchayat work with the help of inspectors and assistant development officers. The suspension and removal of panchayat office-bearers vested in the government and the subdivisional Magistrate usually exercized this power.

Bihar

Immediately after the transfer of power the Bihar Panchayat Raj Act was passed in 1947 for the whole of Bihar except certain specified areas. The declared object was to establish and develop local self-government in the village communities and to improve their social and economic life. The Act, however, came into force only in April 1949, not in 1947.

In the initial stages, *gram panchayats* were formed with a population of 1,000 adult members. With the abolition of the permanent settlement system the Government decided in 1955 that for welfare schemes of rural development a *halka* should be the unit of revenue administration as well as for the execution of development schemes within an Anchal-cum-Development Block, a *karamchari* being in charge of revenue, while a village level worker was responsible for development work in each *halka*.

The formation of *halkas* and *gram panchayats* was to be determined on certain principles: it was laid down that an Anchal-cum-Development Block in a district should ordinarily consist of 10 *halkas*, a number which might, according to local circumstances, go up to 12 or come down to 8. For each such *halka* was to be constituted on the basis of area and population, not of the number of villages. Normally, however–a *halka* consisted of the jurisdiction of two *gram panchayats*, although in exceptional cases it might comprise even three villages. The average size of a *gram panchayat* in north and south Bihar was about 3–4 square miles with an average population ranging between five to six thousand in the north of the State, and two to three thousand in the south.

A *gram panchayat* was to consist of 18 members called *panch*. Of these, a *Mukhiya* and eight members constituted its executive committee, while a *Sarpanch* and the other eight *panchs* were to form a *gram cutchery* or village court (the *Nyaya Panchayat* in U.P.). The *Mukhiya* and four members of his executive committee were elected by secret ballot on adult suffrage, while the remaining four executive positions were set aside for nomination to reserved seats for scheduled castes, scheduled tribes, women and others. The same principle applied to the other half of the *gram panchayats* where the *Sarpanch* and four *panchs* were to be elected by secret ballot, while the other four were nominated to reserved seats according to area and proportion in the local population. The executive committee was to elect one number as *Up-mukhiya* who, during a vacancy in the office of the *Mukhiya* or his temporary absence or incapacity, was to exercise his powers. The Act provided for the appointment of a panchayat secretary also.

The *gram panchayats* were classified into three grades, first, second and third. Their term of office on both executive and judicial sides varied according to their grades, ranging from five, four and three years respectively for the first, second and third category. This classification was consistent with the dominance of the caste order reflected in the social behaviour of the state.

The cognizance of the *gram cutchery* extended to a number of offences covered by the Indian Penal Code, the Bengal Public Gambling Act, the Cattle Trespass Act and the Bihar Panchayati Raj Act. But the offences triable and the punishments authorized varied from panchayat to panchayat according to the grade assigned to it. A *Nyaya Panchayat* or *gram cutchery* of the first grade, for example, was empowered to sentence a convict to undergo simple imprisonment not exceeding one month or a fine not exceeding Rs 100. But in a *cutchery* of the third grade the maximum was not to exceed 7 days or a fine of Rs 50. The same principle applied to the determination of civil suits also.

The Act defined the powers of *Mukhiya* and *Sarpanch* in relation to the preservation of law and order, especially in a state of emergency, and recognized the functionaries of *gram panchayats* as public servants within the meaning of section 21 of the Indian Penal Code, and disobedience to their orders being punishable under the same Code. The Government of Bihar decided in 1955 that under ordinary circumstances all development schemes in the rural areas should be executed through the agency of *gram panchayat*, which began to be implemented soon after that.

In terms of financial resources, the Government decided that 'there shall be formed a pool of a minimum of 6¼ of the rent received by the Government in respect of land and [that] the same shall be distributed to the *gram panchayat*.'[55] The other sources of income provided in the Act were to be grants-in-aid, savings from *gram cutchery* and local development works. Powers of taxation were in addition delegated by the Act to enable *gram panchayats* to levy a compulsory property tax as well as a supplementary tax on vehicles, sales in village markets and fees on registration of animals sold in the village area. The Act further laid down that the *Mukhiya* and members of the executive committee would be individually and collectively responsible for misappropriation or any loss of the *gram panchayat* funds. The Government could in fact institute a case for the recovery of money against the defaulters.

The Act provided for the establishment of a Regional Gram Panchayat Advisory Committee and there was to be a Bihar State Gram Panchayat Board of 26 members. Its function was supervisory and advisory. The central guidance and control was vested in the Gram Panchayat Department, with a Secretary to the Government, a Director assisted by a Deputy Director and one Assistant Director of Gram Panchayats. There was to be one Deputy Director of Gram Panchayats in each district and a Supervisor for every two blocks in the State. In their jurisdiction the Block Development officers were given the powers of a Deputy Panchayat Officer.

The Act made provisions for a village volunteer force in each panchayat. It was to consist of adult members of the *gram panchayat* within the age group of 18 to 30 years, functioning under the command of a chief officer for watch and ward duties. There was to be one instructor of the village volunteer force in each sub-division, one head instructor in every district and one state organizer at the state level. The Act provided for the training of all panchayat functionaries including the village volunteer force and instructors.

The Bihar Panchayat Raj Act was in fact a comprehensive measure, although its provisions remained inoperative in several respects. Conceptually, a *gram panchayat* in Bihar was required to function as a unit of revenue administration with a circle officer for an *Anchal* and a *karamchari* in each *halka*, a unit of judicial administration, a unit of police administration, a unit for the maintenance of law and order, a unit for development works and an agency of social and economic change.[56] However, the role so assumed to have been assigned to *gram panchayats* existed largely on paper, except in matters of revenue administration and the formation of panchayats by election, which enabled *Mukhiyas* to secure contracts for works from block authorities.

In fact, the fear of bureaucratic interference checked *gram panchayats*. The state reserved to itself the power of withdrawing the operation of the Act or any part of it from any local area. The *Mukhiya* and his executive committee were to carry out the behest of the district authorities empowered to recommend their removal or suspension as the case might be. Even the Block Development Office could suspend the execution of any of the resolutions of a *gram panchayat* if he so deemed fit.

Orissa

The *gram panchayats* of Orissa were governed by the Orissa Gram Panchayat Act, 1948.[57] Under this Act each panchayat consisted of about 10 to 25 villages covering a population of not less than 1500, a figure which later rose and ranged between 3,000 to 10,000, although attempts were made to bring it back to the earlier position.

The *gram panchayat* was to be elected by secret ballot from amongst the members of the *gram sabha*, the general body. The panchayat so constituted was required to elect a *sarpanch* and *naib* (deputy) *sarpanch* from amongst its own members. They were comparable to the *Mukhiya* and *Up-Mukhiya* in Bihar. There was in addition an *adalati panchayat*, the judicial wing of a *gram panchayat*, headed by a President elected from amonst the members of the *gram panchayat* itself.

The strength of *gram panchayats* varied from 11 to 25 members, there being no provision in the Act for the reservation of seats for scheduled castes and scheduled tribes. Its term of office was to be normally three years, which could be extended if necessary for a year more by the state government.

The *adalati panchayat* was under the Act vested with powers to try criminal cases covered by several sections of the Indian Penal Code, the Cattle Trespass Act of 1871, the Police Act of 1861, and other cases transferred by the District and Subdivisional Magistrates or any other Magistrate empowered to deal with them under the Code of Criminal Procedure, 1891. The *adalati panchayat* was also to handle civil suits of different categories and limited value.

The panchayats were not authorized to collect land revenue. No percentage on land revenue was, therefore, allowed to them. They, however, received annually one-third of the local cess as well as an aditional cess collected by the government from their areas. Village forests or waste lands belonging to the government were not vested in panchayats. Only such public properties as markets, ghats, ponds and tanks were transferred to them for management, so that they might use them as sources of income.

The tax-revenue of panchayats in Orissa was under the Act to consist of panchayat tax, latrine tax, profession tax, vehicle tax and labour tax. Certain fees such as license fees on brokers, cattle registration fees and the like were also collected. The government on its part also made a substantial *kundu* leaf grant of about three to four thousand rupees to each *gram panchayat* situated in *kundu* leaf-growing areas for development purposes. Loans were in addition granted for the construction of market sheds, street lighting, pisciculture and poultry farming.

Provisions were made for panchayat secretaries who were not to be government servants, but local men holding a middle-pass certificate and paid a monthly salary of Rs 40, met partly from the panchayat fund and partly from a government subsidy. He was appointed by the *gram panchayat*, subject to the approval of the District Magistrate.

Unlike U.P. and Bihar, the administrative set-up of the *gram panchayat* department was headed at the state level by the Chief Secretary-cum-Development Commissioner. Its Director and Deputy Director, on the other hand, united in their office the functions of a Deputy Secretary to the government. Two of its Assistant Directors were likewise invested with secretariat functions of a correspondingly lower rank.

Below the state level, the Revenue Divisional Commissioner, too, was included as part of the *gram panchayat* administrative arrangement. He functioned as Assistant Director of the *gram panchayat*. The district set-up included the District Magistrate and *gram panchayat* Organizer. The Subdivisional Officer was himself in charge at that level. The Block Development Officer who presided over a jurisdiction which in size compared more or less to a *thana* had under him *gram panchayat* Supervisors and Inspectors.

The authority of the District Magistrate, however, remained unimpaired in the administration of his district and the introduction of democratic institutions in local administration was not to weaken that authority. Subject to approval by the State Government, he could, as in other states, order under the Act the dissolution and reconstitution or abolition of a *gram panchayat* or *adalati panchayat* on the ground of neglect of duty or abuse of power. He could by notification remove any member of the *gram panchayat*, its *sarpanch*, *naib sarpanch* or president of the *adalati panchayat*.

Punjab

The administration of rural areas in the Punjab was governed by the Punjab Gram Panchayat Act, 1952,[58] as adapted and amended up to December 1953. The principal Act remained on the whole unchanged, although certain minor modifications were introduced by the Punjab Gram Panchayat (Amendment) Act, 1959.

The Act provided for the formation of a panchayat in any village or group of contiguous villages with a population of not less than 500. Every such *gram panchayat* was to consist of five to nine *panches* or members. The number of panchayat members was determined by the government broadly on a population basis. A panchayat with a population of 500 to 1000 was normally to consist of five members. It was six for a panchayat of 1000 to 2000, and seven for a population of 2000 to 3000. Its size rose to eight members in case population ranged between 3000 and 4000. When the population exceeded 4000, the size of the panchayat rose to nine, the limit laid down by the Act.

The election of members was by direct and single transferable vote through secret ballot. There was reservation of seats for scheduled castes, and that, too, was on the basis of their population in the panchayat areas—one member in case their populaton happened to be 5 per cent or more of the total, and two, if it exceeded 10 per cent.

Only a person of the panchayat area whose name was entered on the electoral roll of the State Legislative Assembly was entitled to vote for the election of the *panches* of *gram panchayats*. Immediately after the election of the *panches* they would elect from amongst themselves a *sarpanch* by direct and single transferable vote through secret ballot. The *panches* and *sarpanch* so elected were to hold office for three years. The *sarpanch* could be removed on a vote of no confidence by a two-thirds majority of the *panches*, subject to approval by the Director of Gram Panchayats.

Under the Gram Panchayat Act of 1952 provisions were made for the exercize of criminal, civil and revenue powers by *gram panchayats*. The Act authorized the government to confer enhanced powers on any particular *gram panchayat* or the elected representatives of a group of *gram panchayats*. In the latter case the representative *panches* elected from amongst themselves by direct voting a panchayat which, when acting in its judicial capacity, became known as an *adalati panchayat*. It was comparable to a *gram panchayat* with enhanced powers. The jurisdiction of both was specified in schedule 1-B of the Act of 1952, while that of an ordinary *gram panchayat* was included in schedule 1-A. The offences mentioned in the two schedules together formed a big list which covered as many as 42 sections of the Indian Penal Code and certain sections of such other measures as the Cattle Trespass Act, the Primary Educational Act, the Northern India Canal and Drainage Act, the Punjab Juvenile Smoking Act, etc. A *gram panchayat* could sentence the accused to a fine not exceeding Rs 100, or, if given enhanced powers, to a fine not exceeding Rs 200 or double the value of the damage or loss caused by his act, whichever was greater.

In respect of civil and revenue powers, the pecuniary limits of a panchayat's jurisdiction were Rs 200 and Rs 100 respectively. The pecuniary limit of an *adalati panchayat* or *gram panchayat* with enhanced powers was, on the other hand, Rs 500 in civil suits and Rs 200 in revenue cases. Civil suits were for the most part limited to recovery of property or its value, of money or goods, the price of contracts or compensation for damage caused to movable property. Revenue suits, on the other hand, related to the recovery of agricultural rent regarding disputes arising from certain sections of the Punjab Tenancy Act, 1887.

As regards the sources of income, there was a panchayat fund vested in each panchayat to enable it to meet such charges as were involved in the performance of its development and other functions under the Gram Panchayat Act, 1952. The sum credited to the Fund included all 'grants from Government or local bodies' and all sums other than judicial fees received on behalf of the *gram panchayat* under the Act. It included also a certain percentage of the land revenue paid by the *gram panchayat* area to the government. Likewise, income derived from the revenue-earning schemes of development undertaken with interest-free loans from the government as well as all profits that accrued to the *gram panchayat* from common village land vested in it, formed part of the fund. The village panchayat was in addition expected to levy taxes and receive contributions for different purposes.

A *gram panchayat* was under the Act authorized to levy any tax which the State Legislature had the power to impose in the state under the Constitution. It could also with prior approval of the adult members of its area impose a tax for the construction of any public work of general utility and exempt any member from its payment who might do voluntary labour in lieu of paying the tax.

The Act provided for the appointment of panchayat secretaries who were essentially the employees for the panchayats and paid by them. The total remuneration of a panchayat secretary amounted to Rs 70 per month in the lowest grade, while higher grades of pay at Rs 80 or Rs 90 were also allowed. The minimum qualification was middle pass, but preference was given to matriculates. They were to be recruited by a selection board consisting of three Assistant Directors of Panchayats, the District Panchayat Officer concerned and one member of the Legislative Assembly. Provisions existed in the state for the training of panchayat secretaries.

The organization of the Directorate at the state level differed little from that in other states. There was under the Director an Assistant Director of Panchayats at each Divisional headquarter. Each district had its own District Panchayat Officer. But below the district level, too, there were panchayat officers to supervize the work of 100 to 150 panchayats each. They were normally stationed at *tahsil*, sub-*tahsil* or Block headquarters according to the number of panchayats or the volume of work in each district. The disciplinary powers to suspend a panchayat or any of its members for neglect of duty was vested in the Director.

Bengal

Before the transfer of power in 1947 the Union Board formed the most practical unit for village administration. It was large enough for purposes of mobilizing financial resources and administrative requirements, and yet small enough to be identified with local feeling and community consciousness. Basically, the Bengal village was linked with the *chaukidari* cess introduced in 1871 for the maintenance of the village police, the *chaukidar*. It was this established tax that later provided a secure basic income for the discharge of functions assigned to Union Boards and their higher echelons under the Act of 1919. The principle of the single village type of panchayat was gradually abandoned. That is why a multiple village panchayat system came to be evolved in course of time. The Union Board of Bengal was a natural corollary.

Since Bengal continued to be subject to a series of political and administrative changes that followed the transfer of power in 1947 and the reorganization of states in 1956, the West Bengal Panchayat Act was passed only in 1957.[59] Executive instructions, however, had in the meantime been issued on the subject of *gram sabhas* and *gram panchayats*, instructions which governed their constitution and later formed part of the Act itself. A *gram sabha* was formed ordinarily with a population that varied from 750 to 1500. There were in addition to be *Anchal Panchayats* established by the State Government, each comprising a number of contiguous *gram sabhas*—ordinarily between five and eight. The population of an *Anchal Panchayat* ranged between 5000 and 8000, although it was without any rigid limits.

A *gram panchayat* was selected by members of *gram sabha* members whose names were included in the electoral roll of the West Bengal Legislative Assembly for the area of the *gram sabha* concerned. An amended provision of the Act, however, laid down in 1959 that if a *gram sabha* failed to elect its representatives to the *gram panchayat* twice consecutively, the State Government might fill the vacancies by nomination.

A peculiar feature of the Act was that it authorized the State Government to constitute, if it deemed fit, the first *gram panchayat* and appoint its members from amongst the *gram sabha* concerned. But a *gram panchayat* so constituted by the government was not to continue for a period exceeding one year from the date of notification, and had to be replaced thereafter by elected members. Another important feature of the Act was a provision under which the State Government might associate with any *gram panchayat* any person possessing special qualifications regardless of whether he was or was not a member of *gram sabha*. The object was to ensure effective functioning of the panchayat concerned. The term of office of *gram panchayats* was four years and their strength was to be not less than nine or more than fifteen, fixed according to a table showing the population and the approximate number of members. There was no reservation of seats in the *gram panchayat*.

The *Anchal Panchayat* was elected through secret ballot from among the members of every *gram sabha* lying within its jurisdiction by the *gram panchayat* concerned, in each case in the ratio of one member for every 250 of the members of the *gram sabha*. An additional member was to be elected if the number of the remaining members of the *gram sabha* was not less than 125. The term of office of its members was four years. The strength of an *Anchal Panchayat* was not fixed as it depended on the number of members of *gram sabhas* constituting it. There was no reservation of seats in the *Anchal Panchayat* also. It was perhaps comparable to the erstwhile Union Board of united Bengal which, besides being responsible for the upkeep of village police, minor roads, water-works and sanitation, exercised judicial functions also.

Under the authority vested by the State Government, every *Anchal Panchayat* constituted a *Nyaya Panchayat* consisting of five members called *Vicharaks* elected by it from amongst the members of the *gram sabhas* within its jurisdiction. Besides several sections of the Indian Penal Code, the powers of the *Nyaya Panchayat* extended to the trial of offences covered by certain sections of the Cattle Trespasss Act of 1871, the West Bengal Panchayat Act, the Police Act of 1861, and the Bengal Ferries Act of 1885. However, the punishment to be imposed could not exceed Rs 25. The class of civil suits the *Nyaya Panchayat* was empowered to hear and try included money suits due on contract, suits for the recovery of movable property or its value, and damage caused by cattle trespass.

The *Anchal Panchayat* was also invested with powers of taxation, compulsory and optional. The compulsory tax was to be levied annually upon persons who were owners or occupiers of lands or buildings or both lying within its jurisdiction. The optional category included a tax on professions, trade and calling fees on the registration of vehicles; fees on plaints, petitions and other processes in suits and cases instituted before the *Nyaya Panchayat*; fees for sanitary arrangements in places of worship and pilgrimage; lighting, and conservancy rates. Though optional under the Act, the first two taxes were to be levied compulsorily under the rules by every *Anchal Panchayat*. Every *Anchal Panchayat* was to meet its cost of administration and the costs of the

Nyaya Panchayat. It was also required to pay the salary of *dafadars* and *chowkidars* and distribute the balance to the *gram panchayats* within its jurisdiction. The grants received by every *Anchal Panchayat* included an amount to meet the pay and allowances of a secretary as well as half the pay of *dafadars* and *chowkidars*. A lump sum of Rs 1000 was, in addition, granted to it for development work.

Secretaries were appointed from a panel of four for each post prepared by the Subdivisional officer. The District Panchayat Officer had the powers to take disciplinary action. But an appeal could lie with the District Magistrate against any action taken by the panchayat officer of the district. The salary of the secretary was paid out of the *Anchal Panchayat* fund. The government, however, made its own contribution towards that payment.

The administrative set-up of village panchayats established under the Act of 1957 seems to have followed the principles recommended by the Rowland Committee in 1945, more especially in so far as it applied to the districts. It was headed at the top by a Director of Panchayats who was also *ex-officio* Joint Secretary in the Local Self-Government and Panchayat Department. Under him was the District Panchayat Officer at the district level. The Block Development Officer at the block level was the *ex-officio* Inspector of Panchayats, with a Supervisor under him. The District Panchayat Officer, who was also in charge of development work, was required to function directly under the supervision of the District Magistrate invested with statutory powers to remove *Pradhans* and hear election petitions, etc. He was kept informed even about what transpired between the Director of Panchayats and the District Panchayat Officer. Divisional Commissioners as well as Subdivisional Officers were kept out of the picture completely, although there was a tendency to involve them also through *ad hoc* executive orders.

On the question of no-confidence issues the Act provided that an elected *Pradhan* or *Up-Pradhan* of an *Anchal Panchayat* or an *Adhyaksha* or *Up-Adhyaksha* of a *gram panchayat* might be removed from office by a resolution carried by a majority of two-thirds of the total number of the *Anchal Panchayat* or *gram panchayat* as the case might be. The *Pradhan* or *Up-Pradhan* could also be removed from office by the District Magistrate, while the power to remove the *Adhyaksha* and *Up-Adhyaksha* of a *gram panchayat* was vested in the District Panchayat Officer.

Other States

Statutory provisions for the establishment of *gram panchayats* were enacted in other states also. These panchayats were based on legislative enactments earlier, and functionally, too, the powers given to them for executive, judicial and developmental purposes were not new. These have already been discussed in the preceding chapter. What was new, however, was the emphasis and importance that village panchayats came to acquire in the 1940's for purposes of increasing food production and the projected post-War development plan. In Bombay, for instance, the 1920 Act was more or less a dead letter as was the Act of 1933 which replaced it. The third Act of 1937 began to make a dent and continued until replaced by the Bombay Village Panchayat Act, 1958. The village panchayats in Madras, besides earlier legislation on the subject under dyarchy, were later governed by the Madras Village Panchayat Act of 1950. The states created after the reorganization of 1956 enacted their own measures in due course of time.

The inauguration of the Community Development Programme and National Extension Service called for immediate recognition of the importance of village panchayats, which had already been emphasized by the Report of the Gorw More Food Inquiry Committee in June 1952. But they continued to form part of the administration of local bodies annexed to departments of local self-government. It was not easy, convenient or practicable to link village panchayats directly to the District Board which was too large a charge to be able to pay detailed attention. In many states a district in fact consisted of hundreds of village panchayats. And even where the panchayats had large jurisdictions their number remained considerable. The link between the District Board and its constituent panchayats was in these circumstances anything but effective and efficient.

The broad objectives of the different Panchayats Acts passed since 1947 in different states were more or less the same, with only minor variations in nomenclature, administrative arrangement, procedure and powers of taxation. All were vested with powers to try civil and criminal cases of a simple nature, apart from certain administrative powers to manage their day-to-day affairs and carry on development work. However, these were not new objectives, for during the days of dyarchy the idea had already been defined variously as 'rural development', or 'uplift', or 'rural reconstruction' all of which aimed at the rejuvenation of village life in its many aspects, especially agricultural and veterinary improvements, the consolidation of holdings, co-operative saving and marketing, the building of roads and wells and the improvement of rural health and education. The movement originated in Punjab in 1923 and spread in due course to the C.P., U.P. and finally to Bombay and Bengal. During 1935–9 rural welfare activities were in fact encouraged financially at an all-India level. They covered the entire range of local bodies from District Boards to village panchayats. Attempts were made almost everywhere to set up *ad hoc* district committees to supervise rural development. In the peculiar context of Indian rural local government, however, local bodies 'had very little share in the new schemes, and when the co-operation of village authorities was called for, they were utilized as agents of the officially sponsored schemes, rather than approached as autonomous local bodies.'[60]

The legislative measures enacted in the first decade after Independence exhibited in principle a shift of emphasis from a mere delegation of administrative powers to a basic change in the character of village panchayats in both organizational and functional terms. This emphasis placed the discharge of 'civil duties' on panchayats as a corporate organization in the same manner as could best be expected from a well-established municipal body. A syndicate study-group report on panchayats assumed in 1959 that their broad objectives, including the performance of their newly emphasized civil duties, were all attainable if only adequate financial resources were made available to them.[61] Little was it realized that the sources of income indicated by the group had mostly been provided earlier for District Boards and, later, under several legislative enactments in the post-Independence period to enable *gram panchayats* to raise their own financial resources through local taxation. But taxation was in both cases avoided, and reliance placed almost exclusively on government grants for a variety of purposes, although in the case of *gram panchayats* statutory provisions were made in some states for a certain percentage of land revenue being set apart to meet their expenditure. In fact, the attainment of quality in the discharge of civil duties was not a function of a formal corporate organization invested with statutory powers to raise financial resources. It depended on a non-acquisitive culture and rational view of public service, a view which clashed with the existing structure of land tenure and the caste system.

The failure of *Nyaya Panchayats* proceeded more or less from similar reasons. The legislative and judicial foundations of the continuing courts of justice established under British rule were all based on 'Contract'. But the sources of law traditionally recognized and naturally acceptable to village communities in underdeveloped societies were not based on this principle. Maine pointed out that, in the Indian situation, where the Village Council had managed to survive despite being 'overshadowed' or 'obscured'[62] at times under despotic rulers, it was 'the obligations of kinship, sanctioned by patriarchal authority' as well as 'custom, or chance', which was considered divinely ordained, and which constituted 'in fact the great sources of law'. It was 'not Contract'[63] The entire modern judicial system was founded on that principle, but the Indian village communities held on to their belief 'that contracts are not completely binding till the State has directed them to be executed'.[64] They continued to be guided in their conduct by custom-bound consensus, which was different from the regular system of *Nyaya Panchayats* established formally under an act of legislature and elected under statutory rules that could not vouch for the qualities of character called for in the traditonal context of custom-based Indian village communities. While investing *gram panchayats* with powers to try cases according to the laws enacted in modern times, no care was taken to see whether the laws so enacted could ever be administered by the village panchayat agencies which, besides being tradition-bound and faction-ridden, lacked both the abilities and resources to ensure justice according to the rule of law. The statutory provisions governing *Nyaya Panchayats* thus remained for the most part inoperative.

As the creation of the 'local fund' had initially been designed to relieve central finance, so was the case with panchayat courts, which were supposed to reduce congestion at the level of the subordinate judiciary. This at least was the thinking of the Civil Justice Committee of 1924–5 which recommended that in all the provinces an endeavour should be made to develop a regular system of panchayat courts. The Committee's object in fact was to put on a sound and permanent footing the judicial functions vested in village panchayats in one form or another. But since they had no training whatsoever in the precise application of an elaborate and complicated body of laws, the Judicial Reforms Committee of West Bengal expressed in 1951 a doubt that was well founded. 'The countryside', it pointed out, 'is now torn with factions—communal, political and personal—and it has become well nigh impossible to ensure an independent and impartial tribunal selected from inhabitants of rural areas. Members of these benches or courts belong to a faction commanding a majority in the district and the courts cannot by reason thereof inspire any confidence in those who belong to the minority faction or factions.'[65]

Even so, the village panchayats in different states were invested statutorily with the trial of cases and punishment laid down by penal and civil enactments. The establishment of *Nyaya Panchayats* was not preceded by a due process of education and economic development in rural areas. The legislation enacted on *gram panchayats* was accompanied by such political propaganda, but could not in fact meet the ends of justice or local peace.

Structural Changes in Community Development Administration

Community Projects Administration

As already noted, the inauguration of the Community Development Programme on 2 October 1952 was preceded by the establishment of the Community Projects Administration on 31 March 1952. Though at the outset attached to the Planning Commission, the organization was soon permitted to have a separate secretariat, functioning as an independent administrative unit under the Administrator appointed for the purpose with certain financial and other powers. The actual implementation of the Community Development Programme, however, was the responsibility of the state governments, the Community Projects Administration being responsible for planning, directing and co-ordinating projects throughout the country under the general supervision of the Central Committee and in consultation with the appropriate state authorities.

The Community Projects Administration initially consisted of a very small staff, but, as a perusal of its files[66] makes clear, the Director himself used his powers to make into a large organization with independent secretariat staff and technical experts. However, S.K.Dey, the then Administrator, attributed this expansion to democratic government which, according to him, precluded any curtailment, more especially because of the 'dissensions' that 'began to grow within the Planning Commission for overlordship in the programme', a trend that grew to such an extent that it became 'impossible to run the programme any longer from within the Planning Commission'.[67] The Administrator does not appear to have had the necessary courage and will to oppose the patronage that led to an undue expansion of the C.P.A. and the steep rise in expenditure on officers, staff allowances, honoraria and other charges. The figures given below indicate the increased expenditure in the first five years of the eastblishment of that organization.[68]

Actual Expenditure (in Rs)

	1952-3	1953-4	1954-5	1955-6	1956-7
1. Pay of Officers	78,638	1,82,514	2,97,350	3,56,000	4,74,000
2. Pay of Establishment	57,848	1,21,815	1,63,101	2,26,000	3,44,000
3. Allowances and Honoraria	84,113	1,64,823	2,73,339	2,95,000	4,17,000
4. Other charges	75,319	2,60,785	1,50,397	7,13,000	4,17,000
Total	2,95,918	7,29,937	8,84,187	15,90,000	16,52,000

The Estimates Committee emphasized that the progressive increase in expenditure must be arrested, and expressed surprise over the sudden and steep rise in the revised estimates for 1955-6 under 'other charges', which were said to include film units, cameras, postage, telephones and staff cars. The Prime Minister was naturally surprised to find that the C.P.A. was no longer prepared to remain attached as a tail to the Planning Commission as orginally intended and as Dey points out in his Introduction to Ensminger's *Rural India in Transition,* he was on 9 September 1956 called by the Prime Minister who was upset by the development. But instead of exercising any check, Nehru agreed to the creation of a new Ministry of Community Development at the Centre.

Ministry of Community Development

In pursuance of clause (3) of Article 77 of the Constitution of India, President Rajendra Prasad accordingly ordered on 18 September 1956 that, with effect from such date as might be appointed by the Prime Minister, a new Ministry to be known as the Ministry of Community Development 'shall be constituted' and that 'the said Ministry . . . shall transact the business of the Government of India which is at present transacted in the Community Projects Administration'.[69]

Under the orders of the Cabinet passed on 20 September 1956 the new Ministry was duly created. The press note issued on the subject, however, gave different reasons to justify its creation.

The activities of the C.P.A. and the N.E.S. are expanding rapidly and there will be further expansion during the period of the Second Five Year Plan. The highest priority has been given to increased food production and a special drive has to be launched for this purpose in the Community Project area and in the national development blocks. The urgency and speed with which measures for increased food production have to be undertaken require concentrated and co-operative effort.

Having regard to the growing magnitude and importance of this work, it has been found necessary to place the C.P.A. under a separate Ministry of Community Development. This will involve no major change in the internal organization of the C.P.A. as it is today. The new Ministry will work in full co-operation with the Ministry of Food and Agriculture, and will, when necessary, take advantage of the resources of that Ministry. The Minister for Food and Agriculture will be responsible for co-ordinating the work of the new Ministry with that of his Ministry. The Central Committee of the C.P.A. will continue to function as heretofore.[70]

However, the creation of the new Ministry involved no loss to the erstwhile C.P.A organization or its Administrator, S. K.Dey; for while it was decided by the Cabinet 'to continue the term Community Projects Administration' so as to avoid confusion in retaining its entire personnel establishment, its Administrator, whose post was abolished, was elevated to the rank of Minister with effect from 20 September 1956.[71]

The establishment of the new Ministry was immediately followed by a Central Advisory Committee consisting of officials and non-officials, including economists, sociologists, psychologists, and several others deemed to 'have given thought to the problem'[72] of Community Development. A new set of officers and staff for the Ministry were soon appointed[73] in addition to those who already formed part of the C.P.A., the emphasis again being on patronage or staff maintenance rather than the service involved in programme activity. The figures below indicate the extent of which administrative expenditure grew further in comparison to 1956-6.[74]

	1956-7	1957-8	1958-9	1959-60
1. Pay of officers	50%	75%	150%	275%
2. Pay of Establishment	—	33%	100%	200%
3. Allowances and Honoraria, etc.	50%	50%	125%	300%
4. Other charges	—	16.7%	83.3%	183.3%

The Mehta Team and Panchayati Raj Institutions

At the beginning of the Second Five-Year Plan the undue expansion of expenditure on the office-oriented Community Development Programme first came to the notice of the Ministry of Finance in the

Government of India. In the course of his Budget speech for 1956–7 the Finance Minister commented on 'the large and growing outlay' of the Plan and emphasized the importance of 'the maximum possible economy' by avoiding 'wastage' arising from delays and inefficiency in the transaction of public business.[75] Following this, the National Development Council constituted a Committee on Plan Projects with the Union Minister for Home Affairs as Chairman and the Union Ministers for Finance and Planning as well as the Deputy Chairman of the Planning Commission, as members. This Committee appointed the Balvantray Mehta Team to report on the Community Projects and National Extension Service with a view to economy and efficiency, especially in terms of personnel requirements and co-ordination between different agencies at the Centre and states.

The principle of administrative reorganization for development was suggested in the Second Five-Year Plan itself. It recommended that village panchayats be organically linked with popular organizations at higher levels and that, democratic bodies gradually take over the general administration and development of districts or subdivisions, perhaps excluding such functions as law and order, the administration of justice and certain functions of revenue administration. In its meeting the National Development Council, too, decided that the Team should carry out a special investigation into the reorganization of district administration on the principle so indicated.

Within the framework of a three-tier system of village panchayats, *panchayat samitis* and *zila parishads*, the Balvantray Mehta Team provided in its recommendations for an 'organic link' between the village panchayat and the *panchayat samiti*, its higher level. It proposed that this higher body should be constituted through indirect elections from village panchayats. The panchayats within a block area were for this purpose to be grouped together in convenient units comparable to *gram sevaks'* circles, and the *panches* of all the panchayats in each unit were to elect from amongst themselves a representative or representatives to the *panchayat samiti*. This body comprised on an average about 20 elected members who were to co-opt a couple of women and a representative of the scheduled castes or scheduled tribes in case their population exceeded 5 per cent of the population of the region. The *panchayat samiti* so constituted was to have an elected chairman.

Apart from the organic link between the village panchayat and *panchayat samiti*, a similar connexion was sought to be established between the village panchayat and *gram sevak* who was to function as 'the development secretary of the *gram panchayat*'. To ensure co-ordination between *panchayat samitis* the Team suggested the organization of a *zila parishad*, its members being drawn from the presidents of *panchayat samitis*, the members of the state legislature and of Parliament representing a part or whole of a district whose constituencies were within the district, and district level officers of the medical, public health, agriculture, veterinary, public health, engineering, education, backward classes welfare, public works and other development departments. The Collector was to be chairman of the parishad, and one of his officers its secretary.[76] The object of the parishad was to replace the district planning committee.

This new three-tier democratic system was to take charge of all aspects of development work in the rural areas. The whole system was to be statutory, elective and comprehensive in the scope of its functions with adequate resources, but not cramped by too much control by bureaucratic agencies. Of the three tiers, the village panchayats and *village samitis* were to be the main local bodies for developmental activities. The compulsory duties assigned to the village panchayat, for instance, included water-supply for domestic use, sanitation, maintenance of village roads and tanks, lighting, land management and maintenance of cattle records, relief work, supervision of primary schools, welfare of weaker sections of society, and the collection and maintenance of statistics. The function of the *panchayat samiti*, on the other hand, was to cover the development of agriculture in all its aspects, provision for local agricultural finance from the government and other sources, minor irrigation, cattle welfare, promotion of rural industries, supply of drinking water, public health and sanitation, medical relief, relief of distress caused by floods and natural calamities, construction and repair of roads, management and administrative control of primary schools, welfare of 'weaker sections,' fixation of wages and the collection of statistics. The Team felt that, having provided for the discharge of these functions, there was little left for any higher executive or administrative body other than the government itself. This argument was directed against the old District Board on the grounds of its large size, inadequate resources and want of a suitable tradition to educate the people in self-government and development work.[77] Its report said: 'The District Board, the district school board and the *janapada sabha* become superfluous, as local interest, supervision and care, necessary to ensure that the expenditure of money upon local objects conforms with the wishes and needs of the locality, are provided by the *panchayat samiti*, which we consider a body of size adequate in population and area. The functions which these [old local] bodies are at present performing will, in our opinion, be performed with greater efficiency by the *panchayat samiti*',[78] an alternative which was being established at the block level, comparable in size and population to the erstwhile *tehsil*, *taluka* and *thana*.

The Rowlands Committee was the first to plead the case against the District Board as an instrument of rural development, especially in the context of the Grow More Food campaign. Its emphasis on the Union Board as a vital link with the reduced jurisdiction of the circle officer was likewise reflected in the Mehta Team's proposed grouping together of village panchayats into convenient units to provide an 'organic link' with a higher block level. Structurally, the effective link between the village panchayat and its higher level for development purposes was no different from the recommendations of the Rowlands Committee. This applied also to the district development committee with the Collector as co-ordinator and chairman.

However, the distinctive feature of the Mehta Team's recommendations lay in its emphasis on what it called 'democratic decentralization', an antithesis of bureaucratic rationalization.[79] It viewed decentralization as 'a process whereby the Government divests itself completely of certain duties and responsibilities and devolves them on to some other authority'. It distinguished decentralization from 'delegation of power', which 'does not divest the Government of the ultimate responsibility for the actions of the authority to whom power is delegated; this authority is under the control of the Government and is in every way subordinate to it'.[80] The Team thus envisaged that once decentralization was effected and power devolved on the elective machinery recommended for development work from the village panchayat upwards, such power should continue to be exercised and such machinery controlled and directed only by popular representatives of the local area, not by agencies of the government. It emphasized that the democratic mechanism so devised 'must have the power to make mistakes' and that 'in the ultimate analysis' it alone must represent 'the local people's will in regard to the local development'.[81] Indeed, it was expected to take over 'the entire general administration of the district with only certain exceptions'.

It was surprising that the Team not only stressed in the same breath the necessity of official 'guidance' to help democratic bodies 'to avoid making mistake', but even recommended that the Collector should preside over the deliberations of the *zila parishad* with one of his officers acting as its secretary. Obviously, the members of the team were in two minds, some acting under an ideological commitment to democracy as an end in itself, and others trying to keep close to the realities of social incoherance as well as the administrative inexperience and financial unaccountability of popular bodies. They recognized that a certain amount of control by the government had to be retained and actually recommended that a *panchayat samiti* could, if necessary, be superseded in the public interest. They likewise felt that even the Collector should be vested with powers to suspend in certain cases a resolution of a *panchayat samiti*. Even so, 'democratic decentralization' was sought to be defined as a process involving a complete transfer to popular bodies of administrative responsibility and control over the necessary resources. In this regard their recommendations betrayed a lack of comprehension both of legal and constitutional dimensions, causing confusion and tending to dilute the responsibility of the bureaucracy without in any way strengthening democracy.

And yet the Mehta Team acted on the assumption that popular bodies, if organized on the principle of democratic decentralization, would be able to gear up the entire existing machinery of general administration for development work. In other words, no separate development services would be needed except a new cadre of Block Development Officer and village level workers, two links established at the end of the administrative chain. Little did the Team realize that the enlargement of the Central Government's involvement in planning and financing development projects, which it emphasized in the course of its report, would mean an augmentation of the Centre's control, an intrusion into the sphere of the states, which the Royal Commission on Decentralization as well as the recommendations of the Montford Report had scrupulously taken care to avoid. The Mehta Team put the lock back by reinvesting the Collector with power to preside ove the *zila parishad*, an alternative to the District Board which dyarchy itself had attempted to set free from the shackles of bureaucracy under the Government of India Act, 1919.

The Report came out on 24 November 1957, and consistent with its recommendations the administration of the village panchayat was transferred to the Ministry of Community Development. The control of 'Co-operation' was similarly transferred to the same Ministry. In its meeting held on 3 December 1958 the Cabinet, at the instance of the Prime Minister, decided that the work connected with co-operation, which at the time was being handled by the Ministry of Food and Agriculture, be transferred to the Ministry of Community Development, because the activities of the latter were intimately connected with the development of co-operation in its various forms. The Ministry of Community Development was, with effect from 30 December 1958, renamed the Ministry of Community Development and Co-operation.[82]

The three-tier system of local government which the Mehta Team commended for acceptance as a model instrument for rural development was called Panchayati Raj by Jawaharlal Nehru. The Panchayati Raj Institutions (PRI) thus included the village panchayat, *panchayat samiti* and *zila parishad*, all linked together organizationally for purposes of development work. It examined whether the existing local bodies could be made to take over and accomplish the new task envisaged by the Community Projects and National Extension Service and decided in the negative, followng officially sponsored and government administered projects under the Ministry. It recommended the replacement of the existing local bodies at *taluka* or district level and felt that the village panchayat was too small in terms of area, population and resources, while the district was too large an area for the people to have their plans locally projected. It, therefore, recommended a single representative and core institution at the block level to take charge of all aspects of development work in rural areas. The institution established for the purpose was, like the village planchayat, a statutory body called the *panchayat samiti*, with an area large enough for functional purposes and yet small enough to engage the interest and service of residents, a principle of administrative reorganization which, as said before, the Rowlands Committee had first suggested in 1945. Organizationally, the budgets of the village panchayats were subject to scrutiny and approval by the *panchayat samiti*, and those of the *samitis* by the *zila parishad*.

The Progress of P.R.I. and Local Variations after 1959

The three-tier system was accepted as a model for rural development and established in most states. It was inaugurated first in Rajasthan in October 1959. Andhra Pradesh and Tamil Nadu followed suit in the same year. Assam and Mysore introduced the system in 1960; Orissa, Punjab and U.P. in 1961; Maharashtra in 1962; Gujarat in 1963; and West Bengal and parts of Bihar in 1964. The following table gives the state-wise variations in Panchayati Raj and its position as in December 1971[83]

Sl. No.	Name of the State/U.T.	Whether three or two-tier	Legislation enacted	Remarks
(1)	(2)	(3)	(4)	(5)
1.	Andhra Pradesh	Three	Yes	
2.	Assam	Three	Yes	Gram panchayat and Anchalik panchayat at block level and Mohkuma parishad at Subdivisional level
3.	Bihar	Three	Yes	Three-tier system established in only three districts out of 17 districts
4.	Gujarat	Three	Yes	
5.	Haryana	Three	Yes	
6.	Himachal Pradesh	Three	Yes	
7.	Jammu & Kashmir	Only gram panchayats	Yes gram panchayats only	The State Government was reluctant to introduce the new pattern of rural administration, as it was engaged in a Cash Agricultural programme
8.	Kerala	Only gram panchayats	Yes gram panchayats only	District Administration Bill, 1971 had been introduced in the State Assembly
9.	Madhya Pradesh	Two	Yes	Though the legislation for higher tiers had been enacted during 1962, zila panchayats at the district level had not so far been established
10.	Maharashtra	Three	Yes	
11.	Manipur	Only gram panchayats	Yes for gram panchayats only	New legislation to set up two-tier system was under consideration
12.	Mysore	Two	Yes	Zila parishads did not exist
13.	Nagalanc	—	—	There was no Panchayati Raj set up, instead area range and tribal councils existed
14.	Orissa	Two	Yes	Zila parishads were abolished in 1968

(1)	(2)	(3)	(4)	(5)
15.	Punjab	Three	Yes	
16.	Rajasthan	Three	Yes	
17.	Tamil Nadu	Three	Yes	
18.	Tripura	Only gram panchayats	Yes for gram panchayats only	New legislation to set up two-tier system was under consideration
19.	Uttar Pradesh	Three	Yes	
20.	West Bengal	Four	Yes	The four-tier system, viz., gram panchayats, Anchal parishads and zila parishads existed
21.	Arunachal Pradesh	Three	Yes	
22.	A & N Islands	Only gram	Yes gram panchayats only	
23.	Delhi	Only gram panchayats	Yes gram panchayats only	New legislation to set up two-tier system was under consideration
24.	Goa, Daman Diu	Only gram panchayats	Yes gram panchayats only	
25.	Pondicherry	—	—	Legislation for setting up the institutions was under consideration
26.	Lacoadive, Minicoy and Amindivi Islands	—	—	Regulations were under consideration for enactment

The Ashoka Mehta Committee's report, which appeared in August 1978, confirmed the fact of continuing variations in the structural and operational aspects of Panchayati Raj, a kind of unevenness that flowed from their historical exigencies in spite of a continued stress on uniformity.[84] Assam, for instance, exhibited shifts in the tiers and functions assigned, the *mohkuma parishad* being recognized as a sub-divisional institution and the village panchayat, an institution commanding a population of well over 15,000. In spite of the limited executive functions in Andhra Pradesh, the *zila parishad* produced good results and the performance of the *panchayat samitis* too was reported to be no less praiseworthy. In Bihar, *zila parishads* were introduced in only eight of the districts, but were soon given up even there. The *samiti* tier worked well initially in Rajasthan which, with

Andhra Pradesh, was the first to establish the three-tier system. Tamil Nadu and Karnataka did not introduce the *zila parishad* in the sense of a body invested with executive functions. But there the *samitis* or *taluka* boards were known for the quality of their performance, especially in such fields as education, water-supply, roads and nutrition. In Kerala, there were only village panchayats, though some were as considerable in size as nearly half a block. Their performance in several municipal and civic matters was worthy of note and despite different political parties being represented on the elected body, the harmony needed for the implementation of development programmes was not found wanting due perhaps to the relatively higher educational and cultural standards in the state. In U.P. a large number of panchayats together with *zila parishads* were set up with limited powers and could not achieve much. The Panchayati Raj enactments of Madhya Pradesh proceeded in a piecemeal way, an approach that proved to be counter-productive. The Bengal pattern was seemingly a four-tier system but was in fact 'weaned away' from that structure to a three-tier arrangement. Maharashtra and Gujarat both deviated from the ideal model for the Mehta report. The three-tier structure was of course there. But the first point of decentralization was at the district level and functioned more effectively than the decentralized arrangements at any of the lower levels. Their success was noticeable especially in the field of planning and development.

C.D. on Decline after 1964

The first five years of Panchayati Raj between 1959 and 1964 were a period of ascendancy, a period of socialistic efflorescence which, though dimmed for a while by the Sino-Indian conflict in 1962, continued to receive the direction and guidance of Jawaharlal Nehru. His death on 27 May 1964, however, dealt a severe blow to the programme, a blow that could be traced no less to the headless bureaucratic expansion of the department, and to vested interests that viewed the C.D. and Panchayati Raj movement as a potential threat to their continued dominance. The period of ascendancy was thus followed by a period of stagnation during 1965-9. Under Indira Gandhi, who came to power in January 1966, the Ministry of Community Development and Co-operation was merged in the sprawling Ministry of Food and Agriculture. It was clear recognition of the primacy which the Department of Food and Agriculture had in the past exercised in the context of the Grow More Food campaign, a primacy which Nehru had for a time delinked by assigning to Community Projects Administration a national stature, much higher than the status of an individual department.

From an article by S.K.Dey in the *Statesman* (New Delhi) of 7 September 1978 it appears that a demand was made in the Lok Sabha to abolish the Community Development Programme and Ministry early in 1965—an indication of the shape of things to come. Even Lal Bahadur Shastri, who succeeded Nehru, 'frankly admitted that he did not share Nehru's faith in the capacity of the people to rule themselves'. The Programme and the Ministry were of course both continued, though not as independent entities. The Conference of Chief Ministers held in Madras in June 1968 also resolved unanimously to continue the Community Development and Panchayati Raj Programmes, but this continuance was not unconditional. In December 1968 a consultative council on Community Development was actually constituted to advise the Centre and the states on the problems relating to its functioning. A similar consultative council was constituted on Panchayati Raj in April 1969. This was soon followed in September by the Consultative Committee of Parliament recommending the appointment of a Commission to look into the working of Community Development and Panchayati Raj Institutions. These successive steps clearly meant that all was not well with these institutions. In fact, schemes for rural development began to be separately organized even outside their infrastructure. A Pilot Research Scheme in Growth Centres was for example started in April 1970, while a Crash Scheme for Rural Employment was introduced a year later in April 1971.[85]

Special Agencies and Programmes

The Fourth Five-Year Plan marked the beginning of a noticeable downward trend in the administration of Community Development and Panchayati Raj Institutions, a trend which not only witnessed the merger of the Ministry with the Ministry of Food and Agriculture in 1966, but led to its actual decline towards the close of the Fourth Plan period in 1970 and the beginning of the Fifth Plan in 1971, when the government started launching separate programmes administered from the Ministry of Community Development and Co-operation. Apart from two plans already mentioned, the Government of India launched in 1970-1 two other schemes to promote the interest of 'weaker sections'. These were Small Farmers' Development Agencies

(SFDA's) and Marginal Farmers' and Agricultural Labourers' (MFAL's) Development Agencies. Their main functions were to identify the participants, study their problems, draw out suitable programmes for them and arrange extension services as well as institutional support for the implementation of the programme.[86]

In addition to the tribal development blocks administered by Panchayati Raj Institution, it was decided in 1970–1 to launch pilot projects in six districts in Andhra Pradesh, Bihar, Madhya Pradesh and Orissa for a period of five years. These projects formed part of the work of Tribal Development Agencies (TDA's), which received grants-in-aid to the tune of Rs 6.90 crores up to June 1975.

The Drought Prone Areas Programme (DPAP) was yet another scheme started in 1970-1, the last year of the Fourth Plan. It applied to 74 districts wholly or partly in as many as 13 states, districts which were identified as chronically drought prone. They represented nearly 19 per cent of the area of the country and accounted for nearly 12 per cent of its poplulation, and applied to Rajasthan and Andhra Pradesh on a particularly large scale. The declared objective was to take up works of a permanent nature in such sectors as irrigation, soil conservation, afforestation and roads on which further development could be planned. The sector-wise allocation of funds on the DPAP was in the course of the Fifth Plan shifted to what came to be known as 'integrated rural development' in agriculture and allied sectors, with a Plan provision for Rs 167 crores to be matched by an equal amount by the state governments, in addition to arrangements for institutional credit to the tune of about Rs 500 crores to be spent on the selected 74 drought-prone districts.[87]

Some other separate agencies organized outside the sphere of Panchayati Raj Institutions included the Pilot Intensive Rural Employment Project started in 1972-3, Agricultural Credit and Marketing to promote integrated agricultural development and reduce rural indebtedness, and a scheme of regional rural banks to meet the credit needs of farmers. The Agricultural Refinance Corporation (ARC) that came into being in 1963-4, was intended to assist the co-operative land development banks. The purpose of the ARC was to step up the pace of investment in agriculture in different regions more particularly in the eastern and north-eastern parts of the country.

The Department of Rural Development

The creation of these separate agencies of rural development, though involving a multi-dimensional effort, signified particular emphasis on the development and conservation of natural resources like land and water as well as the provision of credit and other facilities to raise the living standard of the rural poor. A new Department of Rural Development was, therefore, created in the Ministry of Agriculture and Irrigation in October 1974, a pattern of administrative arrangement which dropped altogether the use of the term Community Development. The Department of Rural Development so created was made responsible for the work of the erstwhile Department of Community Development and also for that relating to agricultural credit and rural indebtedness, including co-operation in the agricultural secrtor. Its main responsibilities were '(a) all aspects of rural development including Community Development and Panchayati Raj, (b) special programmes for the betterment of weaker sections for the community like the small and marginal farmers, the development of drought-prone and tribal and hilly area and for rural manpower planning and employment, (c) agricultural credit and marketing including quality control and development of regulated market.[88]

The Department of Rural Development was in fact to concentrate on special programmes for the weaker sections of society as well as credit and marketing facilities, which made it far more comprehensive than the erstwhile Department of Community Development and Panchayati Raj. The programmes so selected for the purpose on an *area basis* was to be integrated to produce the desired result, with the highest priority being accorded to agriculture and allied sectors. This new structural pattern for integrated rural development was adopted by the state governments also.

The added emphasis on integration between the various agencies of rural development proceeded from the earlier experience of the Panchayati Raj structure where, except in Maharashtra and Gujarat, it had' hardly been given an opportunity to take up planning or implementation work on a sizeable scale'. Even 'the essential idea that all developmental activities should flow only through the block level organizaton lost ground, though the panchayat samiti as a key unit of decentralization was in most cases coterminous with the block.'[89] In practice, the process of development was in the opposite direction, from top downwards, not from the village upwards. Maharashtra and Gujarat were two clear cases of deviation from the recognized norms of Panchayati Raj. Instead of starting planning and implementation from the village upwards to the *zila parishad* at the district level, they proceeded from the district to village panchayat. In other words, the district was in both states made the first key point of democratization, a point where both administrative and technical staff were available for decentralized planning and execution. Both states kept the Collector out of the Panchayati Raj system and took out of his control the district level officers of the various technical departments, who were placed with the *zila parishad* under the administrative control of the Chief Executive Officer (or District Development Officer) functioning as the co-ordinator of all development programmes in the district.[90] Their elected *zila parishads,* with the D.D.O. controlling the entire technical staff, were given complete authority and responsibility and invested with the necessary resources to make a success of the system even at the villlage level. In fact, neither of the two states relied primarily on the village panchayat which, for planning and executive purposes, possessed none of the requisites for development. Maharashtra and Gujarat thus produced good results by reversing the process of decentralized planning and development, a process which the Asoka Mehta Committee also adopted as part of its own recommendation in favour of a two-tier system, the district and the block.

But even in Maharashtra and Gujarat, the special agencies, for example, for small farmers or drought prone areas or for intensive tribal development, were not brought within the purview of elected *zila parishads.* The staff under the *zila parishad* would execute schemes, though the programmes were kept outside their orbit. Again, planning work in respect of these schemes was not entrusted in Maharashtra to *zila parishad*, but to a body outside the *parishad* under the chairmanship of a Minister. Moreover, the implementation of the 'transferred activities' in Maharashtra and elsewhere was subject to a number of separate orders and directions of the state government, which assumed the form of subsidiary legislation reducing the decision-making powers of the elected bodies. Even the staff spared by the state to the district and lower bodies came gradually 'to consist of officers who were not wanted by the state governments'[91] It was in these circumstances that a new Department of Rural Development was created in the Ministry of Agriculture and Irrigation in 1974 to integrate all developmental activities within or outside the purview of the Panchayati Raj Institutions.

Panchayati Raj and District Administration For rural Development

As said before, the Grow More Food Inquiry Committee (1952) and the Planning Commission both emphasized the importance of establishing a nation-wide extension service that called for a re-orientation of outlook and reorganization of district administration to meet the demands of a welfare state. The community development programmes and the national extension service came in the context of this policy objective.

The administrative and organizational issues involved in the execution of the policy objective, however, proceeded in the districts along two parallel hierarchies, democratic and bureaucratic. The former attempted to set up representative institutions at the district and block level in addition to village panchayats established under various state legislations, while the latter proceeded to be reorganized horizontally to facilitate co-ordination at both the district and block level under a generalist administrator co-ordinating the activities of technical departments. This organizational pattern was indicated only in general terms in the First Five-Year Plan. But as the Second Five-Year Plan stressed the relative importance of the democratic hierarchy as an effective instrument of social and economic transformation, it was laid down that the functions of the elected representatives 'would eventually include the entire general administration and development of the area other than law and order, administration of justice and functions specifically pertaining to revenue administration.'[92] The Mehta Team's emphasis on democratic decentralization and its implied superiority of the Panchayati Raj Institutions over government bureaucracy flowed from the new policy objective of the Second Five-Year Plan. The declared goal was to see that the official bureaucracy collaborated with the three-tier democratic organizations, gave them the benefit of its knowledge and experience, and worked with them as a team to make the Panchayati Raj scheme a success. In practice, however, democracy involved not only considerations of the ruling party's political stability, but also its interest in the exercise of patronage through the use of bureaucratic agencies which, it was feared, might not serve that purpose except when placed in a position subordinate to elected bodies, and not as a team on a co-ordinate principle. While the political interest of the Congress at the Centre weighed not a little in the restricted application of the regular three-tier elective system to non-Congrss dominated states, patronage as a lever of power politics called for a control of the bureaucracy on the score of democratic decentralization. It was a typical educated middle-class strategy to rule, not to serve.

To obviate the dangers of a disruptive tendency of specialization and to ensure co-ordination under a single administrative head in the district the Rowlands Committee had in 1945 recommended that the Collector be recognized as the undisputed head of all government agencies operating in the district, except in matters of their internal administration and technical methods. No democratic organization was recommended by the Committee to serve as a check on the bureaucracy, a rule-bound organization accountable for all administrative actions. The Mehta Team envisaged democratic decentralization, but wanted the Collector none the less to preside over the proceedings of the *zila parishad*, the supervisory democratic agency of district development activities. The legislation enacted by state governments, however, did not provide for the Collector to preside over any such *parishad*, except in Madras and Mysore where he functioned as the Chairman of the district development council. The Collector was made a regular member of the *zila parishad* in Andhra Pradesh and a member without voting rights in Gujarat, Orissa, Punjab and Rajasthan. He could attend the meetings of the *zila parishad* without voting rights in U.P. and Bihar. But in none of these states could the Collector ever claim to preside. The elected bodies thus expected co-operation in the form of obedience from the Collector who generally happened to be superior to them in all respects except in the matter of political legitimation acquired through the ballot box by means fair or foul.

The relations of the elected bodies with technical officers were in law found to be equally wanting. These officers were in a number of states given the right to attend the meetings of *zila parishads* and *panchayat samitis*, without being members of these bodies. They had no voting rights. Even the district-level officers could be invited to attend their meetings and give advice without powers to vote. It was only in Mysore (Karnataka) that the district-level technical officers were regular members of the district body. They were doubtless members in Madras (Tamil Nadu) and Assam also, but they had no voting rights.[93]

The legislation enacted on the relationship between Panchayati Raj Institutions and district administration thus discriminated between bureaucracy and democracy. It was not realized that the work of development needed collaboration, and not competition for power and status. No cohesive team for development could in these circumstances be evolved between the elected and the official elements of district administration. Maharashtra and Gujarat, however, were an exception. Their administrative arrangements for rural development not only ruled out the principle of democratic planning from below, but also recognized the importance of the District Development Officer who controlled the entire technical staff at the district level and co-ordinated all the development programmes of the district.

A basic weakness of the Panchayati Raj system was its emphasis on planning from the village panchayat level upwards, a level devoid of both human and material resources. It was in some cases a result of ideological obsession and in most cases a political gimmick and sophistry to cover vested interests, economic or elitist. Whatever the motives, the Panchayati Raj system remained for the most part an utter failure at the village panchayat level. The annual Programme Evaluation Reports pointed out that in spite of the efforts of the Ministry of Community Development 'the people themselves lacked real enthusiasm' and viewed community development 'as a Government programme which required village participation'.[94] Even Gujarat, where the higher levels of Panchayati Raj institutions produced good results, reported in 1960 that villagers had still not 'adopted the development programme as their own with a full sense of responsibility'. They felt that it was, 'after all, a programme prepared by government' and that they were being asked 'merely' to co-operate with it.[95] The Praja Socialist Party of Gujarat made a similar comment on democratic decentralization. It said:[96]

> Though in our State village panchayats are formed since long and have also been given powers . . . to take up a wide range of activities of rural welfare and rural reconstruction, these village panchayats have not still become the true components of decentralised democratic institutions and have not still developed the attitude of common rural welfare; they are still not completely rid of the influence of vested interests and factional local politics.

Rajasthan presented a more or less similar picture of village panchayats. The *Report of a Study Team on Democratic Decentralization in Rajastan*, which was prepared in 1961 under the auspices of the Association of Voluntary Agencies for Rural Development, complained of a serious lack of community consciousness among village panchayats and a total disinclination to levy any taxes to improve their financial resources.[97]

On the nature of the village panchayat and its functioning the *Report of a Community Development Evaluation Mission in India* was specially important and enlightening. The Mission was organized at the request of the Government of India by the United Nations Technical Assistance Administration (TAA). It consisted of M. J. Coldwell (Canada), Professor Renè Fernand Dumont (France) and Dr Margaret Read (United Kingdom). The Mission's field visits began on 17 December 1958 and were carried on until 3 March 1959. The Report came out in August 1959. In the course of its report the Mission threw useful light on India's rural economy. As regards village panchayats, the Mission's observations on the change of attitude among villagers and the degree of popular participation with community development programmes were specially significant.

The Mission found a wide gap between the existing practice and declared policy objectives of the Second Five-Year Plan which extended the scope of panchayats from being a mere unit of local self-government to being a unit of development for all people including weaker sections. For it was not evident that all sections of village society attended village meetings. As its report pointed out, 'Inquiries sometimes brought out the fact that Harijans were not present and did not as a rule, in spite of having a reserved place in the membership, take part in regular panchayat meetings.' The Mission used this as evidence to show that there was little or no change in the attitudes of elected panchayats, the cornerstone of Panchayati Raj. It also noticed that in spite of statutory provisions for the establishment of village panchayats there were variations between states and within different parts of each state in respect not only of financial resources available to panchayats, but also of their responsibility for development and administration in relation to the official staff whose duty it was to guide and supervise their work.

A more interesting disclosure that came to the notice of the Mission was in regard to the membership of panchayats and the actual mode of their functioning, a disclosure that had immediate relevance to an understanding of the problem of popular participation with development plans. Under the conditions caused by the elaborate receptions usually organized for the Mission by village panchayats, it was left with hardly any time to put queries and seek answers to the various administrative and organizational issues involved in community development. Even so, the Mission managed every time to make 'a few inquiries' which brought to light the social complexion of the membership of panchayats and their vested interests which obstructed the flow of popular participation. 'There was little doubt,' its report said, 'that the membership of the Panchayat lay chiefly among the larger landowners—the richer element in the village population—who commanded respect because of their caste and their family connexions, and also because they were relatively well-do-do, and who were interested in development because it would increase their income. This impression is confirmed by the study of panchayats in the Fifth Evaluation Report of the Planning Commission, and by a more detailed study in Uttar Pradesh which dealt with village leadership and interest in development plans and projects.' [98]

Naturally enough, the case of community development and village panchayats was one of continuity rather than change. For, as the Mission's Report added:

> Not only did the panchayat membership chiefly consist of well-to-do farmers and the higher caste groups, it was also a predominantly older group, following the traditional pattern of Indian society. This was evident at almost all meetings attended by the Mission—an impression that was confirmed by the Fifth Evaluation Report study. In the areas covered by that study, only 1.1 per cent of panchayat members were under 25 years of age, and only 38.9 per cent were between 25 and 40 years, the balance of 60 per cent being in the older group. [99]

Interestingly enough, the Working Group on Block Level Planning which the Planning Commission appointed on 5 November 1977 with Professor M. L. Dantwala as Chairman, expressed in its *Report* a view which confirmed the impression of the U.N. Mission about the role of Panchayati bodies in rural development. For, the Group clearly pointed out that 'there is a wide-spread feeling, which we share, that by and large the Panchayati Raj Institutions do not reflect the interests and needs of the weaker sections of the rural community. An extreme view is that they in fact obstruct the flow of benefits to the weaker sections.'[100] This explains the absence of people's full participation earlier emphasized conceptually as a *sine qua non* for the success of community development programmes. For, as the Working Group rightly pointed out:

> It is well known that the public is not a harmonious entity; in reality it comprises groups with conflicting interests. Take as an illustration a plan of minor irrigation. If it is proposed in the interest of improving assets distribu-

tion to deploy a larger than proportionate share of the available underground water for the small and marginal farmers, will the *non-beneficiary* group ungrudgingly acquiesce in the decision? Participation by the beneficiary group may result in non-participation—varying from non-cooperation to civil or not so civil resistance—by the (richer) non-beneficiary group. It is not difficult to surmise in whose favour the summation would be. Briefly, if we wish to plan for the weak, the plan may have to be imposed from above and cannot be a product from below *in which the below is dominated by the rich and the strong.*[101]

The Panchayati Raj Institutions which in practice protected the vested interest of rich farmers and landowners posed serious obstacles to measures intended to alleviate the sufferings of landless labourers, small and marginal farmers, as well as the residents of hill and drought-prone areas. A search for a solution of these problems not only led to the gradual denigration of the Ministry of Community Development and its final replacement by the Department of Rural Development, but also brought about the direct organizational and major financial involvement of the Government of India in the maintenance of several area-based special programmes and agencies.

However, the problems posed by Panchayati Raj Institutions had also another dimension, not less important than the new Central policy direction that emerged in the course of the Fourth and the Fifth Five-Year Plans. It was the organizational dimension of district administration for development which, for purposes of implementation, involved new patterns of relationship between the District Officer and the officers of technical departments, between the administrative bureaucracy and democratic bodies and between district officials and their state departments.

In spite of certain nominal differences in different states, the structural pattern of district administration was mainly characterized by uniformity, with the District Officer recognized as the general controlling authority over the several departments, each with its own vertical hierarchy and separate parent office at the state headquarters. In addition to these, there developed in course of time autonomous agencies like the Electricity Board, State Transport and other special agencies which, as said before, were set up for particular programmes, such as the Small Farmers' Development Agencies, Tribal Development Agencies and Drought Prone Areas Programme, all operating in specific area jurisdictions within the district, with the Collector performing the role of a co-ordinator. It was here that the basic weakness of district administration for development lay. The simultaneous operation of horizontal and vertical links tended not only to split loyalties but also diffused responsibilities, a trend which affected both efficiency and discipline. This was especially so because the Collector's role as a co-ordinator was undefined and informal and particularly limited to implementation. When implementation formed part of the responsibility of the Panchayati Raj bodies, co-ordination of the corresponding departmental functionaries vested in their chief executive officer instead of the Collector. The case of Maharashtra was a typical example.

During the Fourth Plan period the Planning Commission suggested a model for setting up different functional units in the state planning departments. One of the functional units so recommended was the establishment of a regional/district planning unit. The Planning Commission also launched in 1972–3 a Central scheme under which assistance was provided to the state governments to meet two-thirds of the cost involved in setting up these functional units equipped with qualified and competent technical staff. The scheme was, however, confined to the strengthening of the planning machinery at the state level, the personnel resources for planning at the district level being neglected in most states.[102] The Centre could do little to remedy this, its All-India technical services being in most cases provincialized.

In the tangled state of relations between district officials and Panchayati Raj bodies the moribund state of the latter contributed to the continuing dominance of the former, a dominance which flowed not only from the administrative skill and functional expertise of the bureaucracy, but also from the caste-ridden backward-looking behaviour of elected representatives who, unlike the policy-bound officers of the government, acted independently of rules either in self-interest or in collaboration with the classes opposed to the weaker sections of society. The dominance which the bureaucracy so acquired, found expression in two different directions: in dissociating the Panchayati Raj bodies from the actual development process and weakening the horizontal link by an emphasis on the traditional loyalty to departmentalism. 'The officials knew no better than to trust their own fraternity. They would, on one hand, ... be averse to PRIs being entrusted with additional functions and, on the other, would not easily get adjusted to working under the supervision of elected representatives. The new development tasks and their load also became such that the bureaucracy had to commandeer all the available staff and, in the process, withdrew what was available for the block.'[103] Almost all the available staff at lower levels had to be requisitioned back by the parent departments and this withdrawal was used by the bureaucracy as a ground for divesting the elected bodies of developmental functions. They became in fact non-existent in several places.

The functional relations which had from the very beginning developed between Panchayati Raj Institutions and district officials were far from satisfactory. The *Pramukh* or Chairman of a *zila parishad* in Rajasthan, for instance, did not get the assistance of the Collector, as the Act had contemplated. The *Report of the Study Team on Democratic Decentralization in Rajasthan* which the Association of Voluntary Agencies brought out in 1961, viewed with great concern the existing communication gap between the bureaucracy and the elected bodies.[104]

The *Report of the Study Team on Panchayati Raj Finances* (1963) had expressed concern which was even more serious as it applied to all states alike. It pointed out that Panchayati Raj Institutions were 'in a state of flux', not only because legislation had not yet been enacted in some states, but mainly because the pattern of relations between district officials and elected representatives was such that they vied with each for power and patronage. The *Report* regretted that, although certain individual Collectors and S.D.O.s took a keen interest in the working of Panchayati Raj Institutions, and some non-official presidents of *panchayat samitis* and chairmen of *zila parishads* also sought official guidance freely, this was more an exception than the general rule. 'We wish,' as the Report made it clear, 'this were universal, but unfortunately, it is not. The future of Panchayati Raj in any state depends to a great extent on the pattern of relations that develop between it and the District and Divisional Officers.' But this remained a pious wish. 'Cordial relations' could not be maintained 'between the officers and Panchayati Raj bodies'.[105] The bureaucracy remained dominant.

In view of the continued dominance of the bureaucracy and the deficiency of both expertise and staff strength at the lower levels of decentralized administration, the district headquarters came to be recognized as the effective centre of planning, a centre which could take care of block-level planning also. The idea was to pool together the available personnel resources and skills at the district level instead of scattering them in several blocks. Even block-level planning was in fact becoming district-level planning in order to enable the planning team to take a broader perspective of resource potential in terms of personnel, expertise and finance. Thus the whole tendency in practice was towards increasing centralization, although the Dantwala Working Group did not fail to suggest that 'while the technical task of planning itself should be performed by the technical team constituted at the district level, some part of the planning function could be assigned to the block level,'[106] perhaps to associate the *panchayat samiti* in a consultative capacity with development work.

As regards implementation, the agency entrusted with the task involved the whole gamut of district administration, its departmental hierarchies vertically organized, its line of command invested with co-ordination on a horizontal principle, its administrative and financial accountability, and, above all, its rules and procedures which at times overlooked the development goal itself. However, the most serious difficulty of district administration as an executive agency for the implementation of development plans was, as said before, the problem of the vertical and horizontal co-ordination of the programmes formulated at different levels. It is here that district administration called for a radical change in both structure and attitude, a change that still remains unaccomplished.

Rural Development Programme: Progress Mainly in Agriculture

By far the most striking progress made as a result of rural development programmes was in the field of agriculture and food production, a field of activity which had in the past started engaging the special attention of the government, more especially since the appointment of the Royal Commission on Agriculture. After the submission of its report, the provincial governments were obliged periodically to keep the Government of India duly informed of the action taken by each of them to give effect to the recommendations made by the Commission.[107] The food shortages caused in the past by recurrent famines became in the present century more noticeable after the cessation of rice supplies from Burma in 1941 and the Bengal famine of 1943. The Government of India was obliged not only to regulate the supplies of foodgrains but also to increase the production of foodgrains through the Grow More Food Campaign. But food scarcity became none the less accentuated; for after the transfer of power in 1947, 30 per cent of the irrigated area went to Pakistan, which at that stage had 18 per cent of the population of undivided India. Besides, most of the jute producing areas and some of the best cotton producing areas, too, were separated from India. In these circumstances, it became necessary to intensify the production of jute and cotton in addition to the acceleration of food production. There was a rapid expansion in the area under crops between 1950–1 and 1960–1. The gross area sown increased by 20.9 million hectares, of which foodgrains accounted for 18.3 million; the total foodgrains produced in the same period being able to show a rise from 50 million tonnes to 82 million, a figure that further rose to 121 million tonnes in 1975–6 and 126 million tonnes in 1978.

Up to about 1960–1, increased production was secured through such measures as irrigation, reclamation of new lands, plant protection measures and tenurial reforms giving greater incentives to cultivators. Great emphasis was thereafter laid on the intensive production efforts in certain selected districts, a package-programme approach which called for simultaneous use of quality seeds, adequate doses of fertilizers and plant protection measures. In the light of the experience of widespread droughts in 1965–7, a new strategy for agricultural development was adopted in 1966–7, which led to what became known as the 'Green Revolution'. The key elements of the new strategy included the cultivation of high yielding varieties of cereals, multiple cropping and development of irrigation for intensive cultivation, which meant increasing utilization of groundwater resources through tubewells, filter points and pump sets. This was done mainly with the help of institutional credit and investment of private savings.

The adoption of the new strategy for agricultural development, however, initially benefited rich farmers and landholders. In view of the smallness of holdings, low resources, inability to obtain credit from institutional sources and inadequate contact with extension personnel and other government officials, small farmers could not generally take advantage of the new technology. A reorientation of policy was in these circumstances effected in favour of small and marginal farmers. The Fourth and the Fifth Five-Year Plans realized the seriousness of the widening disparities and proceeded to provide for special programmes and agencies to obviate social unrest by making irrigational and credit facilities available to the economically and socially handicapped. It is, however, not yet clear as to how far, if at all, the disparities have actually been removed.

Despite knowing the kind of role the Panchayati Raj bodies had played in the interest of the economically strong and well-to-do, the Asoka Mehta Committee held a brief for such bodies in the name of democracy and recommended that they be revamped and fully involved in the development process. Little did the Committee realize that their ouster from that process in the past was more a result of their own doings than of bureaucratic designs. For the bureaucracy, if it so liked, could function without them, but they could not function without the bureaucracy. It is true that the elected bodies had a useful consultative role to play. But in the country's historical and social context the permanent component of its development process was bound to be officers of the government who alone had the skill and responsibility for implementation. Even so, the Asoka Mehta Committee recommended not only a restoration of the full involvement of Panchayati Raj Institutions in the process of rural development, but a political reinforcement of their authority to enable them to dominate the bureaucracy, a radically novel design to acquire power as an agency of what it called Local Government.

There can be no better example of confused thinking than to insist that a mutually exclusive, caste-based and segmented society like India's can in ten or fifteen years give rise through legislative enactment and constitutional change to a contract-based and territorially conceived democratic structure called Panchayati Raj, to provide an alternative to the institution of Collector that took centuries to mature into its present form. It is understandable if elements of democracy are used as a cover to justify bureaucratic action. It is understandable also when power elites use the party system as a cover for group action on ideological grounds in their elections to Parliament or state legislatures. In both cases their distance from the electorates is quite considerable except at certain limited points of contact on personal or other grounds. But if the party system is carried to the level of Panchayati Raj bodies to reinforce them politically as an anti-bureaucratic lever of power, the experiment is unlikely to succeed at the local level, where the electorates, their representatives and officers of the govenment must all operate locally in close contact with each other.

It would be a step forward if the political party system when carried to the level of Panchayati Raj institutions could organize the weaker sections of society and impart to them a general awareness about their rights and obligations. But experience of the post-Independence period has shown that the practitioners of politics indulge mostly in self-aggrandizement and use power to promote their own interest or the interest of their supporters who are mostly either co-religionists or members of the same caste or group. And since most of the so-called 'freedom-fighters' who enter or entered the portals of power happen to be members of the middle or lower middle class, they find it difficult to maintain their status symbols purely by legitimate sources of income. They often take recourse to unlawful means to amass wealth. Barring a few exceptions, they do not even possess sufficient education, which might otherwise have fitted them for any of the competitive jobs. Politics naturally holds out to such persons the prospect of power, an important source of affluence.

Moreover, as candidates for election depend for success on the coffers of their political parties, so do the parties of the middle classes draw their sustenance from the money-bags of business houses, especially in the current Indian situation where little or no care is bestowed on building a mass base for social service and political support. Far from serving as an agency for the mass education and awareness of the poor, the political party system may in these circumstances cause at the grass-root level not only confusion from conflicting ideologies, but also caste or class riots which may seriously interfere with the peaceful pursuit of development work.

In fact, it is neither bureaucracy nor democracy that can singly provide an answer to the administration and organizational issues involved in the process of development with social justice. It is not the dichotomy of their relationship, a legacy of British imperial tradition, that can resolve those issues. What is called for is a change of attitude on the part of both, a check and balance between the two, a reciprocity based on co-operation, not competition.

VI

PERSONNEL QUALITIES AND RESOURCES

The personnel involved in the process of rural development have generally been of two main categories, the generalist and the technocrat. The former belong to the Indian Administrative Service which succeeded the erstwhile Indian Civil Service in 1946, and the latter are in line with the several All-India Services created from time to time to promote technical development—for example, of education and agriculture, civil veterinary and medical, forest and plublic works. This chapter is confined to a discussion of the generalist administrator, a basically field-based instrument of public service from which the secretariat advisers are even now drawn at both the State and Central levels, not only as field experience is considered relevant to policy formulations, but also because the exigencies of Central supervision are considered necessary for integrated development.

Prior to the outbreak of the First World War in 1914 the administrative bureaucracy in India had for all practical purposes remained free from the social or political influences of the Indian middle classes. Its attitude was typically rule-bound and its whole emphasis was on administrative efficiency, undeflected by considerations of religion or caste. It stood for open competition as the only condition for entry into the superior civil service and refused to accept communal principles as a basis for the distribution of seats in the public service. In spite of the organized pressure of the National Muhammadan Association to have seats reserved for Muslims in the

Indian Civil Service, the bureaucracy did not relent. Lord Dufferin had no alternative but to tell the Association that no Muslim candidate could be exempted from the established rules of educational and competitive tests.

While recruitment to the Indian Civil Service was purely competitive, the political system introduced even for purposes of representative government, for example, under the Indian Councils Act of 1892 remained purely secular. It recognized no claims of religion or caste. It noted the existence of special interests and classes, but the constituencies created were all territorial. In other words, the primary unit of the constitution of the state was the individual, not his religion, community or caste. In spite of the voting pattern of non-official members being typically characteristic of Indian conditions, the bureaucratic majority of the Council held its own point of view. Lord Morley's assessment of the bureaucracy was not wrong when he said that in spite of its ability, honesty and uprightness of conduct it was a 'cast-iron bureaucracy' believing in 'nothing but the virtue of will and arbitrary powers'.[1]

Morley's remarks were not without reasons. A social change was, for instance, taking place in Bengal as a result of the progressive subinfeudation and fragmentation of zamindari lands, producing a lower middle class of half-educated unemployed youths with hardly any means left to support the prestige their ancestors had earlier enjoyed. The social change, so arising from an economic phenomenon, was assuming a political dimension. For the unemployed indulged in revolutionary crimes which were sought to be justified on grounds of nationalism. The bureaucracy took no notice of these developments on a plane other than that of law-and-order, calling for an immediate policy of repression and supporting a 'counter-weight' to the middle class. While the Muslims were for electoral purposes recognized constitutionally as a separate community, landholders were in law treated as a separate interest. The Morley-Minto reforms, which embodied these principles, were, however, a political approach which did not filter down to the administrative level. It was later in 1912 under Lord Hardinge's Government that the Royal (Islington) Commisson examined the existing employment limitations of educated Indians in the public services, limitations which involved social and political questions.

The report was signed only a few months after the outbreak of the first War and its publication was deferred in the hope that the War might soon come to an end. 'When written', said the Montford Report, 'it might have satisfied moderate public's opinion, but when published two years later, it was criticized as wholly disappointing.'[2] The War had not only changed the entire perspective, but created a demand for civil servants far in excess of the supply. Together with the Russian Revolution of 1917, it released the forces of democracy and nationalism in India on a scale that appeared to threaten the supremacy of bureaucratic authority. In a letter to the Viceroy, the Secretary of State for India, Sir Austen Chamberlain, made it clear that the Government could not but take into consideration the constant emphasis the War laid upon repeated declarations that the Allies were fighting for the cause of freedom and liberty.[3] He felt the Indian situation was naturally influenced by the world being 'in a state of revolution', and excited more especially by the Russian Revolution.

The response of the British Government found expression in its policy declaration of 20 August 1917, which promised (i) increasing association of Indians in every branch of administration, (ii) the gradual development of self-governing institutions, and (iii) the progressive realization of responsible government in British India as an integral part of the Empire. The goal envisaged for India before Sir Austen was succeeded by Edwin Montagu in July 1917, had in fact been 'self-government' as an integral part of the British Empire. And on his accession to office Montagu actually started working on the basis of 'self-government' being the goal to be attained through the gradual development of free institutions. The private papers of Sir Austen indicate that the expression 'self-government' was, however, substituted by 'responsible government' at the instance of Lord Curzon who was recognized by the Cabinet as the spokesman on Indian affairs.[4] This substitution whittled down the goal of self-government, for responsible government might be possible even without an independent legislature.

The expression introduced in the Declaration of 20 August 1917 on the advice of Curzon was embodied in the preamble of the Indian Bill. But Montagu's mind none the less kept working on the lines of Dominion Status, a further stage in the constitutional progress of India of which the 1919-Act was only a partial fulfilment. Arrangement was, therefore, made in the Act itself to relax the directive and supervisory control of the Secretary of State over the Government of India and of the latter over the Provinces. Section 19A of the Act, for instance, provided that the Secretary of State might divest himself of his responsibility to Parliament and delegate it to the Government of India in respect of both central and provincial subjects. The only condition attached to such delegation was that the Legislative Assembly and the Government should be in full agreement. Section 45A(d), on the other hand, provided rules for the transfer of reserved subjects to the administration of the Governor acting with ministers appointed under the Act, and for the allocation of revenues or monies for the purpose of such administration. The Government of India itself could effect such transfer, subject merely to draft rules being placed before both Houses of Parliament for approval by means of a 'resolution' only.

The political advance so envisaged by Montagu created insecurity among European Civil Servants. But a more serious and direct provision that worried them was Section 96B(2) of the Act which tended to make them subject to legislative control. For it laid down that although it was the Secretary of State in Council who was authorized to make rules governing their recruitment, conditions of service, pay and allowances, that rule-making power might be delegated to the Governor-General in Council or even to Local Governments. Alternatively, the Secretary of State in Council might also authorize 'the Indian Legislature to make laws regarding the public services', laws to which every civil servant appointed after the passing of the Act would remain subject.

It was within the framework of these constitutional changes that the bureaucracy in India was expected to function, a framework that reflected the influence of politics on both government and administration. And in its letter of 13 May 1920 the Government of India actually proceeded to operationalize these changes by asking the Secretary of State to divest himself of his controlling authority in respect of the transferred subjects under the draft rules sent to him for his approval.

It was in these circumstances that the bureaucracy asserted itself, and although the Home authorities had clearly recognized that Section 19A provided for the Secretary of State being divested of control over subjects other than transferred provincial subjects, the bureaucracy strongly resisted any such divestment of control over the executive authority in India. The Government of India, too, was in full agreement with the views of its bureaucracy who sounded caution against the growing friendship between the Congress and the All-

India Muslim League on the question of Turkey's involvement in the War against Britain.[5] The Congress–League Pact of 1916 and the Hindu–Muslim *entente* on the Khilafat question may not have been deep, but it presented the appearance of national unity.[6] The non-cooperation movement came in the same context and symbolized that unity, though for a short while only.

Thus, while British policy in India was aiming at a gradual devolution of power from London to New Delhi to facilitate the growth of provincial autonomy, the emotion-bound Congress leadership was forging an alliance with the pan-Islamic group in a bid to seize power with their help. These developments which resulted in the arrest of Gandhi and the resignation of Montagu, led the British to be cautious and adopt a go-slow policy, a policy which was further reinforced by the Swarajist attitude to enter the Legislative Assembly and wreck the reformed constitution from within. The projected divestment of the Secretary of State's control over the executive authority in India and the transfer of subjects from the reserved list were both stalled. The bureaucracy took advantage of the wrong moves of the Congress and prevented the Government from carrying out the intention of the Act for further reforms. Some of its members even retired prematurely to forestall subjection to popular control.

Racial Politics and Decline of Efficiency

The racial politics emerging from the rigid attitude of a section of the bureaucracy and the anti-British struggle for self-government could not but leave its mark on the future course of development in terms of personnel, morality and efficiency. Professionally, the beginning of a decline of administrative standards proceeded basically from nationalist demands for the extended employment of Indians in the public services. There were doubtless other causes. But political and power motivations involving racial dimensions were by far the most important trends which dyarchic democracy released to the great prejudice of recognized professional norms. Communal and caste considerations followed as a natural sequence. The bureaucracy was consequently ceasing to be viewed as a group of administrators bound together professionally to carry on the business of government independently of social or political complexions. In the colonial situation they were first identified racially as Europeans and Indians, which was later vitiated by considerations of religion or caste. Though in reality a fight for position and power in the post-1919 situation, the Indo-European tangle in the public services was being used as a lever on both sides for political or personal gain. Administrative decisions were in certain cases naturally affected by extra-professional considerations. As the evidence collected by the MacDonnel Committee showed, there were instances where 'the Government of India, embarassed by hostile agitation and confronted by the difficulties of introducing great constitutional changes, have tended in certain cases to postpone the maintenance of law and order in deference to political considerations'.[7] The professional norms of public administration had thus begun to yield place to the irrationality of politics, especially in the districts where officers acted under a belief that their position would be altered under dyarchy and that they would not be defended by ministers in the exercise of authority. A Note in the form of a warning which the Home Member recorded on 18 December 1920 was a clear indication of the situation emerging from the impact of politics under the partial democracy of dyarchy:

> If our officers are treated with consideration and justice by Ministers, defended when they are unjustly attacked in Council and supported in the proper discharge of duties, then very few men will want to go; but if by reason of racial antipathy or a dislike of the European element in the service, or in order to meet political exigencies in the Council, our officers are not properly treated and are not defended in the discharge of duties . . . . there are many who will face poverty and discomfort rather than sacrifice their good name and self-respect.[8]

In spite of the warning, however, a good number of European civil servants retired for conscientious reasons. Politics had begun to pressurize the bureaucracy.

As a result of the interaction with democracy even on a limited scale the old standards of bureaucratic efficiency, for instance in Madras, showed a marked decline. The bureaucracy could not adjust itself to the frequency of changes in the formulation of new policies in the transferred field under Indian ministers. Inefficiency proceeded from another factor which became especially noticeable in the post-Reform era. That was 'the general unsettlement of the minds of permanent officials'. They had been brought up earlier 'to carry out definite policies without questioning the underlying reasons for them'. But they became 'uncertain' about what was to be done and not done when 'the policy of every department' under ministers began to be 'pulled up by the roots and examined *ab initio*' from considerations other than purely public. This and the revision of salaries and allowances prompted a spirit of 'questioning of authority and demurring to rules and orders', which rendered administration difficult. Their spirit of questioning flowed also from their loss of confidence in the morality of the legislative authority in the province. For there was a sudden and 'large increase of expenditure, not only in the office of the Legislative Council, but also on the travelling allowances of members',[9] which was sought to be met by increasing taxation. Democracy was proving more burdensome to the tax-payer than bureaucracy.

The report of the Government of Bihar and Orissa, on the other hand, referred to the difficulties arising from 'bureaucratic supremacy and popular control' in the transferred field. The authors of the Joint Report had contemplated that the bureaucracy would for many years continue to guide and, to an extent, mould 'the proceedings of the Ministers and the Council'. But this hope seemed 'doomed to frustration'. Though the knowledge and experience of the services were for a time indispensable to ministers, they could not 'remain in leading strings for an indefinite period'. The superior services in fact seemed to 'foresee in the India of the not very distant future no place for them as services in the sense in which they previously existed', and it was precisely 'this feeling more than anything else which [was] responsible for premature retirements and for pessimism as to the expediency of future recruitment'. The technical services, too, shared the same feeling because of 'the spirit of racialism' underlying the pressure the Legislative Council maintained 'for the abolition of the higher appointments'.[10]

An important effect of even limited democracy was a division of the bureaucracy itself on racial lines. Even those European officers who were 'most hopeful of India's future and most willing to be of service to her, felt that no man cares to go on working when his services are not wanted'. They recognized that it was the 'distrust of the services regarding the future which is responsible for the birth of numerous service associations and particularly of the European Government Servants' Association'. This vogue of service associations took 'a racial turn'. It led to 'the formation of a similar association for the Indian members of the superior services'.[11] Racialism was thus being used as a lever to secure a commanding position in the superior services, a development that was neither 'legal' nor 'rational' in the Weberian sense. It was, however, not entirely unjustified, for Indians had in the past been deprived of their due share in the higher services.

Speaking generally of the kind of relationship that developed between ministers and the permanent services, the *Report of the Reforms Inquiry Committee, 1924,* referred to the evidence received from several Local Governments, but preferred to illustrate the position best by a quotation from the report of the Government of the United Provinces.

The spirit and the outlook of the services are not what they were. It may be difficult to specify the precise extent to which they have been affected, or to disentangle the various causes. But of the broad fact there can be little doubt. In the heated political atmosphere of the first fifteen months after the inauguration of the Reforms, the European services were the object of constant vilification and abuse in the press and on the platform; indeed as will be seen from the published proceedings, in the Legislative Council also, where though criticism was more restrained, it was often hostile and prejudiced. During the more peaceful period, which followed the collapse of the campaign of disorder, matters have much improved; and from various quarters keen appreciation has been expressed of the capacity of European officers to handle a difficult and dangerous situation. But there is still a tendency to look very sharply into any mistakes or shortcomings of hard-pressed European officers, and to ignore their reasonable claims. More than one resolution has been passed which, if carried out, would have deprived them of appointments to fill which they had been recruited. It is not suggested that the Legislative Council has deliberately sought to inflict injustice on European officers. The constitution of the all-India services is not well understood, and many members of the legislature are influenced by the feeling (for which there is justification) that in the past Indians have not received their fair share of the higher appointments. The natural effect, however, of the attitude of the legislature has been to create in the minds of Englishmen serving in India an impression of hostility and a feeling of insecurity, which make it difficult for them to give of their best. There are distinct signs that the services are losing their former keenness. Since they no longer have the power of shaping policy to the extent which they had, they no longer feel that the progress of the country depends upon their efforts, nor indeed that any efforts of theirs are likely to have abiding results. Enthusiasm and energy have also been sapped by financial pressure and by the cloud of uncertainty, which hangs over the future of the country for which they have given their lives.

The Reforms Inquiry Committee agreed with the views of the U.P. Government. It did not deny that during the months following the inauguration of the Reforms the services were 'subjected to much unjust criticism'. It however felt that the criticism of the services was inevitable in the existing state of India's constitutional development, although it emphasized that in India's own interest a 'contented permanent service and a return to that keenness which it is said is being lost' were both of great importance.

Decline in Recruitment Standards to meet the Demands of Indianization

The problem of Indianizing the public services in India has been discussed in some depth in another work.[12] What is relevant to our purpose here is to point out that the politics of Indianization which began with the recommendations of the Islington Commission and gained in urgency with the Montford Report, led to a review of the methods of recruitment, which, though designed to accomplish the immediate object of satisfying social and political urges, could not but compromise the quality of personnel selection.

The Islington Commission's recommendation was for a minimum of 25 per cent Indians in the superior posts of the Indian Civil Service. This was to include appointments made by promotion from the Provincial Civil Service as well as direct appointments to superior judicial posts from the Bar. This percentage was, however, to exclude Indians recruited to the Service on the basis of the competitive examination held in London. Owing to the delay caused by the War in carrying out this recommendation the Montford Report raised the percentage of Indian recruitment from 25 to 33 from 1918 onwards, not from an earlier date. This proportion was to rise annually by 1.5 per cent for ten years, to a maximum of 48 per cent, an all-round figure to cover total Indian recruitment from all sources other than the London competition.

In recommending this limited increase in the percentage of Indian recruitment the Joint Report was guided by considerations of quality: 'The qualities of courage, leadership, decision, fixity of purpose, detached judgement, and integrity in her public servants will be as necessary as ever to India. There must [therefore] be no such sudden swamping of any service with any new element that its whole character suffers a rapid alteration.' Consistent with the principle so suggested, the Joint Report recommended an annual rise of 1.5 per cent and sounded a warning that it would be absolutely 'unwise to create a demand in excess of the supply', more especially from the provincial services, where the number of candidates of higher quality was 'strictly limited'. Although it was recognized that 'the opening of the more attractive services' might be expected 'to stimulate the supply', it was still felt 'necessary', if the existing quality of the services was not to be 'unduly impaired, to take special steps to see that recruits are of a satisfactory standard'.[13]

But since the existing methods of recruitment in England for both

Europeans and Indians could not supply enough Indian candidates, there was no alternative but to rely on a system of appointment in India to supplement it. The increased proportion of the Indian element to be so recruited for superior posts in India was confirmed by the Government of India Act, 1919 and soon formed part of a Resolution adopted by the Government of India on 1 December 1920 which increased the methods of recruitment. In addition to the competitive examination in London, the Resolution of 1 December 1920 laid down four other methods of recruitment. These were separate competitive examination in India, nomination in India, promotion from the Provincial Civil Service, and appointment from the Bar to the higher judicial posts held by members of the Indian Civil Service.

There was no compromise with the standard of recruitment in London, which continued to be the main channel of admission to the Indian Civil Service. In a Minute recorded by Sir Charles Innes, Member of the Executive Council of the Governor-General, this service 'was regulated by what was generally recognized to be the most difficult competitive examination in the world',[14] the object being to secure officers of the highest quality combining both intellectual and moral excellence.

Separate Examination in India. A separate competitive examination in India was recommended by the Islington Commission as an important source of increasing Indian recruitment, a source which was recognized by Section 97 of the Government of India Act, 1919. It was to be held under the rules made by the Secretary of State with the advice and assistance of the Civil Service Commissioners. In comparison to the examination held in London, its range or area of competition was, however, limited. But a more serious limitation arose from India's regional and communal imbalance in terms of educational and economic development, an imbalance that tended to withdraw its support from the projected separate examination being even an all-India competitive test. For the educationally backward regions and communities feared the continued dominance, for example, of Madras, Bombay and Bengal. The Chief Commissioner of the Central Provinces emphasized that unless the examination was provincial, an all-India competition would seriously affect the interest of that area. Though otherwise advanced, Bengal, on the other hand, felt concerned about its backward Muslim community. It urged that if there was to be an all-India examination the Local Government must reserve 25 per cent of the vacancies for Muslims by publishing two lists, one showing Muslims in order of merit among themselves, and the other the remaining successful candidates.

The Government of India, while recognizing the force of arguments in favour of provincial competition, found it necessary to have one all-India competitive examination to obviate any noticeable fall in standards. A compromise, however, had to be devised at the suggestion of the provinces. A principle of nomination provided under Section 97(6) of the 1919 Act was accepted as a subsidiary method for securing what might be considered due representation of the various provinces and communities in the Indian Civil Service. No reservation was thus made on regional or communal grounds in the all-India competitive examination which commenced at Allahabad in 1922.

Nomination. The use of nomination as a mode of recruitment was a departure from the Weberian canons of a rational bureaucracy which emphasized open competition as an essential condition. Qualifying tests, including a period of training for two years in England, were of course prescribed to reduce the gap arising from the application of two different standards of recruitment for the same service. Even so, the gap remained. Nomination merely acted as a palliative, an expedient to meet the exigencies of politics arising from regional backwardness and social separatism. None the less, it was an essential device which made some employment opportunities available to the backward areas and communities without the competitive service being swamped by reservationists.

Promotion from the P.C.S. Apart from nomination, the other mode of recruitment which injected into the Indian Civil Service the interests of backward regions and communities was promotion from the Provincial Civil Service, a service based on a lower standard of recruitment in terms of educational attainments and intellectual equipment. The infiltration of the provincial element into the superior service began formally under the Regulations of 21 April 1892. Under these Provincial Civil Service men were, on the basis of the extent and quality of their performance, promoted to certain reserved or 'listed' superior posts in the Indian Civil Service without being entitled to its membership. In spite of promotion they continued to be members of their own parent service. Moreover, as it was generally late in life that they got a chance of promotion to a substantive post of Collector or District and Sessions Judge, they were practically excluded from the prospect of rising to higher positions in the administrative or judicial lines. The Government of India Resolution of 1 December 1920 permitted promotees to take rank with I.C.S. officers and be eligible with them for all posts borne on the civil service list. This again was a compromise, for the 'competitionwallahs' retained their structural status, although the provincial promotees gained functionally.

Appointments from the Bar. Recruitment from the Bar was a worse form of surrender to political pressure. The Local Governments as well as the Judges of the High Courts and Judicial Commissioners unanimously opposed any proposal to reduce the number of listed posts to accommodate the Bar, which they did not consider a suitable source of recruitment for District and Sessions Judges.[15] Under its Resolution of 1 December 1920 the Government of India accordingly made it clear that Local Governments themselves could appoint to these posts persons who were not members of the Provincial Civil Service.[16] But in no case was their appointment to exceed one-fourth of the total number of listed posts.

I.C.S. Saved but All-India Technical Services Provincialized. In spite of the pressure of politics, the Government of India and the India Office together devised means to save the competitive character of the Indian Civil Service. The revised methods of recruitment to accelerate the pace of Indianization left certain scars on the Service and injected into it such elements as compromised its position in terms of administrative morality and efficiency. Even so, they were not recognized as its integral part and the status acquired through open competition remained inviolable.

But the Service had to reckon with two main difficulties arising from the introduction of the constitutional changes of 1919. The first was political. The Reforms envisaged democracy, though partial and limited at the beginning. The political system so envisaged was territorial and secular in concept, but Indian society was not so. It was segmented, communal and caste-oriented. There was an obvious dichotomy between the political and social systems. Secondly, the premier administrative service that had over the years developed in the country, was based on competition. Indian society, where it was called upon to operate was, on the contrary, status bound and non-competitive. The tradition-bound national politics of the period which gained in mass popularity as an anti-Western cultural and social reaction, threatened both secular democracy and open competition as a basis of recruitment. It was in face of these odds that the still dominant European elements of the bureaucracy maintained administrative standards within the framework of dyarchy. Their success was partly due to the co-operation extended to them by those of their ministers who were men of education and status, experience and understanding.

None the less the racial antagonism did not cease. In response to political pressure for increasing Indianization the Lee Commission recommended in 1924 an increase in promotions from the Provincial Civil Service from 'a maximum of 16 per cent of the total cadre' of the Indian Civil Service to '20 per cent of the recruits'. The Government of India interpreted this recommendation as a discontinuance of the erstwhile listed post system and its replacement by a system of regular annual appointments from the Provincial Civil Service to the extent of 20 per cent of the vacancies available. In a circular addressed to Local Governments on 5 August 1924 it suggested that the system of listed posts be discontinued and that officers selected from the Provincial Civil Service be introduced at the lower levels of the Indian Civil Serivce as its regular members.[17]

In a Note recorded on 27 February 1925, James Crerar, the Home Secretary, raised serious objections to the earlier interpretation sent for comment to Local Governments. He emphasized the continuance of the existing practice, with the percentage of the reserved listed posts raised from 16 to 20. His arguments against the circular of 5 August 1924 were guided not only by regard for the interest of senior members in the Provincial Civil Service, but by a concern to preserve the integrity of the Indian Civil Service, which was already being seriously affected. 'The solidity and uniformity of the Service,' he regretted, 'have already to some extent been broken, but a Service which consisted of (i) Europeans, (ii) Indians recruited in England, (iii) Indians directly recruited in India [through separate examination], (iv) Indians promoted to inferior [Civil Service] posts, and (v) Indians promoted to superior posts [Judicial Branch] would hardly be a Service at all, but rather a collection of separate Services.' He expressed apprehension that the Indian Civil Service might in course of time lose its identity altogether and get 'replaced by a provincial counterpart'. But he emphasized that so long as it continued in its existing form as an all-India Service no promotee from the junior officers of the Provincial Civil Service should be allowed to enter it on a definite recruitment basis with a title to the full membership of the Service, Crerar, therefore, insisted that the existing practice of promotion to listed posts must continue, so that there was no question of promoted officers being recognized as Indian Civil Service officers. A.P. Muddiman, the Home Member, agreed with Crerar and accepted his view that promotion of provincial officers should be straight to superior posts, not to the lower grades of the Civil Service, and the Secretary of State accepted this position. No promotee from the Provincial Civil Service was thus to be permitted to write 'I.C.S.' after his name, which privilege could be acquired only by passing the open examination. The 1892 arrangement thus continued to operate with the percentage of promotion to reserved superior posts raised from 16 to 20. Cases none the less occurred[18] where Provincial Civil Service officers stole a march over certain I.C.S. officers. For politics favoured provincialization as a step in the direction of Indianization.

However, the all-India services which became immediately subject to provincialization were those operating in the field of 'nation-building' activities. It is true that there was a case for decentralization of these services for development purposes under the control of Local Governments. But, as said before, the execution of development projects called for a well-organized central machinery of supervision and co-ordination in each field to ensure integrated planning and implementation. Instead of provincializing the all-India technical services their provincial counterparts could have been created for co-ordination between the provinces and the Government of India, the controlling agency of the all-India services. But since national politics in the imperial situation acted more on sentiment than reason, the higher echelons of the British bureaucracy in India saw no harm in accepting its demand for provincialization as a form of Indianization, a demand that hit development work more than the interest of Europeans employed in these technical services. For one of the conditions for provincialization was that no change was to be made in the position of the existing members of such services. They retained all the rights of officers of an all-India service in respect of pay, pension, allowances, etc. Their duties alone were provincialized, not their status or conditions of work. The Local Governments were not to touch their privileges, but were simply to build up provincial services by degrees to take over those duties. The technical services so provincialized included the Indian Educational Service, the Indian Agricultural Service, the Indian Veterinary Service, the Indian

Forest Service, the Indian Medical Service (Civil), and the Roads and Buildings Branch of the Indian Service of Engineers. These were to cease to be all-India Service from 1925 onwards under the recommendations of the Lee Commission.

The nationalist agitation against the all-India services was guided by racial and political overtones but not reinforced by concern for developmental requirements or administrative exigencies. This extra-professional overtone persisted even after the transfer of power, when the Indian Administrative Service was created as a substitute for the Indian Civil Service. A question arose in the Drafting Committee of the Constituent Assembly concerning protection of the rights of the erstwhile Secretary of State's all-India officers: the article drafted by the Committee in October 1948 dealt with the Secretary of State's Services as well as members of the Indian Administrative Services and the Indian Police Service. This, however, evoked a controversy and led to the safeguards being restricted to the Secretary of State's Services only. Even this restriction became subject to severe criticism, but Vallabhbhai Patel's intervention was crucial in this matter:

> Learn to stand upon your pledged word, and also, as a man of experience I tell you, do not quarrel with the instruments with which you want to work. It is a bad workman who quarrels with his instruments. Take work from them. Every man wants some sort of encouragement. Nobody wants to put in work when everyday he is criticized and ridiculed in public. Nobody will give you work like that. So, once and for all decide whether you want this Service or not. If you have done with it and decide not to have this Service at all, even in spite of my pledged word, I will take the Services with me and go.[19]

The provincialization of the all-India technical services was also reviewed after the transfer of power. There had, for instance, been no provincialization of the duties of the Irrigation Branch of the Indian Service of Engineers and the whole cadre of the Indian Service of Engineers in Assam. In the field of agriculture, the Indian Council of Agricultural Research was responsible for co-ordination after the Indian Agricultural Service was provincialized. The Administrative Reforms Commission (1966–7) reviewed the situation regarding the all-India services in the technical field and noted with satisfaction that the constitution of 'three new Services—the Indian Forest Service, the Indian Service of Engineers and the Indian Medical Service—had been agreed to by Parliament and [that] the Indian Forest Service has entered the state of actual constitution.' In addition, the *Report of the Study Team on Personnel Administration* affirmed that the 'constitution of two more services—the Indian Educational Service and the Indian Agricultural Service' were 'under the active consideration of Government'.[20] The necessity of reviving the all-India services earlier provincialized under the recommendations of the Lee Commission in response to nationalist pressure was thus clearly recognized.

Consistent with the provisions of the Indian Forest Service (Initial Recruitment) Regulations, 1966, special selection Boards were constituted for each state cadre to make appointments to the Indian Forest Service at the initial constitution.[21] The new all-India Medical and Health Service, on the other hand, was created with effect from 1 February 1969, when the initial recruitment regulations and cadre rules were framed. The constitution of the new Service was preceded by the establishment of the Central Health Service (Amendment) Rules notified in September 1966,[22] the rules for the constitution of the Service being already made and announced in 1963. One of the feature of the scheme for constituting the new all-India Service was that persons holding Class I posts in the Central Health Service would be notionally allotted to the various state cadres, and, after the Service was constituted, be treated as on deputation to the Central Government subject to being reverted to the State Governments on the expiry of tenure. In other words, the scheme recognized that there would be a regular flow of officers between the Centre and the States, a principle that governed the functioning of all the all-India services. Although Tamil Nadu and Mysore had not by then agreed to participate in the scheme, the new Service was constituted, as under the All-India Services Act, 1951, it was not essential that the cadres for all states should be formed simultaneously.

The recognition of the need to revive the all-India technical services in the post-Independence period was clear admission of the error committed in the 1920's under the obsession of nationalism and racial politics, an error which affected in no small degree the progress of the 'nation-building' departments.

Recruitment on Communal and Caste Basis

Minority Communities

Muslims. The racial approach of the non-cooperation and Khilafat movements to build a Hindu-Muslim nationalist front against the British was on the whole based on emotion and political strategy, bereft of either social or economic content. It was, in political terms, time-serving and transient, ebullient and effervescent. The Punjab Muhammadans, like those of Bengal, 'found themselves committed by the Lucknow compact [1916] to accept somewhat less than their numerical proportion of representation; it was nevertheless clear, even before they attained the power the new franchise [of 1919] gave them, that they were not content to accept Hindu leadership, and would insist on a fuller recognition of their claims in every sphere.[23] Far from the two communities remaining united, they fell apart against each other after the settlement of the Turkish question, which dispensed with the necessity of Hindu support for the Khilafat. Communal riots broke out in the Punjab where the urbanized Hindu minority controlled the social and economic power, the Muslim majority being educationally backward and engaged for the most part in agricultural pursuits. Analysing the state of mutual distrust and communal fanaticism that developed after the suspension of the non-cooperation movement in March 1922, an official estimate thus pointed out the effect on both communities:

> Educated Muslims, who hitherto would willingly have given their adhesion to the generality of the nationalist programme, were deeply and honestly perturbed by the consequences of these developments to the political future of India as a whole. But they also began to reflect more deeply on the implications to their own community of the swaraj programme or even of an acceleration of the reforms programme, under conditions such as these. On reflection followed a clear appreciation of the danger to their community latent in any unregulated political advance [like the non-cooperation movement] and a greater insistence on the production of substantial guarantees for its protection in both the political and the administrative spheres; and in the latter, more particularly, for its adequate representation in all grades of the public service.[24]

In fact, once the bureaucracy was sought to be divided into Europeans and Indians according to racial categories, the demand for its division into Hindu and Muslim counterparts became a natural corollary.

As said before, the revised mode of recruitment by nomination was employed to meet the demands of backward regions and communities under the Government of India Resolution of 1 December 1920. In spite of a series of resolutions passed by the Central Legislative Assembly the Government did not agree to represent minority communities, such as Muslims, Sikhs, Anglo-Indians or domiciled Europeans. Instead it agreed to prevent a preponderance of one class or community in the services under its direct control. And even in using nomination an attempt was to be made to maintain the highest possible standard of qualifications by selecting candidates who had attained a qualifying standard in the open competition in England or India.[25]

However, this precaution against the admission of men of inferior attainments was taken at the instance of the Secretary of State to neutralize the effect of a 'pledge' already given by the Home Member, Sir Alexander Muddiman, on 2 March 1925 to satisfy the Muslim members of the central legislature who demanded reservation in the services for the minorities. In spite of the care that the Home authorities took to preserve the standards of recruitment even while trying to satisfy social and political urges, the pledge given by the Government of India to reserve one-third of all direct appointments in the services for 'minorities' marked the beginning of a process which made it difficult to reconcile considerations of merit with those of social justice; the Indian Legislature pressurized the Government of India regularly from 1925 onwards to submit reports on the employment statistics of each minority community.[26]

Other Minorities. There was no rigid allocation of seats although it was recognized that Muslims were entitled to a lion's share. A Resolution of 4 July 1934[27] set apart 25 per cent of all vacancies for Muslims, and the remaining 8⅓ per cent that were 'reserved', for other minorities. But since the existing position of Anglo-Indians was at the instance of the Secretary of State to remain unaffected, they continued to have 8⅓ per cent of the direct appointments for themselves. The previously sanctioned unit of 33⅓ per cent for all minorities was thus covered by Muslims and Anglo-Indians alone. The Resolution of 4 July 1934 therefore provided for an additional 6 per cent reservation to satisfy the demands of minorities other than Muslims and Anglo-Indians. Naturally, the standard of efficiency was further weakened by reservations on communal grounds. Of the minority communities, Muslims, however, were the greatest beneficiaries.[28]

Scheduled Castes. Amonst other matters, the Government of India Act of 1919 had also provided for the representation of special classes and interests. Bombay had on this basis created such political categories amongst Hindus as Brahmins and non-Brahmins, the later being further sub-divided into Marathas and backward castes, including 'depressed classes' of untouchables, who were for the first time categorized systematically at the time of the 1931 Census. They were renamed by M.K.Gandhi as 'Harijans', his object being to counteract the MacDonald Award of 1932 which recommended separate electorates for the Depressed Classes. Under Gandhi's influence they were recognized by caste Hindus as members of the traditional Hindu order and this recognition was embodied in the Poona Agreement of 1932, which recommended a fair degree of representation for them in the public services. But in view of their level of education, it was felt that no useful purpose could be served by reserving for them a specific percentage of the vacancies set apart for Hindus as a whole, although duly qualified candidates were not to be deprived of opportunities for appointment merely on the ground of failure in open competition. Such qualified candidates as could not compete successfully could straight away be absorbed by nomination in accordance with the rules made under the Resolution of 4 July 1934. The Depressed Classes were renamed the 'scheduled castes' under the Government of India Act, 1935, and various scheduled castes were listed and notified in 1936 for appointment to the public services.

The Resolution thus marked an important stage as far as the reservation and distribution of seats in the public services on communal and caste considerations is concerned. It was, however, a limited, job-oriented approach to socio-economic problems, which acted merely as a palliative, and that, too, at the cost of efficiency.

Steps to maintain Efficiency

An analysis of the bureaucracy in India up to 1947 thus brings out two main developments that affected administrative integrity and efficiency—the increasing pressure of politics for promotion to the Indian Civil Service from the Provincial Services, and communal representation through nomination. The British Government in India [29] foiled the attempts of both to become members of the Indian Civil Service, and remained firm concerning the standards of open competition where merit alone counted.

Considerations of merit also determined promotion. The principle of reservation was doubtless recognized and appointment made by nomination to accommodate regional or communal sentiments. The standard of recruitment could not but be eroded, more especially when it came to the recruitment of scheduled caste men who, in terms of educational advancement, were by far the most backward. But the principle of promotion on pure merit acted as an effective check on a sudden deterioration in standards.

Moreover, the Government of India, by its Home Department Memorandum of 6 August, 1935, excluded from the scope of its Resolution of 4 July 1934 certain services and posts which called for the maintenance of high qualifications. 'In paragraph 6 of the Resolution', the Memorandum pointed out, 'it has been made clear that the rules do not apply to certain services and posts requiring high technical or special qualifications.' These services and posts were listed and 'specifically excluded from the scope of the orders regarding communal representation in the services'.

The major threat to administrative standards was, however, the rising pressure of politics for accelerated promotion from the Provincial Civil Services, especially from 1923 onwards when provincial governments were empowered to appoint their own P.C.S. men to listed posts, subject to the Secretary of State being informed within twelve months of the appointments so made. Cases occurred where P.C.S. men were appointed to the posts reserved for I.C.S. officers and allowed to hold them for several years without the approval of the Secretary of State.[30] Since promotion to listed posts thus came to be made by Local Governments with the Public Service Commission having little or no direct control over the selection initially made by them, it became a matter of serious concern to the Government of India and the Secretary of State. They finally agreed that the principles governing promotion to listed posts should include rigid selection of P.C.S. officers of moderately senior standing, appointment to listed posts by the Governor in his individual discretion, subject to prior consultation with the Federal Public Service Commission set up in 1937 under the 1935 Act and promotion being ordinarily restricted to officers who still had a reasonable period left for service.[31] The principles so settled were necessarily meant for a select list of P.C.S. officers which was sought to be formed for promotion to listed posts.

However, objections were raised by Bombay which preferred seniority to a 'select list' and by Assam which, in view of the provincial autonomy introduced under the 1935 Act, regarded it more appropriate to consult, in the formation of the list, the provincial public service commission and not the Federal Public Service Commission. In fact, the criterion of merit underlying the formation of the select list did not find favour with some on the ground that it involved the exercise of discretion and gave freedom to ministers of Congress governments in the provinces to push the claims of such officers as possessed political pull. It was feared that once the principle of selection allegedly on merit was conceded, the door would in practice be left open to favouritism. Seniority was, therefore, emphasized by certain provinces as the safest course to pursue. The Secretary of State none the less accepted the Government of India's proposed method of selection on merit, a selection made by experts, subject to prior consultation with the Federal Public Service Commission. It provided incentive to the improvement of the quality of the Provincial Services and checked a decline in the quality of P.C.S. officers promoted to the Indian Civil Service. No select list was perhaps prepared in advance of the P.C.S. officers who were deemed to be fit and qualified for promotion to the Indian Civil Service.

Effect of the War on the I.C.S. and P.C.S.

The Second World War which created conditions for the transfer of power, turned the tables against the Indian Civil Service, the strength of which was depleted by European retirements in 1947 and Muslims partially opting for Pakistan. The shortage of officers had naturally to be made good by recourse to the Provincial Civil Services; for men could not be recruited direct to superior posts in the general administration. Some preliminary training and experience was essential to the efficient discharge of 'superior' duties.

The indispensability of the Provincial Civil Services as a major source of direct recruitment to the superior posts of the Indian Civil Service had already been envisaged by the Government of India in a Home Department circular letter dated 12 May 1945 addressed to all Provincial Governments for advice and guidance. The broad picture that had by then emerged was that 'whereas the I.C.S. cadre provided for 820 officers capable of holding superior posts', the number of such posts had increased by 159 according to figures available with the Government of India up to 1943, the increase since then being greater because of the stoppage of recruitment by open competition. The augmented war-time demand for additional officers had been met 'by the ban on retirement, reduced facilities for leave, accelerated promotion of junior officers, and recourse to the Provincial Services'.[32] These were all steps which could not but affect administrative standards.

But the post-War problem of reorganization posed an even greater threat to efficiency. On a conservative estimate it was calculated that when the ban on ordinary retirement was raised and restriction on the grant of leave removed, 'the reduction in the number of superior offices available for duty in 1947' would be of the order of 'somewhere between 200 and 300'. There were no substantial sources from which to meet the inadequacies of man-power that would be so caused. The Home Department letter concluded that

the shortage of officers in the immediate post-War years must be met from the Provincial Services. The alternative, should it be suggested that the Provincial Civil Services cannot produce sufficiently suitable men in adequate numbers, is to maintain restrictions on I.C.S. leave and retirement to the extent that the Provincial Civil Services fail to produce the number of men required. For, it should be noted, the demand for men here under examination is a minimum demand for carrying on the administration on its present basis as determined by war-time conditions. It is a demand that must be met even though it may involve some lowering of administrative standards.

As noted in Chapter V, the Government of India was at this very period thinking actively in terms of post-War development plans. Its Home Department circular letter was, however, concerned with the manpower requirements of the immediate post-War general administration itself. It did not take into account 'the expansion of the Services which the planned development of post-War India may require'. Its emphasis on the Provincial Civil Services as the main source of recruitment was confined to the needs of ordinary existing administration alone. The letter made it clear that 'the Provincial Civil Services will not be able to meet both demand for maintaining the administration at its present level and the additional requirements of development. From the administrative points of view, expansion must be a gradual process the pace of which will be determined by the number of men available to fill superior posts as and when produced by new recruitment'.[33] In view of the substantial increase contemplated in the number of the P.C.S. officers promoted to the superior posts of the Indian Civil Service, it was suggested that the strength of the Federal Public Service Commission should temporarily be increased to assist in the formation of an advance list of suitable P.C.S. officers, a list from which men could be drawn on a substantive basis as and when vacancies were created. The shortage of officers for superior posts in fact led the Government of India to suggest additionally that it would be undesirable to oblige promoted officers to revert to their permanent posts in a Provincial Civil Service after a period of five years or so, for 'they could not reasonably be expected to adjust themselves to the fall in status and in pay after so long a period of higher rank'.[34] The conditions created by the War were thus immediately responsible for the P.C.S. rise to importance in spite of the risk of lowering administrative standards.

Post-War Situation Worsened

The difficulties of the post-War situation were even worse than those visualized in the Home Department Note of 1945. Recruitment to the Indian Civil Service, which had been stopped after 1943, had not yet revived, and the successor Indian Administrative Service was designed in 1946. The all-India Service so constituted, however, suffered from several weaknesses. On account of the additional shortage[35] created by the retirement of Europeans and the transfer of Muslims to Pakistan. The 'war service' candidates were the first to be selected to the new Service, in addition to the temporary officers possessing some administrative experience. Even officers belonging to the Central Secretariat and other services were promoted to it, in addition to officers of the Provincial Civil Services who filled the gap in their respective provinces. A certain percentage of the shortage was met even by emergency recruitment from the open market, regardless of age restriction. The Indian Administrative Service, right from its start, thus hardly emerged as a Service.

The quality of the Indian Administrative Service was further diluted by certain structural changes which had never applied to the Indian Civil Service. These changes signified increased infiltration by the provincial element not only of promotions but also a rise in status. The Memorandum regarding the constitution of the Indian Administrative Service, for instance, raised the percentage of promotion from the Provincial Civil Service from 20 to 25 and invested the Provincial Government itself with powers to fill within that limit such number of 'superior posts' as were allocated to it in the schedule. The rules regulating the promotion of the P.C.S. officers to the Indian Administrative Service were to be framed by the Provincial Government concerned. The Federal Public Service Commission, as the Memorandum said, was merely to be consulted. And, unlike the tradition of the Indian Civil Service, an officer, who was promoted to a superior post included in the schedule, became entitled to the membership of the Indian Administrative Service, unless the vacancy was not likely to last for more than three months, or if in the opinion of the Provincial Government concerned there was no suitable officer of the Indian Administrative Service available for the post.

The increasing representation of scheduled castes was yet another source of weakness. Instead of making special provisions for them to improve their qualification and competence for employment in the civil service the government was pressurized by politics to provide for their employment as a pre-condition to educational advancement. The British, however, used caution, and made no reservation of scheduled caste seats for superior posts in the civil service under the Government of India Resolution of 4 July 1934.

There was none the less a change of policy in 1943, when the Government decided for political reasons that some reservation might encourage scheduled caste candidates to improve their qualifications and become eligible for government posts and services.[36] The percentage worked out on the basis of their population in the country came to 12.75. But since a sufficient number of scheduled caste candidates were still not forthcoming, in spite of age concessions and reductions in fees, the extent of reservation did not exceed 8⅓ per cent. The position was reviewed again in 1946, when the percentage was raised from 8⅓ to 12.5.

A new situation emerged with the formation of Pakistan which made the Muslims of India a smaller and less powerful group; for Pakistan absorbed more than 60 per cent of the Muslim population of the subcontinent. The communal riots that broke out set the tone against the mainstream of separatist politics, the minorities themselves being led to adopt an attitude of self-denial for the creation of what might appear as a politically homogeneous society. In view of the report of the Advisory Committee of the Constituent Assembly the erstwhile principle of separate electorates was given up, but care was taken to protect the interests of the minorities, especially the Anglo-Indians and the scheduled castes and tribes.

Apart from a reservation of 12.5 per cent of direct recruitment to vacancies in the civil service, the scheduled castes enjoyed under the Government of India Resolution of 21 August 1947[37] some special concessions, such as relaxation in the maximum age limit by three years and reduction to the extent of one-fourth in the payment of admission fees. Under the recommendations of its Advisory Committee, the Constituent Assembly put an end to the system of reservation or special representation of the different religious and racial communities. But the privileges extended to scheduled castes remained unaffected. The Constitution of India promulgated on 26 January 1950 not only confirmed the concessions already granted, but provided that where recruitment was made otherwise than by open competition the reservation for scheduled castes was to be fixed at 16 2/3 per cent. Reservations to the extent of 5 per cent of direct recruitment was for the first time provided for the scheduled tribes in 1950.

Schedule caste officers and promoters from the Provincial Civil Services were the two elements mainly responsible immediately for the erosion of administrative standards in terms of both morality and independence of judgement. For both were subject to political pulls. They were, with certain exceptions, prone to the irrationality of caste or group influences, their rise in the service being a result of ministerial discretion rather than of merit. Though conscious of the political compulsions of democracy, the Indian leadership also recognized the necessity of a competition-based civil service. The creation of the Indian Administrative Service and safeguardes for the rights of the erstwhile Indian Civil Service in the midst of emotion-charged dissent in its own ranks were clear expression of that recognition. Even so, the defect remained. It arose not so much from a lack of appreciation of open competition as the basis of recruitments as from a lack of political will to resist provincial pressure.

Trends Towards Further Decline

New trends towards further decline in the standards of administration developed after the attainment of Independence and the introduction of a formal democracy. These trends were the result of a dichotomy that surfaced noticeably with the transfer of power in 1947. While the institutional frame of the political system reflected the principles of Western Liberalism, the product of an advanced capitalist economy that emphasized the rule of law and the rationality of administrative norms, the human agency which became invested with the management of the political machine represented a variegated society which, for historical reasons, existed at different levels of social and economic development, besides being, as a whole backward-looking and caste-oriented in respect of loyalties and affiliations. In spite of adult franchise, however, the first couple of decades were characterized by the balance being weighted more on the side of liberalism than social reaction. Men like Rajagopalachari, Nehru and Patel exercised their influence in favour of reasonable political and administrative standards and counteracted pressures for patronage. Even so, democracy had its say, and, in the context of Indian society, effected a shift of balance from meritocracy to nepotism.

Administrative Expansion. From an administrative point of view the development of planned projects should have been a gradual process of adjustment to the quality of personnel selected for implementation. But, as already noted, little care was taken to relate work to staffing. There was suddenly an enormous increase of employees, leading to the transformation of the Community Projects Administration, for example, into a full-fledged Ministry with its Administrator raised to the position of Cabinet Minister. The original policy orientation came to be vitiated by considerations of patronage rather than service to the community.

The growing tendency towards administrative expansion did not leave even the Indian Administrative Service unaffected. The number of candidates appointed to the I.A.S. on the results of the competitive examinations held during 1947–59 was 616[38] but the size of the annual recruitment was rising gradually. However, as against the average of 47.4 appointments a year during 1947–59, in 1962 the figure was sought to be raised by the State Governments to anywhere between 80 and 85. Some States in fact pressed for an annual recruitment of 100 candidates, for the Ministry of Home Affairs itself had been increasing the annual rate of recruitment, having recruited 87 candidates in 1961 and 99 on 1962.

V. T. Krishnamachari, who at the instance of the Planning Commission completed a study of the problem of personnel administration in 1962, made it clear in his report that 'the annual intake should not be increased to a level at which the quality of the selected candidates is likely to suffer'.[39] He fixed a limit at 90 in view of the fact that mean percentage of the aggregate marks obtained by the ninetieth candidates during 1947–61, a period of fifteen years, was 50.3, the cummulative mean percentage difference between the thirtieth and ninetieth candidates being only 5 per cent. The limit of an annual intake of 90, together with appointments made to vacancies reserved for members of scheduled castes and tribes could give a total of about 100 recruits from the 'generalists' 'without any significant dilution of quality'.

The I.A.S. cadres which included direct recruitment and promotion posts in the State Governments and at the Centre, provided for deputation, leave and training reserves. The actual posts and the reserves together formed the total authorized strength of the I.A.S. cadres. The rate of increase from 1948 to 1962 was as follows on January:[40]

Year	Authorized strength	Year	Authorized strength
1948	803	1958	1676
1950	897	1959	1785
1952	1201	1960	1862
1955	1542	1961	2010
1957	1672	1962	2147

The estimated requirements for I.A.S. personnel during the Third Plan period up to April 1966 were worked out in terms of the total authorized strength of the cadre at the round figure of 2,400. This calculation was made on the basis of the total authorized strength of the cadre on 1 July 1962 being 2, 252, made up of 1862 from direct recruitment and 390 promotion posts. Taking into account all the indications of an increse in the strength of the I.A.S., the Krishnamachari report suggested that the total authorized strength of the cadre should not exceed 2,400 by the end of the Third Plan period in 1966. It held out a hope 'that the cadre may be expected to be stabilised at this figure'. the report emphasized that in framing a recruitment programme 'it has to be borne in mind that a fresh entrant to the Service needs practical experience for some years before he can fill a cadre post effectively.'[41]

However, there is no evidence to show that the Government of India took serious notice of this advice. Not only was the limit of 2,400 crossed earlier than expected, but the authorized strength of the cadre went on rising instead of being stabilized as suggested. This is clear from the figures given below.[42]

Year	Authorized strength on 1 January
1963	2,278
1964	2,470
1965	2,567
1966	2,855
1967	2,882
1968	3,035
1969	3,234
1970	3,199
1971	3,225
1974	3,794
1975	3,884
1976	4,195

The annual intake of recruits to the I.A.S., which was estimated at a maximum of 100 to be attained towards the close of the Third Plan period in 1966 recorded a marked increase in strength much earlier. Reports of the Union Public Service Commission show that, while in 1963 the total number of candidates recommended in order of merit for appointment was 105, the number so recommended for appointment rose to 152 in 1967, and to 157 in 1972. Apart from the dilution of quality caused by an increasing annual intake and heedless rise in the cadre strength of the I.A.S, the efficiency of administration became further weakened by a higher rate of promotion from the State Administrative Services (old P.C.S.). Until May 1977 the promotional quota from State Administrative Service personnel was 25 per cent of the total annual intake into the I.A.S. This quota was raised to 30 per cent in 1977. Promoted I.A.S. officers were expected to be more tractable than 'competitionwallahs'.

In his report V. T. Krishnamachari had of course visualized the possibility of occasional gaps in the I.A.S. cadre. But the remedy he had suggested was not to raise the percentage of promotion from the State Services. On the contrary, he expected the various governments to consider a system of 'promotion by a special competitive examination', a system recommended by the Second Pay Commission for 'serving civil servants'. This proposed competitive examination was to be conducted by the Union Public Service Commission to fill a certain proportion of the all-India and Class I vacancies. The age-limits of such candidates might be between 24 and 30 years and the period of qualifying service of 5 years. The essential part of the proposed scheme was 'that only those who are nominated by their Departments, should be permitted to take the examination; and the criteria for departmental nominations should be not only good work and good conduct, but also exceptional promise'. The scheme suggested that in order to ensure fair nomination a State Government might appoint a selection committee as a necessary safeguard. However, the examination was to be open not only to employees of State Government, but also to those of the Central Government, public corporations and other undertakings in the public sector. The idea was to facilitate 'some amount of lateral mobility' to bring into the higher services men of ability and competence, and to reduce, to howsoever small an extent it might be, the barriers which divided the service in one department from those in others.[43] The scheme, however, remained largely inoperative, for the State Governments generally viewed it as an infringement of their right to patronage.

Gradual Weakening of U.P.S.C. Control. Under Section 96(c) of the Government of India Act, 1919 provisions were first made for the establishment of a public service commission to look after the conduct of the projected separate I.C.S. examination in India. The Public Service Commission (India), as it was first named, was actually established in 1926. It consisted of four members in addition to its Chairman, Sir Ross Barker of the Home Civil Service of the United Kingdom, who sought to build the Commission on the model of the Civil Service Commissioners of his country. The Commission so established came to be known as the Federal Public Service Commission under the Government of India Act, 1935, which also provided for the establishment of a Public Service Commission for each province, or one for a group of provinces. The Federal Public Service Commission was under the Constitution of India reconstituted into the Union Public Service Commission which came into operation on 26 January 1950.

The control of the U.P.S.C. became weakened initially in respect of the category of cases where it was not necessary for the Government to consult it, cases which under Article 372(1) of the Constitution purported to be temporary appointments for periods not exceeding one year. In its very first report the U.P.S.C. regretted the manner in which Ministries and Departments misused the discretion so provided:[44]

> This provision has been invoked by Ministries and Departments of Government far too indiscriminately. There have been too many cases in which posts have been filled by the appointment of Ministries' nominees on the ostensible ground that the posts were temporary. A little reflection would, however, have shown that most of these posts were not likely to be done away with after one year. In many cases the Ministries' nominees have been kept in office for periods far in excess of one year without any reference to the Commission. Such nominees of Government cannot be denied an opportunity to compete for the post when it comes to be filled regularly on a competitive basis. The experience which they gain of the duties of the post, at the cost of the tax payers, gives them an undue advantage over candidates from the open market. This state of things is the direct consequence of Ministries and Departments not making use of the provision properly and has naturally evoked severe and widespread public criticism. The Commission are blamed for what is'really the default of Ministries or Departments of Government'.

The Commission, however, could merely request the Government to divest itself of its power to make temporary appointments without consulting it, a request which rarely received the recognition it deserved.

Irregularity in personnel recruitment became in fact a general feature in the administration of the country after the transfer of power to popular Ministries. Even in a much later report of 1971 the U.P.S.C. regretted the lowering of standards due to patronage and expressed 'concern over the persistence with which cases of irregular appointments continue to occur'. These irregularities proceeded mostly from a continuing practice of *ad hoc* appointments 'made and continued for long periods'. This, as the U.P.S.C. explained, happened because 'direct vacancies, which should be filled on the results of competitive examinations or through recruitment by selection, are not reported to the Commission. As is to be expected, all these have an adverse effect on the quality and morale of the public services.' When allowed to continue over a period, *ad hoc* appointments and promotions vitiated 'the pace of subsequent recruitment causing, inevitably, imbalances in cadre structure which, in turn, raise a chain of other problems'. [45]The withholding by Ministers of direct recruitment vacancies from the U.P.S.C., it was added, not only 'denies' the State 'personnel of requisite quality but has a direct bearing on the employment opportunities which should morally be available to fresh graduates coming out of Universities, technical institutes, etc.[46]

There was yet another consequence of *ad hoc* appointments continued for longer periods. The Twenty-First Report of the Commission pointed out that 'where recruitment to Services is made on the basis of the competitive examinations, appointment of persons on *ad hoc* basis (sometimes for periods of five or six years, or even more) has often led to suggestions for relaxation of age limits so as to render such candidates eligible to take the examinations.'[47] The Commission could not but yield to the suggestions so made. It agreed to recommendation No. 14(1) of the Administrative Reforms Commission in favour of raising the upper age limit to 26 years for recruitment to the non-technical higher services by open competition Accordingly, orders 'raising the upper age limit from 24 to 26 years for admission to the Indian Administrative Service, etc. examination were issued by Government on April 11, 1972'.[48] It was raised to 28 years for the examination of 1979. Rules of recruitment themselves were thus changed to suit the convenience of ministerial nominees.

Another serious anomaly which impaired the quality of recruitment was 'continued uncertainty' about the manpower requirements of the government. In spite of the instructions of the Ministry of Home Affairs, Ministries and Departments generally failed to inform the U.P.S.C. in advance of their needs. Instances continued to occur where the number of vacancies reported initially did not bear any relation to the number of vacancies finally reported to be filled on the results of the examination. As the following table shows, there was a very wide disparity.[49]

Name of Examination	No. of vacancies notified	No. of vacancies finally reported
1. Indian Administrative Service, etc. Examination, 1972	158	455
2. Engineering Services Examination, 1972	139	403
3. Engineering Services (Electronics) Examination, 1972	78	241
4. Assistants' Grade Examination, 1972	44	263

In these circumstances the U.P.S.C. was obliged to express itself against unhealthy trends in personnel management, although there had over the years been no 'major change in the basic pattern of the examinations'. 'The somewhat persistent tendency to make *ad hoc* appointments and to allow them to continue without adequate justification, the lack of adequate care in the assessment of man-power requirements, and the failure on the part of controlling authorities of certain Services to convey timely intimation regarding their requirements to the Commission, are features that tend to weaken the administrative machinery and vitiate the process of personnel recruitment'.[50]

Apart from these trends, a decline in the quality of recruitment flowed also from a steady fall in the standards of university education, an enormous rise in the number of candidates who appeared at the examinations, and, above all, from an increasing number of cases where candidates attempted to seek admission by producing forged and false documents, particularly age certificates, or where candidates resorted to unfair means in the examination hall. The annual reports of the U.P.S.C. draw attention to these and other developments which impaired the recognized norms of recruitment and lowered the standards of administrative efficiency and morality.

Reservation By-Passing Merit. The adverse effects of the policy of reservation in the public services has already been noted. The first list of Scheduled Castes after the transfer of power was drawn up in 1950; it was a revised version of the list approved under the Government of India (Scheduled Castes) Orders of 1936. The test applied for drawing up the list was social, educational and economic backwardness. The 'primitive tribes' were, like the 'depressed classes', also listed for the first time by the 1931 Census and their first list after Independence was likewise prepared in 1950.'

The special concessions granted to members of the Scheduled Castes and the Scheduled Tribes in 1950 were later extended. The percentage of reservation in direct recruitment made by open competition on an all-India basis was by 1974 raised to 15 in the case of Scheduled Castes and to 7½ in the case of Scheduled Tribes. The vacancies reserved were even sought to be carried forward for three recruitment years if sufficient numbers with prescribed qualifications were not forthcoming for the posts advertised. The rules governing reservation laid down that in the case of vacancies filled through the U.P.S.C. or by advertisement it was necessary to have recourse to two alternate advertisements. The first advertisement was to be issued inviting applications in respect of reserved posts only from the candidates belonging to Scheduled Castes and/or Scheduled Tribes as the case might be, and not from general candidates. If, as a result of the first advertisement, the number required for such posts was not selected, the remaining reserved vacancies were to be re-advertised, inviting applications on the second occasion from general candidates also. But the general candidates were to be considered only when Scheduled Castes and Scheduled Tribes candidates did not happen to fulfil the minimum conditions stipulated for appointments to the reserved vacancies.

Where recruitment was, on the other hand, made by interview the interview of Scheduled Castes and Scheduled Tribes candidates was to be held on a day or sitting of the Selection Committee other than sitting fixed for the general candidates, so that 'Scheduled Castes and Scheduled Tribes candidates are not judged in comparison with general candidates and the interviewing authorities and boards are prominently aware of the need for judging the Scheduled Castes and Scheduled Tribes candidates by relaxed standards'.[51]

Reservation did not leave promotion unaffected. There was provision for 15 and 7½ per cent respectively for Scheduled Castes and

Scheduled Tribes in promotions made on the basis of limited competitive examinations for Class II, III and IV posts. The qualifying standard of examination for these posts was relaxed in their favour and even those who did not possess general qualifications were considered. With effect from 20 July 1974, reservation was provided by selection not only in Class II, but up to the lowest rung of Class I posts also. Scheduled Castes and Schedules Tribes candidates were on the basis of reservation included in the 'select list' for promotion even to posts within Class I carrying an ultimate salary of Rs. 2,000 or less.

Besides reservations, the Scheduled Castes and Scheduled Tribes candidates have been allowed to enjoy certain other concessions also. Their is, for instance, relaxation in age in matters of recruitment, which provides that the upper age-limit prescribed for direct recruitment to a service or posts may be enhanced by five years in the case of candidates belonging to Scheduled Castes and Scheduled Tribes. The concessions of age limit under the notification issued for the All-India Civil Services Examination of 1979 in fact ranged between three years to eight for different categories of candidates, the Scheduled Castes and Scheduled Tribes candidates being entitled to the maximum of eight years in case they happened to be displaced persons from East Pakistan. They have also been allowed a reduction to the extent of one-fourth in the fees prescribed for admission to any examination or selection to a service or post.

To ensure that the reservations and other orders relating to concessions in the All-India and Central Services were scrupulously followed, provisions were made for the appointment of liasion officers whose duty was to see that the instructions issued from time to time were duly complied with. The Constitution, too, provided under Article 338 for the appointment of a Special Officer whose responsibility is to investigate matters relating to the safeguard provided for the Scheduled Castes and Scheduled Tribes. In addition, there was to be a Parliamentary Committee to go into various aspects and report to Parliament. Electoral considerations have also dictated the expediency of having a High Power Committee with the Prime Minister as Chairman. The whole policy direction was in fact on job reservation to satisfy political ends independently of its repercussions on the quality of administrative personnel.

The number of candidates from the Scheduled Castes and the Scheduled Tribes who applied for admission to the combined competitive examination for the all-India and higher central services showed a steady increase over the years, as is clear from the figures given below:

Year	Number of Scheduled Castes Candidates	Number of Scheduled Tribes Candidates
1963	1,057	221
1964	1,372	239
1965	1,582	263
1966	1,828	320
1967	1,986	445
1968	2,219	597
1969	2,445	631

While the number of candidates belonging to the Scheduled Castes had more than doubled in a period of seven years, candidates from the Scheduled Tribes nearly tribled during the same period. It was, however, not an expression of social mobility while the politics of reservation tended to stabilize the erstwhile social distinctions and provide an incentive to caste riots, the steady inroads into the best methods of recruitment have seriously tended to impair the quality of the higher civil service that sets the norms of administrative behaviour in the country. The irrationality of politics filters down to the rational level of administration.

Distortion of Original IAS Objectives

The main objectives underlying the formation of the Indian Administrative Service were to provide a body of officers of high calibre, possessing an all-India outlook but common to the Union and the States for purposes of ensuring a uniform system of administration throughout the country. The conference of the 'Premiers' of all the provinces that met on 21 October 1946 under the presidentship of Sardar Vallabhbhai Patel, the then Home Minister, took the final decision to constitute the Service and summed up the reasons in the following minute:[52]

> The reason which prompted the decision in favour of an All-India Administrative Service was mutual advantage both to the Centre and the Provinces. It would facilitate liaison between the Centre and Provinces, ensure a certain uniformity in standards of administration and maintain the central administrative machinery in touch with realities. The provincial administrative machinery would on its part acquire a wider outlook and obtain the best

material for the higher posts. The Home Minister emphasized that there was need for ensuring contentment and security in the Services and for seeing that the Services were free from communal or party bias.

The Study Team on 'Centre-State Relationships' recognized the continuing validity of an elite servide and pointed out that quality was the *raison d'etre* of the existence of such a service, or in fact, of all higher management, especially when the tasks of development called for a combination of both generalist and specialized talents in the superior civil service.

The mechanism employed earlier and suggested originally even in the case of the Indian Administrative Service sought to achieve the objective mainly by three different methods:[53]

(1) by structuring the cadre in such a way that 79 to 80 per cent of the senior posts went to direct recruits selected on the basis of a difficult all-India competitive examination and the remaining 21 to 20 per cent to promotees from the state services. The underlying idea was that the combined competitive examination limited to candidates between the age group 21–24, should throw up 80 per cent of the senior officers of the cadre.

(2) by a recruitment policy that controlled numbers.

(3) by ensuring an attractive environment of work in terms of prestige and conditions of service.

As discussed before, this mechanism underwent severe distortions on account of too heavy a rate of recruitment, imbalance in the structure and composition of the Service, and deterioration in the environment of work.

The structuring of the cadre did not proceed in accordance with the mechanism originally devised, the promotees from the State Services being admitted to an increasingly greater share, in spite of their lower standard of recruitment as the Lee Commission observed in 1958. 'Having regard to the part played by the Public Service Commission in the selection of the subordinate judiciary', the Commission pointed out, 'we took care to examine as far as possible, the Chairman and some of the members of the Public Service Commissions in various States. We are constrained to state that the personnel of these Public Service Commissions in some of the States was not such as could inspire confidence, from the point of view of either efficiency or impartiality. There appears to be little doubt that in some of the States, appointments to these Commissions are made not on considerations of merit but on grounds of party and political affiliations.' Irregularities naturally occurred in the appointments made by State Public Service Commisions, and in one case the Supreme Court had to 'annul wholesale certain appointments made on the recommendatios of one of the State Public Service Commissions'.[54] Even so, according to a survey made on 1 November 1965, 'the recruits admitted as a result of the open competitive examination accounted for only 43.2% of officers of the I.A.S. in the senior scale and above instead of the original expectation of 80%'.[55] Apart from the increasing percentage of promotees from the State Services, this imbalance in the composition of the I.A.S. proceeded from a series of *ad hoc* recruitments, so that 'the direct recruitment quota which was intended originally to be filled entirely by officers recruited through the annual competitive examinations has come to be composed of various elements. The mixture in the senior scale of the I.A.S. of variously state cadres, as surveyed on 1 November 1965 shows that . . .State Service officers . . .accounted for anything from 27.6% (Madras) to 52% (Rajasthan)'.[56]

As said before, this *ad hocism* was a result of an absence of planning. the integration of states in 1949 and their subsequent reorganization did call for an increase of the I.A.S. cadre, and so did the advent of the five-year development plans. But for nearly a decade or so the policy of recruitment remained more or less conservative. When it was discovered that the cadre needed considerable expansion, it was done in a sudden and haphazard manner. The Special Recruitment of 1956 which was intended to fulfil the demand, was again on an *ad hoc* basis. The excessive recruitment which later followed to increase the annual intake, was a reaction in the opposite direction. The annual intake 'increased from 33 in 1947 to 138 in 1965', and, according to a report of 1968, it was being 'targetted' at 160 thereafter. This order of recruitment, as the report said, was bound 'to take its toll in terms of quality', which, according to the Study Team on 'Centre-State Relationships', had by 1966 'declined to a point when it must cause concern'.[57] The situation worsened still further when the promotional quota from the State Services was raised formally from 25 to 30 per cent and the authorized strength of the I.A.S. cadre increased enormously from 803 in 1948 to 4,195 in 1976, partly from ex-cadre posts being sought to be filled by cadre officers.

Prestige as a bulwark of the civil service is not an independent variable. It is in fact closely related to the collective merit of the group to which the officers belong, the values and traditions to which they subscribe, the degree of responsibility discharged by them, their standard of performance and, above all the homogeneity and balance in the structure and composition of the service to which they belong. Mere salary scales and conditions of service do not add up to the intangible elements that constitute what is generally meant by prestige. In the course of this chapter it has been shown how the quality of recruitment has steadily been declining and the homogeneity of the Service becoming a thing of the past. The old prestige was natually bound to diminish as it did.

As regards the degree of responsibility, the civil service had earlier functioned more or less as rulers, the governor and the permanent service being vested practically with the final say in policy matters. Democracy, even in its limited form of dyarchy, brought ministers into the picture. In the field allotted to them their orders were expected to be duly carried out and if a govenor wanted to veto such order, he had to convince the ministry of the correctness of his stand. The civil service was for the first time obliged to treat a minister as the source of power by virtue of his being an elected representatives of his constitutents and voters. The ministries formed under the Government of India Act, 1935, marked a further advance of democracy and enhanced the position of ministers.[58] The 'special responsibilities' of the governor, however, operated as a check on the misuse of power and deviation from the established rules of administrative business. An interesting case, for example, occurred in Bihar where ministers ordered officers to carry out their directives independently of any reference to the Secretariat. In the famous Brett Circular of 1937, the Chief Secretary of Bihar, Brett, advised executive officers that such ordes should not be carried out unless duly authorized and issued from the Secretariat. The Chief Secretary was right and within the limits of his authority, for the responsibility, for any directive on behalf of the Government was that of the Cabinet, not of a single minister. The final arrangement, however, was that the officer should carry out the orders if it happened to be within the portfolio of the minister. All that an officer could do was to ask for written orders in case he had any doubts. Brett viewed this arrangement as highly irregular and susceptible to corruption. He resigned and left. The degree of responsibility which the bureaucracy earlier exercised by a strict adherence to administrative formalities was, with the growth of democracy, being sought to be superseded by ministers. Brett's resignation was an expression of bureaucratic firmness in the exercise of its responsibility.

The dichotomy in the relationship between administrative rationality and political informality was heightened after 1947. The transfer of power and the establishment of parliamentary democracy on adult suffrage reduced the permanent civil service to a position of subordination to ministers. Policy matters and their implementation became two separate and distinct categories, the former being recognized as the concern of ministers, and the latter as the legitimate sphere of civil servants who were expected to be free from political influence or party affiliation. The neutrality of the civil service was considered essential to the functioning of parliamentary democracy where the political complexion of the party in power was subject to periodic changes. The ministerial superiority of the political wing was, however, recognized without a corresponding provision for checks by rule to ensure ability, honesty of conduct and a minimum degree of understanding, if not intellectual insight, in the formulation of policies. The education which politicians generally got in the post-Independence period was in the streets, in organizing agitations against any group or party in power. Their capacity to learn from circumstances and gain experience was their only aid. They generally had little theoretical perception of a recognizable moral code as a guide to conduct.

But since the civil servants, unlike politicians, continued to be as a class more advanced educationally in addition to their being rule-bound and subject to disciplinary action, the political wing of the machinery of government, even at the level of governors and ministers, generally compared poorly with them in respect of intellectual and moral standards. Thus the degree of responsibility which civil servants exercised in the post-1947 period was a function not so much of their subordinate position in constitutional terms as of ministerial dependence on them for a knowledge of public affairs and policy decisions. It was a case of a new bureaucratic despotism, born of ministerial incapacity and political uncertainty.

The general decline of fitness in the civil service as a whole, however, led to a reduction in its importance. The exigencies of development administration, which called for a capacity to appreciate complicated situations involving a knowledge of both human and material management, especially in an age of technological advance, drove in the same direction. The new task of development necessitated a measure of specialization, not technical expertise in a single field but a broad grasp and understanding of the essentials of related functions.

However, in operation this involved questions of seniority and promotion, which in turn required a review of the erstwhile practice of the tenure system of deputation to the Centre. Soon after the transfer of power and for a number of years thereafter the Government of India lost sight of the need for its top administrators to keep in touch with the field in districts. Once deputed to the Centre, they remained there without any attempt being made to maintain contact with the states. Steps were later sought to be taken to set right the error by a strict adherence to the tenure rule. None the less, a result of the weakening of the Indian Administrative Service was that a considerable number of ex-cadre officers came to hold cadre posts, and secretariat jobs at all levels were held by non-I.A.S. officers. The position at the Centre in 1970 was as follows:[59]:

	Held by I.A.S. Officers	Held by others
Secretary's posts	32	12
Addl. Secretary's posts	15	13
Joint Secretary's posts	80	68
Deputy Secretary's posts	84	186
Under Secretary's posts	51	420

This change-over started even before the transfer of power in 1947, when recruitment to the Indian Civil Service had stopped in 1943 and posts were being kept in abeyance for war-service candidates. In the scientific services, too, care was being taken to observe the principle that officers should be technocrats. The advance of technology and decline in the general standards of the administrative services were in fact gradually reducing the operational area of the civil service.

But since the task of planned development called for a broad grasp and understanding of related functions, the importance of the generalist administrator could not but continue to be recognized not only by virtue of his general education in the humanities and social sciences, but also by the kind of training imparted to the direct recruits, some of whom still showed evidence of an admirable quality of mind. What was needed was a degree of specialization already alluded to, a kind of specialization necessary for development work, not for technical expertise in a strictly professional sense.

This specialization is a product of training, of a foundational course and professional training on the job. The exigencies of development administration dictated the necessity of periodical in-service courses, and their success depends on the co-operation and efficiency of administration in the states. Such training has none the less already started in the Indian Institute of Public Administration at New Delhi, the Administrative Staff College at Hyderabad, and the National Institute at Mussoorie.

VII
CERTAIN BROAD CONCLUSIONS

The first phase of rural development under the British began with the administration of revenue itself. It was concerned not merely with the collection of land revenue, but also with a comprehensive scheme of land survey. The surveys and settlement operations which Collectors had to undertake as part of their immediate duties furnished information which constituted a basis for agricultural policy, land reforms and measures for agricultural improvement. It was no doubt a dilatory process, and the immediate financial concern of the government was always evident, but the experiences of recurrent famines proved beyond doubt the indispensability of statistics on agricultural production and the landed classes in enabling the government to take protective and preventive measures against agricultural distress. The administration of revenue was in fact fairly complex, involving not only measures of relief against natural calamities but also positive action to promote rural development. Despite the opposition of landowners, tenancy reforms were enacted and cadastral survey operations started even in areas of zamindari settlement.

The idea of rural development through the government was initially a search for an alternative to *laissez faire*, a profit-based economic principle which failed to provide relief to famine-stricken people and necessitated some bureaucratic intervention in restricting free trade. But as official policy remained generally opposed to interference with trade, it was given only to individual Collectors to control the market on humanitarian grounds. The report of the

Deccan Riots Commission (1873-4) was amongst the first documents to question the soundness of *laissez-faire* as a guide to community welfare. The necessity of rural development, more especially of rural financing through institutional channels, began to be realized by the government, which suggested the need for more control over the operation of the free trade principle.

The new attitude towards rural development found expression mainly in two directions, namely, a reorganization of the internal administrative arrangement and a delegation of some responsibility to self-governing local bodies. The former included, for example, a move towards the establishment of a separate department of agriculture at the Centre and in the provinces, a scheme of financial decentralization to enable provinces to find means to promote their own development work in the various technical departments, the organization of a number of All-India specialized Services to ensure uniformity and efficiency in the direction and supervision of technical departments in the provinces, and, finally, an attempt to provide some kind of training in agriculture for I.C.S. officers. Though partly motivated by political considerations, the local bodies, too, were designed to relieve imperial finances for purposes of local development.

Though steady, the progress remained slow, however; for the European pressure-group against control was reinforced by Indian private enterprise, and together they opposed the centralization which Lord Curzon had pushed to an extreme through several measures of reform designed to promote irrigation and co-operatives, agricultural education and experimental farms.

Apart from the opposition of business communities to bureaucratic control, the demand for decentralization had also a political dimension arising from a downward filtration of higher education and the consequent emergence of educated elites at the lower levels of society who sought both employment and a share in the exercise of power. Collaborators in business and politics tended to become competitors under the banner of nationalism. The exigencies of rural development, too, called for both administrative and financial decentralization, a situation which not only led to dyarchy in the provinces at the political level, but, more significantly, to the provincialization of the various all-India Services of a technical nature, with their branches extended in due course to the district also.

What dominated the provincialization of the all-India technical services was, however, racial politics, the politics of replacing Europeans by Indians in the public regardless of considerations for quality or even organizational requirments. It was, of course, not wholly without justification: there would be little or no scope for the development of indigenous talent if the dominance of Europeans continued unabated. Morley had already sounded a warning in 1906 and suggested reliance on Indian resources for development purposes. Even so, the practice of importing European expertise remained unaffected. The provincializing of all-India Services was, however, no answer, although the case for separate provincial services for development could not be denied. The standard of provincial recruitment was of necessity inferior, for the range of competition was narrowed down to provincial limits and there were, in addition, enormous regional variations in the level of social and economic development which the all-India Services could alone have counter-acted. The Government of India was, in fact, shorn of its administrative agencies of control and supervision without being relieved of the responsibility to finance development projects. The national political leadership hardly realized the baneful character of provincial politics and encouraged provincialism as a means to get into the corridors of power.

With the appointment of non-official chairmen and considerable increases in the strength of their elected representatives, district boards, too, became subject to the influence of nationalist politics, especially during the non-cooperation movement.

After 1919, district boards were thus generally deprived of the services of the Collector's revenue staff, a situation which worsened with the continued financial crisis arising not only from rise in prices and the cost of administration, but also from political involvements and the mismanagement of funds. Politics tended to bedevil the administration of the provinces also. But while provincial governments had the advantage of a reasonably efficient bureaucracy, there was no such administrative cadre in the local bodies which could save them from the pernicious effects of ministerial interference, which, from personal, caste or communal motives, further increased under provincial autonomy.

The inefficiency of district boards as an instrument of development came to the surface especially during the second World War. Experience established beyond doubt not only the very weak state of their entire system of communication, but also the ineffectiveness of the health and other services they were required to provide for war purposes. What in fact led the government to describe them as *functus officio* was their utter failure to contribute to the 'Grow More Food' campaign, which was not only designed to win the War but also meet the acute shortage of food and fodder for the civil population. Experience in this campaign led to a shift of emphasis from district boards to village panchayats and Union Boards, lower units of local bodies which were immediately in contact with the food-producing rural masses.

The importance of planning and direct government involvement in development work, which was first recognized during the 'Grow More Food' campaign, was sought to be intensified on the publication of the report of the Grow More Food Inquiry Committee in June 1952. The Community Development Programme inaugurated in October the same year and the National Extension Service introduced a year later were both expressions of the concern felt by the Government of India for the continuing shortage of food and the neglect of the rural masses, a concern which was further reinforced by Article 40 of the Constitution of India directing every state government to establish village panchayats for development purposes. The panchayats so established no doubt remained attached for a time to local bodies as part of the department of local self-government, but they were finally integrated in 1958 with the Community Development and National Extension Service.

Another step in the attempt to secure popular participation was what the report of the Balvantray Mehta Team called 'democratic decentralization'. It was a three-tier administrative arrangement from the village upwards to the district, designed to involve the people's elected representatives in the process of planning from below, with members of the official hierarchy functioning at each level as mere adjuncts. This general plan for rural development held out the hope that the status assigned to elected representatives would in time create confidence in the people and induce them to treat the community development programmes as their own. But the expectation was not fulfilled. The people continued to believe that these were all government programmes and that they were being asked merely to co-operate. Formal democracy and decentralization acted as a lever to power and privilege for a few and bore no relation to popularity based on service to the community, honesty and integrity of conduct. The Mehta Team's democratic decentralization was in fact an aexpression of the dichotomy that had over the years developed under

British rule between the power-wielding bureaucracy and jail-going nationalists who, on the attainment of Independence, pressed for a reversal of the erstwhile power relationship. The old complex generally continued and only in Maharashtra and Gujarat were three exceptions; these states did not start planning from below, nor did they show any prejudice against the bureaucracy. The Chief Executive Officer, a civil servant, controlled the entire technical staff in the district.

There was in fact a general falling-off in the expectations originally entertained. The independence of the Ministry of Community Development and Co-operation began to be slowly loosened until it was tagged to the Ministry of Food and Agriculture in 1966 and finally replaced by the Department of Rural Development in 1974. Several special programmes had in the mean while branched off and came to be organized separately on an area basis under guidance and assistance received directly from the Centre, although programme implementation had originally formed part of the responsibility of state governments. The Department of Rural Development so created was naturally vested with the integration of all such special programmes as came to be separately organized at central initiative towards the close of the Fourth Five-Year Plan period and the beginning of the Fifth.

But the Centre also had serious limitations in providing an efficient administrative agency of control and supervision. The British had for development purposes created in the technical field a number of all-India Services with a standard of recruitment comparable to that of the I.C.S. The members of these Services in the special departments worked as the eyes and ears of the Government of India who used them both in the formulation of policies and their execution. Like officers of the I.C.S., they constituted a link between the secretariat and field administration, an arrangement which kept the Centre duly informed of trends of progress made by special departments in the provinces. The provincialization of these Services under the pressure of national politics, however, deprived the Government of India of a central machinery of inspection that was necessary not only in providing an all-India view in determining the rate of progress in the provinces, but more especially for raising the standard of knowledge and performance in the technical branches of development. The error committed by the national leadership getting in these services Indianized through provincialization was realized by the

States Reorganization Commission (1956) and the Administrative Reforms Commission (1966). Both recommended a revival of the several erstwhile all-India services in the technical field, but provincialism had gone too far to admit of such a revival. Strengthened and reinforced initially by the national leadership, provincialism did not spare even the I.C.S. and the Indian Police. However, Vallabhbhai Patel stood in the way and saved the situation by creating their two successor All-India Services. Even so, quality was considerably diluted by the increasing infiltration of provincial elements.

The problems of rural development in fact raised serious administrative and financial issues in respect of both centre-state and state-district relationships. This study makes it clear that no development was possible without the active involvement of the Government of India in administrative and financial terms. Administrative decentralization was no doubt a necessity for purposes of implementation raising local resources for development. The history of India's financial administration, however, shows that, while the dependence of the provinces 'or states' on the Centre was a common experience, the local bodies and village panchayats without exception expected provincial grants and cesses rather than imposing even statutory obligations to improve their own financial resources for fear of unpopularity. A resort to central resources was thus usually the only substantial lever to progress in rural development. And yet the Government of India was denied its rightful claim to reconstitute its own all-India Services to control and supervise that progress. On the contrary, movements have arisen to transfer part of the Central cake as of right to the states, to be locally shared for political advantage. This trend is perhaps a continuation of the political dimension of decentralization that began after 1905 in the wake of Lord Curzon's administration.

The problems which confronted district administration for development under Punchayati Raj Institutions were mainly related to the level of planning, to vertical and horizontal linkages for the purpose of co-ordination, and the relations of officials with elected bodies at each level of the three-tier system. In the absence of expertise and resources at the village level the Balvantray Mehta Team's recommendation in favour of planning from below remained no more than a mere day dream. The Asoka Mehta Committee recognized this limitation and expressed itself in favour of a two-tier system, the *mandal* (block) and the district, the latter being in practice more real than the former in terms of the availability of personnel and technical resources for planning, not exclusive, of course, of blocks themselves. The question of vertical and horizontal links remains unresolved; while the former has the sanction of history for all disciplinary and promotional purposes, the latter is a new and *ad hoc* arrangement designed to achieve specific goals of development in rural areas through integrated efforts and co-ordination at block and district levels. It is not merely a problem of the relationship between the co-ordinator and the technical staff serving under him; the loyalty of both to the goal of national reconstruction can alone reconcile the two links in district administration for development. This problem of linkage poses in fact the much wider issue of the relations between 'administration', a rational category, and 'politics', which partakes of the character of 'irrationality'. In other words, the issue is not merely one of administrative re-adjustment, but also political.

However, the quality of bureaucratic performance was also a variable dimension. It kept changing over the years with the changing patterns of government and politics. In order to keep the bureaucracy free from colonial political attitudes Morley suggested in 1906 the expediency of relying on indigenous expertise for purposes of development work. In 1909 the royal Commission on Decentralization had also advised similar action to meet the demands of employment-motivated politics and to safeguard administrative standards. But since progress on this front remained slow and tardy, the political constitution of government itself was sought to be changed in 1919 as a means to satisfy the demands of nationalism by promoting the Indianization of the higher echelons of the public Services. It led to the organization of separate Services associations for Europeans and Indians in the civil service for the protection of their rights and privileges, the object of the latter being especially to get into key positions in the administration. A strict regard for administrative neutrality had thus begun to give way to the extra-professional irrationality of politics. The fall of recognized bureaucratic norms had begun even with the introduction of partial and restricted representative institutions.

Once the bureaucracy became initially divided on racial grounds under nationalist influence, its further division on a communal basis and then again into caste categories could not be prevented. Muslim reservation in the public Services, followed by reservations for members of the Scheduled Castes and Scheduled Tribes, all came in the same context. The method employed for recruitment to the superior Services was that of 'nomination', a principle which also covered promotion from the provincial Services, whose percentage increased from 16 in 1892 to 30 in 1977. Further, the back-door entry through ministerial machinations, which, as the annual reports of the Union Public Service Commission point out, kept increasing inthe post-Independence period, the authorized strength of the I.A.S. cadre itself rising from 803 in 1948 to 4,195 in 1976. The quality of administrative personnel immediately invested with the task of promoting development thus naturally suffered a serious setback.

Some weakening in the standards of administration was perhaps inevitable in a democracy or government by consent. But it is difficult to accept a situation where the expansion of development activities remained unrelated to the availability or otherwise of able and trained manpower resources. This popular, though unsound, trend began soon after Nehru had taken over as Prime Minister in 1946 itself. He suggested the expediency of 'special procedure' to secure the services of those whom he considered 'competent' and possessed of 'technical qualifications' even though the Prime Minister was not strictly invested with powers to make such appointments. 'All appointments in India to Governments service and posts', he was reminded by the Cabinet Secretariat, 'are done by the Federal Public Service Commission after open advertisement. Government informs the Commission of the vacancies to be filled, and the qualifications of the candidates they require, and the Commission do the recruiting'. However, the practice of the government itself appointing individuals on a temporary basis for a number of years and merely submitting them later to the Commission for approval continued. The quality of the manpower recruited even for development purposes was hardly sought to be related to job requirements.

In these circumstances the I.A.S., recruited by open competition, was the only hope. Through increasing emphasis on the observance of the rules governing the tenure system, its members are made available to the states to which they are obliged to return after the expiry of their deputation. They constitute the real strength of the administrative infrastructure for purposes of rural development in the states, although the lowering of standards for the Scheduled Castes and

Scheduled Tribes remains a serious professional handicap. The basic weakness of modern Indian administration under parliamentary democracy has in fact been its failure to sustain its professional character in the face of changing norms of social and political behaviour, a failure that is mainly attributable to a steady fall in the standards of recruitment.

NOTES

I. EVOLUTION OF DISTRICT ADMINISTRATION UP TO 1858

1 Forrest, *Selections*, ii, p. 454.
2 *Sixth Report*, Vol. IV, p. 301a (1804 edn.).
3 See specially B. B. Misra, *The Central Administration of the East India Company, 1773–1834* and *The Judicial Administration of the E.I.C. in Bengal, 1765–82.*
4 Orissa included at the time only the district of Midnapore and a part of Hooghly, or, more accurately, the tract lying between the rivers Subarnarekha and Rupnarain. Orissa proper was conquered and annexed from the Marathas by Lord Wellesley in 1803. See *Report on the Administration of Bengal*, 1901–2, p. 45, para. 107.
5 Clive to the Court of Directors, 28 Sept. 1765, I. O. MSS Eur. E. 12., pp.76–7,
6 Vol. IV, p. 300b (1804 edn.).
7 See Misra, *The Central Administration of the E.I. Co.*, p. 111 (Case of interposition by the Supervisor of Nadia against Raja Krishna Chandra, the local zamindar).
8 See Misra, *Central Administration*, pp. 177–82.
9 See Misra, *The Judicial Administration of the E.I. Co.*, pp. 264, 269.
10 See Misra, *The Judicial Administration of the E.I. Co.*, Ibid. Chap. IX.
11 See Misra, *Central Administration*, pp. 128–30.
12 Ibid. p. 132.
13 Ibid. p. 156. The number of districts placed under Supervizors in 1769 was only 11 for Bengal and 5 for Bihar, a Supervizor being in some cases placed in charge of a couple of districts. Edward Golding had, for instance, the charge of Saran and Champaran with headquarters at Chapra. See Misra, *Judicial Administration*, pp. 35–41. The number of districts in Bihar alone rose to 31 in 1976.
14 Ibid. p. 157.
15 The Zamindari rights of the Company in these villages were based on a grant made to it by the Mughal Emperor, Farrukh-siyar in 1717. But on account of the opposition of the then Nawab of Bengal, Murshid Quli Khan, they could not be taken possession of.
16 *Fourth Report from the Committee of Secrecy* (24 March 1773), Vol. IV (1804–Print), p. 115b.
17 Ibid. p. 115 b.
18 Ibid. p. 115 b.
19 Ibid. p. 116 a.
20 Ibid. p. 116 a

21 Ibid. p. 252a
22 Ibid. p. 235b.
23 *Sixth Report*, op. cit., pp. 309ab.
24 Ibid. p. 309a.
25 See *Report of the Administration of Bengal, 1901–2*, p. 48, f.n.
26 See Misra, *The Central Administration of the E.I. Co.*, Chap. VI.
27 See Misra, *The Central Administration of the E.I. Co.*, p. 214.
28 See Parl. Papers (HL), No. 445 of 1853, p. 136, paras 6–7.
29 *Selections from revenue records of the N.–W. Prov.*, iii, p. 63.
30 See Philips, *Introduction to the Correspondence of Lord William Cavendish Bentinck*, Vol. 1.
31 See *Report of the Administration of Bengal*, 1901–2, p. 52.
32 See *Notes on Police in the Decentralization Committee for the Royal Commission on Decentralization, 1907–9*, para 1.
33 See Col. Baird Smith's report about U.P. cited in the *Report on the Famine in Bengal and Orissa* (1866), p. 1.
34 See *Report of the Administration of Bengal, 1901–2*, paras 130–1. See also Misra, *The Central Administration of the E.I. Co.*, pp. 161–3.
35 Para 14 of the Decentralization Comtt. Note on Police.
36 See *Our Indian Empire*, quoted in Misra, *Administrative History*, p. 485.

Size of Districts in 1858

Province	Average area in sq. miles
Madras	6,784
Bombay	6,070
Bengal	3,373
N.W. Provinces	2,047

37 *Selections from the Revenue Records of the N.W. Provinces*, iii, p. 63.
38 See Alexander Rogers, *The Land Revenue of Bombay* (1892), p. 9
39 George W. Forrest (ed.), *Selections from the Minutes and Other Official Writings of the Honourable Mountstuart Elphinstone*, Bombay, 1884 (Extracts), p. 57.
40 Ibid. pp. 59–60.
41 Ibid p. 62 .
42 Ibid. p. 63
43 All the land which did not belong to peasant proprietors (*mirasidars*) or occupant-cultivators, belonged to the government or to those to whom the government assigned it. Elphinstone's report (as Commissioner) on the territories conquered from the Peshwa made it clear that the property of the zamindars in the soil had not been introduced or even heard of in the Maratha country. Ibid. p. 279.
44 *Administrative System of the Marathas*, 2nd ed., Calcutta, 1925, p. 214.
45 See G. W. Forrest (ed.) *Selections from the Minutes and other official writings of the Honourable Mountstuart Elphinstone*, 1884, p. 61 (Extracts).
46 Ibid. pp. 68–9.
47 Ibid. p. 67.
48 *Report of the Administration of Bengal, 1901–2*, p. 55.
49 See pp. 55–61.
50 *Report of the Royal Commission upon Decentralization in India*, 1909, p. 19.
51 See Misra, *The Administrative History of India*, p. 327.
52 See Misra, *The Indian Middle Classes*, p. 114.
53 See Minute by J. P. Grant, 24 July 1854, Home (Public) Cons. 11 Aug. 1854, No. 53.

54 See Minute by G. G., 12 July 1854, Home (Public) Cons., 11 Aug. 1854, No. 51.
55 See Home (Public) Cons., 9 Feb. 1855, No. 45.
56 See Notes (on the P.W.D.) of the Decentralization Committee for the Royal Commission upon Decentralization 1907–9, pp. 2–3.
57 See Extracts taken from the *Report of the Bengal and Orissa Famine Commission* (1866), Calcutta, 1867, p. 14.
58 See Chap. VI.
59 H. Sharp (ed.), *Selections from Educational Records*, Part I, 1781–1839, Calcutta, 1920, p. 116.
60 See paras 4 to 8 of Court's Despatch to the Madras Government of 29 Sept. 1830 (*Evidence* of 1832, App. I, No. 21, quoted in Sharp (ed.) *Selections*, p. 179.
61 J. Long (ed.), p. 304.
62 J. A. Richey (ed.), *Selections from Educational Records*, Part II, Govt. of India, New Delhi, 1965. p. 65.
63 Ibid. p. 65.
64 See Sharp, *Selections*, Part I, p. 130.
65 Ibid. p. 142.
66 See J. A. Richey, *Selections*, Part II (1840–59).
67 Educational Despatch No. 4, 7 April 1859, Ibid. p. 427, para 5.
68 Ibid. para 41.
69 See B. B. Misra, *The Bureaucracy in India: An Historical Analysis of Development up to 1947*, pp. 139–57. The Imperial (Indian) Educational Service, as distinct from the Provincial Educational Service, was created in 1896.
70 See Rep. Sel. Com. HL, 1852, [19(88)] Qs. 1187–88, 1190, 1192–93. See Misra, *The Indian Middle Classes*, pp. 181–3.
71 See Note (on Medical) of Decentralization Committee for the Royal Commission upon Decentralization (1909), pp. 1–4.
72 From Sanitary Commission to Home Sec., Govt. of India, No. 620, dated 5 Sept. 1964, Home (Public) A File (1965), Nos. 2–3, pp. 1–2.
73 Ibid. p. 2.
74 See Despatch from the Govt. of India, No. 75, 1 Nov. 1862 (referred to by the Committee for the Decentralization Comn. para 2)
75 See *100 Years of Indian Forestry (1861–1961)*, Volume One Souvenir, p. vi.
76 See Home (Public) Progs., April, 1870, p. 12.
77 See A. R. Tucker's Note on Forest Administration in Decentralization Committee for the Royal Commission upon Decentralization, para 2.
78 *Report of the Indian Commission (1880)*, Part I, p. 104.
79 See B. B. Misra, *The Indian Middle Classes*, p. 101.
80 See Ibid. pp. 104–7.
81 See B. B. Misra, *The Administrative History of India, 1834–1947*, pp. 538–64.

II. RECURRENT FAMINES AND RURAL DEVELOPMENT, 1858–1905

1 See Appendix A.
2 *Famine Commission Report (1880)*, Part I, para. 72, p. 25.
3 Ibid. para. 49, p. 12.
4 Ibid. Part I, para. 47.
5 Ibid. Part I, para. 49.

6 Extracts taken from the *Report of the Commissioners Appointed to Enquire into the Famine of Bengal and Orissa*, No. 74.
7 Ibid.
8 For instance, of 2,782 deaths in the Balasore charitable dispensary alone from May to October 1866, dysentery and diarrhoea together claimed 2,669. See Ibid. No. 74.
9 *Famine Commission Report (1880)*, Part I, para 55.
10 Ibid. para 55.
11 Ibid. Part I, para 57.
12 Ibid. Part I, para 61.
13 See *Famine Commission Bengal Replies*, Agriculture Branch, Revenue Department—Famine—Darjeeling, 5 July 1878.
14 Ibid. p. 130.
15 Ibid. p. 130.
16 Ibid. p. 133.
17 Ibid. p. 158. The Sub-Divisional Officer who strongly opposed the principle of relief work was C. J. O'Donnell who held charge of Siwan in 1878. According to him, the temporary remission of land revenue, the free grant of loans in cash and the stimulation of ordinary trade and grain supply were the best form of famine relief.
18 Ibid. p. 185.
19 Ibid. p. 243 (Answer to Question 33).
20 Extracts taken from the *Summary of the Administration of Lord Curzon ... in the Department of Revenue and Agriculture*, p. 3.
21 Ibid. p. 3.
22 Ibid. p. 4.
23 Ibid. pp. 4–5.
24 See Ibid. pp. 5–6. See also despatch No. 73 of 30 October 1902 to Sec. of State, and despatch No. 210 of 26 December 1902 from the Sec. of State; also Govt. of India Res. No. 7/7/4 of 21 March 1903 in the Depart. of Revenue and Agriculture.
25 See the *Report of the Famine Commission (1880)*, Part I, para 43.
26 Ibid. Part I, para 44.
27 Ibid. Part I, para 45.
28 Ibid. para 45.
29 *Report of the Commission*, Vol. I, para 19, p. 5 (extracts).
30 Ibid. Vol. I, p. 5 (extracts).
31 Ibid. Vol. I, p. 4 (extracts).
32 Ibid. Vol. I. p. 337 (extracts).
33 Ibid. Vol. I, p. 344 (extract).
34 Ibid.
35 Extracts taken from the *Report of the Commissioners Appointed to Enquire into the Famine in Bengal and Orissa in 1866*, pp. 17–19.
36 Ibid. para 66, p. 19.
37 Ibid. para 51, p. 13.
38 Ibid. para 57, p. 15.
39 Ibid. para 57, p. 16.
40 See J. A. Voelcker, *Improvement of Indian Agriculture*, Abstract of Report, p. 462.

41 See Ibid. p. 446.
42 See Home (Public) Progs., July 1881, No. 19 of 1881 (Sec. of State of Govt. of India, No. 55—Revenue—16 June 1881.)
43 See para 124 of the *Famine Commission's Report*, Part I, in Home (Public) A Progs., July 1881, No. 31.
44 See Ibid. para 125, No. 31.
45 Home (Public) A Progs., July 1881, No. 19 (para 4 of the letter).
46 Ibid. para 4.
47 Home (Public) A Progs., Nos. 131–4, dated 10 June 1871.
48 Ibid. (despatch from Sec. of State, No. 61 dated 22 Sept. 1870), paras 2–4.
49 Ibid. para 6.
50 See Home (Public) Cons., No. 91–102 (Govt. of India Letter No. 40 dated 6 April 1870, para 5).
51 Ibid. para 4.
52 Ibid. para 11.
53 This constitution of a separate Secretariat was authorized by the Sec. of State under his despatch No. 16, dated 27 April 1871. See Home (Public) Cons., Nos. 131–4 (10 June 1871).
54 Quoted by C. L. Tupper of the I.C.S. in his Note on the same subject. See *Report of the Indian Famine Commission* (1880), Part I (Famine Relief), Appx. I, Sec. III—Agricultural Training.
55 See Misra, *The Bureaucracy in India*, pp. 78–80.
56 *Report of the Indian Famine Commission (1880)*, App. I, Sec. III—Agricultural Training (Note on Agricultural Training for Civilians by C. L. Tupper).
57 Ibid. Note on Agricultural Departments in India by E. C. Buck.
58 See Commission's Report, Part II, Chap. 14, Sec. III.
59 See Home (Public) Progs., July 1883, Nos. 188 to 192, dealing not only with agriculture, but also with the training of junior civilians in surveying, which the Govt. of Bengal considered essential for purposes of cadastral survey in the permanently settled districts.
60 See Ibid.
61 See Home (Public) Progs., Sept. 1883, Nos. 70 & 71 (letter to S/S dated 1 Sept. 1883).
62 See Ibid. paras 3–5.
63 Quoted in Ibid. para 10.
64 See Revenue and Agriculture Dept., Sept. 1886 (Agriculture Progs., Nos. 2 to 3½), File No. 122, Serial Nos. 1 & 2. Buck emphasized the importance of the study of agriculture as part of a regular system of education in India where increasing unemployment arising from literary education had started causing political discontent.
65 Comparable to the present Block Development Officer or Circle Officer who preceded him.
66 See J. A. Voelcker, *Report on the Improvement of Indian Agriculture*, 2nd ed., p. 454.
67 Ibid. p. 455.
68 Ibid. p. 462.
69 Ibid. p. 463.
70 Ibid. p. 464.
71 Ibid. p. 364.

72 Ibid. p. 466.

73 *Summary of the Administration of Lord Curzon*, Jan. 1899 to April 1904, p. 3, para 4.

74 Ibid. para 5, p. 3.

75 See Govt. of India Res. No. 11–294–3 of 20 December 1900.

76 See *Summary of the Administration of Lord Curzon*, Part I, para 10, pp. 7–8. The first Inspector–General was J. Mollison, at the time Deputy Director of Agriculture, Bombay. By 1884 every major province had an Agriculture Department under a Director, but the work of these departments was mainly confined to the simplification of revenue settlement procedure and improvement of the land records system. See *Royal Commission on Decentralization* (1907–09), para 318 (Agriculture).

77 *Summary of the Administration of Lord Curzon*, Part I, p. 13. These principles later found expression in the *Report on Vocational Education in India (1937)* by Wood and Abbott, and subsequently in Gandhi's concept of basic education. But the poor quality of teaching personnel and the manner in which these principles were applied could not accomplish their aims. See Misra, *The Indian Middle Classes*, pp. 296–9.

78 See Rev. and Agril. A Progs., Sept. 1905, Nos. 14–18.

79 Earlier, Madras and Bombay had each a European Deputy Director. A Deputy Director was sanctioned for U.P. in 1901, for Bengal in 1904, and for the Punjab and the Central Provinces in 1905. A limited number of experts, such as agricultural chemists and economic botanists, were also in Madras and Bombay. See *Summary of the Administration of Lord Curzon*, Part II, chap. III, para 2.

80 Ibid. Part I, para 17.

81 Ibid. Part II, Chap. III, para 8, p. 50.

82 Ibid. Part I, para 16, p. 11.

83 Chapters V and IX provide an analysis of rural classes and their changing relationships under the impact of land legislation in modern times.

84 *Summary of the Administration of Lord Curzon*, Part I, para 38.

85 Ibid. para 38.

86 The Commission consisted of J. B. Richey, A. Lyon, A. Colvin (All civil Servants) and Shumbhoo Prasad Luxmeelal. Colvin was later sent to the North–Western Provinces and replaced by Carpenter, a Bengal Civilian, who died suddenly. See *Report of the Committee on the Riots in Poona and Ahmednagar (1875)* submitted by J. B. Richey to the Bombay Govt.

87 Chapt. I, para 12 of the *Deccan Riot Commission Report*.

88 Ibid.

89 Ibid. para 17.

90 *Deccan Riot Commission Report*: App. B (Preliminary Digest of Evidence, pp. 353–65), p. 353.

91 Ibid. pp. 54–5. The Administration Report of Bombay for 1873–4 also admitted that only 14 per cent of the cases were contested, 69.5 per cent being decreed or dismissed *ex-parte*. Ibid. p. 357.

92 Ibid. p. 355.

93 Ibid. pp. 363–4.

94 *Report of the Deccan Riot Commission*, App. A, para 44.

95 See *Report of the Deccan Riot Commission*: Minutes by J. B. Richey, G. W. Carpenter, A. Lyon and Shumbhoo Prasad Luxmeelal, pp. 43–6.

96 Ibid. p. 53.
97 Ibid. p. 102 (IV. Reduction of Enhanced Assessment by the Govt.).
98 See Misra, *The Administrative History of India, 1834–1947*, pp. 538–57.
99 See Misra, *The Indian Middle Classes*, chap. XII.
100 See Home (Judl.) A Progs., March, 1874, No. 280, para 6.
101 I.O. MSS. Eur. C. 144, no. 17, F. 2, 23 June 1886.
102 Ibid. no. 17, F. 2.
103 See *Summary of the Administration of Lord Curzon*, para 41, p. 24.
104 See Misra, *The Indian Middle Classes*, pp. 355–6.
105 See *Summary of the Administration of Lord Curzon*, Part I, para 42, pp. 25–6.
106 See Govt. of India letter no. 1130–176–3 of 27 July 1905 to the Govt. of United Provinces, cited in the *Summary of the Administration of Lord Curzon*, Part I, para 43, p. 27.
107 Ibid. para 44, p. 27.
108 Ibid. para 46, p. 27.
109 Ibid.
110 Ibid. para 49.
111 See *Report of the Royal Commission on Decentralization (1909)*, Chap. IV, p. 79.
112 Under the Govt. of India Res. No. 13–61–16 dated 13 September 1901.
113 *Summary of the Administration of Lord Curzon*, (Confidential) in the Public Works Dept., para 8, p. 4.
114 Ibid.
115 Ibid. paras 79–81.
116 Ibid. para 82.
117 See despatch to the Sec. of State, No. 36 of 7 December 1905, and enclosures, in the Dept. of Rev. and Agriculture.
118 *Report on Indian Constitutional Reforms* 1928 reprint, Cd. 9109, p. 3.

III. DECENTRALIZATION AND DEVELOPMENT, 1905–35

1 See 3 & 4 Will. iv. S. 39.
2 Financial Progs., 15 Dec. 1843, Nos. 1–4.
3 Colchester, *History of the Indian Administration of Lord Ellenborough*, in Correspondence with the Duke of Wellington, p. 445.
4 Under the arrangement of 1882 the Imperial heads in major provinces included customs, salt, opium, posts and telegraphs, and the bulk of receipts from railways and irrigation. The divided heads, on the other hand, were forests, excise, the licence (later income) tax, stamps, and registration (previously provincialized). The receipts classified as 'Provincial rates' were made entirely provincial. The balance of provincial outlays was met from land revenue, which was otherwise classed as Imperial. See Misra, *The Administrative History of India*. pp. 380–1.
5 Ibid., p. 384.
6 See *Report of the Royal Commission on Decentralization*, pp. 25–6.
7 The covenanted and the uncovenanted services of general administration have been discussed at length in *The Administrative History of India, 1834–1947*, Chap. II, and in *The Bureaucracy in India: An Historical Analysis of Development up to 1947*.
8 See *Report of the Royal Commission on Decentralization*, p. 77.

9 See Ibid. pp. 107–8.

10 Burma and the Central Provinces had, in addition, a Chief Conservator.

11 These grades were as below:

	Extra-Deputy Conservators	Extra-Assistant Conservaters
1st Grade	Rs 600	Rs 350
2nd Grade	Rs 550	Rs300
3rd Grade	Rs 500	Rs 250
4th Grade	Rs 450	Rs 200

See A. R. Tucker's Note on Forest Admn. in the Committee for Decentralization Comn., para 7.

12 See *Report of the Royal Comn. on Decent.*, p. 106.

13 Ibid. p. 108.

14 See A.R. Tucker's Note on Forest Admn. in the Committee for Decentralization Comn., para 28.

15 See *Report of the Royal Commission on Decentralization*, p. 109.

16 See Decentralization Committee for the Royal Commission on Decentralization (Education) para 11.

17 See Home (Medl.) File No. 41A of March 1885. The designation of IGCH was approved by the Sec. of State in his Military letter No. 12 of 22 Jan. 1885, para 32. The earlier designation in the case of Bengal, N.–W, Provinces and Punjab was Deputy Surgeon-General, which became IGCH in 1885.

18 Ibid. (Medl.), Part IV, para. 11. See also Home (Pub.). File Nos. 88–101A, Sept. 1867; also Home (Pub.) A File Nos. 2–3, 5 Sept. 1865.

19 See Home (Sany.) File Nos. 88–89A of May 1884 (Despatch in Finance and Commerce Dept. to Sec. of State, No. 52 of 26 Feb. 1884, para 2. The Deputy Surgeon-General was, before 1885, the administrative head of the medical dept. in Provinces other than Madras and Bombay.

20 Ibid.

21 It formed part of 'Medical Research Laboratories' intended for the study of health problems in India on the basis of bacteriological experiments. The Central Research Institute had originally been proposed to be established at Mukteshwar in the Himalayas. But on objections raised by the Sec. of State the site was changed to Kasauli. See Home (Medl.) File Nos. 39–43A of Feb. 1901.

22 Madras and Bombay appointed their own Sanitary Commissioners. See *Report of the Royal Comn. on Decentralization* (1909), paras 377, 383, 384.

23 See Home (Rev. & Agr.) A Progs., Nos. 12–44, Nov. 1905 (File No. 81 of 1905), from Govt. of India to Sec. of State, No. 356 of 26 Oct. 1905, paras 1–2.

24 Ibid. paras 1 and 3. Rs 20 lakhs were set apart annually for research in addition to budgetary allocation which had increased from Rs 9½ lakhs in 1902–3 to 18 lakhs in 1905–6.

25 Ibid. para 31.

26 See home (Rev. & Agr.) A Progs. Nos. 1–8, Aug. 1906 (file No. 66 of 1906), Letter from Sec. of State to Govt. of India, No. 17 (Rev.) of 26 Jan. 1906, para 2.

27 See Home (Educ.) A Progs., Nos. 55–7, dated March 1904.

28 Cited in Home (Rev. & Agr.) A Progs., Nos. 14–18, dated September 1905 from Home (Educ.) A Progs., Nos. 19–26, dated August 1896.

29 See Home (Rev. & Agr.) A Progs., Nos. 14–18, dated Sept. 1905, p. 4.

30 The Director of Agriculture was to be a member of the I.C.S.
31 See Rev. & Agr. A Progs., Agriculture, Nov. 1906, Nos. 1–20 (India Office to Sec., Govt. of India, 14 Sept. 1906).
32 From Sec. of State to Govt. of India, No. 17 (Feb.) dated 26 Jan. 1906, para 7, in Agr. A Progs., Nos. 1–8, Aug. 1906 (File No. 66 of 1906).
33 Ibid. para 4.
34 See Ibid. Serial Nos. 7 and 8 (A Progs., Aug. 1906, 1–8, F. 66).
35 From Sec. of State to Govt. of India, No. 226 (Rev.), 14 Dec. 1906, para 4. (A Progs., Nos. 38–9, Jan. 1907, F. 14 of 1907).
36 See Govt. of India, Finance & Commerce Dept. Res. No. 3353 of 30 Sept. 1881 and letters to Local Govts., 10 October 1881. See also Misra, *The Administrative History of India*, Chap. VIII, giving an account of the pre-British position and its modification in the early British period with subsequent developments.
37 See I.O. MSS. Eur. C. 144/3, p. 122 (Ripon to Kimberley, 21 May 1883).
38 Ibid. para 5.
39 *Decentralization Committee for the Royal Comn. on Decentralization*, Note on Local Boards, pp. 2–3.
40 Ibid. p. 5.
41 See India Act I of 1883 and XVI of 1903 for the Central Provinces; India Act XX of 1883 and XX of 1891 for the Punjab; U.P. Act I of 1900 and III of 1906; Bengal Act III of 1884 and III of 1885; Madras Act IV of 1884 and V of 1884; Bombay Act I of 1884 and III of 1901.
42 See para 25 (p. 14) of the *Report*. The Indian Council Act (1909) provided for an Executive Council for each of the Lieutenant-Governorships also. It partially comprised Indian Members functioning in the context of a non-official majority in the local legislature. With the local leaders appointed to their Executive Councils the Lieutenant-Governorships were induced to assert themselves in the same way as Madras and Bombay earlier did in provincial matters.

With the annulment of the Partition of Bengal the Bengali speaking divisions of the old province were reunited and placed under a Governor in Council with its capital at Calcutta in April 1912, the seat of the Govt. of India being removed to Delhi. Bihar and Orissa formed a separate Lieutenant-Governorship while Assam became a Chief Commissionership.

43 See Misra, *The Bureaucracy in India*, pp. 93–151; *The Administrative History of India*, pp. 215–26
44 See Misra, *The Administrative History of India*, pp. 496–7.
45 Burma and the Punjab had each a Financial Commissioner. The Central Provinces which had earlier no Board of Revenue, later adopted the Punjab arrangement by appointing a Financial Commissioner.
46 See Misra, *The Bureaucracy in India*, Chap. III.
47 See *Report*, para 487, p. 171.
48 Ibid. para 492, p. 173.
49 Ibid. paras. 551–2, p. 193.
50 Ibid. paras 392–3, p. 138.
51 Ibid. para 537, p. 188.
52 Ibid. para. 490, p. 172.
53 Ibid. para. 527, p. 185.
54 Ibid. para 529, p. 185.

55 Ibid. p. 187, f.n.
56 Ibid. para. 523, p. 184.
57 Ibid.
58 Quoted in Montford Report, p. 6.
59 See *Report*, para. 674, p. 231.
60 Home (Pub.) Letter to Sec. of State, No. 7 of 21 March, 1907, I.O. MSS. Eur. D. 573 (Council Reforms), para. 43).
61 Ibid. para. 46.
62 The contributory factors and the circumstances that led to the announcement of 20 August 1917 have been examined by the author in *The Administrative History of India 1834–1947*, pp. 57–69.
63 See Misra, *The Bureaucracy in India*, p. 214.
64 Chamberlain Papers, AC., 22/91 (Secret Minute by the Sec. of State for India). See also Misra, *The Indian Political Parties*, Chap. III on the beginning of mass involvement in politics.
65 Morley to Minto, 8 Jan. 1908, I.O. MSS. Eur. D. 573/3, P. 8.
66 Pp. 70–1.
67 Of the total number of 1,387 Europeans and Indians employed in the I.C.S. on 1 July 1922, Indians held only 208 or 15 per cent of the I.C.S. posts. See Misra, *The Bureaucracy in India*, p. 235.
68 Ibid. p. 238.
69 Ibid. p. 252 and Home (Ests.) File No. 178 of 1924 and 28 Feb. 1925.
70 Sec. of State to Govt. of India, No. 17 (Rev.) dated 26 Jan. 1906, para 4.
71 See File No. 67 of 1911 (Agr.), B Progs., for Feb. 1911, Nos. 49–51. The information in the chart contains designations, names of incumbents, dates of birth, dates of appointment to the department, pay and allowances.
72 From Sec. to Govt. of India to Local Govts. Nos. 650–6 dated 16 June 1911, para. 2 (A Progs., Nos. 1 to 3, Agriculture, July 1911), File No. 194 of 1911.
73 Ibid. (From Sec. of State to Govt. of India, No. 52 (Rev.) of 12 May 1911, para. 2–3).
74 See Agr. A Progs, Nos, 13 to 18 (May 1912), File No. 294 of 1911.
75 Ibid. para. 1, p. 349.
76 Ibid. para 2.
77 Ibid. para.3.
78 Ibid. para. 4.
79 See Ibid. tel. from Sec. of State to Viceroy dated 1 Nov. 1911.
80 See Ibid. Serial No. 4.
81 Ibid. Serial No. 6 (Finance Despatch No. 82 of 1912 to Sec. of State).
82 See Agr. A Progs., Aug. 1921, Nos. 14–19 (File No. 393 of 1920).
83 See Ibid. and General A Progs., Oct. 1919, No. 1 to 6 in File No. 204 of 1919 (Dept. of Rev. and Agr.)
84 See Home Dept. File No. 28/27-Special.
85 See Govt. of India Resolution No. 826–Agr. of 23 March 1929, Agr. A Progs., July 1929, Nos. 75–83.
86 Home Dept. File No. 101/28–Special, para. 2. The pre-Reforms position of agricultural development in the provinces is described in their Administration Reports for relevant years.
87 Ibid. paras. 5–6, pp. 7–8.
88 See tel. to Sec. of State, No. 635–AGRI, dated 24 April 1929 and Govt. of India

Resolution No. 826 AGRI, dated 23 May 1929 (Agr. A Progs., July 1929, No. 75–83).

89 The Council was registered under the Registration of Societies Act XXI of 1860, not constituted under an Act of the Imperial legislature as recommended by the Royal Commission.

90 The representatives elected by the Inter–University Board were Dr N. N. Ganguli, Khaira Professor of Agriculture, Calcutta University; Dr Leslie Coleman, Director of Agriculture, Mysore; C. T. Mudaliyar, Principal, Agricultural College, Coimbatore; and K. K. Hyder, Professor of Economics, Aligarh Muslim University.

91 See Agr. B (Print) Progs., July 1930, Nos. 81–3.

92 See Dept. of Educ., Health and Lands File No. 57–15/39-A, Serial Nos. 1–5.

93 See Agr. B (Print) Progs., 1930–39 containing the class of powers delegated and the Govt. of India's orders thereon.

94 See General Summary (Review) No. 2 of 1935 (New Delhi, 6 March 1935).

95 Cited in Home (Sany.) Progs., Oct. 1895, no. 164, p. 29.

96 Ibid. p. 27.

97 See Ibid. p. 30.

98 Dr Simpson was at the time Health Officer of Calcutta.

99 Ibid. p. 3.

100 Ibid. p. 1.

101 See Ibid. pp.. 27–31.

102 Of the 247 districts in British India and Burma in 1936, only 128 employed medical officers of health; in the remaining 119 districts the Civil Surgeon functioned as district medical officer, responsible for public health administration. See Blunt (ed.), *Social Services in India*, p.196.

103 Home (Med.) Part B Progs., March 1914, Nos.68–9.

104 Hom (Med.) Part B Progs., March 1914, No. 68, pp. 2–3.

105 See Home (Med.) File Nos. 37–55A, Dec. 1910, pp. 260–3

106 Ibid. p. 255.

107 See File Nos 6–7 B Home (Med.), June 1914, containing Resolution of the Govt. of India, Nos. 888–908, dated 23 May 1914, paras 13–16. It is very comprehensive Resolution on the progress of public health.

108 Ibid. para. 7.

109 Ibid. para. 4.

110 See Home (Sany.) File 9D, May 1919, giving an account of the Imperial grants to the Local Governments for urban sanitation from 1911 onwards.

111 See Home (Health) A Progs., May 1925, Nos. 17–28.

112 Ibid.

113 See Blunt, *Social Services in India*, p. 194.

114 See Appendix to the Sixth Report from the Provinces on the action taken by each of them to give effect to the recommendations of the Royal Commission on Agriculture during 1936 and 1937, in respect of item Nos. 47 and 48, Recommendations 12–13, 15–17 and 19.

115 See Govt. of India, E. H. & Ls. Dep. to the Govt. of Bihar, Rev. Dept., No. F. 243/37-A, dated 27 Aug. 1937 in reply to Bihar Govt. letter No. 243/37 raising a question whether under the federal constitution of 1935 it was open to central legislative to discuss provincial subjects and call for the supply of information on the same.

IV. LOCAL BODIES AND RURAL DEVELOPMENT

1 See B. B. Misra, *The Administrative History of India*, p. 327.
2 Maine, *Village-Communities in the East and West*, 7th ed., 1913, pp. 107–9.
3 See pp. 388–9 (1905 ed.).
4 *Village-Communities in the East and West*, pp. 122–3.
5 Ibid. p. 124.
6 Ibid. p. 125.
7 *The Indian Village Community*, p. 3. See also Misra, *The Administrative History of India*, pp. 414–22, where the village communities of joint proprietors, the main features of land tenure in the. N. W. Provinces, have been discussed in some depth.
8 See Ibid. p. 9.
9 See Misra, *The Administrative History of India*, pp. 412–14.
10 See Baden Powell, *The Indian Village Community*, pp. 14–15. The village accountant was called *patwari* in U.P., Bengal and Bihar. In Madras he was known as *Karnam*. The equivalent post in Bombay was that of *kulkarni* or *talati*.
11 See Misra, *The Administrative History of India*, p. 435.
12 See Misra, *The Central Administration of the East India Company, 1773–1834*, p. 42.
13 See Misra, *The Administrative History of India*, p. 4.
14 Sharp, *Sets*:, p. 116.
15 *Moral and Material Progress Report*, 1881–2, p. 145.
16 See MacDonnell's Note in Home (Pub.) Progs., April 1888, Nos. 31–8, para. 44.
17 Ibid. paras. 59–60.
18 Ibid. para 65.
19 Ibid. para 78.
20 See Misra, *The Administrative History of India*, pp. 622–3.
21 *Report of the Administration of Bengal*, 1891–2, Part II, p. 95. The area covered by the districts was 110,043 square miles with a population of 61,787,908.
22 See Ibid. pp. 95–6.
23 See Ibid. p. 96.
24 Ibid. p.97.
25 *Report on the Administration of Bengal*, 1892–3. Part I (Survey and Settlement), pp. 54–7.
26 See the Reports from Commissioners of Divisions on the Working of District Boards in Bengal during 1908–9, *Statistics of British India*, Part VIII (Local Funds), pp. 53–4.
27 See Reports from Commissioners of Divisions on the Working of District Boards in Bengal during 1893–4 (Resolution No. 4294, L.S.G., Calcutta, 3 Dec. 1895), para 12.
28 See Ibid. for 1907–8, p. 52, para. 275.
29 The income derived from civil works, education and medical for the same year was Rs 11,98,685, Rs 47,900 and Rs 62,912 respectively.
30 See Reports from Commissioners of Divisions on the Working of District Boards in Bengal during 1908–9, Statistics of British India, Part VIII–Local Funds, pp. 54–5.
31 See Ibid. p. 57.
32 See Ibid. p. 59.
33 See Misra, *The Administrative History of India, 1834–1947*, p. 628.

34 Report of the Administration of the Madras Presidency, 1935–6, p. xii.
35 Ibid. xii.
36 See *A Review of the Administration of the Presidency of Bombay, 1922–3*, pp. 95–6.
37 Ibid.
38 *Administration Report of Bombay*, 1920–1, p. 58.
39 See Letter to Govt. of Bengal, No. 70 L.S.G., dated 9 Aug. 1920. See Also *Reports of Local Governments on the Working of the Reformed Constitution*, 1923, I.O. Part. Papers, Cmd. 2361 [Report from Bihar & Orissa, Letter No. 1362-C, dated 14 Aug. 1923, para 33 (i)]. The Bihar & Orissa report points out that 'the transfer of local administration from official to non-official hands had already commenced before the Reforms Scheme was inaugurated, but the process has perhaps been expedited by the Constitutional Change'. The privilege of having a non-official chairman was first given to the District Boards of Patna, Bhagalpur and Cuttack before 1919.
40 See Resolution No. 4294. L. S. G., dated 3 Dec. 1895, para. 62.
41 Ibid. para. 62. The Commissioners of Dacca and Patna were in full agreement with Westmacott. The Patna Commissioner even went so far as to affirm that 'with a few notable exceptions' District Boards 'are not fit, and probably never will be fit, to be left to manage their affairs themselves'. Ibid. para 62.
42 From J. T. Renkin, Comr. Dacca Div., to Govt. of Bengal, No. 4847 J, dated 8 Sept. 1920, para. 31.
43 See Views of the Divisional Commissioners contained in the Reports and Resolutions of Bengal Government in the Local Self-Govt. Dept. for 1891–2, 1893–4, 1894–5, 1919–20, 1923 and so on.
44 See Comr. Presidency Div. to Govt. of Bengal, No. 70 L. S. G., dated 9 Aug. 1920, para 18.
45 See Chapter XIV, 'The Village', paras. 401–3, 411.
46 The letter enclosed the Report of the Govt. of Bihar on progress during 1936–7 in giving effect to the recommendations of the Royal Commission on Agriculture in India—See para. 101 of the Report.
47 Comr. Presidency Division to Govt. of Bengal, No. 70 L. S. G., dated 9 Aug. 1920, para. 17.
48 See Letter from Cmr., Dacca Division to Govt. of Bengal, No. 3980–J., dated 18 Aug. 1923, para. 17.
49 Comr., Dacca Division to Govt. of Bengal, No. 4847J, dated 8 Sept. 1920, para 6.
50 Ibid. para 31 (General).
51 See I. O. Parl, Papers, Comd. 2361 of 1925.
52 See Ibid. Cmd. 2362 of 1925.
53 See Ibid. Cmd. 2360 of 1925: I. O. Record Dept. No. (19) 4964.
54 See *Indian District Boards Administration Report*, 1921–2, pp. 1–2.
55 See Ibid. pp. 3–4.
56 *Resolution Reviewing the Reports on the District Boards in Bengal during 1923–4*, para 3, p. 1.
57 See Bengal Govt. Resolution (No. 143 L. S. G.) of 25 Jan. 1923, para 12. The names of important District Board Chairmen mentioned are: Raja Moni Lal Singh Roy, C. I. E. (Burdwan); Rai Abinash Chandra Banerji Bahadur (Birbhum); Babu Baroda Prosad De (Hooghly); Rai Ashutosh Bose Bahadur

(Howrah); Rai Sahib Bama Charan Ray (Bankura); Raja Reshicase Law, C. I. E. (24–Parganas); Maharaja Kshaunish Chandra Ray Bahadur (Nadia); Babu Bijoy Krishna Mitra (Jessore); Rai Amrit Lal Raha Bahadur (Khulna); Nawab Khajeh Muhammad Yusuff, Khan Bahadur (Dacca); Khan Bahadur Maulvi Syed Hossain Chaudhury (Mymensingh); Khan Bahadur Hemayatuddin Ahmed (Bakarganj); Maulvi Majibal Hyder Chaudhury (Noakhali); Khan Bahadur Maulvi Emaduddin Ahmed (Rajshahi); Rai Bahadur Kali Pada Banerji (Jalpaiguri); Khan Sahib Syed Riyazuddin Qazi (Bogra).

58 Govt. of Bihar and Orissa (Ministry of Local Self-Government) Resolution No. 3233 L. S. G., dated 22 March 1923, para 15.

59 Ibid. para 6 (b).

60 Ibid. para. 7.

61 The rise of Indian capitalism was recognized by the appointment of the Indian Industrial Commission in 1916 and the development of science and technology that followed. See Misra, *The Indian Middle Classes*, p. 293, 333–4.

62 The local rates, as the table indicates, increased from Rs 23,56,721 in 1912–13 to Rs 70,20,011 in 1921–2. See Govt. of Bihar and Orissa (Ministry of Local Self-Govt.) Resolution No. 3233 L.S.G., dated 22 March 1923, para 7.

63 *Report of the Local Government on the Working of the Reformed Constitution*, Cmd. 2361 of 1924, para 32.

64 Report of the Indian Statutory Commission, IX, 442.

65 See U.P. Local Self-Govt. Resolution No. 212/IX–7–1922, dated 16 March, 1923, para 2–3.

66 Ibid. para. 3.

67 See Ibid. para. 5.

68 See Resolution of the U.P. Govt. in the Local Self–Govt. Dept., No. 609, 25 June 1925.

69 Ibid. para. 10

70 Ibid. para. 12.

71 Ibid. para. 13.

72 See Hugh Tinker, *The Foundations of Local Self-Government in India, Pakistan and Burma*, p. 135.

73 See *Report on the Administration of the Punjab*, 1919–20, para. 37.

74 See *Punjab Administration Report*, ii, Chap. iii, para. 21. The volume deals with the functioning of Local Self-Government during 1921–2.

75 Ibid. para. 22.

76 Ibid. para. 25.

77 Local Self-Govt. Dept. Resolution (No. 383/192–VIII, 15 February 1923). Reviewing the Reports on the Working of District Councils in the Central Provinces and Berar for 1921–2, para. 6.

78 See Govt. of Bihar, Development Dept. to Sec., Govt. of India, Dept. of Education, Health and Lands, No. 1122–D, dated 5 May 1938.

79 See Govt. of Bombay, Rev. Dept. to Govt. of India, Dept. of Education, Health and Lands, No. 1446–A/28, 21 July 1938, enclosing *Sixth–Reoprt showing the Progress made in giving effect to the recommendations of the Royal Commission on Agriculture in India up to the end of 1937* [For official use only].

80 See Govt. of C. P. and Berar, Agr. Dept. to Govt. of India in the Dept. of Education, Health and Lands, No. 1063. 933–X, dated 18 June 1938 enclosing *Statement showing the action taken by Central Provinces and Berar Govt. on the Recommenda-*

tion of the Royal Commission on Agriculture during the years 1936, 1937.

81 The reports consulted were those of Bengal, Madras, Punjab and U.P.

82 See Resident for Rajputana to Govt. of India in the Dept. of Education, Health and Lands, No. 45–G/38, 15 Feb. 1938, para 4 (f).

83 See Govt. of Bengal, in Rev. Dept. to Govt. of India, in the Dept. of Education, Health and Lands, No. 3892–Misc., 21 Feb. 1938, para 1.

84 Govt. of Madras in the Rev. Dept. to the Govt. of India in the Dept. of Education, Health and Lands, No. 546, 26 Feb, 1938, enclosing memorandum on economic condition, agricultural distress and relief measures, in reply to Govt. of India, No. 17–1/38--A, dated 21 Jan. 1938. See also annexure on press communique under Govt. Order No. 2627, dated 16 Dec. 1937, indicating the scope of the Collector's functions in terms of relief against agricultural distress.

85 See Appendix to the *Sixth Report from the Provinces on the action taken to give effect to the recommendations of the Royal Commission on Agriculture* in regard to item No. 47, Recommendation No. 12 (Rural Medical Relief).

86 *Bihar and Orissa in 1926–7*, pp. 5 and 32.

87 Ibid. p. 5. Congress leaders like A. N. Sinha and Sri Krishna Sinha were chairmen of one or other of the District Boards in Bihar before they got elected to the provincial legislature.

88 Ibid. pp. 7–8.

89 Ibid. p. 8.

90 *Bihar in 1937–8*, pp. 126–7.

91 See *Report of the Administration of the United Provinces*, 1942, XI, para 46.

92 Ibid, p. 24.

93 *Report of Bengal Administration Enquiry Committee 1944–5*, p. 17.

94 Ibid. p. 18.

95 Ibid. p. 18.

96 Ibid.

97 Ibid. p. 21.

98 Ibid. p. 22.

99 Ibid. pp. 110–11.

100 Ibid. p. 111.

101 Bihar and U. P. enacted legislation on panchayats in 1947; Orissa in 1948; Punjab in 1952; Bengal in 1957, and Maharashtra in 1960. See File No. 4/2/60 (Training I) Dept. of Community Development, Govt. of India.

102 Extracts from notes on Political Dept., File No. 449–R(S)/44, Serial No. 1 and Serial No. 2 in Secret File No. F. 30/45–R, Secretariat of the Govt. Gen. (Reforms).

103 From Chief Sec., Madras, to Govt. of India (Home Dept.), No. 532 of 28 July 1924, para 31 (*Reports of Local Govts. on the Working of the Reformed Constitution*, 1924, p. 45.)

104 See *Memoranda submitted to the Indian Statutory Commission by the Government of India*, Chap. IV (Communal Representation in the Legislature and Local Bodies), pp. 121–83.

105 Chief Sec., Bombay, to Govt. of India, No. 4206–C, 19 July 1927 in *Views of Local Governments on the Reforms*, 1927, p. 117.

106 Ibid. See also *Report of the Local Governments on the Working of the Reformed Constitution*, I. O. Parl. Papers, Cmd., 2361 and 2362 of 1925.

107 Chief Sec., U. P., to Govt. of India, 3 July 1924, para. 12, p. 167.

108 Tinker, *Foundations of Local Self-Government in India, Pakistan and Burma*, p. 312.
109 See *Views of the Local Governments on the Working of the Reforms*, 1927, I. O. Parl. Papers, Cmd. 70–230, pp. 16–35
110 *Report of the Committee Appointed by the United Provinces Legislative Council to Cooperate with the Indian Statutory Commission*, 1929, p. 54.

V. ALTERNATIVES TO LOCAL BODIES AND RURAL DEVELOPMENT

1 No. F. 2–/42–A. of the Dept. of Education, Health and Lands, New Delhi. See Govt. of Bihar, Development and Employment Dept. (Agriculture Branch) File No. 10A–16/43, B Progs., Dec. 236–275/43.
2 See Ibid.
3 See Bihar Govt., Development and Employment Dept. File No. 10 A–52/42, Progs., No. Dec. 568–71/42 (enclosing letter from Joint Sec., Bihar Landholders' Assn. to Sec. to Govt.).
4 Letter from the Govt. of India (Dept. of Education, Health and Lands), No. F. 20–22/44–P, 22 June 1944, para 10.
5 Ibid. para 2.
6 Ibid. para 8.
7 Ibid. paras 10–11.
8 Govt. of Bihar, Development and Employment Dept. File No. 9A–3 of 1944, Progs., Nos. Dec. 1558–1577/1946. E. R. J. R. Cousins was Chairman of the Committee.
9 Ibid.
10 Ibid.
11 Addressed to the Chief Sec. Bihar Govt., the letter of 24 November 1945 was included in its Rev. Dept., L. R. Branch File No. IVM–565/45, Progs. No. 181–6/468, para 1.
12 Ibid. para 2.
13 See *Report of the Grow More Food Inquiry Committee*, published in June 1952. It emerged in fact as a 'Rural Development Committee', giving rise to the community development programme and the national extension movement. See Note by Thakurdas Bhargava, M.P., a members of the G. M. F. Inquiry Commission. See Supplement to the Report, p. 1.
14 See *Revised Post-War Development Plan for Bihar*, No.53–1/50: *Post-War Reconstruction and Development Programme, 1948–49*, Govt. of Bombay (Sinha Library, Patna, Records Nos. 1475 and 1721; also No. 1456).
15 *Report of the Bengal Administration Enquiry Committee*, 1944–5, para 384.
16 Ibid. para 386.
17 Ibid. para 11.
18 See V. T. Krishnamachari, *National Extension Movement*, CPA Series, No. 27, p. 4.
19 See *Report*, 1944–5, para 18.
20 The co-ordination of the 'machinery of government' included such matters as personnel management and conditions of service, not the general policy which belonged to the Cabinet.

21 See *Report*, para 58.
22 The Balvantray Mehta Committee Report was signed on 24 November 1957.
23 *Report of the Bengal Administration Inquiry Committee*, 1944–5, para 36.
24 Ibid. para 83.
25 Ibid. para 65.
26 Ibid. para 77.
27 See Granvills Austin, *The Indian Constitution* (OUP, 1972), p. 35.
28 See Govt. of India File No. 11/57–58–Adm., pp. 5–7 (Transfer of the subject of village panchayats to the Ministry of Com. Development). Co-operation was added to it and the Ministry renamed the Ministry of Community Development and Co-operation. See Govt. of India File No. 7(3A)/59–Adm.
29 Govt. of India, Min. of C.D. and Co-operation File No. 4/6/60–Trg. Sec. I, p. 37.
30 Ibid. p. 21.
31 Ibid. pp. 37–8.
32 Govt. of India, Min. of Com. Development, File No. 11/125/58–Admn. I, p. 67.
33 Memorandum No. CPA/A/40/52 (3 Nov. 1952), p. 16.
34 See Appendix I to Estimates Committee Thirty-Eighth Report on Ministry of Community Development (CPA), Part I, pp. 66–79.
35 See Memorandum No. CPA/A/40/52 (3 Nov. 1952), pp. 14–16; also File No. CPA/A/36/(1)/52 (5 April 1952), paras 1–4.
36 See File No. CPA/A/36/52 (5 Aug. 1952), p. 20.
37 See File No. CPA/A/36(1)/52, pp. 1–2.
38 See File No. CPA/A/40/52, p. 17.
39 See File No. F. 11/125/58–Admn. I, Govt. of India, MCD, p. 60.
40 Douglas Ensminger, *Rural India in Transition* (March 1972), p. 6 (Introduction by S. K. Dey).
41 See V. T. Krishnamachari, *National Extension Movement* (Govt. of India, CPA Series No. 27), pp. 2–7. It was issued in September 1955. See also Ensminger, *Rural India in Transition*, pp. 34–47.
42 Ibid. p. 5 of *National Extension Movement*.
43 See Govt. of India, Ministry of Community Development File No. F. 11/125/58–Adm. I.
44 Ibid. p. 64.
45 See Ibid. p. 71.
46 Ibid. p. 75.
47 Ibid. p. 76.
48 See File No. 3/30/60—Training Sec. I (Govt. of India, Ministry of Community Development and Co-operation), p. 186.
49 See File No. F. 11/125/58–Admn. I (Govt. of India, Min. of C.D.), pp. 79–81.
50 See *Community Development Programme in India, 1952–72*, Govt. of India, Ministry of Agriculture, Department of C. D., pp. 21–2.
51 See Estimates Committee, Thirty-Eighth Report (B. C. No. 34). pp. 34–7. Balvantray G. Mehta was its Chairman.
52 Ibid. p. 38, para 301.
53 Ibid. pp. 38–9, para 302.
54 *The Statesman*, 23 Aug. 1978 (Hyderabad), p. 7.
55 See Govt. of India, Ministry of Com. Development and Co-operation, File No. 4/2/60, Trg. Sec. I, pp. 132–3.

56 See Ibid. p. 136.
57 See Ibid.
58 See Ibid.
59 See Ibid.
60 Hiugh Tinker, *Foundation of Local Self-Government in India, Pakistan and Burma*, p. 208.
61 See Govt. of India, Ministry of C. D. and Co-operation File No. 4/6/60, Trg. Sec. I, pp. 21–32.
62 H. S. Maine, *Early History of Institutions*, (7th ed.), p. 388.
63 H. S. Maine, *Village Communities in the East and West* (7th ed.), pp. 110–11.
64 Ibid. p. 111.
65 Govt. of India. M.C.D.C., File No. 4/2/60, Trg. Sec. I, App. D. p. 182.
66 See File Nos. CPA/A/144/53, CPA/A 144(1)/53, CPA/A/36(5)/53, CPA/A/326/54, CPA/A/1(3)/55, CPA/A/10(1)/55, CPA/A/1(8)/55, CPA/A/1(17)/55, and CPA/A/1(22)/55
67 Introduction by S. K. Dey to Ensminger's *Rural India in Transition*, p. 7.
68 Report of the Estimates Committee, 1956, para 38.
69 MCD/A/85/(1)/56.
70 Ibid.
71 See Estimates Committee Report (38th), 1956–7, on the Ministry of C. D. and Community Projects Administration, 1956, part I, p. 15. See also File No. M.C.D./A/1(35)/56. All C.P.A. posts were continued except the post of Administrator.
72 Ibid. p. 14, para, 35.
73 See File No. M.C.D./A/85(1)/56, pp. 3–6.
74 See Govt. of India, Min. of C.D. and C. File No. 13/64/(A) 59 CT, Correspondence, p. 5, para, 4.
75 See *Report of the Team for the Study of Community Projects and National Extension Service*, Vol. I, p.i.
76 See Ibid. Chap. II, paras. 2.15, 2.27 and 38.
77 See Ibid. pp. 5–6, paras. 2.3 to 2.5.
78 Ibid. p. 19, para. 2.38.
79 See B. B. Misra, *The Bureaucracy in India*, where the concept of bureaucratic rationalization has been explained in Chapter III.
80 *Report*, Vol. I, p. 7, para. 2.8.
81 Ibid. p. 6, para. 2.5.
82 See File No. 7(3A)/59–Admn., pp. 5–7.
83 See *Community Development and Panchayati Raj in India 1952–72*, pp. 67–8.
84 See *Report of the Committee on Panchayati Raj Institutions*, pp. 3–4.
85 See *Community Development and Panchayati Raj in India*, 1952–72, pp. 63–4.
86 See *Rural Development*, Directorate of Advertising and Visual Publicity, Ministry of Information and Broadcasting, Govt. of India.
87 See Ibid. pp. 6–7.
88 Ibid. pp. 1–2.
89 *The Asoka Mehta Committee Report*, p. 4.
90 See *Report of the Dantwala Working Group on Block Level Planning*, Planning Commission (cyclostyled), p. 159.
91 *Asoka Mehta Committee Report*, p. 5.

92 V. T. Krishnamachari, *Report on Indian and State Administrative Services and Problems of District Administration* (Aug. 1962), p. 33.
93 See Ibid. p. 47.
94 *A Guide to Community Development* (Revised), Govt. of India, March 1962, p. 2.
95 *Report of the Democratic Dacentralization Committee*, Gujarat State, Part II, p. 24.
96 Ibid. Schedule 9, p. 118.
97 See p. 16 of the *Report*.
98 *Report of a Community Development Evaluation Mission in India*, para 306, p. 70.
99 Ibid. para 315, p. 71.
100 *Report of the Working Group on Block Level Planning* (cyclostyled), Govt. of India, Planning Commission (1978), pp. 139–40.
101 Ibid. p. 37.
102 See Ibid. p. 18.
103 *Report of the Asoka Mehta Committee* pp. 5–6.
104 See pp. 18 and 19 of the *Report*.
105 See Part I of the *Report*, pp. 44–5.
106 See Report of the Dantwala Working Group, p. 23.
107 I consulted the 'Sixth Report' submitted by Provincial Governments for the years 1936 and 1937 as also a report of the action taken by the Centre. The coverage of the provincial reports and their appendices are indicative of the great care that was being taken to promote agriculture before the outbreak of the Second World War.

VI. PERSONNEL QUALITIES AND RESOURCES

1 Morley to Minto, 6 June 1906, I. O. MSS Eur. D. 573/1, p. 119.
2 *Report on Indian Constitutional Reforms* (reprint, 1928) p. 199.
3 See Chamberlain to Chelmsford, 2 May 1917, I. O. MSS. Eur. AC 22/91, p. 9.
4 See Hailey's Note in Hailey Papers, I. O. MSS. Eur. E. 220/30, pp. 174, 175.
5 See Home (Pol.) B Progs., 23 Sept. 1916 (Muhammadan Affairs, para 7).
6 See Home (Pol.) B Progs., March 1920, No. 183.
7 Home (Ests.) File No. 965, p. 9.
8 Home (Ests.) A Progs. May 1921, Nos. 370–6.
9 See *Reports of the Local Governments on the Working of the Reformed Constitution* (Madras), 1927, pp. 433–4.
10 Letter from Chief Sec. Bihar and Orissa, No. 1362 C, dated 14 Aug. 1923, to Sec. to the Govt. of India, Home Dept. I. O. 2361 of 1925, pp. 183–4.
11 Ibid. p. 184.
12 See Misra, *The Bureaucracy in India: An Historical Analysis of Development up to 1947*, Chapter V.
13 *Report on Indian Constitutional Reforms* (reprint, 1928), para. 314, pp. 200–1.
14 Home (Ests.) Progs., 28 Feb. 1925, pp. 55–6.
15 See Home (Ests.) A Progs., March 1920, Nos. 336–408, pp. 482–4.
16 This power was first given to Local Governments under Govt. of India (Home Dept.) Notification No. 598 of 21 June 1918, which authorized them to list additional posts reserved for the I.C.S. with the prior sanction of the Govt. of India and the Sec. of State in Council.

17 See Home Dept. letter No. F. 178/2/24, dated 5/8 Aug. 1924 in Home (Ests.) File No. 178 of 1924.
18 See Misra, *The Bureaucracy in India: An Historical Analysis of Development up to 1947*, pp. 255–62.
19 Quoted in B. Shiva Rao (ed.), *The Framing of India's Constitution: A Study*, p. 721.
20 See para. 3.75 of the *Report of the Study Team on Personnel Administration*, August 1967.
21 See *Seventeenth Report of the Union Public Service Commission*, 1 April, 1966 to 31 March, 1967, para 28 (iii), p. 39.
22 Ibid. para. 28 (i), p. 39.
23 *Reports of the Local Governments on the Working of the Reformed Constitution* (Punjab), I. O. Parl. Papers, Cmd. 2362 of 1925, p. 196.
24 Home (Pol.) File No. 82 and K. W. of 1925, Part I (Confidential), para 10, p. 10.
25 See Home (Ests.) File No. 3 of 1925 (Govt. of India to Sec. of State, 4 June 1925); the exigencies of nomination to the I. C. S. had in fact arisen in the course of the War in 1915, which called for the bulk of appointments being made through nomination. See Memorandum by W. R. Barker, Chairman, Public Service Commission, 1928, in *Indian Statutory Commission Report*, Vol. XV, p. 197.
26 For the definition of the term 'minorities' see Home (Ests.) File No. 14/34, (Confidential, Simla Records, 3).
27 See Home (Ests.) File No. 14/17–B 33, Serial Nos. 1–14. The Resolution is recorded under Serial No. 12.
28 See Misra, *The Bureacracy in India*, pp. 381–2.
29 See *The Government of India (Scheduled Castes) Order*, 1936. It was supplemented by Home (Ests.) Resolution No. 31/14/ (S), 6 Feb. 1945
30 See Misra, *The Bureaucracy in India*, pp. 263–4.
31 See Home (Ests.) File No. 39/4/38 of 1938, pp. 2–3.
32 Secretariat of the Gov.-Gen. (Reforms), File No. 119/45–R (Recognisation of Services to suit Post-War Conditions), para 2.
33 Ibid. para. 7.
34 Ibid. para. 10.
35 The total number of Europeans who so retired was 254. See the Constituent Assembly of India (Legislative) Debates, 19 Nov. 1947, Vol. I, pp. 187–8. As regards Muslim Civilians, there were about 100 before Partition, but only 12 remained in India.
36 See Home (Ests.) Res. No. 23/4/42 of 11 Aug. 1943.
37 See Home (Ests.) Res. No. 16/10/47, 21 Aug. 1947(R).
38 See V. T. Krishnamachari, *Report on Indian and State Administrative Services and Problems of District Administration*, Aug. 1962, p. 72. Krishnamachari, a retired listed post holder, completed this study at the instance of the Planning Commission and with the concurrence of the Ministries of Home Affairs and Community Development.
39 Ibid. p. 10.
40 Ibid. pp. 68–9, Statement I. The I. A. S. cadre included I. C. S. personnel merged with it after the transfer of power.
41 Ibid. p. 8.
42 See Avasthi–Maheshwari, *Public Administration*, 9th ed., pp. 407–8.
43 Cited in V.T. Krishnamachari, *Report on Indian and State Administrative Services and Problems of District Administration*, p. 11.

44 *First Report*, p. 3.
45 *Twenty-First Report of the U.P.S.C.*, pp. 61–2, and *Nineteenth Report*, p. 75.
46 Ibid.
47 *Twenty-First Report of the U.P.S.C.*, p. 62.
48 *Twenty-Second Report of the U.P.S.C.*, p. 25.
49 See *Twenty-Third Report of the U.P.S.C.*, p. 26–7.
50 *Twenty-Second Report of the U.P.S.C.*, p. 49.
51 See S. K. Krishnan, *Reservation in Services*, a paper for trainees at the Institute of Secretariat Training and Management, Establishment Division of the Dept. of Personnel and Administrative Reforms, Govt. of India, 22 August 1974.
52 See *Report on the Management of the Indian Administrative Service*, Vol. I, Dept. of Administrative Reforms, Ministry of Home Affairs, Govt. of India, May 1968 (cyclostyled copy), App. I.
53 Ibid., para 1.3.
54 *Report of the Study Team on Recruitment . . . and Taining,* with Lt.-Gen. S.P.P. Thorat as chairman, June 1967, p. 29.
55 *Report on the Management of the Indian Administrative Service*, May 1968, Vol. I, para 1.10
56 Ibid.
57 Ibid., para 1.6.
58 See Misra, *The Bureaucracy in India*, Chapter VI
59 See B. Sivaraman, *The Role of the Civil Services in the Administration of India* (typed), Training Div., Dept. of personnel, Cabinet Secretariat, New Delhi, Sept. 1970, pp. 27–8.

SELECT BIBLIOGRAPHY

MANUSCRIPTS

INDIA (COMMONWEALTH RELATIONS) OFFICE RECORDS

INDIA (COMMONWEALTH RELATIONS) OFFICE RECORDS

MSS Eur. E, 12	Clive to Court Correspondence.
MSS Eur. C. 144	Dufferin to Northbrook
	Ripon to Kimberley, 21 May 1883.
MSS Eur. D. 573	Council Reforms.
MSS Eur. D. 573/3	Morley to Minto, 8 Jan. 1908.
MSS Eur. D. 573/1	Morley to Minto, 6 June 1906.
MSS Eur. AC.	Chamberlain to Chelmsford, 2 May 1917.
MSS Eur. AC. 22/91	Secret Minute by Sec. of State.
MSS Eur. E. 220/30	Hailey Papers—Notes on Admn.

GOVERNMENT OF INDIA FILES CONTAINING NOTES AND PROCEEDINGS

Home (Pub.) Cons. No. 53 of 11 Aug. 1854 (Minute by J. P. Grant, 24 July 1854 and by Gov.–Gen., 12 July 1854).

Home (Pub.) Cons. No. 45 of 9 Feb. 1855.

Home (Pub.) A file, Nos. 2–3 of 1865 (From Sanitary Commissoner to Govt. of India, No. 620 of 5 Sept. 1864).

Home (Pub.) file, Nos. 88–101A of Sept. 1867.

Home (Pub.)Cons. No. 91–102 (Govt. Letter No. 40 of 6 April 1870).

Home (Pub.) A Progs., Nos. 131–4 of June 1871.

Home (Judl.) A Progs., No. 280 of March 1874 (Importance of excutive action to provide relief).

Home (Pub.) Progs., No. 19 of July 1881 (S/S to Govt. of India (Rev.) No. 55 of 10 June 1881 on tenancy reform).

Home (Pub.) Progs., No. 31 of July 1881.

Home (Pub.) Progs., Nos. 70–1 of Sept. 1883 (Govt. of India to S/S, 1 Sept. 1883).

(Agr) Progs., Nos. 2–3 of Sept. 1886, File No. 122, Serial Nos. 1 and 2 (Emphasis on the Study of Agriculture).
Home (Sanitary) File Nos. 88–89A, May 1884 (Letter to S/S, No. 52 of 26 Feb. 1884).
Home (Sany.) File, Oct. 1887, Nos. 168–79 A.
Home (Pub.) Progs., April 1888, Nos. 31–8.
Home (Pub.) Progs., Nos. 188–192 (Training of Civilians in cadastral survey).
Home (Medical), File No. 41A (Medical Service).
Home (Medl,) File, June 1888, Nos. 137–46 A.
Home (Sany.) Progs., Oct. 1895, Nos. 164.
Home (Medl.) File, June 1895, Nos. 16–17B.
Home (Medl.) File, Oct. 1901, Nos. 71–72A (Position of officers in the Indian Medical Service (Civil).
Home (Medl.) File, Feb. 1901, Nos. 39–43A (Medical Research Laboratories and public health).
Home (Edn.) A Progs., March 1904, Nos. 55–7 (Rural Edn.).
Home (Rev. & Agr.) A Progs., Sept. 1905, Nos. 14–18.
Home (Rev. & Agr.) A Progs., Aug. 1906 (File No. 66 of 1906 (Correspondence with S/S).
Home (Rev. & Agr.) A Progs., Nov. 1905, Nos. 12–44 (File No. 81 of 1905 (Correspondence with S/S on agricultural development).
Home (Rev.) A Progs., Jan. 1907, Nos. 38–9 (File 14 of 1907).
Home (Medl.) Progs., Dec. 1910, Nos. 37–55A (Recruitment).
Home (Agr.) B. Progs., Feb. 1911, Nos. 49–51 (Agricultural Devt.).
Home (Agr.) A. Progs., July 1911 (File No. 194 of 1911—Advice to Local Govts. under Letter Nos. 650–6 of June 1911).
Home (Agr.) A Progs., May 1912, Nos. 13 to 18.
Home (Medl.) File, June 1914 (Govt. of India Resolution 888–908 of 23 May 1914, tracing the state of public health in an historical perspective).
Home (Sany.) File, May 1919, No. 91 (Imperial grants since 1911).
Home (General) A Progs., Oct. 1919, Nos. 1 to 6 (Rev. & Agr. File No. 204 of 1919).
Home (Pol.) B Progs., March 1920, No. 183 (Communal question related to development).
Home (Pol.) B Progs., Sept. 1920 (Muhammadan Affairs).
Home (Ests.) A Progs., March. 1920, No. 336–408 (Recruitment).
Home (Ests.) A Progs., May 1921, Nos. 370–6 (Official attitude).
Home (Agr,) A Progs., Aug. 1921, Nos. 14–19 (Agr. and dyarchy).
Home (Ests.) File No. 178 of 1924 (Letter to S/S).
Home (Ests.) File No. 178 of 28 Feb. 1925.
Home (Pol.) File No. 82 and K. W. of 1925, Part I (Conf.).
Home ((Ests.) File No. 3 of 1925 (Recruitment by nomination).

Home (Ests.) Progs., 28 Feb. 1925 (Recruitment by constitution).
Home (Special) File No. 28/27 (Dyarchy and development).
Home (Special) File No. 101/28 (Pre-Reforms position of agricultural development).
Home (Agr.) A Progs., July 1929, Nos. 75–83 (Govt. Resolution No. 826 of 23 March 1929).
Home (Agr.) B Progs., July 1930, Nos. 81–3.
Home (Ests.) File No. 14/34 (Minorities defined).
Home (Ests.) File No.14–17–B/33 (Recruitment).
Home (Easts.) File No. 965/33 (Political expediency in recruitment).
Home (Ests.) File No. 39/4/38 of 1938 (Nominations).
Home (Agr.) B (Print) Progs., 1930 to 1939 (Delegation of powers and Govt. orders).
(Education, Health and Lands) File No. 2–4/42-A (Importance of food and fodder supply during Grow More Food Campaign).
Home (Ests.) Resolution No. 23/4/42 of Aug. 1943 (Reservation).
Home (Finance) Progs., 15 Dec. 1943, Nos. 1–4 (Decentralization).
G.-G (Reforms) File No. 119/45–R (Reorganization of Services for post-war development).
Home (Ests.) Resolution No. 16/40/47–R (Relaxation in recruitment standards).
Home (Ests.) File No. 60/220/49 (Deviation from established norms of recruitment).
Community Project Administration (CPA) Files of 1952, 1958 and relevant files of the Ministry of Comminity Development and Cooperation (MCDC).
(MCDC) File No. 11/25/58–Administration I.
(MCDC) File No. 4/6/60 (Training).
(MCDC) File No. 4/2/60 (Training I, including Panchayat Acts of the several States).
(MCDC) File No.11/57/58 (Village Panchayats transferred to MCDC).

REPORTS AND PRINTED RECORDS

1. Fourth Report from the Committee of Secrecy of House of Commons, 24 March 1773 (1804 Print).
2. Sixth Report from the Committee of Secrecy (HC), 26 April 1773 (1804 Print).
3. Philips, C. H. (ed.), *The Correspondence of Lord William Cavendish Bentinck*, Vol. I (1828–31) and Vol. II (1832–35), OUP 1977.
4. Sharp, H. (ed.), *Selections from Educational Records*, Part I, 1781–1839, Cal. 1920.

5. Richay, J. A. (ed.), *Selections from Educational Records*, Part II, New Delhi, 1965.
6. Report of Select Committee (HL), 1852.
7. Report of the Commissioners appointed to enquire into the famine in Bengal and Orissa, 1866.
8. Report of the Deccan Riots Commission (1875), including appendix and minutes of evidence.
9. *Selections from Revenue Records of the North–Western Provinces*, Vol. III.
10. Famine Commission—Bengal Replies, Agricultural Branch, Revenue Department, Darjeeling, 5 July 1878.
11. Report of the Indian Famine Commission, 1880.
12. *Moral and Material Progress Report*, 1881–82.
13. Forrest, G. W. (ed.), *Selections from the Minutes and other official Writings of . . . Mountstuart Elphinstone*, Bombay, 1884.
14. Reports of the Administration of Bengal, 1891–92, Part II and 1892–93, Part I (Cal. 1894).
15. Reports from the several Commissioners of Divisions on the Working of District Boards in Bengal during the year 1893–94, including Resolution No. 4294½, L. S. G., Calcutta, 3 Dec. 1895.
16. Report of Administration of Bengal, 1901–2.
17. Summary of the Administration of Lord Curzon in the Department of Revenue and Agriculture.
18. Report of the Royal Commission upon Decentralization, 1909 (including the report of its Decentralization Committee on several nation-building subjects like education, agriculture, health, etc.).
19. Report of the Indian Constitutional Reforms, 1918 (1928 reprint)
20. Report of the Administration of Punjab, 1919–20 and 1921–2.
21. Report of Divisional Commissioner, Dacca, to Bengal Govt. No. 4847J dated 8 Sept. 1920.
22. A Review of the Administration of the Presidency of Bombay, 1922–23.
23. C. P. and Berar, L. S. G. Resolution No. 383/192–VIII dated Nagpur 15 Feb. 1923.
24. Indian District Boards Administration Report, 1921–2.
25. Resolution Reviewing the Reports of the District Boards in Bengal, 1923–24; Rev. and Agr. Resolutions No. 7/7/4 of 21 March 1903, No. 13–61–16 of 13 Sept. 1901 and No. 11–294–5 of 20 Dec. 1900.
26. Report of the Reforms Enquiry Committee, 1924, Cmd. (19)4694.
27. Report of the Local Governments on the working of the Reformed Constitution, 1923, 2361. Also Cmd., 2362 and 2360 on the same subject (1924–25).
28. Views of the Local Governments on the working of the Reforms, 1927.
29. Memoranda submitted to the Indian Statutory Commission by the Government of India.

30. Report of the Administration of the Residency of Madras, 1935–38.
31. Bihar in 1937–38.
32. Report of the Administration of the United Provinces, 1942.
33. Report of the Bengal Administration Enquiry Committee, 1944–45.
34. Government of India (Scheduled Caste) order of 1936, supplemented under Resolution No. 31/14 (S) of 6 Feb. 1945.
35. Government of Bombay Post-War Reconstruction and Development Programme.
36. ARC Report of the Study Team on Personnel Administration (1966–67).
37. Report of the Study Team (Throat) on Recruitment and Training (1967).
38. Report of the Grow More Food Enquiry Committee (1952).
39. Report of the Balwantray G. Mehta Committee on Panchayati Raj, November 1957.
40. Report on Indian and State Administrative Services and Problems of District Administration (V. T. Krishnnmachari), Aug. 1962.
41. Report on the Management of the Indian Administrative Service, Vol. I, May 1968.
42. Annual Reports of the Union Public Service Commission.
43. Home Public Despatch from S/S, No. 61 of 22 Sept. 1870.
44. Rev. and Agr. despatch to S/S, No. 36 of 7 Sept. 1905.

RECORDS OF CERTAIN LOCAL GOVERNMENTS

1. Government of Bihar and Orissa L. S. G. Resolution No. 3233 of 22 March 1923.
2. Central Government Letter to Bihar Government in the Department of Education, Health and Lands, No. F. 243/37 dated 27 Aug. 1937 re. Centre's power to discuss provincial subjects under 1935 Act.
3. Bombay Government (Rev. and Agr.) to Govt. of India, No. 1446–A/28 of 1938, enclosing Sixth Report showing progress in giving effect to the recommendations of the Royal Commission on Agriculture for agricultural development. Similar reports from Bengal, Madras, Punjab, C. P. and U. P.
4. Bihar to Govt. of India (Education, Health and Lands) No. 1122–D, dated 5 May 1938.
5. Bihar Govt. (Development and Employment) Progs., Dec. 568–71/42 (Landholders Assn. view on food production).
6. Bihar Govt. (Development and Employment) File No. 10A-16/43, B. Progs., Dec. 236–275/43 (Grow More Food Campaign).
7. Bihar (Development and Employment) File No. 9A-3, Progs., Dec. 1558–1577 of 1946 (Grow More Food Compaign).
8. Bihar (Rev.) Progs., No. 151–86/46B (Grow More Food Campaign).

Pre-1947 Panchayat Acts

India Act I of 1883 and XVI of 1883 for C. P.; India Act XX of 1883 and XX of 1891 for the Punjab; U. P. Act I of 1900 and III of 1905; Bengal Act III of 1884 and III of 1885; Madras Act IV of 1884; Bombay Act I of 1884 and III of 1901.

SOME SECONDARY WORKS

Austin, G., *The Indian Constitution*, 1972.
Badan-Powell, B. H., *The Indian Village Community*, 1896.
Blunt, E. (ed.) *Social Services in India*, 1938
Dubhashi, P. R., *Rural Development Administration in India*, 1970.
Ensminger, D., *Rural India in Transition*, (March 1972).
Krishnamachari, V. T., *Nationl Extension Movement*, C. P. A Series, No. 27.
————, *Reservation in Services*, Aug. 1974.
Maine, H. S., *Village Comunities in the East and West*, 7th edition, 1973.
————, *The Early History of Institutions.*
Mathai, John., *Village Government in India* (London, 1915).
Misra, B. B., *The Central Administration of the East India Company, 1773–1834*, 1959.
————, *The Administrative History of India, 1834–1947*. 1970.
————, *The Bureaucracy in India*, 1977, 1980.
————, *The Indian Middle Classes: Their Growth in Moden Times*, 1961.
————, *Government and Bureaucracy in India, 1947–75.*
Moreland, W.H., *Agrarian System of Moslem India*, 1929.
Rogers, A., *The Land Revenue of Bombay*, 1892
Sivaraman, R., *The Role of Civil Services in Administration of India* (Typed Copy, Dept. of Personnel, 1970).
Tinker, Hugh, *The Foundations of Local Self-Government in India. Pakistan and Burma*, 1954
Voelker, J. A., *Improvement of Indian Agriculture* (ICAR copy used).

INDEX